Comparative Law in Eastern and Central Europe

Comparative Law in Eastern and Central Europe

Edited by

Bronisław Sitek, Jakub J. Szczerbowski
and Aleksander W. Bauknecht

CAMBRIDGE
SCHOLARS
PUBLISHING

Comparative Law in Eastern and Central Europe,
Edited by Bronisław Sitek, Jakub J. Szczerbowski and Aleksander W. Bauknecht

This book first published 2013

Cambridge Scholars Publishing

12 Back Chapman Street, Newcastle upon Tyne, NE6 2XX, UK

British Library Cataloguing in Publication Data
A catalogue record for this book is available from the British Library

ISBN (10): 1-4438-4898-0, ISBN (13): 978-1-4438-4898-5

TABLE OF CONTENTS

Private Law

Public Law

INTRODUCTION

Comparative law is a research methodology that has been increasingly fashionable in recent decades. Comparisons between common law and civil law dominated the comparative law landscape. Many methods of comparative law were in use: comparison of legal rules, comparison of cases, comparison of legal theories. Each of them had strong proponents and opponents. Dogmatic comparisons of rules were criticized for not giving the whole picture of law in action, but praised for being the first and the only truly legal step in comparative research. Case-based comparisons were praised for enabling us to compare the true understanding of rules by courts, yet the critics of this method pointed out that only the higher courts' decisions are the subject of comparison, and most cases do not reach this stage. Comparisons of legal theories were praised for enabling us to know the spirit of the laws, yet the opponents would argue that many countries sharing the same theory would draw opposite conclusions from it.

The problems of comparative law did not stop it from becoming a mainstream method and subject in legal research. The objectives of comparative law varied from researcher to researcher. For Christian von Bar, unification of law by creation of just, efficient, secure, freedom-promoting private law was the aim of comparative research. For Tomasz Giaro, comparative law was a tool for acquiring deep knowledge about how the law works, and questioning the classical divisions between common and civil law. The whole spectrum of views on the purpose of comparative law varies greatly, from enthusiasts seeing in it the solution to all legal problems, by transplanting the best rules, to critics viewing it as a waste of time and money that has neither practical application, nor theoretical value. The scope of this book is, irrespective of your view of comparative law, unprecedented and useful. The science of comparative law in the East was extremely underdeveloped due to the Iron Curtain. Many areas of law, although known to the eastern academics, constitute an uncharted territory from the comparative point of view.

This book is a result of the attempted (and successful) introduction of comparative law into the region of Eastern and Central Europe. The subject has induced interest beyond expectations. It opens with a chapter on the unification of law, both from the perspective of institutional unification by such supra-state organizations, spontaneous and institutionalized unifications between two or more legal systems, and the methods of choosing the right rules in the unification process. Chapters two and three follow the classical division of private and public law, proposed by the brilliant Roman lawyer Ulpian. The chapters comment on the current topics discussed in by academics in Eastern and Central Europe.

UNIFICATION OF LAW

THE STRUGGLE FOR A EUROPEAN LAW OF CONTRACT

CHRISTIAN VON BAR

UNIVERSITY OF OSNABRÜCK, GERMANY

It means a lot to me to be able to stand here before you today in Olsztyn to speak about a European project, which looks likely to assume historical importance. Where, if not here in the former Allenstein, can the impetus driving the creation of the European Union and the purposes served by the creation of a zone of freedom, security and justice be more evidently grasped? We, and especially those of us who are from Germany, which brought so much misfortune to this part of the world, should always remember this. I am extremely grateful for your hospitality and if I may, I would like to proudly advert to the fact that for many years, my home town of Osnabrück and Olsztyn have enjoyed a warm and fruitful partnership.

In the second half of 2011, the Republic of Poland will assume the Presidency of the European Council. Ensuring that the project that I wish to discuss today, namely the creation of a European Law of Contract and a common frame of reference (extending beyond contract law), will be lent a receptive ear by the European polity, and legislature thus hinges on Polish prowess! For the first time in its history, it appears that the European Union is about to create its own -European- contract law. Moreover, the creation of a tool box for the European legislature that would perhaps exist alongside a European Law of Contract is also mooted. As a minimum, this option constitutes a viable alternative provided that the consultations on this matter go well. This would create a set of European model rules possessing a terminological and systematical coherence, which would in all likelihood be referred to by the European and national legislature when drafting new laws involving private law.

However, we have not yet reached this stage. The struggle for a common European law of contract is not yet over. The Vice-President of the Commission and Commissioner for Justice, Mrs. Viviane Reding, will deliver a speech on the 3rd of June in Leuven detailing the initial findings and recommendations of the consultation process and outline the legislative instrument that the Commission has in mind to implement a European law of contract. We reckon that by October or November there will be a proposal to implement an Optional Instrument in the form of a Regulation. However, much can happen in the meantime. The political tug-of-war continues to play a significant role in this process; not all European Ministries of Justice are visionaries. The never-ending back and forth, the untold prejudices and particular national interests of some stakeholders, the attempts to lobby members of the national parliament, the fear that European jurists have of the unknown, the palaver about the competition between the various legal systems and the ignorance of what has already been achieved – all of the foregoing is not only an annoyance and depletes energy, but in the worst case scenario, may also be effective. The world already looks towards Europe in the hope of seeing a clear signal from the continent that gave birth to private law. The Union should not fail to grasp this historic opportunity!

The conference in Olsztyn is a conference on comparative law. In the light of this, may I first of all state that the fact that so many are currently discussing the drafting of a new European private law is a veritable triumph for modern comparative law. Almost thirty years to the day have passed since a plan was hatched to establish the Commission on European Contract Law under the leadership of its Danish chairman Ole Lando; almost twelve years have passed since the founding of the Study Group on a European Civil Code; and six years since the Study Group joined forces with another research group, the Acquis-Group. Meanwhile, the establishment of a European Law Institute is just around the corner; we hope to put the finishing touches on the necessary documents in Athens in April and then establish it in Paris in the month of June.

The matrix of issues raised during today's discussions originated from or were proposed by scholars from the centre of European legal science, and everything so far is the product of research projects on comparative law. At the European level, the traditional lone legal researcher has been replaced by a research team. Teamwork encourages new insights. For me personally, the decisive point is that we once again, become conscious of our common private law heritage and we have attempted to bring this to light in the fundamental principles, definitions and in commentaries and annotations on the Model Rules. Whether one agrees with every aspect of the texts drafted is not that important. Neither this project nor an academic career will hinge on the outcome of the endless academic discussion on some detail in sales law. For Europe as a whole, this is of secondary importance. By contrast, it is paramount for Europe and its people that the internal market functions smoothly, not only the internal market for goods but also that for services, which even today remains a problem area. The Euro can only remain strong and secure in the long term if it is the currency of a genuine internal market, if it matches the economic performance of the actors on the internal market and if everyone can do what they can best, unimpeded, and receiving adequate recompense for their services.

Perhaps, this economic aspect is not pivotal; instead cultural aspects may be more significant. We must take decisive steps towards creating a European culture of communality, especially we lawyers. We should not be deterred by opponents, who state that this project will sound the death-knell for competition between legal systems and will result in the loss of national legal cultures. This is because contract law (quoting Ole Lando) is not the stuff of folklore, and legal orders can neither run nor jump. Legal systems are not competing to win beauty pageants or to earn money. Their point of reference is solely justice as an absolute value; without this they would not be legal orders. I shudder to think that I should speak of legal systems in terms of winners and losers. If their respective triumphs and failures should be seriously evaluated, i.e. by means of statistical data, then at the very most, only where party autonomy under the conflict of laws permits choice of law. The yardstick would then be the frequency by which the parties chose a legal system designed to govern cross border transactions. The winner would be the system that was most frequently chosen to govern contracts. However, we are not in the possession of such numerical data and therefore will never know who has won this race. Moreover, we have no chance of discovering such information. We can only surmise that the legal systems of countries with large populations are statistically more likely to be chosen over legal systems of countries with smaller populations. Who or what will prove this conjecture? It serves to demonstrate that only economies and companies compete with one another, not legal systems. Any indicator of quality, however framed, cannot be derived on this basis. The Estonian private law is, for example, a monumental testament to intellectual prowess - only, who would choose it?

So where do we stand today? I think I may assume that you are all well-versed with the genesis of the Draft Common Frame of Reference (DCFR) as well as with the key parameters of the 20 year long political debate surrounding the creation of a European law of contract. If you recall, initially, there was even talk of creating a wholesale European private law and in the Parliament, even talk of a European Civil Code; therefore, the latter idea is mentioned in the Green Paper to which I will turn in a minute. Moreover, the Study Group on a European Civil Code, on whose work a major part of the Draft Common Frame of Reference is based, also examined the entire law of obligations, i.e. contract law in its entirety, extra contractual obligations and even ventured into areas of property law, relevant to the internal market. Even today, it remains hard for me to comprehend why this work of the Study Group, especially the proposed rules on proprietary security rights in movable assets has been side-lined in recent debates. I also do not see any genuine political movement on this issue.

It is true that the Vice President and EU Justice Commissioner, Mrs. Reding, did opt to limit the substantive scope to contract law, but politically speaking the term 'contract law' also permits an array of other interpretations and could potentially include the regime of proprietary security rights within its remit and could certainly also include the law on dissolution of contracts. We find ourselves in the midst of a complex political process, in which the proponents of a European private law must finally speak out loud and clear. It is, in my view, quite straightforward: companies and their umbrella associations, who wish to trade unimpeded by extraneous legal barriers within the internal market in their economic sector, should now become more vocal. There is no good reason to confine this project to sales law; no legitimate reason to exclude the service sector entirely. Vice President Reding tentatively supported this view in an article written for the German newspaper 'Handelsblatt'. In the article, to illustrate an argument, she spoke pointedly of 'a … medium sized company that manufactures and offers, if necessary, repairs of washing machines'.[1] The noteworthy aspect of this example is the mention of a repair service; the mention of this, we must deduce, was not simply a matter of chance.

In the Green Paper mentioned earlier, entitled 'Policy options for progress towards a European Contract law for Consumers and Businesses', the Commission has identified seven (or indeed nine, depending on interpretation) possible means of making contract law in the EU more cohesive:

(i) The online publication of **model contract clauses** (non-binding) which be employed in contracts within the internal market.

(ii) A (binding or non-binding) *toolbox*, to which the EU legislator would have access when drafting new legislative proposals having a bearing on EU contract law, the aim here being to ensure consistency and coherence in legislation.

---

[1] Viviane Reding, *We don't have an Internal Market*, 5/6 Handelsblatt 72 (2010).

(iii) A **Commission Recommendation on Contract Law**, addressed to Member States encouraging them to incorporate 'an instrument on European Contract law into their national laws' based on the model of the Uniform Commercial Code.

(iv) An **optional instrument for European Contract law** (…), which might be chosen voluntarily by consumers and businesses. This optional instrument is conceived as an alternative to the existing national regimes of contract law and would be available in all of the official languages. The optional instrument might be applicable to cross border transactions only, or in both cross border and domestic contracts. The optional instrument would need to guarantee a high level of consumer protection and offer legal certainty for the entire duration of the contract.

(v) **Harmonisation of national contract law** pursuant to an EU Directive.

(vi) **Wholesale harmonisation of national contract law** on the basis of a EU Regulation, and,

(vii) The introduction of a **European Civil Code**, which would replace national contract law.[2]

It will have immediately been apparent to anyone keenly following the discussions of the past few years that this list contains all the options which have already featured in the cut and thrust of this debate. The Commission appears to have taken all of them into consideration, if one discounts a further theoretical option that two or three States would adopt a uniform contract law to regulate factual matrixes with cross-border elements, which are of interest to them, with reference to a text drafted in Brussels and invited other States to participate. However such a project would not make much sense in the realm of contract law, as to have nationality as the connecting factor would be completely unacceptable. Therefore, this option was befittingly left out of the Commission's compendium of options.

Yet, several of the proposals put forward by the Commission do not appear to embody particularly realistic options. Right from the outset I have been of the view that the Commission is unlikely to simply make do with option (i) (model contractual clauses published on the Internet), nor do I believe that a strong political will exists for option (vii) (European Civil Code). One option is too restrictive whereas the other is too expansive. A 'European Civil Code' which would only take the place of national **contract law**, would, in reality, not amount to a 'Civil Code', owing to its narrow substantive scope. Without further elaboration, I

[2] See also http://tinyurl.com/2cesa5b.

cannot readily grasp the distinction between Option (vii) (European Civil Code) and Option (vi) (Regulation establishing a European Contract Law). Option (v) (Directive on European Contract Law), in my view, does not seem to constitute an appropriate instrument. A directive would not address an array of issues in the national legal systems and would therefore, not bring about reform where reform is needed. Indeed, a directive would only serve to heighten the complexity of contractual negotiations rather than diminish them, because lawyers from both sides would have to deal with the numerous national variations on the same area of law.[3]

The policy option inspired by the American experience with the **Uniform Commercial Code** (Option iii) is original, and has, to date, not featured significantly in academic discussion. However, it must also, in all probability, be dismissed as a non-viable option. In my view, this solely constitutes an interesting theoretical experiment, and does not constitute a workable option as it has little chance of being realised, owing to the different challenges faced by America and Europe. Based on a recommendation from Brussels, the Member States would not set in motion, on their own initiative and, to a certain extent, at their own risk, the necessary legislative machinery. For such a proposal, Europe has 'too many Louisianas';[4] few Member States would subscribe to such a massive harmonisation project.

It is now more than likely that the next phase on the way to a European contract law will not take the form of any measure of harmonization in the strict sense. The harmonisation idea has, temporarily at any rate, been put on the back burner, and has given way to a new trend. The signs have been evident for quite some time that for the foreseeable future, it will not be possible to harmonise or unify the contract law regimes of the Member States by way of EU legislation. The political as well as practical complexities associated with such a task still present huge obstacles. Therefore, other solutions are required. Fundamentally, there are two options that present themselves: the gradual incorporation of European

---

[3] Simon James correctly points out this problematic in a Clifford Chance Client Briefing, *European Contract Law: Coming out* (July 2010), available at http://tinyurl.com/43cbzob.

[4] The Uniform Commercial Code has been adopted by all of the US States. However, Louisiana has not adopted a number of important articles on sales law and leases owing to the fact that they were inconsistent with its civil law tradition (see further http://tinyurl.com/l2dc9).

texts into the national legal systems by the Member States themselves, or the creation of a new additional system of law.[5]

In this respect, the alternatives are (ii) (**toolbox**) and (iv) (optional instrument for contract law). The **toolbox**-solution (Option ii) has been debated for a long time and was, for a time, the frontrunner. The wording of the Commission Decision setting up the Expert Group also speaks of a common frame of reference. It states: 'the Group should assist the Commission in preparing a proposal for a Common Frame of Reference for European Contract Law which should include consumer and business contract law using the Draft Common Frame of Reference as a starting point [...]. In particular, the Expert Group should assist the Commission in selecting parts of the Draft Common Frame of Reference, which are of direct or indirect relevance for contract law, restructure, revise and supplement the selected parts'.[6] Only the appointees themselves are cognisant of whether the Expert Group had indeed freedom to choose the relevant parts of the DCFR, or whether in fact, the Group's remit was already defined by others. At any rate, nowadays, one may perhaps cautiously, and fully conscious of the fact that nothing final has been decided yet, state that the Common Frame of References has turned out to be a project beset with both political and practical challenges. Most likely, it is not an objective that may be easily described in political terms and easily championed publicly, nor is it one that can be straightforwardly implemented given the multifarious resistance to the project. I personally am nonetheless persuaded that the concept of a Common Frame of Reference or tool box is right and proper. The fact that the political scales are weighted in favour of an Optional Instrument does not automatically connote that the idea of a common frame of reference will be dropped. Favouring one approach does not mean adieu to another. National and European legislatures are beginning to cite the DCFR, which is purely an academic text. It is easy to appreciate just how much more influential a political CFR, extending beyond the narrow confines of contract law, would be!

I ought to emphasise once again: that nothing has been decided yet in the political realm. As I speak, 300 responses from governments, national parliaments, professional bodies and lobby groups are being evaluated by

---

[5] It is, for example, complete nonsense for the general press to claim that the Commission is hell-bent on 'unifying contract law on a European wide basis'. (according to Laurenz Schmitt & Stephan Balthasar, *Pläne für ein europäisches Vertragsrecht haben erhebliche Mängel*, Frankfurter Allgemeine Zeitung (August 11th, 2010).

[6] Clifford Chance Client Briefing, *European Contract Law...* (July 2010).

the Commission. However, material decisions need to be taken before long. The mandate that has been given to the Expert Group did not extend beyond the remit of a feasibility study. Therefore, the text which will soon be submitted by the Expert Group is not at all conclusive and the Commission will amend parts of that text. Therefore, some time shall pass before a final text will be laid before the Council and Parliament (which will entail, as is well known, that the Commission shall lose sovereignty over the text). Nonetheless, it may be inferred that the optional instrument for European contract law, that is Option (iv), has the best chance of being implemented, and I wish to stress the importance of it being a success. The idea of an optional instrument, that is, an optional legal system tailored to meet European requirements, offers, strategically, greater potential for expansion into other legal fields extending far beyond the narrow remit of contract law. For example, it could also lead to the creation of an optional instrument for European family law or securities over immovable property.

With that, I have nearly come full circle. I am convinced that the Optional Instrument can only be a success when its field of application is sufficiently broad. In my view, three decisions are imperative: firstly, that the Optional Instrument is not restricted to intra-Union cross-border contracts, rather that it shall also apply in purely national or domestic cases. Second of all, that its ambit is not merely confined to sales or even to consumer sales contracts. Instead, a core area ought to embrace services relevant to the internal market. Thirdly, the Optional Instrument ought not to be limited to B2C-contracts and ought, primarily to serve the interests of SMEs, to encompass B2B contracts. The private law within the internal market needs its own profile, otherwise it cannot in the long run develop into a self-contained composite alongside UN Sales Law and the law based on EU Directives. Additionally, from its inception, it must be so structured that it can organically extend into areas that are not as yet within its remit.

Finally, if it is to be implemented as *lex contractus*, it must be made clear that the optional instrument is truly law and not simply a set of standard term and conditions. The legislative instrument required to create such a law is a Regulation. In turn, opting for a Regulation will raise the thorny issue of the relationship between the law laid down by the Regulation and the national law in the Member States. The narrower the scope of application of the Optional Instrument, the more scope for the ensuing void to be filled by the national laws of the Member States. It is therefore essential to clearly prescribe the parameters between European law and national law. This is an issue that is currently being carefully addressed by the responsible working unit within the Commission's DG Justice. In my view, the crucial point is that the Optional Instrument does not really deal with a type of 28th legal system as is often inferred; rather, it stands on its own and is completely innovative. A '28th legal system' would stand, like all other 27 legal systems, **under** the regime created by the Rome-I-Regulation; the Optional Instrument however, must rightly stand above it, i.e. only subject to its own rules on the choice of law.

Allow me to conclude by saying that I am still concerned about the eventual composition and indeed the territorial scope of application of the grandiose sounding 'European contract law', which is currently the hot topic of conversation. It behoves all those involved, representatives from academia, industry, consumer agencies, the legal profession, officials from the Department of Justice and above all, political representatives to ensure that this ambitious and worthwhile project intended to facilitate creating a true internal market does not fail on account of a small number of 'know it alls'.

CONSIDERATIONS ABOUT THE DCFR IN THE LIGHT OF THE EUROPEAN LEGAL TRADITION

ALDO PETRUCCI

UNIVERSITY OF PISA, ITALY

Preliminary observations on reasons for creation of the Draft Common Frame of Reference (DCFR), its structure and content

As we all know, the year 2003 was crucial in planning a reappraisal of part of patrimonial private law of the Member States of the European Union, as in that year it started the process leading to the publication of the Draft Common Frame of Reference, concluded by an interim outline edition in January 2008, and followed by the final edition in 2009.[1]

In the Communication of February the 12th, 2003, the European Commission, based on information obtained as responses to the Communication of July the 11th, 2001, activated a more precise plan. The aim was to achieve a better coherence in European contract law, recognizing a fundamental role in such development to a Common Frame of Reference (CFR), in which principles, concepts and common terms relating to this part of law might have been included.[2]

---

[1] The current version first appeared online (February 2009) under the title Christian von Bar et al., *Principles, Definitions and Model Rules of European Private Law. Draft Common Frame of Reference* (2009), limited to the text of the Project preceded by a brief introduction; in October the full version was published with commentary in six volumes: Christian von Bar & Eric Clive, *Principles, Definitions and Model Rules of European Private Law. Draft Common Frame of Reference* (2009).

[2] For events before 2003 there is an extensive collection of literature in Guido Alpa & Giuseppe Conte, *Riflessioni sul progetto di Common Frame of Reference e sulla revisione dell'Acquis communautaire*, Riv. Dir. Civ. 141ff. (2008); some references can be found even in my article Aldo Petrucci, *Introduzione. Il Progetto di Quadro comune di riferimento (DCFR)* in Giovanni Luchetti & Aldo Petrucci

According to the Commission's intention, the main point of the CFR would be to increase constancy of the acquis communautaire (meaning existing common European legislation) in the field of contractual law in the nearest future, to support uniform application of law, which is intended to correct the functioning of 'cross-border transactions, and by that to complement internal market'. However, the CFR should have to 'create the basis for further deliberations of an optional instrument in European contract law' according to the opinion expressed by the Economic and Social Committee on July the 17th, 2002, with the purpose of establishing a uniform and general law in this field, based on the instrument called opt-in, which is binding only if it is voluntarily adopted by the EU Member States.

The Commission, in the same Communication, also proposed the creation of standard contractual clauses to be used on the European scale. They should be broadcast among businessmen and professionals in electronic form, in order to show that the objectives of European contract law shall be implemented not only through traditional regulatory instruments, but also with the help of practical ones.

This kind of action plan has gained an appreciation from the European Council and Parliament, so that the Commission, in a new Communication of October the 11th, 2004 entitled 'European Contract Law and the Revision of the Acquis: Prospects for the future', defines directions of development of the CFR that will provide 'a conceptual legal tool box, which provides tools essential to proceed at revision of actual acquis, at introduction of new regulations, elaboration of standard conditions and clauses … and at projecting of European Civil Code'.[3]

For the implementation of a draft of the CFR, the Commission decided to finance a three-year research, by means of the foundation of a network (DCFR-Network), giving this task to two already existing groups: the Study Group on a European Civil Code and the Acquis Group (Research Group on Existing EC Private Law), whose workshops and meetings were scheduled and not only involved researchers and academics, but also experts and representatives of associations and interested groups of the EU Member States (currently 27) and other European countries, such as Switzerland and Norway. The work began on December 15th, 2004 and was conducted in the years 2005-2007 until the interim edition of 2008 and the full edition of 2009.

(eds.), *Fondamenti romanistici del diritto europeo. Obbligazioni ei le Radici contratti dalle romane al Draft Common Frame of Reference* 8ff. (2010).

[3] See Guido Alpa & Giuseppe Conte, *Riflessioni sul progetto...* 158 (2008).

Reasons for the creation and publication of the interim edition of DCFR in 2008 were explained by the authors in The Introduction: there was a need to realize the commitments received in 2004 by the European Commission (that was the financing unit), to complete a three-year work and to gain opinions, suggestions and critical remarks through conferences, workshops and University courses that would have an influence on the final edition.[4] On the other hand, the content of the interim edition was incomplete compared to the original plan, because it did not include typical figures of contracts in Book IV (except for sales and lease of goods), and lacked Books VIII, IX and X dedicated to acquisition and loss of ownership of goods, on proprietary security on movable assets and on trusts.

The final edition is not only complete, but also contains many observations made during discussions of the interim text and reflections performed by members of the Groups. It has three parts:

a) ten books including Model Rules;

b) a separate part of Principles;

c) an annex devoted to Definitions.

To refer to the content of each part, we may use indications supplied by the same authors in The Introduction.[5]

As for the Principles (which in the outline edition are before Model Rules) it considered the experience of Principes directeurs du droit européen du contrat formulated by the Association Henri Capitant and Société de législation comparée and included in two books published in Paris in 2008,[6] but the choice was fully independent. They are as follows:

1. Four **Underlying principles** consisting of freedom, security, justice and efficiency;
2. **Overriding principles**, originating from the four mentioned above, and adding others like those of a highly political nature, for example: protection of human rights, promotion of solidarity and social responsibility, preservation of cultural and linguistic diversity, protection and promotion of social welfare, and promotion of the internal market.

---

[4] In the Introduction of the provisional version Christian von Bar et al., *Principles, Definitions and Model Rules...* 4ff. (2009).

[5] *Ibid.*, 12ff. (2009).

[6] See Bénédicte Fauvarque-Cosson & Denis Mazeaud (eds.), *Principes contractuels communs. Projet de cadre commun de référence* (which constitute the first part of Principes directeurs) and *Id.*, *Terminologie contractuelle commune. Projet de cadre commun de référence* (2008).

Model Rules are distributed in ten books of the Project and do not have any normative force, but are considered as 'soft law' rules such as those of PECL (Principles of European Contract Law) written by the Lando Commission and might be used as a model for European and national legislations for the improvement of the coherence of the acquis communautaire and internal laws.

Model Rules are contained in 1023 articles in total.

Book I consists of only ten articles (from I.-1:101 to I.-1:110) and collects some **General provisions**, that apply to all the DCFR, including those relating to its application (I.-1:101), interpretation and development (I.-1:102), good faith and fair dealing (I.-1:103), reasonableness (I.-1:104), regulations regarding consumers and entrepreneurs (I.-1:105), regarding the meaning of expressions 'in writing' and 'signature' (I.-1:106 and I.-1:107) and calculation of time (I.-1:110).

Book II on **Contracts and other juridical acts** is composed of nine chapters, Book III on **Obligations and corresponding rights** contains seven chapters, and in Book IV, entitled **Specific contracts, rights and obligations arising from them**, some types of contracts are regulated, such as: sales, lease of goods, services, mandate contracts, commercial agency, franchise and distributorship, loan contracts, personal security and donation.

Books V, VI and VII contain, in order, **Benevolent intervention in another's affairs, Non-contractual liability arising from damage caused to another, and Unjustified enrichment**.

Finally, Book VIII deals with **Acquisition and loss of ownership of goods**, Book IX concerns **Owners security on movable assets,** and Book X is dedicated to **Trusts.**

Definitions have a function of suggestions for the development of the uniform legal language and terminology at European level.

Definitions that relate particularly to important concepts are part of Book I of the Project. For the others, Article I.-1: 108 refers to the Annex, which contains a list of 164 definitions and becomes an integral part of the Project: 'The definitions in the Annex apply to all the purposes of these rules unless otherwise results from the context'.

From the substantive viewpoint, these definitions are taken from the acquis and Model rules. The reason this location was chosen, is connected with the need to maintain the brief character of Book I and enable eventual extension of the list in the future without the necessity of modifying and distorting all of the Project.

As can be seen in this short description, DCFR, although it excludes from its area of application the number of private law matters provided in

Article I. - 1:101 (2),[7] goes far beyond the intentions reserved to the Common Frame of Reference by the European Commission, because of the addition of parts relating to non-contractual obligations (from benevolent intervention in another's affairs to unjustified enrichment and non-contractual liability arising from damages), to acquisition and loss of ownership of goods, owners security on movable assets and the trust, in order to point out the independence of the 'academic work' from the constraints of 'politic choices'.[8]

A final note concerns the language. The adoption of English for the publication of the final edition of the Project is justified by the language of the editors' Groups. However, it is accentuated that English is not the only official language, because a large number of translations into other European languages are expected. Therefore, editors have made the effort to chose a terminology that was accurate, precise, and at the same time accessible and clear, in a broader perspective of providing effective 'model–rules' for national legislators.

Implementation of DCFR and previous legal tradition

The main purpose of my paper today is how to place this new hypothesis of a unification of large sections of European private law, in the context of more than two thousand years of legal tradition of our continent, in order to estimate, whether the DCFR is something totally unrelated and independent, or whether we can see in it some roots of such long tradition, more or less consciously taken into account. For this reason it is extremely important to start from explicit statements made by the same editors of the DCFR in the Introduction.

In fact, after pointing out the autonomy of the Project as 'academic text' with reference to the destiny of a future Common Frame of Reference, the editors of DCFR hope that it will promote the knowledge of European private law at the level of an overall legal order, as well as develop legal education thereon. In particular the Project can: 'help to show how much national private laws resemble one another and have provided mutual

---

[7] Status and legal capacity of private persons; will and succession; family relationships, including marriage; bills of exchange, checks, promissory notes and other negotiable instruments; employment relationships; the ownership of, or rights in security over, immovable property; creation and regulation of companies and other bodies corporate or incorporated; matters relating primarily to procedure or enforcement.

[8] Cf. Christian von Bar & Eric Clive, *Principles, Definitions and Model Rules...* 3 (2009).

stimulus for development *directed to unification* and indeed how much those laws may be regarded as regional manifestations of an overall common European legacy'.[9]

This function is strengthened also by the publication of comments and notes to all Model-rules. It should reveal just a small number of cases in which European legal systems produced quite different answers to common problems.

So the same editors are conscious of the existence of a 'common European legacy', emphasized by the various national private laws, classified as simple regional variations of it, thus greatly facilitating the task of elaborating uniform rules and principles.

Even if it is not said which one this common legacy is, in obedience – it seems - to a spreading contemporary, there is no doubt that this must be identified with the complex of rules and principles inherited from Roman law and the subsequent Romanist (or Roman–canonical or Roman-German) tradition, which have represented for centuries the *ius commune Europaeum*.

We do not intend now to go into the details of an investigation intended to find those historical roots and some points of contact in relation to the various parts of the DCFR, as this is the objective that we intend to achieve in specific studies.[10] Instead of this, here we limit ourselves to some general remarks regarding the structure of the Project and its systematic exposition.

The first is the evident choice made in favour of a 'code solution', through the adoption of Model rules in ten books that may be considered as a kind of 'codification' between a 'code of principles' and a 'code of rules'.

Despite the deep difference of contemporary historical context from that in which the 'codification movement' arose in the 19th and the first half of 20th century, it is clear that the DCFR expresses a type of codified law in contrast with solutions in favour of a non-codified private law.[11]

---

[9] So Christian von Bar & Eric Clive, *Principles, Definitions and Model Rules...* 4 (2009).

[10] See, in addition to Giovanni Luchetti & Aldo Petrucci (eds.), *Fondamenti romanistici del diritto europeo. Obbligazioni ei le Radici contratti dalle romane al Draft Common Frame of Reference* (2010) also the more recent one: Id. (eds.), *Fondamenti di diritto contrattuale europeo. Dalle radici romane al Draft Common Frame of Reference* 3 (2010).

[11] For further information see Guido Alpa & Giuseppe Conte, *Riflessioni sul progetto...* 161ff. (2008) (with references to bibliography) and for earlier legal tradition Sandro Schipani, *La codificazione del diritto romano comune* (1999).

The second remark relates to the decision of separating the 'Principles' and 'Definitions' from the body of Model rules and of locating them, respectively, in an autonomous 'section' and in the attached Annex.

It is true that this choice to separate the Principles was inspired by the French Principes Directeurs of 2008, and for Definitions by the example of the acquis communautaire.

But it is also true that something that cannot be ignored, even if omitted by the editors, is the obvious connection with some systematic choices existing in the Codification of Justinian (Corpus Iuris Civilis).

Without going into detail, we can observe that the first title of the Institutiones (I. 1, 1) and of the Digest (D. 1, 1), both entitled *de iustitia et iure*, give some basic principles for all the Compilation; then the concept of the *principium* located in D. 1, 2, 1 has the sense of the initial element, necessary to understand the historical development of all the rules, but at the same time even the meaning of their foundation (*et certe cuiusque rei potissima pars principium est*);[12] finally at the end of the Digest, like Appendices, we find Title 50, 16 (*De verborum significatione*), containing definitions of more used terms and concepts, and Title 50, 17 (*De diversis regulis iuris antiqui*), which includes a list of more general rules, both applied all over the body of law.

The third remark concerns the existence of a general part of obligations (Book III of the DCFR), including a framework applicable not only to those arising from contract, but also to those arising from damages caused to another (Book VI), of benevolent intervention in another's affairs (Book V) and of unjustified enrichment (Book VII).

This leads to the unity of the concept of obligation and of its legal regime, even when it does not derive from a contract (it is not a coincidence that in the project 'non-contractual obligations' are mentioned), with a strong reaffirmation of the Roman law based (or civil law) 'model' in opposition to the common law system, which excludes, as is known, non-contractual liability (torts law) from the law of obligations.

It seems appropriate to set out what is said by the same authors in the Introduction: [13] 'The *DCFR* also covers other private law rights and obligations within its scope even if they do not arise from a contract. It

[12] On this concept see: 3 Sandro Schipani, *Principia iuris, potissima pars principium est. Principi generali del diritto. Schede sulla formazione di un concetto in Normazione formazione e interpretazione del diritto dall'età romana alle esperienze moderne. Ricerche dedicate al Professor Filippo Gallo* 649 ff (1997).

[13] Christian von Bar & Eric Clive, *Principles, Definitions and Model Rules...* 11 (2009)

covers, for example, those arising as the result of an unjustified enrichment, of damage caused to another and of benevolent intervention in another's affairs. It also covers obligations, which a person might have, for example, by virtue of being in possession of assets subject to proprietary security or by virtue of being a trustee... Book III contains some general rules which are applicable to all obligations within the scope of the DCFR, whether contractual or not. The advantage of this approach is that the rules in Book III may be taken for granted, or slightly modified where appropriate, in the later Books on non-contractual matters. The alternative would be an unacceptable amount of unnecessary repetition'.

Such a choice reflects, as is known, the systematization adopted from Justinian's Institutions 3,13,2 (and before, at least in its core, from Gaius' Institutions 3,88)[14] and from European codifications of the 19th and 20th centuries. The reasons that led to this adjustment do not consist of a formal respect of the legal tradition, but in a 'mere advantage', emphasized by the words of the same editors' Groups, when they outline that any other alternative would have meant 'an unacceptable amount of unnecessary repetition'.

We may just discuss why it was decided to put Book II, on contract and other juridical acts, before Book III on the general part of obligations and Book IV on typical contracts. As there is no 'official' explanation and without omitting an influence, perhaps unconscious, of the systematization of Gaius' and Justinians' Institutions, where for contracts a priority exposition was reserved compared to grounds for termination of obligations, we can think of two hypotheses.

Firstly, that this is due to the original motivation of the oldest projects of unification of European private law, concentrated on contract as an essential legal instrument to facilitate the integration of EU's internal market. The reasons would be understandable, in this interpretation, for the precedence of its legal discipline in comparison with this of obligations. An obvious example, on the other hand, is the expositive order of *PECL*, in which the discipline for contract is contained in Parts I and II, while the obligations are set out in Part III.

The second hypothesis is based on the precise choice of a model, i.e. that of the German Civil Code (BGB), in which the regulation of the legal

[14] *Gai 3, 88*: omnis enim obligatio vel ex contractu nascitur vel ex delicto [In fact, each obligation arises out of a contract or a delict]; *I. 3, 13, 2*: sequens divisio <obligationum> in quattuor species diducitur: aut enim ex contractu sunt aut quasi ex contractu aut ex maleficio aut quasi ex maleficio [a subsequent division <of obligations> outlines four species: in fact or they arise out of contracts or of quasi-contracts, or of delicts or of quasi-delicts].

transaction (*Rechtsgeschäft*), including contract, is found in the general part of Book I (§§104ff.), while the regulation of obligatory relations in general is placed in the introduction of Book II, dedicated to them, followed by the typical contractual figures.

Another important remark relates to the identification of the negotiorum gestio as a category of source of non-contractual obligations (Book V: **Benevolent Intervention in Another's Affairs**), restoring and maintaining a tradition dating back to Gaius' work *Aurea* in D. 44, 7, 5 and to Iustinian's Institutions (I. 3, 27, 1). A similar observation may also be applied to unjustified enrichment (Book VII: **Unjustified enrichment**), where instead the conservation of Roman roots (*indebiti solutio, actio de in rem verso* and restitution obligations in *id quo locupletior factus est*)[15] is not reflected directly, but passes through the filter of the elaboration of German legal studies (Pandectistic) in the construction of the category of the *ungerechtfertigte Bereicherung* (§§ 812ff. BGB).

We may also mention a general tendency to concentrate as much as possible on and to order under a limited set of criteria (the concept of legally relevant damage, accountability, causation, defences and remedies) the system of obligations for damages caused to others and its liability (Book VI: **Non-contractual liability arising out of damage caused to another**, in a total of 57 articles), with an evident preference for a model much closer to the Roman tradition, deriving from *lex Aquilia* (in both French and German interpretations), and completed by some special provisions of greater severity,[16] rather than for a model characterized by a series of exaggerated and fragmented rules proceeding from the system of common law torts.[17]

Finally, the last remark relates to the place reserved for ownership of goods (Book VIII) and proprietary security of movable assets (Book IX), both located after contracts and obligations. This may, on one hand, reflect the fundamental distinction in patrimonial private law - of Roman origin - between property law and rights and obligations law (expressed, as we know, in the combination of *actiones in rem / in personam*

---

[15] For the *indebiti solutio* see *D. 44, 7, 5, 3* (Gai. 3 aur.); *I. 3, 27, 6-7*; about *actio de in rem* verso the title *D. 15, 3* and the obligations of reimbursement of enrichment, for ex., *D. 5, 3, 25, 11ff.* and *D. 14, 3, 17, 4* (Paul. 30 ad ed.).

[16] See. eg, Vincenzo Zeno-Zencovich, *La responsabilità civile* in Guido Alpa et al., *Diritto privato comparato. Istituti e problemi* 273ff. (2004); Sandro. Schipani, *Contributi romanistici al sistema della responsabilità extracontrattuale* (2009).

[17] See, e.g., Vincenzo Zeno-Zencovich, La responsabilità... 281ff. (2004); Ugo Mattei, *Il modello di Common law* 224ff. (2004)

actiones),[18] on the other hand, the influence is clear, once again, of the model of the German Code, in which rules of property and proprietary securities are collected in Book III, which immediately follows Book II on obligatory relations.

Future prospects of the Project: doubts and certainties

What is the predictable destiny of DCFR in the near future? After two years from its publication there have been many critical and favourable voices. We may perhaps deduce something from two recent decisions of the European Commission on the way to prepare and to adopt the Common Frame of Reference (CFR) for EU.

With reference to criticism, it came from many directions.[19] Great hesitation was due to two 'strong initial conditioning factors', related to this as well as to all other projects of integration and harmonization of contract law or, more generally, in patrimonial private law in the EU, developed according to the requirements specified by the Community Bodies. Because their goal is to pursue the achievement of the unified market, hindered by differences between national legal systems, the first conditioning factor is the imposition of a 'suspect, much too unequivocal correlation between economic activities and legal forms', thus relegating projects of harmonization of private law rules to an ancillary position in regard to the economic needs.

The second conditioning factor derives from the exclusion in the perspective of a future integration of entire areas of private law, such as family relationships, inheritance, ownership of immovable property, intended to stay 'on the edge of this evolutionary process', creating a 'European private law strongly unbalanced in its parts', with some areas covered by common principles and rules, and others still covered by individual national – and sometimes regional - legal systems and cultural traditions.

Severe complaints about the systematic and methodological choices of DCFR were made by a large proportion of the European academic world.[20]

---

[18] See e.g., *Gai. 4, 1-5*; *I. 4, 6, 1-2*.

[19] A general view is found in Guido Alpa & Giuseppe Conte, *Riflessioni sul progetto...* 146ff. (2008) (with extensive references), to these two authors belong the expressions quoted in the text. Adde U. Perfetti, *Presentazione* in *Il Draft Common Frame of Reference del diritto privato europeo* XVII (2009).

[20] See, R. Zimmermann et al., *Der Gemeinsame Referenzrahmen für das Europäische Privatrecht. Wertungsfragen und Kodifikationsprobleme*, Juristenzeitung 529ff. (2008); Bénédicte Fauvarque-Cosson, *Présentation des*

Such criticism concerns both specific issues and background problems, such as:

1. the absence of a clear identification of the guiding principles, of their content, scope and hierarchy in case of conflicts among rules;
2. the character of a synthesis of existing codes (with a certain primacy to the BGB) and existing acquis, rather than a new project intended to give specific solutions (at least) to the most significant problems of contemporary European contract law;
3. the excessive use of general clauses, such as reasonableness, and as a result too much discretion left to judges, which reduces legal certainty;
4. tendency towards a hard and unpredictable limitation of contractual freedom of the subjects;
5. total deficit of social justice;
6. incompleteness and imperfection of the contents of the *Annex Definitions*, which do not include all the concepts contained in the Model rules and do not specify many of them;
7. unclear role reserved for practical application of good faith and fair dealing;
8. the lack of coordination between the provisions of Book III on the general regime of obligations and those of Books V, VI and VII on non-contractual obligations, in consequence making the former virtually inapplicable to the latter.

Furthermore, additional doubts arise from a more cautious attitude (almost 'a step back') expressed by the European Commission during the drafting of the Project. In its report of September the 23rd, 2005, it is specified that the Common Frame of Reference should have as a priority a revision of acquis in contractual matters and in particular in the field of consumer protection, thus revealing a direction towards slowing down or resizing the purposes of the Project. A similar stance was taken in a following report of July the 25th, 2007, where it was also added that DCFR was not designed to achieve a large-scale harmonization of European private law or even to become a continental Civil Code. The same caution was shared in 2008 by other Community Bodies: the Council's report of April the 18th and the European Parliament's resolution of September the 3rd have returned to attribute to *DCFR* a role only in contract law

travaux du Groupe Association H. Capitant des amis de la culture juridique française/ Société de législation comparée in Adde U. Perfetti, *Il Draft Common Frame...* 63ff. (2009); Stefan Grundmann, *The structure of the DCFR – Which approach for today's contract law?* in *Ibid.*, 85ff.

considering it as a simple 'University document' and possible basis for the future non-binding action of the Community legislature in this area.[21]

The explanations for such caution have been identified in three factors:[22] a) the extent and complexity of the Project, leading to concerns about its short term success, b) the initial lack of clarity on certain aspects of the real scope of the Draft Framework, and c) the lack of political will in support of the work of harmonization, in respect of which it more often expressed a Council attitude of opposition and mistrust.

Despite the aforementioned criticisms and concerns, the implementation of the DCFR is not a purely theoretical and academic exercise, because there are some important elements that reveal the future driving force in the reconciliation (or even unification) of the private law of our continent.

Firstly, the fact that Community Bodies wish to limit the function of the DCFR to a future Common Frame of Reference extended only to the contract sector is not necessarily a handicap. It is always a step towards a Project intended not only to affect the review of EU consumer law, but also to harmonize, at least, the general provisions on contracts of Member States.

Furthermore, even if the functions of the Project only had the purpose of reviewing the acquis, it would still be an important moment in the process of harmonization of national legal systems, contributing to significantly accelerate that of contractual law. In fact, as is noted,[23] the start of this process is unlikely to be stopped and 'it is reasonable to expect that it will soon produce its effects on the future Community legal order'.

The same beliefs also leaked from the introductory remarks of the authors of the DCFR, who not only clearly emphasize the potential of improving the acquis, but also highlight the role that the model can play in the Community legislature in order to develop the future CFR and in national legislatures in order to standardize and integrate their internal private law.[24]

---

[21] See Bénédicte Fauvarque–Cosson, *Présentation des travaux du Groupe Association H. Capitant des amis de la culture juridique française/ Société de législation comparée: terminologie, principes directeurs et révision des principes du droit européen du contrat* in Adde U. Perfetti, *Il Draft Common Frame...* 58ff. (2009).

[22] See Guido Alpa & Giuseppe Conte, *Riflessioni sul progetto...* 169ff. (2008).

[23] Guido Alpa & Giuseppe Conte, *Riflessioni sul progetto...* 173 (2008).

[24] Christian von Bar & Eric Clive, *Principles, Definitions and Model Rules...* 19ff. (2009).

Finally, two additional positive elements of the Draft should not be underestimated. The first one is given by the 'functional' approach, followed by the editors in its preparation and very much inspired by Christian von Bar, which led to enhancing more common elements than differences among the various legal systems. This approach, despite receiving harsh criticism, has a great deal of realism and pragmatism, certainly to be appreciated in such a context as the European one, if it is expected to achieve some results. The second element is the inclusion in one set, the rules on contract law in 'general' and on contract law for consumers, in order to overcome artificial fragmentation and build a unified system.[25]

I conclude remembering two initiatives taken by the Commission in the first half of 2010. The first is the establishment, by a decision of April 26th, 2010, of a Group of experts (independent, not more than twenty) with the task of helping the Commission to prepare the Common Frame of Reference in the field of European contract law, by selecting the corresponding parts of the DCFR and improving them in the light of the acquis and further studies. The second one is the publication, on July 1st, 2010, of a Green Paper on possible options in the adoption of European contract law for consumers and companies or professionals, in order to consult ordinary people, organizations and Member States, on what would be the most appropriate common legal instrument to achieve this aim: an immediately binding (Regulation) or one that requires the mediation of national legislators (Directive or Recommendation).

---

[25] In this sense Stefan Grundmann, *The structure of the DCFR – Which approach for today's contract law?* in Adde U. Perfetti, *Il Draft Common Frame...* 100. (2009), which also expresses a very negative opinion on the Project.

SOME PREJUDICES ABOUT THE LEGAL TRADITION OF EASTERN EUROPE

TOMASZ GIARO

UNIVERSITY OF WARSAW, POLAND

Uncertainties about the legal tradition of Eastern Europe

Prejudices and stereotypes sometimes occur even in the best historical scholarship and, a fortiori, in legal historiography. However, a legal historian is also obliged to question and eliminate them. Let us consider in this spirit several common prejudices about the legal tradition of Eastern Europe, which are in circulation above all in the western part of the continent. Some of them are explicitly formulated, but most rather constitute a kind of background knowledge, if not background ignorance, of the western legal historian.

As a matter of fact, in respect of Eastern Europe the picture of our knowledge is all but clear. First of all we do not even know whether this region ever existed and still exists as a distinct legal area. If we may trust a stereotype of European legal historiography, from the high Middle Ages right up to the civil codifications of the 19th century[1] or, according to a somewhat different formulation, until the so-called *usus modernus Pandectarum*, the phase of legal development immediately preceding the codification,[2] the legal area of Europe formed a wholly undifferentiated unit.

Is Eastern Europe supposed to be included in this homogeneous area? And if so, precisely to what extent? Indeed, Eastern Europe could have been equally excluded, particularly if it is deemed to be identical to Byzantium, frequently considered the decadent offshoot of the Roman Empire and a natural enemy of Europe. The stereotype just cited represents evidently an innovation with respect to the well established

---

[1] Reinhard Zimmermann, *Das römisch-kanonische ius commune als Grundlage europäischer Rechtseinheit*, 47 Juristen-Zeitung 11 (1992).

[2] Reinhard Zimmermann, *Roman Law and the Harmonization of Private Law in Europe* in Athur S. Hartkamp et al. (eds.), Towards a European Civil Code 25 (3rd ed. 2004).

doctrine of legal history and comparative law, according to which European legal unity has always been compromised by two divisions: civil versus common law and Western versus Eastern Europe.

Given that the majority of actual opinion makers of European legal history reside in the continental West, in the name of Western legal tradition the division between civil law and common law is usually underestimated, [3] while the division between East and West is overestimated.[4] Anyway, the heartland of Europe and the central stage of its legal history is, indeed, the Western part of the continent which roughly embraces the current day territories of France, Benelux, West Germany, Italy and Spain. This region was traditionally distinguished from Eastern Europe as a 'new' or 'younger' post-Carolingian Europe, born only in the 9th-10th century.[5]

Regrettably, the process of nation-building was delayed in the East and less successful. Hence, up to World War I continental Europe was composed of several strong nation-states in the West and few polyethnic empires, i.e. Austria-Hungary, Russia and the Ottoman Empire, in the East. In connection with this, the question may be posed whether Eastern Europe is a truly autonomous legal area, generated by the historical *longue durée*, or merely a construct of western hegemonial discourse, born with the very term 'Eastern Europe' during the Enlightenment [6] and strengthened by the Cold War of 1945-1989.

Eastern Europe was identical with the legal area of Byzantium

Since the Eastern Roman Empire, governed from the city of Byzantium, was historically the first rival of the Western Empire, and subsequently of the Roman Papacy, the concept of Byzantium is often used in the metonymic sense to designate the whole European East. Following the medieval religious divide between Latin and Orthodox Christendom, cherished particularly by the German legal historian Helmut Coing (1912-2000), the founder of the Max-Planck-Institute of European

[3]Reinhard Zimmermann, *Roman Law, Contemporary Law, European Law* 184, 188 (2001).

[4] Id., *Roman Law and Comparative Law*, 16 The Journal of Legal History 26 (1995).

[5] Henryk Samsonowicz, *From 'Barbarian Europe' to 'Younger Europe'* in Jerzy Kłoczowski & Hubert Łaszkiewicz (eds.), *East-Central Europe in European History* 87-95 (2009).

[6] Larry Wolff, *Inventing Eastern Europe. The Map of Civilization* 6ff. (1994).

Legal History in Frankfurt am Main, there is only 'Europe', East Central Europe included, and 'Byzantium' which embraces the Balkans and Russia.[7]

The historical reality behind this scholarly European geopolitics seems to be, however, somewhat more complicated than the theory. The Eastern part of Europe has had, indeed, just as little homogeneity as the Western. Speaking with more precision, East and West must be distinguished also within Eastern Europe. As a matter of fact, as subject of legal history from the middle ages onwards this region has been composed of at least three distinct sub-regions: (1) South Eastern Europe; (2) East Central Europe; (3) Russia.[8]

(1) The borderline between the Eastern and Western Roman Empire, established in 293 AD by Emperor Diocletian, became the divide between Eastern and Western Europe only during the 6th century, as the Southern Slavs begun to settle on the Balkan Peninsula.[9] At the end of the 9th century, when their Christianization started,[10] the Slovenes and the Croats on the western side adopted the Catholic confession and the Latin script, whereas the Serbs on the eastern side adopted the Orthodox confession and the Cyrillic script. The famous schism between both Churches, called the Great Schism, has perpetuated this division since 1054.

Thus, already in the second half of the 9th century in Eastern Europe some empires arose proselytized from Byzantium, particularly – proceeding from the East to the West – in 865 the First Bulgarian Empire, in 863 Great Moravia, and in 988 Kievan Ruš. In Great Moravia, however, western and eastern influences merged. Also, the founder of the Serbian state, Grand Prince Stefan Nemanja (1167-1196), received his crown from the Catholic legate as well as from the Byzantines. Even so, Serbia remained within the Orthodox orbit, exactly as did Bulgaria.

As a matter of fact, during the 8th century, as in the East the traditional Latin-Greek bilingualism eventually disappeared to the benefit of Greek alone, the political division between East and West became a cultural one. Consequently, the key historical process of the late Middle Ages in South Eastern Europe was the decline of the Byzantine Empire which, in the second half of the 15th century, together with the neighbouring Southern

---

[7] Helmut Coing, *Von Bologna bis Brüssel* 3 (1989).

[8] Johann P. Arnason & Natalie J. Doyle (eds.), *Domains and Divisions of European History* (2010).

[9] Florin Curta, *Southeastern Europe in the Middle Ages 500-1250* 53ff. (2006).

[10] Ludwig Burgmann, *Das byzantinische Recht und seine Einwirkung auf die Rechtsvorstellung der Nachbarvölker*, 26 Südosteuropa-Jahrbuch 287 (1996).

Slavs, was subjugated by the Ottoman Turks who subsequently maintained their rule over the whole Balkan Peninsula up until the 19th century.

(2) East Central Europe is the Roman Catholic westward-looking part of Eastern Europe with a legal culture oriented towards the Latin European model.[11] Its Gelasian doctrine of two equal ‘swords’, the spiritual and the temporal, implies a political independence of Church and State, legal and ecclesiastical culture resting upon the relationship of mutual autonomy. This structure was reproduced in the whole area of Latin Christendom whose reception in East Central Europe, accomplished through the mediation of the Roman Papacy, could be accompanied by the rejection of Roman law as the legal system of German emperors.

Around the turn of the millennium in East Central Europe, several Christian Kingdoms were founded. Besides Bohemia and Poland, where Christianity already became dominant during the 10th century, Hungary converted to the Roman Church at the beginning of the 11th century, as did the states of Denmark, Norway and Sweden in the North. In the wake of the Christianization of Poland and Hungary, Canon Law began to apply there, becoming the main bearer of Roman Law. The situation was therefore similar to that in the Nordic countries where Roman Law was never recognized as a subsidiary *ius commune*, whereas the two learned laws of the West (*ius utrumque*) were represented exclusively by canon law.[12]

Another bearer of Roman law in East Central Europe was the German town law. In the 13th century the inner colonization of Germany extended towards the East. The border of the Holy Roman Empire moved from the River Elbe to Oder, eastwards from which numerous towns and villages of German law were established.[13] Thus, the German-speaking world was the primary transmitter of Western ideas to the East. Magdeburg rights were granted to more than 100 cities, first of all in Poland and Lithuania, but also in Russia, Ukraine and Moldavia. As a final result of this first Europeanization of eastern borderlands, East Central Europe adopted the economic and legal models of the West.[14]

East Central Europe initially shared the general delay of the East towards the West. Given the scarce urbanization and the correspondingly

---

[11] 1 Harold J. Berman, *Law and Revolution. The Formation of the Western Legal Tradition* 92, 279, 504, 521 (1983).

[12] Ditlev Tamm, *Roman Law and European Legal History* 216ff. (1997).

[13] Lonnie R. Johnson, *Central Europe. Enemies, Neighbors, Friends* 37-42 (2nd ed., 2002).

[14] Robert Bartlett, *The Making of Europe* 172ff., 298-300, 306-314 (1994).

weak position of the burghers,[15] the medieval Eastern Europe did not require legal Romanization, driven in the West by the towns as the third engine of reception, next to the Holy Empire and the Latin Church. Also the feudal fief system was less developed in the East and the emancipation of towns belated.[16] However, during the High Middle Ages the colonization, urbanization and agricultural improvement, as well as the introduction of Canon Law and German Law reduced the civilizational gap that divided East Central Europe from the West.[17]

(3) By contrast, in respect of Russia, which participated in the process of the international circulation of Canon Law and German Law to a lesser extent, the same gap widened. Usually either identified with Eastern Europe in a narrower sense or, on the contrary, excluded from the concept as an extra-European territory,[18] Russia remained occupied by the Mongols between 1240 and 1480. The liberation from this 'Tatar yoke' was accomplished only by Grand Prince of Moscow and subsequently 'of all Russia' Ivan III the Great (1440-1505). Due to this hegemony of Moscow over all Russian lands under Ivan III, its government took on a new autocratic form.

Both Christian Orthodox component parts of Eastern Europe, namely Russia and South Eastern Europe, displayed a close symbiosis between Church and State. Due to the Orthodox Church, as early as the Middle Ages, the secular Roman-Byzantine Law was always received in one package with the Canon Law of the Byzantine Empire. Because of the unsophisticated nature of the societies populating the Byzantine world, which were predominantly of Slavic origin, this legal-ecclesiastical package primarily fulfilled an elementary civilizing function.

Only since Peter the Great (1682-1725) Russia became, at the expense of Sweden and Poland-Lithuania, a European power, developing an absolutist system even stronger than the Western one. Whereas the latter was based on a progressive alliance between the monarchy and the cities, the former consisted, in a strong parallel to Brandenburg-Prussia, of a reactionary coalition between the monarchy and the gentry. In spite of the 'enlightened' reforms initiated by Empress Catherine the Great (1762-

---

[15] Maria Bogucka, *The Towns of East-Central Europe* in Antoni Mączak et al. (eds.), *East-Central Europe in Transition. From the 14th to the 17th century* 97ff. (1985).

[16] 1 Antoine Leca, *La république européenne. L'unité perdue 476-1806* 289ff. (2000).

[17] Michael G. Müller, *Where and When Was (East) Central Europe?* in Johann P. Arnason & Natalie J. Doyle (eds.), *Domains and Divisions...* 115 (2010).

[18] Cf. Robert Bideleux & Ian Jeffries, *A History of Eastern Europe* 8ff. (1998).

1796) at the turn of the 18th century, Russian society remained feudal, the economy backward, and the government autocratic.

Eastern Europe never experienced the reception of Roman Law

Lack of reception of Roman Law is recognized as a distinguishing feature of the Eastern European legal tradition, exactly as in the case of the English Common Law.[19] Therefore, during the whole period preceding the European civil codifications of the 19th century, there was a general presumption of the binding force of Roman Law in the continental West and merely isolated cases of Romanist influence in the East. The Austro-German legal historian Paul Koschaker (1879-1951) even coined the reductive catchphrase 'Europe and Roman Law', corresponding to the title of his monograph, first published in 1947.

Koschaker's influential book, which also appeared in Italian and Spanish translations, is an early symptom of the German post-war integration in the West. Told in one sentence, according to Koschaker, only Western Europe is the true Europe, because only that region experienced the real reception of Roman Law in the Middle Ages.[20] However, as troubadour of the Western legal culture,[21] Koschaker does not take into account that this defect of Eastern Europe was compensated during the 19th century, when the massive transfer of Western codes and legal doctrines to the East occurred.

Yet despite this fact, Eastern Europe retains in the eyes of Koschaker a somewhat suspect, peripheral status. At present, the idea of labeling certain regions of Europe as non-European is rarely represented in an explicit manner, but in Western Europe, books entitled 'European legal history' completely excluding the East, are still being written, such as the book by Randall Lesaffer, published by the Cambridge University Press in 2009. Perhaps as a remedy a more differentiated view on the reception of Roman Law in East and West should be adopted? Indeed, in the recent decades the concept of reception has been relaxed.

---

[19] Tomasz Giaro, *Westen im Osten*, 2 Rechtsgeschichte 124 (2003).

[20] Critical Trajan Ionasco & Valentin Al. Georgesco, *La réception du droit romain de Justinien* in 3 *Atti del Convegno Internazionale Studi Accursiani* 1236f. (1968); Tomasz Giaro, *Europa und das Pandektenrecht*, 12 Rechtshistorisches Journal 326ff. (1993).

[21] Tomasz Giaro, *Der Troubadour des Abendlandes* in Horst Schröder & Dieter Simon (eds.), *Rechtsgeschichtswissenschaft in Deutschland 1945 bis 1952*, 31-76 (2001).

According to the new concept, advocated particularly by the German legal historian Franz Wieacker (1908-1994), even the West of the continent never experienced a direct transfer of ancient legal rules, but merely a process of a scholarly intellectualization of local legal orders.[22] Nonetheless, from the end of the 11th century onwards, Roman Law remained in Western Europe the subject of continuous study and gradual interpretive adaptation to new social needs, whereas the Byzantine world offers quite the opposite; a static picture.

However, the first reception of Roman Law occurred paradoxically in the East, due to the Byzantine emperor Justinian I the Great (527-565) who turned the old western law, written in Latin between the 1st century BC and the 3rd century AD, into a compilation. Regrettably, in the post-Justinianic age the East and the West drifted apart still further. The compilation, published in the middle of a Greek-speaking world, was an Occidentalizing reception of foreign law. But as quickly as Justinian's later years its first acculturation through the Greek works of law professors from Beirut and Constantinople took place.

Within the framework of the so-called Macedonian Renaissance, during the 9th century Byzantium experienced a second reception of Roman law. It also produced works, which contained some post-Justinianic elements. Thus to the older *Ecloga legum* of 741 two younger law books, the *Eisagoge* and the *Prochiron*, both published between 867 and 886, were added. However, the most important were the *Basilica*, a Greek periphrasis of the whole Justinianic legislation, compiled around the year 888 in 60 books.[23]

Despite this process of Hellenization the compilation of Justinian never acquired a factual validity in the East. Although it still enjoyed a high symbolic value, from the substantial point of view it was rather a kind of black box, which remained permanently unopened, because the reception of Roman Law in Byzantium was not accompanied by the reception of the Western art of interpretation. Byzantine jurists were not even able to create for their legal science a Greek technical terminology.[24]

The Hellenization of Roman Law in Byzantium was followed, in all of South Eastern Europe, by its Slavization as a means of Christianization of

[22] Franz Wieacker, *A History of Private Law in Europe* 96f., 176f. (1995); other citations in Tomasz Giaro, *Comparemus!, Romanistica come fattore d'unificazione*, 19 Rivista Critica del Diritto Privato 539f. (2001).

[23] Marie Theres Fögen, *Roman Law. Byzantium* in *Brill's New Pauly. Classical Tradition IV* 1085f. (2009).

[24] Francisco J. Andrés Santos, *Le langage juridique Byzantin* in Bart Coppein et al. (eds.), *Modernisme, tradition et acculturation juridique* 51-60 (2011).

the Slavonic tribes. In contrast to the learned Latin law of the West, the use of local language secured for the Byzantine Law received in Eastern Europe a strongly marked popular character. Yet the process of abridging and simplification deprived the Roman originals almost entirely of their dogmatic subtlety. The valid law of the Balkans consisted, indeed, of short summaries completely devoid of any doctrinally elaborated casuistry. In consequence, the Eastern reception of Roman Law was purely symbolic, in contrast to its dynamic reception in the West.

Thus, despite the unsophisticated character of Byzantine Law its practical effectiveness remained problematic. Already its normative substrate differed from the Latin *Corpus Iuris Civilis*. Objects of reception in the Balkan area were, indeed, beside the ecclesiastic *Nomocanones*, 'extracts from extracts', such as the *Ecloga*, the *Prochiron* and the *Epitomai* of the *Basilica*, written in Old Church Slavonic.[25] The most important document of the reception of Byzantine Law in the Balkans is Dušan's Code of 1349-1354 which originated in St. Sava's *Nomocanon* of 1219, a compilation of Roman and Canon Law, based on the legislation of the ecumenical councils, organizing the young Serbian kingdom and its Church.

As far as Russian territories are concerned, Kievan Ruš was also traditionally influenced by Byzantine Law in its usual version, which mixed religious and secular aspects as well as the elements of public and private law. It was the Russian clergy who applied this law in ecclesiastical courts where already in the second half of the 13th century the full translations of the *Ecloga* and the *Prochiron* were used. By contrast, not only the original Latin text of the *Corpus Iuris Civilis*, but also the Greek *Basilica* remained unknown in Russia until the end of the 17th century.[26]

The nucleus of Western reception was the intellectualization of local legal orders, accomplished by the learned jurist, provided with university education in Roman Law. However, until the middle of the 19th century in the Byzantine world there were no universities except for the University of Moscow, founded relatively late, in 1755. Therefore the region had no

---

[25] Kirill Maksimovič, *Byzantinische Rechtsbücher und ihre Bedeutung für die Rechtsgeschichte Osteuropas* in Tomasz Giaro (ed.), *Modernisierung durch Transfer* 1-32 (2006).

[26] Vladimir Gsovski, *Roman Private Law in Russia*, 46 Bullettino dell'Istituto di Diritto Romano 369 (1939); Gianmaria Ajani, *Alcuni esempi di circolazione di modelli romano-germanici nella Russia imperiale, Studi Gino Gorla* 967f. (1994).

juristic literature and no legal profession at all.[27] In the Byzantine world the only reception vehicle was the Orthodox Church, which, blending statute and law as well as religion and morals, by no means contributed to an intellectualization of legal knowledge in the East.

The early reception of Roman Law created in the West a kind of synthesis between Roman and Germanic legal concepts. As a means of compromise between both systems, some typically continental institutions of private law emerged, such as the acquisition of movables in good faith from the non-owner as well as the rule 'sale does not break hire'. Further synthesis was achieved by the law of Reason, represented in particular by 'Introduction to Dutch Jurisprudence' of Hugo Grotius. This work, published in 1631, for the first time organized the jurisprudence as a homogeneous system, consisting of Roman and Germanic elements.

By contrast, the whole of Eastern Europe lacked a legal doctrine of the Western type and level, except perhaps to some extent the Byzantine doctrine of Canon Law.[28] In consequence, the Eastern reception of Byzantine Law, cut off from its original Roman sources and therefore purely symbolical, remained unable to induce any kind of manageable synthesis between the written law of the Byzantine Empire and local folk laws.[29] The largely not collected or recorded and, as a result, not Romanized, customary law of Slavonic origin flourished.

Eastern European law was not backward, but simply different

The above-mentioned may certainly justify the qualification of Eastern Europe as an economic and legal periphery of the Western centre. However, many contemporary historians of European legal development, in line with political correctness, refuse the concepts of delay, of backwardness, and similar, as excessively value-laden.[30] Regrettably, this attitude ignores the existence of sound indicators of backwardness, such as

---

[27] Critical Trajan Ionasco & Valentin Al. Georgesco, *La réception du droit romain...* 1234 (1968).

[28] Valentin Al. Georgesco, *Développement du droit dans le Sud-Est de l'Europe* in III.5 Helmut Coing (ed.), *Handbuch der Quellen und Literatur der neueren europäischen Privatrechtsgeschichte*, *Das 19. Jahrhundert. Südosteuropa* 32f. (1998).

[29] Trajan Ionasco & Valentin Al. Georgesco, *La réception du droit romain...* 1235 (1968); Tomasz Giaro, *Europa und das Pandektenrecht...* 335 (1993).

[30] Jani Kirov, *Prolegomena zu einer Rechtsgeschichte Südosteuropas*, 18 Rechtsgeschichte 140ff. (2011).

indices of industrial and agricultural production, the level of illiteracy, the book-printing and reading statistics etc., which together make these criteria a hard historical fact.

Indeed, a parallel history confronting East and West shows exactly the same things happen in both parts of Europe, viz. state building and Christianization, feudalization, recording customary law, founding towns, cities and universities, abolition of slavery and mitigation of serfdom, development of capitalism and industrialization as well as constitutionalist movement and codifications. These processes have, however, always been accomplished earlier in the West, following in the East only after a certain delay. As a result, European history, general as well as legal, is asynchronous, made by pioneering societies in the West and only imitated by Eastern latecomers.

This advance of the West may be explained through elements of Roman continuity, represented by the culture of the universal Church and the Roman infrastructure, such as brick-built towns, hardened roads and navigable rivers, all of which were completely absent from the East. Outside the gates of Constantinople, the Byzantine Empire presented an entirely rural landscape. Only King Casimir the Great (1333-1370) is said to have found Poland built in wood and to have left it built in stone. Warlords with political ambitions, such as the first Frankish King Clovis (466-511), appear in the West 400 years earlier than the comparable eastern figure of the Bulgarian Khan Boris I (852-889).

The economic and social backwardness of Eastern Europe was attested by its early political decline.[31] At the end of the 15th century, South Eastern Europe fell under Ottoman rule, for half a millennium remaining cut off from the European circulation of legal models. Conversely, in East Central Europe the territory eastwards of the Rivers Elbe and Leitha was re-feudalized in the 16th century and, together with the recently discovered America, turned to the agrarian periphery of western capitalism. Eastern European neo-serfdom became a reservoir of cheap manpower and raw materials for the English-Dutch centre.[32]

In contrast to South Eastern Europe and Russia, in East Central Europe there were universities founded at a relatively early date,[33] namely in Prague in 1348, in Cracow in 1364 and in Pécs in 1367. However, during their somewhat phantasmal existence they did not fully participate in the western world of learning. As a matter of fact, they functioned with

---

[31] Michael G. Müller, *Where and When Was (East)...* 116 (2010).

[32] Witold Kula, An Economic Theory of the Feudal System. Towards a Model of the Polish Economy 1500-1800, London 1976, 129-133.

[33] Manlio Bellomo, *The Common Legal Past of Europe 1000-1800* 110 (1995).

considerable intermissions, leaving their chairs of Roman law vacant for long periods. Their modest level is confirmed by continuous peregrinations of Czechs, Poles and Hungarians to Western universities, which continued up to the 19th century.[34]

In South Eastern Europe the lack of political autonomy within the Turkish Empire excluded horizontal relations between its provinces. Therefore, their local law was preserved throughout the centuries exactly as it was at the moment of their subjugation. This 'mummification' of Slavic legal systems[35] embraced also the Byzantine Law of Greece and Rumanian Principalities. As far as Russia is concerned, it was less urbanized and less agriculturally advanced than East Central Europe. Consequently, prior to the 19th century, no learned law, no juristic literature, and no legal profession were known throughout Russia and South Eastern Europe.[36]

In the East of Central Europe the re-feudalization of the 16th century was still stronger than in East Germany. In the West the alliance of monarchy with the bourgeoisie, legally disadvantaged but economically ascending and protected by the dominant ideology of mercantilism, opened the road to absolutism. By contrast, in Poland and Hungary the gentry suppressed the royal power almost entirely. The system of noble democracy was in both countries strictly connected with the rejection of Roman Law; regarded as an instrument of absolutism.

The watershed of the 'second serfdom' at the turn of the 15th century also brought serious political consequences. All the countries of East Central Europe initially retained their political independence, but the early modern division of labour made them in to suppliers of cheap agricultural goods to the West. This process of re-feudalization in the East, obviously accompanied by de-urbanization, reopened the civilizational gap. As the final consequence, all the states of East Central Europe sooner or later became victims of the transfer of their sovereignty to foreign imperial powers.[37]

---

[34] Tomasz Giaro, *Legal Tradition of Eastern Europe. Its Rise and Demise*, 2.1 Comparative Law Review. Special Issue: The Construction of Legal Traditions 6 (2011).

[35] Giannantonio Benacchio, *La circolazione dei modelli giuridici tra gli Slavi del Sud* 70ff. (1995).

[36] Valentin Al. Georgesco, *Développement du droit...* 32f. (1998).

[37] Michael G. Müller, *Where and When Was (East)...* 115f. (2010).

The political decline of East Central Europe took place in stages.[38] In Hungary and Bohemia the political domination of the Habsburg dynasty ended with their almost complete disappearance as independent states. In 1687 the Hungarian Parliament conferred the crown heritably to the Habsburgs. Within the dual monarchy, Hungary remained an autonomous legal area, since its noblemen managed to preserve the Tripartitum, a feudal collection of customary laws recorded in 1514. However, the position of Hungary was strengthened only in 1867 by the Compromise (*Ausgleich*) concluded with Austria.

In Bohemia the same expansion of the Habsburg dynasty, guided by Archduke Ferdinand I (1556-1564), who in 1526, immediately after the battle of Mohacs, was elected also to the Bohemian crown, and inaugurated the almost total loss of independence of the country. Only one century later, in 1627, following the defeat suffered by Bohemian Protestants during the Thirty Years War in the battle of the White Mountain, the Holy Roman Emperor Ferdinand II (1619-1637) made Bohemia a hereditary land of the Habsburgs.

The Polish-Lithuanian Commonwealth (1572-1795) enjoyed the longest political existence. It developed to the extreme the western constitutional model of estate monarchy, dominated by the gentry, proud of the old Polish *liberum veto*, the legal right of each deputy to nullify all acts of the parliament passed at its session.[39] After the political reforms introduced by the Constitution of May 1791, the first written constitution in Europe and the second in the world, Polish statehood was destroyed by Prussia, Russia and Austria, which in 1795 wiped Poland off the map of Europe.

In view of a close interrelation between the presence of Roman Law and the strength of state power in a given country, the partitions of Poland-Lithuania were frequently ascribed *inter alia* to the failed reception of Roman law.[40] It was the gentry that rejected this law as an agency of over-strong government, even if it would have probably constrained anarchy and modernized the country. Its legal order was characterized by a

---

[38] On the following see Tomasz Giaro, *Legal Tradition of Eastern Europe...* 13f. (2011).

[39] The erroneous information on the *liberum veto* in Tomasz Giaro, *Poland*, IV The Oxford International Encyclopedia of Legal History 330 (2009), is due to an unhappy intervention of the editors.

[40] Romuald Hube, *O znaczeniu prawa rzymskiego i rzymsko-bizantyńskiego u narodów słowiańskich* 387 (1868); Ignaz v. Koschembahr-Łyskowski, *Zur Stellung des römischen Rechts im ABGB, Festschrift zur Jahrhundertfeier des ABGB* 293 (1911).

considerably longer persistence of the traditional customary law, uncodified and strongly differentiated according to local conditions and to particular social 'estates'. On the eve of the partitions, the Polish-Lithuanian legal system still remained largely medieval in character.[41]

Prior to the codifications of the 19th century, in the whole of Eastern Europe the learned judge of commoner origin, typical for Germany, remained completely unknown. In East Central Europe, justice was administered by the noble lay judges and in Russia, as in South Eastern Europe, by the orthodox clerics.[42] Due to its town law as well as Canon Law and public law, East Central Europe was better integrated into the western legal culture than the South East and Russia.[43] Nonetheless, the knowledge of Roman Law ascertainable in East Central Europe prior to the codifications was scarce. Such a modest legal scholarship was unable to reshape the local private law to its modern western form, equal for the whole society.

The civil codes destroyed a unitary legal culture of Western Europe

Some Western legal historians mourn the 19th century as the time of decay of the pan-European *ius commune* or at least of the unitary legal culture.[44] In reality rather the opposite is true. The unity of the old *ius commune* never existed, because neither in the Byzantine world nor in Western Europe were the Pandects of Justinian directly applied. Moreover, the controversial law of European jurists implied even more uncertainty than the ancient Roman Law did. Only the pre-revolutionary France knew some hundreds of local customary laws, whereas for successful models of civil codes in the 19th century there were exclusively two: the French *code civil* and the Austrian ABGB.[45]

Consequently, it should be remembered that these few codes, which suppressed the variety of local laws (*iura propria*), effected a standardisation on a national scale. Hence, the codes of the 19th century are justly regarded as the signature of the continental legal tradition.

---

[41] Tomasz Giaro, *Legal Tradition of Eastern Europe*... 14 (2011).

[42] Tomasz Giaro, *Europäische Privatrechtsgeschichte*, 21 Ius commune 14f. (1994).

[43] Tomasz Giaro, *Legal Tradition of Eastern Europe*... 16 (2011).

[44] Reinhard Zimmermann, *Roman Law and the Harmonization*... 21f. (3rd ed. 2004).

[45] 3 Carlo A. Cannata, *Legislazione, prassi, giurisprudenza e dottrina dal XVIII al XX secolo, Ricerche Filippo Gallo* 28f., 35ff. (1997).

Nonetheless, their most important outcome, easily forgotten when deploring the demise of the pan-European *ius commune*, is undoubtedly a relative uniformity of private law reaching far beyond national borders: in the East and the West of the continent. A similar harmonizing role was played somewhat later by the German Pandect science, which also embraced, in the second half of the 19th century, Eastern Europe, from Greece to Russia.

All this consolidated the civilian tradition on a basis significantly enlarged to the East. The Prussian ALR of 1794 and the Austrian ABGB of 1811 were evidently imposed on the recently partitioned Polish territories simultaneously with their entry into force in their respective fatherlands, whereas the civil code was introduced in the Napoleonic Duchy of Warsaw only with a slight delay of three years. Also in the Balkan Peninsula the galloping reception of Western civil codifications swept away the old feudal mosaic of customary laws only a few decades later than in Central Europe.

Obviously, in Eastern Europe the imposed or borrowed codification could not be considered – at variance with the famous saying of Jean-Etienne-Marie Portalis (1746-1807), the chief architect of the civil code – a 'compromise' (transaction) between the old and the new law or between French custom and Roman law books.[46] On the contrary, in the East the change was much more radical: the indigenous law was replaced by a foreign one, the consuetudinary law was replaced by a statute, the law proper to a given social 'order' was replaced by the unitary code and the lay judge was replaced by a professional one.

At the same time, the modernizing professionalization of legal education in Eastern Europe occurred. The university of Moscow, established in 1755, was flanked by the new ones in Kiev (1834) and St. Petersburg (1819), whereas in South Eastern Europe the law faculties emerged somewhat later: in 1837 in Athens, in 1860 in Jassy, in 1864 in Bucharest, in 1874 in Zagreb, in 1892 in Sofia, and in 1904 in Belgrade.[47] Contemporarily the old universities of East Central Europe were revitalised. In Poland and Hungary, the traditional strongholds of lay justice, already during the second quarter of the 19th century legal reviews, 'Themis Polska' (1828-1830) and the Hungarian 'Themis' (1837-1839), as well as lawyers' associations were founded.

---

[46] Cf. Pier Giuseppe Monateri et al., *Le radici comuni del diritto europeo. Un cambiamento di prospettiva* 135 (2005).

[47] Tomasz Giaro, *Modernisierung durch Transfer – Schwund osteuropäischer Rechtstraditionen*, in Id. (ed.), *Modernisierung durch Transfer zwischen den Weltkriegen* 285 (2006).

However, the legal development of Hungary and the Russian Baltic provinces displayed decisively more continuity than the development of Bohemia and Poland. The latter were, indeed, subject to the general legal order of the Danube Monarchy and, in the case of Poland, also to the legal order of Prussia, and subsequently of the Second German *Reich*, as well as of the Russian Empire. The modernization of these systems obviously also embraced their peripheries, where the imposition of western statutes was accompanied by the reception of the corresponding legal doctrine.

Similarly to Hungary, the legal Westernization of the Russian Empire, which started only at the beginning of the 19th century, was in constitutional and private law limited to the doctrinal level,[48] as well as to the civil cassation judicature of the Ruling Senate in St. Petersburg, which stood under the influence of the German Pandect science. The further influence of the Pandect science culminated in the Russian drafts of the civil code, published in 1905 and 1913, which took into consideration also the French code civil and the Baltic Code of private law, compiled in 1864 by Friedrich Georg von Bunge.[49]

A general difference between the modernization of private law in East and West should be noted. Whereas the Western process of gradual amalgamation of local Germanic laws with the learned Roman Law, inaugurated by the medieval Gloss and crowned in the 19th century by the codes, was a process of extremely long duration, in Eastern Europe the same 19th century brought an abrupt breach of local traditions. Western legal imports clashed here with pre-industrial societies. Even the legal historians willing to condemn the codifications in the West as destructive of the good old *ius commune*, must recognize that their shock effect in the East was incomparably greater.

In South Eastern Europe the retreating Ottomans left a legal vacuum behind, because the old local customary law mixed with some Byzantine accretion was absolutely unsuitable for the needs of a capitalist economy. Hence, most new Balkan states exchanged overnight their outdated Byzantine model against the well-modernized western one.[50] To the codifications, which ensured a legal unity of the territory, a western constitution was added, completing the fashionable pattern of the nation-

[48] Olimpiad S. Ioffe, *Soviet Law and Roman Law*, 62 Boston University Law Review 723ff. (1982); William E. Butler, *Russian Law* 26ff. (1999).

[49] William Butler, *supra* 333; Anatolij A. Tille, *Die Kodifikation des russischen Zivilrechts und die praktische Rechtsvergleichung*, 35 Osteuroparecht 8 (1989); Tomasz Giaro, *Legal Tradition of Eastern Europe...* 16 (2011).

[50] Holm Sundhaussen, *Europa Balcanica*, 25 Geschichte und Gesellschaft 641-643 (1999).

state. The new modes of legislation and government as well as the state monopoly on legal training and adjudication disempowered the Orthodox Church.

However, legal modernisation through imported codifications could not induce an effective social change. The traditional Balkan societies remained incomplete. Unlike Prussia and Bohemia, they had no middle class nor, as in Russia, Hungary and Poland, an aristocracy. Their social structure was a duality, counterposing the mass of peasants on one side and the bureaucratic-military elite on the other. In the absence of a middle class the legal reforms undertaken 'from above' did not lead to an efficient social transformation.[51] The Balkan as well as the Russian modernization of the 19th century recalls the medieval reception of Byzantine Law, which remained purely symbolic in character.

In comparison, the modernization of East Central Europe, which traditionally stood in a narrow exchange with the West, was more successful. Nonetheless, the 19th century brought to all the countries of Eastern Europe a decisively stronger inclusion into the continental system.[52] Not only the eastern periphery was penetrated through the capitalist market economy of the West, which replaced the traditional rural ways of social and economic life, such as the Balkan *zadruga* and the village community. Also in the legal respect this radical change of model eliminated from contemporary law of Eastern Europe, both private and public, all national elements pre-dating the 19th century.[53]

The East made no contribution to the European legal tradition

The long list of Eastern European borrowings and legal transfers from the West, which occurred between the Middle Ages and the present day,[54] may possibly justify a completely passive receptive image of the private law in the East. In this sense, the East would have made no substantial contribution to the European legal tradition. Yet this is not the whole truth.

---

[51] Holm Sundhaussen, *Institutionen und institutioneller Wandel in den Balkanländern* in Johannes Papalekas (ed.), *Institutionen und institutioneller Wandel* 46ff. (1994); Rumen Daskalov, *Development in the Balkan Periphery Prior to World War II*, 57 Südost-Forschungen 239f. (1998).

[52] Pier Giuseppe Monateri et al., *Le radici comuni del diritto europeo. Un cambiamento di prospettiva* 136-142 (2005).

[53] Tomasz Giaro, *Alt- und Neueuropa, Rezeptionen und Transfers* in Id. (ed.), *Modernisierung...* 305 (2006).

[54] Cf. Gianmaria Ajani, *Il modello post-socialista* 21-33 (2nd ed., 1999).

Of course, during the inter war period 1918-1939 the intense circulation of western legal models continued throughout Eastern Europe, except Soviet Russia. Almost everywhere, new legislation was needed, because further states emerged or the borders of the old ones changed.

During the inter war period, Eastern Europe definitely dismissed its old law stemming from the period of *ancien regime*. In the Balkan countries, already in the 19th century liberated from the secular 'Turkish yoke', a return to their indigenous law, mummified in its medieval conditions, proved to be virtually impossible. However, the rapidity of legal development excluded a return to the old law also in Poland, reborn after the partitions of 1795-1918 which definitely interrupted the Polish legal tradition. The same holds for Czechoslovakia where already in 1811 the Austrian ABGB abrogated the old *ius bohemicum*.[55]

The new western codes of private law, besides the German BGB, the Swiss civil code (ZGB) of 1907 and the Swiss code of obligations of 1911, determined the preparatory works for codifications in Eastern Europe. Regrettably, the achievements were not particularly great:[56] Yugoslavia with its six legal areas produced only drafts of the civil code in 1934 and of commercial code in 1937; Romania with its four areas published both drafts in 1938, and Czechoslovakia with its Austro-Hungarian dual system in 1937. The simple receptions, typical of the 19th century, were now sometimes substituted by syntheses of western models. Such an objective was targeted in the law of obligations for the Slavonic states, discussed in 1933 at the congress of the Slavonic Jurists in Pressburg.[57]

The congress refused, however, to adopt the Polish code of obligations which in 1933 by means of a modern synthesis unified the disparate legal systems inherited in Poland from the partition era. Yet this code must be considered the greatest achievement of the European doctrine of private law between the wars. Indeed, the Poles acknowledged the necessity to codify in the first place the law of obligations, whose unity was essential for the economy and trade, whereas they excluded the possibility of extending one of the foreign codes to the whole country. The comparative

---

[55] Tomasz Giaro, *Westen im Osten...* 133f. (2003).; Id., *Modernisierung...* 326f. (2006).

[56] Tomasz Giaro, *supra* 136; Id., *supra* 318f.

[57] Vidan O. Blagoyévitch, *Rapport sur l'unification du droit des obligations dans les Etats slaves*, 63 Bulletin de la Société de Législation Comparée 138ff. (1934); Helmut Slapnicka, *Österreichisches Recht ausserhalb Österreichs* 79f. (1973).

approach made the Polish code of obligations a work of compromise, recently defined as the first truly European codification.[58]

As a matter of fact, the main drafters of the code came from all the Polish partitions whose legal systems varied between themselves to a great extent: Ernest Till (1846-1926) and Roman Longchamps de Bérier (1883-1941) from the Austrian area, Ludwik Domański (1877-1952) and Henryk Konic (1860-1934) from Central Poland, where the French Code civil was effective, and finally the Roman lawyer Ignacy Koschembahr-Łyskowski (1864-1945) from the German partition. However, Longchamps, who in 1907-1908 spent one year in Berlin studying with Josef Kohler and Theodor Kipp, was an expert in German and in French civil law too.

The Polish code of obligations gathered inspirations from all the continental legal families of the time.[59] Nonetheless, it is a widespread opinion among Polish civil lawyers that Romanic inspirations found their place in several provisions of the general part of the law of obligations, whereas the Germanic ones did so rather in the special part. The code contained, indeed, a kind of general part which consisted of its first five titles: I. Sources, nature and types of obligations (art. 1-28), II. Formation of obligations (art. 29-167), III. Passing of obligatory rights and duties (art. 168-188), IV. Extinction of obligations (art. 189-287) and V. Debtor's acts damaging the creditor (art. 288-293).

However, in opposition to the Swiss code of obligations, but following rather the model of the German BGB, the above-mentioned parts of the Polish code of 1933 are not gathered under a single heading. By contrast, as far as the method of regulation is concerned, the drafters of the Polish code were guided rather by the French, Austrian and Swiss method of legislating through principles than by the German method of providing for every possible case.[60] Also the chief reporter, Roman Longchamps de Bérier, stressed the paramount role of the Swiss law of obligations, perfectly reconciling French and German elements, as the principal source of the Polish code.[61]

The code adopted the *clausula rebus sic stantibus*, which still had been present in some older European codes: the Prussian ALR (I.5 § 380) and,

---

[58] Filippo Ranieri, *Europäisches Obligationenrecht. Ein Handbuch* 106 (3rd ed., 2009).

[59] Leonard Górnicki, *Prawo cywilne w pracach Komisji Kodyfikacyjnej* 438-462 (2000).

[60] Bronisław Hełczyński, *The Law in a Reborn State*, in Wenceslas J. Wagner (ed.), *Polish Law throughout the Ages* 142 (1970).

[61] Roman Longchamps de Bérier, *Le nouveau code polonais des obligations*, 64 Bulletin de la Société de Législation Comparée 329f. (1935).

limited to preliminary contracts, the Austrian ABGB (§ 936). However, the *clausula* was omitted by the French *code civil*, according to which (art. 1134) contracts bind the parties exactly like the statute, as well as by the German BGB and in principle by the Swiss code of obligations.[62] Nonetheless, having considered the experience of German judicature, which during the 1920s in reference to the 'basis of the transaction' (*Geschäftsgrundlage*) was forced to resort to the general clause of good faith (§ 242 BGB), the Polish lawgiver preferred to formulate a special provision on supervening events.

Pursuant to this provision (art. 269) of the Polish code of obligations if 'the performance has become excessively difficult or threatens one of the parties with a crippling loss, which could not have been foreseen at the time of the formation of contract, the judge can, if he considers that it conforms to the principle of good faith and fair dealing, after having considered the interests of both parties, prescribe a manner of performance, fix the amount of damages or even terminate the contract'. To the discretion of the judge are also left numerous questions of fact relative to the institutions of unjustified enrichment (art. 123-127) and of undue performance (art. 128-133).[63]

The tort law of the Polish code of obligations relies on the principle of fault (art. 134-167). An exception is stated only for the liability of the possessor of a building or other structure (art. 151 § 1), responsible 'for the damage caused by the crumbling of the building or the detachment of a part thereof, unless he can prove that the accident happened not because the building had been neglected or because its construction was faulty, but for some other reason out of his control'. Moreover, a presumption of liability rested with owners of businesses run by natural power and with owners of plants, where explosives were used (art. 152), as well as with owners and users of mechanical vehicles (art. 153-154).

The Polish code of obligations was well received in the majority of European countries. In his preface to its French translation, Henri Capitant (1865-1937) evaluated it decisively higher than the somewhat earlier Franco-Italian draft law of obligations, published in 1927. Whereas this draft aimed only at 'rejuvenating the French and Italian codes' by means of a new judicature, the Poles were in a position similar to the draughtsmen of the *code civil*, and eventually they managed to produce equally a 'work

---

62 Konrad Zweigert & Hein Kötz, *An Introduction to Comparative Law* 518ff. (3rd ed., 1998).

63 Zygmunt Nagorski, *Codification of Civil Law in Poland 1918-1939* in *Studies in Polish and Comparative Law* 63f. (1945).

of compromise'.[64] There were also some positive echoes from Germany.[65] Without obviously touching the English Common Law, the Polish code of obligations of 1933 seems to have achieved the greatest synthesis possible within the continental system.

'The real socialism' was a blackout of European legal history

The continuity of private law in Eastern Europe under the socialist regime still remains controversial. However, according to a stereotype of legal historiography in East and West, 'the real socialism' was a historical regression; indeed a kind of blackout of European legal history. As such, the law of real socialism aligns neither with the preceding nor with the following system and should be forgotten straight away. On the other hand, according to some experts, in the Polish legal order 'there are still numerous offspring' of 'the real socialism'. [66] Regrettably, from the European perspective, things do not seem that simple.

As a matter of fact, after the communist revolution of 1917 Soviet Russia tried again to step out of the Western legal world. However, in the realm of private law the Russian jurists relied on the above-mentioned projects of the tsarist time, influenced by the Pandect science. The civil code of the Russian Republic (RSFSR), published in 1922, with its general part as well as with its general clauses on the social function of law and on the abuse of rights, bears the imprint not only of the Pandect science, but also of the 'juristic socialism' of Léon Duguit (1859-1928) and Anton Menger (1841-1906).

After World War II the whole of Eastern Europe fell under communist rule: the periphery of western capitalism became a periphery of the Soviet Empire. At its centre an upheaval of economic and social structures occurred. At the periphery prevailed a moderate climate of an 'as-if

---

64 Henri Capitant, *Préface* to: *Code des obligations de la République de Pologne* V-XX (1935); cf. Henri Mazeaud, *Les dispositions du code polonais des obligations relatives à la responsabilité délictuelle*, 63 Bulletin de la Société de Législation Comparée 193-223 (1934).

65 See citations in Helmut Slapnicka, *Österreichisches Recht...* 20f. (1973); Tomasz Giaro, *Europäische...* 17f. (1994).; Claudia Kraft, *Europa im Blick der polnischen Juristen* 113 (2002).

66 Rafał Mańko, *Is the Socialist Legal Tradition Dead and Buried?* in Thomas Wilhelmsson et al. (eds.), Private Law and the Many Cultures of Europe 103 (2007).

thinking' of imported ideology. [67] Nonetheless, the communists expropriated large landholdings and nationalized industry and commerce, thereby repeating the failure of Balkan modernization in the 19th century, to attempt an industrial revolution before a rationalization of agriculture. Even if the Soviet-style constitutions were based on the principle of unity of state power, in the ordinary legislation, particularly in the Hungarian and the Polish civil codes, of 1959 and 1964 respectively, many traditional institutions survived.

At the beginning the old law was being adjusted with the help of general clauses and vague concepts. They made it possible to substitute the traditional free exercise of subjective rights with their exercise 'according to their social scope' and the traditional equal protection of private and public property with the 'special protection' of the latter. The method of general clauses became dominant as well in East Germany until 1975, when the BGB, a 'late born child of the Pandect science and of the national-democratic liberalism',[68] was abrogated. Due to its abstraction, the code could be applied by the communists as well as by the Nazis.

The general clauses preserved their role also after the socialist codifications of civil law, which were completed in Czechoslovakia in 1950, in Hungary in 1959, in Russia and Poland in 1964 and in East Germany in 1975. For instance in the Polish code of 1964 the 'social-economic scope of a right' and the 'principles of social life' formed criteria for the exercise of rights and the fulfilment of duties (art. 5 KC). However, as far as the new civil law is concerned, the legalist way of thinking became in principle the obligatory doctrine.

Contrary to the prejudice that the real socialism was strictly unitary in character, the new legal family covered an inhomogeneous territory, which previously belonged partly to the border area of the reception of Roman Law (East Germany and Bohemia), partly to the Byzantine world (Bulgaria and Romania), and finally to the area occupied only during the 19th century by the natural law codes and the Pandect science (Poland and Hungary). This lack of homogeneity was stressed by the followers both of the autonomy of socialist law and of its affinity to the Romanist family.

Moreover, some legal historians drew a line between the socialist countries of Latin background, including the legal culture of the *ius commune* on one side, and those of Greek Orthodox background, cut off

---

[67] Kazimierz Wyka, *Life as if*; cf. Janina R. Wedel, *The Unplanned Society* 59 (1992).

[68] Franz Wieacker, *Industriegesellschaft und Privatrechtsordnung* 15 (1974); cf. Id., Wieacker, *A History of Private Law*... 379 (1995)

from the rest of Europe by Ottoman occupation, on the other;[69] thus the medieval religious divide between Europe and the Byzantine world, dear particularly to Helmut Coing,[70] was revaluated. Some other scholars distinguished the market-oriented countries, such as Yugoslavia, Hungary and Poland, from those preferring the administrative control of economy, such as Russia, Czechoslovakia and East Germany.[71]

Poland and Hungary proved most faithful to the civilian tradition. They justified the cultivation of the Pandect science with the hermeneutic distinction between the traditional form and the socialist content. Also the Soviet civil law, in particular the Russian code of the NEP-period, was drafted by pre-revolutionary jurists in a traditional manner. For this reason, despite the political leadership of the Soviet Union, other countries sometimes overtook the piloting doctrinal role. Even if the fundamental doctrine on types and forms of property emerged during the 1930s in Russia, after World War II truly socialist civil codes were promulgated only in 1964 by Czechoslovakia and in 1975 by East Germany.

The second Czechoslovak civil code of 1964 was accompanied by the code of economy, which regulated the socialist property. The civil code contained some ideological innovations. In particular art. V imposed 'mutual rights and duties' not only between the parties, but also 'with respect to society'.[72] The maxim remained, however, merely an interpretation tool, because the society may hardly be considered a subject of civil law. Moreover, the code abandoned the category of right *in rem*, understood as a direct legal power over things and therefore proscribed because of the Marxist aversion to the capitalist commodity fetishism. The categories of the code followed not the structure of legal institutions, but their social function and scope.[73]

Also the East German code of 1975 was structured according to the states of affairs, lacking a sharp distinction between property and obligations. There was neither a clear distinction between ownership and possession nor between ownership and *iura in re aliena*. Hence, only 'lawful possession' was protected (§ 33.3) and a general notion of 'property

---

[69] Tomasz Giaro, *Aufstieg und Niedergang des sozialistischen Zivilrechts* in Gerd Bender & Uli Falk (eds.), *Enteignung* 227 (1999).

[70] Helmut Coing, *Geschichtliche Grundlagen des Rechts im kontinentalen Europa und im Common Law* in Klaus J. Hopt (ed.), *Junge Juristen und Wirtschaft* 18 (1991); Helmut Coing, *Von Bologna...* 3 (1989).

[71] Hubert Izdebski, *La tradition et le changement en droit: l'exemple des pays socialistes*, 39 Revue Internationale de Droit Comparé 877 (1987).

[72] Theodor J. Vondraček, *Commentary on the Czechoslovak civil code* 3 (1988).

[73] Tomasz Giaro, *Aufstieg und Niedergang...* 289 (1999).

and interests therein' applied (§ 295). A special law on the contract system in the socialist economy of 1965 and 1982, explained sometimes with the Weimar tradition of a distinct business law (*Wirtschaftsrecht*),[74] created a mixed regulation, which reflected the dual nature of the state as industry owner and holder of power as well as the consequent intertwining of economy and politics.

Communism intended to reverse the Westernization of Eastern Europe, but the pre-revolutionary continental influence on Russian civilians was very profound. Facing the question of subjective rights, vested in state enterprises with reference to the fractions of national property entrusted to their care, they tested without a definitive success all the conceptual tools of legal history and comparative law: the state as the sole holder of a one-man company, agency, divided property, *peculium*, *trust*, limited interests in property, possession and finally the mostly diffused specific right of operative administration. The reason for this failure was, however, the very formulation of the question according to the simplistic nature of property in the civil law countries, based on the Pandect science, rather than in the flexible case-law style.[75]

There is still a distinct legal tradition of Eastern Europe

A final question concerning the legal tradition of Eastern Europe should be obviously posed, namely how deep the traces left by the experience of 'real socialism' are in the legal systems of particular Eastern European countries which had previously been members of the so-called Eastern Bloc.[76] Some scholars of this region argue to the positive,[77] insisting that these infamous traces are to be eradicated as soon as possible. However, in my opinion, already today the socialist tradition can only be considered as effectively dead and buried.

As a typical representative of private law systems of East Central Europe, the Polish civil law currently does not differ essentially from its western counterparts, which provided its building materials in the 19th century and the interwar period. The Polish civil code of 1964 was amended several times, particularly in 2003, in order to remove the

[74] Hubert Izdebski, *La tradition et le changement...* 862, 877 (1987).

[75] Katlijn Malfliet, *The Hungarian Quest for a Valid Theory of 'Socialist' Property,* 13 Review of Socialist Law 261ff. (1987); Tomasz Giaro, *Aufstieg und Niedergang...* 279 (1999).

[76] Gábor Hamza, *Continuity and Discontinuity of Private Law in Eastern Europe after World War II*, 12Fundamina: A Journal of Legal History 48-80 (2006).

[77] Rafał Mańko, *Is the Socialist Legal Tradition...* 83 (2007).

remnants of 'the real socialism'.[78] Lawyers in Eastern Europe are now kept busy primarily by the same task as in the old Member States of the European Union: the implementation of directives on consumer protection. The on-going differences between legal life in East and West are a matter of legal culture and juristic style rather than of substance of the law.[79]

To sum up, after the fall of communism, the independent states of the East are back again at the European legal stage, but their traditions prior to the 19th century, which disappeared long ago, seem impossible to resuscitate. After Harold J. Berman had extended the concept of western legal tradition not only to East Central Europe, but also to communist Russia, unfortunately forgetting to mention South Eastern Europe as well, the European character of Soviet law became widely recognized.[80] Given its Romanist, or better Pandectist, constitutive elements, Soviet civil law was undoubtedly part and parcel of the continental legal family[81] and remains today a chapter of western legal history.[82]

In keeping with the general experience of social history the centre-periphery structure tends always to consolidate, because the centre is used to become more and more central, whereas the periphery becomes necessarily still more peripheral. This insight reveals itself, however, not to be entirely exact with respect to legal families. Contrary to Koschaker's slogan 'Europe and Roman law', which proclaimed the restriction of the continent to its western part, the failed reception of Roman law had been supplied in the East already during the 19th century.

Evidently, this law was received in its modern shape of western codifications and legal doctrines. Since then the old threefold legal map of Europe, consisting of the British Isles as well as the western and the eastern part of the continent,[83] was replaced by a simpler dual system, confronting the English Common Law with the homogeneous continental

---

[78] Dorota Kempter, *Der Einfluss des europäischen Rechts auf das polnische ZGB* 53ff. (2007).

[79] Rafał Mańko, *The Culture of Private Law in Central Europe*, 11 European Law Journal 527ff. (2005).

[80] Ludwig Burgmann, *Das byzantinische Recht...* 539 (1996).; Christopher Osakwe, *Rethinking the Nature of Soviet Law*, 19 Comparative Law Review 110 (1985).

[81] John Quigley, *The Romanist Character of Soviet Law* in Ferdinand J.M. Feldbrugge (ed.), *The Emancipation of Soviet Law*, 27ff. (1992).

[82] Albert J. Schmidt, *Soviet Civil Law as Legal History. Essays Ferdinand Feldbrugge* 46 (1996).

[83] Tomasz Giaro, *Roman Law Always Dies with a Codification* in Antoni Dębiński & Maciej Jońca (eds.), *Roman Law and European Legal Culture* 18 (2008).

area. It is exclusively this duality of the Western legal tradition and not its alleged, but anyway obsolete, opposition to Eastern Europe which remains the chief obstacle to the present harmonization of private law of the Member States, pursued by the European Union.

TO UNIFY OR TO SYNCHRONIZE LAW IN EUROPE?

BRONISŁAW SITEK

UNIVERSITY OF WARMIA AND MAZURY IN OLSZTYN, POLAND

Introduction

To unify or to synchronize law in Europe? To build a new legal system irrelevant to European legal culture based on Roman Law and medieval *ius commune*? What system of values should be the base of the European legal space? Should it be based on traditional values, such as human dignity, individual autonomy, respect for property, or perhaps human rights, specifically tolerance, respect for all minorities, the primacy of the individual over society, in particular economic value, especially profit? These are indeed Hamlet's questions about the further development and shape of the European legal space. For at least fifty years these questions have been raised by the lawyers dealing with the unification of European law, particularly in the area of the civil law.

Intensification of research in this area occurred after the Second World War. The main reason was a globalist trend, initiated with the unification of technical standards. The discovery and definition of the universal principles of economics was an undoubted contribution. Hence, the idea of unification is not absent in other cultures, which are particularly subjected to globalist tendencies.[1]

The subject of this study was limited to analysis and evaluation of trends in unifying the European legal space such as unification and synchronization connected with decodification of law. These are typical phenomena for the process described as the Europeanization of law. The basic feature of the unification trend is the internationality of legal

---

[1] See Robert Cooter & Thomas Ulen, *An Economic Analysis of Law*, Polish translation J. Bełdowski, K. Metelska-Szaniawska, XVIff. (2009). About the origin of economic analysis of law also see Tomasz Giaro, *Leon Pietrażycki Economic Analysis of Law. Materials for Further Consideration* in *Learning and Teaching Law. Tradition and Future* 211ff. (2009).

standards.[2] In order to show the rationality of proposed solutions unifying the European legal space, it would be appropriate to analyze a case from South African law.

Non-institutional work of unification

Unifying the European legal space is a reflection of global trends. Restatements could be examples, which since the 1930s are a subsidiary source of law on the grounds of the American Common Law.[3] In 1980, The United Nations Commission on International Trade Law (UNCITRAL) adopted the so-called Vienna Convention that contains standards for the international sale of goods. Work on a common regulatory framework within the civil law is conducted by the

---

[2] See Kazimierz Lankosz, *European Legal Space on the Threshold of the 21st Century* in *Contemporary Challenges of the European Legal Space. Commemorative Book to Mark the 70th Birthday of Professor Eugeniusz Piontek* 33 (2005).

[3] The main function of restatements is to systematize the bases, commonly accepted legal rules belonging to separate areas of law. This term comes from the verb to restate that means re-presentation or drafting. Although restatements are devoid of binding character and cannot be incorporated into national legal systems, it is used in all U.S. states. Prepared drafts of rules take the form of set of characteristic structure and accompanied by commentary (Comments). The actions of these principles are illustrated with cases' examples (Illustrations). In addition, the provisions are included in 'annotate rapporteurs' preparing the draft restatements (Reporter's Notes). Restatements play an important role in the practice of lawyers. They are widely used in the jurisdiction of the courts and reported in published legal opinions. Restatements have also become the basis for the introduction of new units in the editorial work of the Commission of Ole Lando or the Christian von Bar Group. The text of the restatements is based on the chapters, sections, which is reflected in the typical method of numbering articles, e.g. art. 1:101 is article 1 of section 1 chapter 1. Restatements cover a range of issues as civil law that is regulated by the continental system of codes (contract law, property law and tort law) and international relations not directly related to this field of law. First restatements, issued in 1932, were devoted to contracts (Restatement of Contract). To that time, a second edition of restatements was prepared (restatements 'Second'), and in some cases the third edition has been developed (restatements 'Third'). Some restatements were included in the first edition and were not preceded by the Second and Third version. The structure of restatements issued in recent times is much more extensive. Compared to the initial studies the number of specific facts increased. See Maria Kaczorowska, *The Role of Restatements in the Process of Europeanization of Private Law*, http://tinyurl.com/3za5jem [February 7th, 2011].

International Institute for the Unification of Private Law in Rome (UNIDROIT), which developed the principles of international trade agreements. Fundamental importance in the European Union was accorded to the so-called Lando Commission (The Commission on European Contract Law) [4] which operated during the years 1980-2003. The Commission developed the Principles of the European Contract Law (Principles of European Private Law - PECL). One of the members of that Commission was Christian von Bar, a German lawyer, who coordinated the work of the study dealing with the European Code of Civil Law (Coordinator of the Study Group on the European Civil Code). It was a base on which the Study Group was set. Its main objective was to elaborate the European Civil Code (Study Group on European Civil Code).[5] Its purpose is to prepare the European Civil Code.

Research on unifying the European legal system is also being carried out by other groups of lawyers.[6] These groups should be mentioned: The Common Core of European Private Law, a group of prominent lawyers, which has been operating since 1995, first in Trento, now in Turin. The work of the group is chaired by U. Mattei and M. Bussani.[7] They deal with contract law, property law and tort law. Another group of lawyers involved in the unification of European law is the European Research Group on Existing EC Private Law (Acquis Group),[8] the Project Group on

---

[4] About the work of this Commission, see: Ole Lando, *Contract Law in the EU. The Commission Action Plan and the Principles of European Contract Law* in http://tinyurl.com/3rhwp7c [February 2nd, 2011].

[5] See. Maria Kaczorowska, *The Role of Restatements...*; Christian von Bar, *Drafting a European Civil Code,* 10 State and Law 44ff. (2000); Ewoud Hondius & Aneta Wiewiórkowska-Domagalska, *The European Civil Code (Analysis of the Study Group Work)*, 6 State and Law 28ff. (2002); Rafał Mańko, *The European Civil Code - the Status of the Project and Prospects for Further Development*, XLIII Studies Iuridica 141ff. (2004).

[6] All these groups operate on the basis of the principle of European legal culture. However, they are starting from a different source base. As an example the concept of good faith in the light of the proposals contained in the individual projects should be analised. See Wojciech. Dajczak, *'Treu und Glauben' im System des Gemeinsamen Referenzrahmens und die Idee einer 'organisch vollzogenen' Privatrechtsangleichung in Europa*, 2 Gemeinschaftsprivatrecht 63ff. (2009).

[7] More about the activities of this group see http://www.common-core.org [February 7th, 2011].

[8] The group's activitie began in 2002. It was a response to European Union action in the field of contract law. A characteristic feature of this working group is the search for common elements in the civil law of the Member States. They are seeking possible solutions in the framework of the acquis communautaire. Effects

the Restatement of European Insurance Contract Law (Insurance Group),[9] the Research Group on the Economic Assessment of Contract Law Rules, or the so-called Economic Impact Group.[10]

The European Union towards the unification of civil law

Work on the unification of law or approximation of the Member States of the European Community, now the European Union, is undoubtedly related to the creation of the internal market. Regulations of the European Union include the area of public law as well as the economy. In accordance with article 3 paragraph 3 of the consolidated version of the Treaty on European Union[11] 'the Union establishes the internal market. It works for the sustainable development of Europe. Its base is balanced economic growth and price stability, highly competitive social market economy, aiming at full employment and social progress, a high level of protection and improvement of environmental quality. Supports scientific and technological advance. This phrase clearly indicates the problematic area, which deals with the Union, notably the European Commission'.[12] It includes the issues of both public law and civil law.[13] We are particularly interested in the second part, the common market[14] and protection of consumers.

---

of the work were published in the Principles of the Existing EC Contract Law. More about the activities of this group see http://www.acquis-group.org [February 7th, 2011].

[9] This group has been working since 1992 at the University of Innsbruck. It deals essentially with insurance contracts. Work is being done in close conjunction with a group of Christian von Bar and the American system of restatements. See http://tinyurl.com/3msdjpd [February 7th, 2011].

[10] The work of this group is associated with the Dutch University of Tilburg. The research group focused on the economic regulation of the market. This is a typical school dealing with the economic analysis of law. They are looking for a solution to the most recent economic problems, using legal instruments. http://tinyurl.com/4ym3txx [February 7th, 2011].

[11] *O.J. C 83, 30.3.2010*, p. 15.

[12] More about the Commission's rights in the unification of European law writes, Roberto Adam, *General Features of Community Law* in 1 Antonio Tizzano (ed.), *The Private Law of the European Union* 27ff. (2006).

[13] See Tomasz Pajor, *Civil Law and the Law of the European Union* in 6 Michał Seweryński & Zbigniew Hajn (eds.), *European legal studies* 58ff. (2002).

[14] See Tadeusz Skoczny, *European Competition Law - the Improvement of Modernization to the Direction of Transformation?* in *Ibid.*, 112ff.

From the point of view of international law, the European Union is not a state, but a specific international organisation with characteristic features and the ability to evolve and to create its own constitutional identity.[15] This state of affairs is also reflected in relation to the civil law. The European legal space is made up of different legal cultures built on the basis of the continental or common law. The foundation of the first is largely Roman law, although we cannot deny the cultural heritage of later epochs, especially the Enlightenment and German *Pandectarum*.[16]

The Europeanization of the private law is accomplished in many areas, unnoticed even by an experienced recipient of legal norms. The European legislative activity and its impact on the practice, significantly impinges on the legislation of the Member States, especially on the modification of the fundamental principles of these systems. We may point out numerous areas in which unification of legal standards has already taken place across the European Union, such as competition law, company law, intellectual or industrial property, labour law, banking law and public trading in securities law, contract, protection of consumers, financial services, Internet law, in particular electronic trading law. The Europeanization of law is also gradually covering different issues related to family law.[17]

The European Union has also joined the process of harmonization of the European legal space institutionally.[18] In 2001, The European Commission issued the Announcement on European Contract Law.[19] The intention was to launch a public consultation about the problems arising from differences in the contract law of the Member States and possible actions in this regard. The collected responses enabled the Commission to establish a plan of action in 2003.[20] The basic instrument to achieve this aim was to develop a common framework (the Common Frame of Reference - CFR): common principles, terminology and rules. In the Communication of the Commission from 2004 about European contract law and revision of the acquis: development, it was proposed to remove

---

[15] See Jacek Barcik & Aleksandra Wentkowska, *Law of the European Union Including the Lisbon Treaty* 15ff. (2008).

[16] The opposite thesis states Kazimierz Lankosz, according to that the current legal system has its origin in the 17th century and has no connection with Roman law and Christianity. See Kazimierz Lankosz, *European Legal Space...* 29 (2005).

[17] See 1 Antonio Tizzano, *The Private law of the European Union* VII (2006).

[18] See Rafał Mańko, *EU Institutions and the Idea of a European Civil Code* 2 European Law Review 47ff. (2004); Jerzy Rajski, *New stage of development of European private law*, 1 Private Law Quarterly 111ff. (2006).

[19] COM (2001) 398, 11.7.2001.

[20] COM (2003) 68, 12.2.2003.

inconsistencies and fill loopholes in the law of contracts between a businessman and a consumer. At the end of 2008 the Study Group of the European Civil Code led by Christian von Bar released a draft of the common framework of references (the Draft of a Common Frame of Reference – DCFR),[21] which included the principles, definitions and model rules of European civil law. The proposed solution is related to trade agreements as well as businessman and consumer agreements.

In 2010, the Commission published a Green Paper on policy options in a scope of progress towards the establishment of the European law of contract for consumers and businessmen.[22] In this document, the Commission presented the status of the unification of the European legal space, and new challenges for the internal market.

Another instrument is the EU Stockholm Program for the years 2010-2014,[23] which has stated that the European judicial area has to promote economic activity in the domestic market.

Hence, it is necessary to accept the draft of a common frame of reference and to conduct further analysis of issues of the law of contract. An important element of the internal market is to help entrepreneurs and consumers to conclude agreements with partners from the other EU countries and to reduce transaction costs. These matters are also described in another of the Commission's documents, 'Europe 2020'.[24] According to the Commission, reduction of the cost of the operation may be achieved by harmonization of standards of the contractual clauses and creation of the optional European law of contract. Permanent economic benefits can be achieved through creation of the European Digital Agenda,[25] a project approved under 'Europe 2020'. This action will achieve sustainable economic and social benefits for the internal market by eliminating the fragmentation of the legal stratification.

Actions taken so far by the Union have caused the Commission to set up an expert group[26] to examine the feasibility of a user-friendly

---

[21] Christian von Bar & Hans Schulte Nölke (eds.), *Principles, Definitions and Model Rules of European Private Law. Draft Common Frame of Reference (DCFR)* (2009). Available at http://tinyurl.com/3kldjxf [January 31st, 2011].

[22] COM (2010) 248, 01.07.2010.

[23] Council's document from December 2nd, 2009 no. 17024/09.

[24] COM (2010) 2020, 03.03.2010.

[25] European Commission Communication Digital Agenda - COM (2010) 245, 19.5.2010.

[26] Commission's decision from April 26th, 2010 established an expert group on a common framework of reference for European contract law, OJL 105, 27.04.2010, p. 109

instrument of the European law of contract, which would bring benefit to consumers and businesses, and would also guarantee legal certainty. This group shall mainly deal with the contract law and the possibilities of using designed elements of the common framework of references prepared by Ch. von Bar's group.

Previous works on the unification of the civil law within the EU raise the question of its subjective scope. This issue was raised by W. Dajczak in 'Von diesem Hintergrund darf für die Diskussion über die Grenze der Kompetenz im Bereich der Union nicht ohne Bedeutung des Zivilrechts sein, dass es *keine Sparte der Rechtswissenschaft gibt, die so einen ausgesprochen europäischen Charakter hat, wie die Privatrechtswissenschaft'*.[27]

Issues to solve

The idea of unification and synchronization of private law in the European Union causes specific practical and research problems that must be solved. The most important of them include clarifying the form of unification and synchronization of law and the rules for its interpretation.[28] Resolution of these issues ultimately determines the choice of the direction of the European legal space. But this is not the end of the problems that will need to be solved. New and no less important problems arise when one selects a path of development of the European legal space. In the case of unification through codification a new issue and mass legal education shall come into being not only on the faculties of law, but above all in education for judges, prosecutors, lawyers and other entities applying law. It is difficult to imagine that only the implementation of the European Civil Code would be equivalent to a common understanding of its content and numerous links to non–Code regulations that exist at the EU level or the national level.[29]

---

[27] Wojciech. Dajczak, *Vom Beruf der Europäischen Union für die Kodifikation des Zivilrechts*, 5 Gemeinschaftsprivatrecht 201 (2009).

[28] The problems of interpretation of the law within the European legal space, considered among others by Polish researchers at a conference organized by the Faculty of Law and Administration February 27th, 2004 See summaries of these materials http://tinyurl.com/3pftjez [January 30th, 2011]. See Tomasz Giaro, *Interpretation as a Source of Law - in the Past and Today*, 7 Studia Prawnoustrojowe 243ff. (2007).

[29] See Naděžda Royehnalová & Jiří Valdhans, *A Few Observations on Choice of Law* in Alexander Belohlavek & Naděžda Rozehnalová, 1 Czech Yearbook of

Further issues will be identified when considering extension of the European Union over new countries outside the European culture, such as Turkey or Tunisia. One of the issues to be tackled will be the content and interpretation of the principle of good faith, which is fundamental to the Western legal culture, and completely unknown in the system of Islamic law. The question of individual autonomy, which is fundamental to the law of contract in the continental legal system, not necessarily accepted in the system of Islamic law, will need to be defined.[30]

Uncoordinated actions in the area of standardization of the European legal space, particularly through the introduction of the European Civil Code lead to the vulgarization of the law, unless the legal community is properly prepared. A similar phenomenon took place in ancient Rome, when in 212 A.D. Emperor Caracalla granted citizenship to all residents of the Roman Empire, except for *peregrini dediticii*. This action violated the principle of personality of law. Everyone was obliged to obey the law of the state applicable to the nationality that one possessed. Few people had the citizenship of the Roman Empire, and only they knew and respected the Roman Law. The other inhabitants applied their own law. Granting citizenship to all inhabitants of the Empire led to the compulsory use of the Roman Law by persons who did not know this law. This was the beginning of the fall or vulgarization of the Roman legal culture.[31]

The harmonization of the European legal space may be made through unification and synchronization. In the case of unification, the simplest method is to enact by an act or a code. This concept is promoted by a group of lawyers gathered around Ole Lando and Christian von Bar.[32]

Codification of law gives the feeling of security, especially to the legislative authority applying law and also to the courts or administrative authorities. We may not forget that codification of law causes fossilization

---

International Law (2010); Id., *Second Decade Ahead: Tracing the Global Crisis* 3ff. (2010).

[30] More about Islamic law, see *Islamic Law of Contract*, http://tinyurl.com/3l8awtk [February 6th, 2011]; Susan Rayner, *The Theory of Contracts in Islamic Law* (1991).

[31] The process of vulgarization of Roman law described by Franz Wieacker, *Vulgarismus und Klassizismus im Recht der Spätantike* 7ff. (1995); Mario Bretone, *Storia del diritto Romano* 475 (2001); Gerhard Dulckeit et al., *Römische Rechtsgeschichte* 292ff. (1989). The reasons vulgarization of Roman law during post-classicism were more than one and should include the impact of foreign rights, especially the rights of the East Germanic peoples.

[32] See Jarosław Bełdowski, *Towards a European civil Code?*, 6 Juridical Education 7 (2005).

of its rules, and eventually the whole system.[33] After a while the legislature does not respond properly and quickly enough to the changing reality. It cannot be unseen that the idea of codification in recent years is in crisis, which is emphasized by many European thinkers, including N. Irti,[34] A. Petrucci,[35] T. Giaro[36] and F. Longchamps de Berier. Hence, the creation of the European Civil Code does not seem to be the best solution.[37]

Another possible way to harmonize the European legal space is synchronisation of the existing legal systems. This concept emerges from the analysis of the previously mentioned documents of the European Commission, in particular the action plan announced by the Commission in 2003. In order to understand the idea of law synchronization and opportunities of carrying it out, it is worth referring to one of the mixed legal systems existing today which was created due to the synchronization of different legal systems. A good example is South Africa's legal system, which is a combination of multiple legal traditions. It will be necessary not only to present the sources and rules of the system, but also analysis of a specific example, which will enable better understanding of the process of unification of law in the Union.

South African legal system

The South African legal system is included in mixed systems, which are also-called hybrid systems. This type of law is in force in: Scotland, Zimbabwe, Zambia, Ceylon and Guyana. South African Common Law consists of the Roman-Dutch Law, the principles of Roman Law and customs derived from Germanic Law. Jurisprudence is not unimportant.

---

[33] See H. Konarski, Perspectives of Codification of the European Contract Law, 3 Commercial Law Review 32 (2004); Rafał Mańko, *Private Law in the European Union. Prospects for the Future* 37 (2004); Ewa Rott-Pietrzyk, *Concept of Reason in the Draft European Civil Code* in Leszek Ogiegło et al. (eds.), *Law Dissertations*.

[34] Natalino Irti, *L'età della decodificazione* 3-97(1999).

[35] Giovanni Luchetti & Aldo Petrucci, *Fundamentals of European Contract Law. Roman Roots to the Draft of the Principles of European Contract Law of the Lando Commission* 23 (2006).

[36] Tomasz Giaro, *Interpretation without the code* in *Interpretation of the law. Conference materials* 25ff. (2004). Summary of materials located on http://tinyurl.com/3pftjez [January 30th, 2011].

[37] See Rafał Mańko, *Private Law in the European Union. Prospects for the Future* 38 (2004).

This system evolved in the 17th and 18th centuries, due to lawyers and the decisions of courts in the Netherlands. The mixed system, in the last two centuries was significantly influenced by English Common Law, its jurisprudence and legislation.[38]

The main sources of South African Law are: legislation, customs, court decisions, legal treatises and Roman Law. The secondary important sources are legal regulations derived from English Law, or the Anglo-American, Dutch, French, German and Swiss Law, whereby those sources are merely used to facilitate finding a suitable solution for one's case. Such application of law, actually codification of others, stems from the fact that the system of South African Law is deprived of a quoting act, nor is there a *numerus clausus* of law sources.[39]

South African legislation has a decisive nature. Its Parliament establishes law, although it follows examples of English Law.[40] Thus, it is not an object of European interest. In South Africa, as in England, an Act is an exception in the legal system and fills existing loopholes in law. The role of the Act follows from the fact that in South Africa's legal system is not possible to supplement the loopholes with analysis of the intent and purpose of the legislature, or by analogy. Wider interpretation is not in use.[41]

Jurisprudence has a significant meaning in the South African legal system, based on an English case law. This solution is unknown to the continental legal culture. In relation to Anglo-Saxon Law, South African case law is applied with a limited scope. Only some decisions of courts may be considered as precedents, being judgments of the Supreme Court. The court may issue decisions, which amend or differ significantly from judgments in similar cases. A characteristic feature of South African processes is that, while they proceed as in the English model, they have kept institutions from the Formula Procedure of Ancient Rome, such as *contestatio litis* or *res iudicata.*[42]

---

[38] See Francois du Bois (ed.), *Wille's Principles of South African Law* (9th ed. 2007); Willem Joubert et al., *The Law of South Africa* (2004); Reinhard Zimmermann & Danie Visser, *Southern Cross: Civil Law and Common Law in South Africa* (1996).

[39] See Bronisław Sitek, *Roman-Dutch Law. Contemporary Use of Roman Law* in Tadeusz Maciejewski (ed.), *This justice* 1933-1945 (1999); Walter Pollak, *The South African Law of Jurisdiction* 143 (1937).

[40] See G. MacKerron, *The Sale of Goods in South Africa* 243 (1935); Bronisław Sitek, *Roman-Dutch Law....* 33-45 (1999),

[41] See Bronisław Sitek, *Roman-Dutch Law....* 33-45 (1999).

[42] See James Mackintosh, *Roman Law in Modern Practice* 88ff. (1934).

In some decisions the Supreme Court of South Africa refers in its cases to the Privy Council, thus is similar to the royal court in England. This type of court was unknown in the system of Roman-Dutch Law, and this practice came after 1910, after the formation of the Southern Union. This practice originated due to the fact that the majority of South African judges and lawyers had studied in England. Hence, it is much easier for lawyers to reach for the well-known precedents and textbooks from their student days or from the practice held in the UK. Unwillingly, they go back to books from the 16th and 17th century, which are written in Latin and thus incomprehensible to modern lawyers. Also, it is easier for lawyers to operate within already known techniques of precedents than refer to old books or make law qualifications using antique books. This practice was banned in 1950.

Jurisprudence, which is understood as a doctrine of law, nowadays performs a different role than in the Roman Law system, especially during the Principate.[43] Doctrine of law in Ancient Rome was the source of law, which in the continental and Anglo-Saxon legal systems is unthinkable. *Prudentes* to increase their authority did not refer to judgments or other acts, such as the imperial constitution. All citations of other solutions adopted in the imperial constitutions, especially in *rescripts*, had an informative or interpretive character.[44]

In justifications for the judgments it is possible to refer to Roman jurists' opinions, as well as those of contemporaries. In the case of older works, courts cite opinions from Inleidigen by H. Grotius, Paratitla Juris Novissimi by S. van Leeuwen, Rechtsgeleerd, Practicaal, en Koopmans Handboek by J. van der Linden. Then, in the situation when quoted authors differ from each other, or do not express themselves in a specific case, the court has the liberty of choosing another lawyer's point of view, or contemporary ones. It should be noted that judges easily decide that a particular case cannot be resolved on the basis of Roman-Dutch Law, but under English Law or another contemporary law. They quote Cujacius, Donolleus and German Pandektysts, such as F.C. v. Savigny,[45] C.F.

[43] Principate period is important because then the Roman jurisprudence reached the highest stage of development. Hence it is regarded as the classic period of Roman Law.

[44] See Wojciech Dajczak, *The Issue of 'Timeless' Nature of the Rules of the Roman Law. Remarks in the Discussion on 'the New European Legal Culture'*, 5.2 The Law UKSW Papers 7 (2005); Tomasz Giaro, *Dogmatische Wahrheit und Zeitlosigkeit in der Römischen Jurisprudenz*, XXIX BIDR 1ff. (1987).

[45] Das Recht des Besitzes, System des heutigen Römischen Rechts.

Glück,[46] K.A. Vangerow[47] or B. Windscheid.[48] Among today's lawyers not only law professors are quoted, such as B. Beinart and P. van Warmelo, but also the South African Supreme Court's judge F.P. van den Heevera who died in 1956. Apart from the Dutch and German legal literature **also Italian, Spanish and French literature is quoted,** but because of the limited knowledge of these languages in South Africa, it has limited range.

The basic principle while quoting the legal literature is the preference of Dutch lawyers' works. Others lawyers may be quoted only when Dutch lawyers do not express their opinions in discussion. The stronger position of the 16th and 17th century Dutch lawyers results from the conviction of their high knowledge of Roman Law.

The final source of law in South Africa is customary law. In contrast to the continental European legal culture, its roots are in judgments. Thus, the South African case law performs a legal function similar to that of case law in the English legal system.

State v. Ebrahim case

There is a possibility that a particular case resolution may be made even with the existence of multiple regulations from different legal systems, the harmonization of which has taken place as a result of centuries of coexistence. The example of different legal systems functioning in so-called mixed system is the State v. Ebrahim case, settled by the appellate court judgment of 26th February 1991 (Supreme Court of South Africa - Appellate Division). In its sentence the court referred among others to the provisions of Roman Law, applying it to citizenship of South Africa.[49]

Facts

Ebrahim, was born in South Africa in 1964. He was held for 15 years in prison for activities against the State, for participation in the illegal armed organizations, especially in the African National Congress (African National Congress-ANC). Imprisonment was in a place considered to be the most severe in South Africa, which was located on the island

[46] Ausführliche Erläuterung der Pandecten.

[47] Lerbuch der Pandecten.

[48] Lerbuch des Pandectenrechts.

[49] http://tinyurl.com/855rftb.

Robbeneiland (Robben Island). He came out in 1979. After leaving prison, the authorities in Pinetown in Natal were conducting an investigation against the prisoner, but in another case. Fearing re-trial and conviction, he fled to the small kingdom of Swaziland, located inside the territory of the Republic of South Africa near the border with Mozambique in 1980. In December 1986 he was abducted by two black men. During the arrest they informed him that they were representatives of the South African police. He was bound, they put a bandage over his eyes, and gagged his mouth. After crossing the border he was handed over, this time to a group of armed white males, who took him to Pretoria. During the journey he was questioned about his activities in the African National Congress. The people accompanying him repeatedly made it clear that they were representatives of the police. This was confirmed by the fact that, although the car often encountered police surveillance along the road, the convoy was not inspected. Jan Cronje, head of South African services, was constantly informed about the operation. The detainee was taken to police headquarters, where he was greeted by the police chief and other officers. When he began appealing to complain that he had been abducted, the answer he heard was that the whole action had been carried out on the basis of sec. 29 of the Internal Security Act of 1982 with academic precision. The applicant complained that he had been kidnapped by the South African police or security service. Yet, neither the police nor the South African security service admitted any abduction. It was relevant to the case that the authorities of Swaziland lodged a protest with the authorities of RPA because of the abduction of the South African plaintiff.

An analysis of the facts

In the light of the evidence it must be assumed that the South African police were not involved in the abduction of the appellant. The persons who abducted the applicant were members of the secret services of South Africa. Such reasoning is based on the belief that such people are not known to the police. Thus, the Court of Appeals based its resolution on the fact that he was abducted by agents of the special services of South Africa.

The establishment of the term 'agent' was of key importance to the case. According to the Court of Appeal, the term 'agent' refers to a person acting on the instructions and within the power of state agencies. In the period after World War II the activities of the special services were implemented through the various agencies. The manner in which the plaintiff was kidnapped unequivocally shows that an agency was responsible. State involvement in such an activity also occurs when the people responsible undertake their activities without the knowledge and approval of the highest state authorities. The actions taken by these bodies must be regarded as a manifestation of state action. Its authorities are acting through delegated authority. This also applies to administrative bodies of special services (agency). Therefore there are no doubts that the abduction was a work of one of the agencies, not the police.

In the light of these facts, it is necessary to consider the issue of the jurisdiction of the court to settle this case. Was the abduction a violation of the principles of international law? Violation of these rules would mean that the trial court was not competent to examine the issue. The court hearing the case was entitled to consider only the issues resolved in the light of national legislation. However, the court was found to be competent because the regulations of international law are part of the national South African law. Thus, a fundamental question must be to identify the rules of national law, which have been violated.

Analysis of legal status

The court of appeal decided to rely on several sources of Roman Law that relate to the competence of provincial governors.

Roman law

Paul. 1 ad ed. (D.2.1.20): *Extra territorium ius dicenti impune non paretur. Idem est, et si supra iurisdictionem suam velit ius dicere.*

(The official is not entitled to judicial power outside his territory. Similarly, when a judge performing his judicial power exceeds his competence). [50]

Paul. L. 13 ad Sab. (1.18.3): *Praeses provinciae in suae provinciae homines tantum imperium habet, et hoc dum in provincia est: nam si excesserit, privatus est. Habet interdum imperium et adversus extraneos homines, si quid manu commiserint: nam et in mandatis principum est, ut curet is, qui provinciae praeest, malis hominibus provinciam purgare, nec distinguuntur unde sint.*

(The governor has authority over the men only in his province, and only when he is there. If he crosses its boundaries, he becomes a private person. Sometimes he is entitled to have authority over people outside the province, if they committed an offence. Indeed, in the Imperial mandates for the governor of the province there an injunction to those who govern

[50] Own translation.

the province to take care of removing criminals from the province, no matter where they come from).[51]

Both texts show that competences of provincial governors in ancient Rome were limited only to the areas assigned for them. Such a practice was followed, despite the existing diversity of ethnic and cultural backgrounds. The authority of the governors was enclosed within the province. Exceeding the boundaries of the province by the governor meant that he became a private person. The execution of his jurisdictions' rights beyond the borders of the province is cause to dispute competencies

Macer l. 2 de off. praes. (D. 48.3.7): *Solent praesides provinciarum, in quibus delictum est, scribere ad collegas suos, ubi factores agere dicuntur, et desiderare, ut cum prosecutoribus ad se remittantur: et id quoque quibusdam rescriptis declaratur.*

(In a case when the governor of the province where the offence was committed wants to pursue the offender residing in another province, he should refer to his colleague in writing, to hand the offender over to him. This procedure has been written in rescripts many times).[52]

From Macera's text it follows that the governor could not decide arbitrarily about criminal cases, exceeding the territorial authority assigned to a particular province. Thus, already in the classical period, the procedure of arrest of offenders residing in another province was generated. This procedure was finally described in the Justinian Novels 124 cap. 5. According to this procedure, the governor, competent to prosecute the offender, started the whole procedure of publication of an edict calling on the offender to appear in front of the court in his province. If the offender did not report himself, the judge (the governor) could notify the governor of the province where the wanted person was sought, and ask for his arrest and for him to be sent to his (the requesting governor's) tribunal. If the governor did not comply with this request he was liable to a fine, loss of office, and exile.

System of Roman-Dutch Law

The position developed in Roman Law was adopted into Roman-Dutch Law, which is demonstrated in a commentary of Voet Johannes (1647-1713), one of the most famous lawyers of that system.[53] A similar position

---

[51] Polish translation Bartosz Szolc-Nartowski, *Justinian Digest* 115 (2007).

[52] Own translation.

[53] Johannes Voet, *Commentarius and Pandectas, Commentary to D. 48.3.2* (1940).

was taken by other representatives of Roman-Dutch Law mentioned in the verdict, for example:

(1) Antonius Matthaeus II (1601-1654) *Tractatus de Criminibus*, Commentary to D. 48.14.1.3.

(2) Dionysius Godefridus van der Keessel (1738-1816) *Praelectiones ad Jus Criminale*, Commentary to D. 48.3.2.

(3) Johannes van der Linden (1756-1835) *Supplementum to Voet's Commentarius ad Pandectas cited in Gane The Selective Voet*, vol 1, p 296, note (b).

(4) Pieter Bort (1615-1674) *Tractaat handelende van Arresten*. Commentary to D. 3.3.4.

(5) Berlichius (Mathaeus Berlich 1586-1638) *Conclusiones Practicabiles* (part 1, concl 74, nn 54-55).

It should be concluded that in Roman Law and the Roman-Dutch Law system, unlawful detention of a pursued person outside the jurisdiction of the judge (the governor) was treated as a serious breach of law, and said act was treated as an abduction.

South African legal system

The South African legal system is significantly associated with the *Roman-Dutch Law* system. Thus, South African Law does not entitle the courts or other state authorities to detain persons prosecuted outside the borders of their jurisdictional territorial, even when they are outside South Africa. This solution also results from national laws, especially sec. 39 of criminal procedure law from 1977 and sec. 19 of law on the Supreme Court from 1959. Moreover, it is reflected in a number of earlier, similar cases, such as Abrahams v. Minister of Justice 1963 (4) SA 542 (C).

Legal status opinion

The above analysis is based on a number of legal principles, such as human rights, respect for peaceful relations between states, justice based on the principle of legality and the prohibition of unlawful arrest or detention of the accused and not to exceed the competence of judicial authorities. Furthermore, the sovereignty of States or other administrative units should be respected, legal proceedings should be based on the principle of transparency and legality and avoid any abuse in the justice system. If the state is a party of the proceedings, it is necessary to maintain the rule of 'clean hands'. This last principle has been breached, in particular by the state authorities in the case in South Africa. In this situation, the Court of Appeal overturned a verdict of the court of first instance and held that the detention and conviction of the appellant was unlawful.

Summary

Globalization processes include ever more areas of social life, also those that are regulated by law. The abolition of political boundaries between states, and consequently the legal barriers, especially customs barriers, has raised particular problems that need to be solved. Generally they are associated with the use of law in the course of trade. One of the sources of the emergence of new problems is freedom of contracts concluded by consumers and businesses in the legal area without borders. The European Union is one such area, where legal systems of Member States, based on the so-called Continental Law and Common Law are still in use. Cultural distinctiveness of the different legal systems raises practical problems for businesses and consumers themselves, such as the uncertainty on the side of consumers, increase of the transaction costs of trade, and loss of citizens' trust in EU institutions and the integration process. Hence, the EU is increasingly interfering in different fields of law, including civil law.

The need to standardize law in Europe by synchronization or codifications was noticed expressly in the eighties. Previous activities implemented within the codification of the Union may be divided into synchronizing and unifying actions in the European legal space. The first of them are in order to develop common solutions to specific legal problems based on solutions developed within the existing legal culture of individual Member States, with reference to Roman Law; activities intended to unify and create a new European Code of Contract Law and European Civil Code, even in isolation from the existing legal culture.

An example of unifying the European legal space is the work of the so-called Lando Commission of the Group of Ch. von Bar. The Commission headed by O. Lando (The Commission on European Contract Law), has formulated the Principles of European Contract Law (Principles of European Private Law). In turn, Ch. von Bar's Study Group chaired the European Civil Code (Study Group on European Civil Code), whose goal is to prepare the European Civil Code. The result of this working group is a draft of a common framework of references (Draft of a Common Frame of Reference - DCFR).

The activities of the European Union are at the stage of the codification of European Law, without specification of its form; that is, synchronization or uniform codification. In this regard, there were a number of EU documents, which are mentioned in the Commission's Green Paper on policy options in regard to progress towards the establishment of European contract law for consumers and businesses.

The last issue to resolve is the question of choosing the way of unification of the European economic space. It seems that the most appropriate way will be synchronization of the existing legal systems. Choosing this path seems to be extremely clear due to the lower economic costs. The introduction of the European Civil Code will required new training in the law for all bodies applying the civil law, and thus judges, prosecutors, advocates and others. Construction of a uniform system of jurisdiction based on the existing legal traditions is possible. An example of this is being investigated from the precedent for a mixed system in force in South Africa. Also, the European Union could have this kind of legal system, and use it without exposing it to allegations of preferring one solution over another.

ECONOMIC ANALYSIS OF LAW AS A METHOD IN COMPARATIVE RESEARCH: EXAMPLE OF PURE ECONOMIC LOSS

JAKUB J. SZCZERBOWSKI

UNIVERSITY OF WARMIA AND MAZURY IN OLSZTYN, POLAND

Introduction

The field of law and economics started with an interesting analysis of social cost by Coase[1] and has undoubtedly changed the way scholars think about legal rules. However, the use of L&E in comparative research is not as widespread as I think it should be. Methodology of comparative law provides various tools for researchers. 1) The text-based dogmatic method, most widely used by lawyers and scholars, is responsible for as much growth of the discipline as for mistakes and misunderstandings. One of them is a still common view, that the institutions of common and civil law are incomparable because of their different dogmatic structures. 2) The functional method, to the contrary, represents the approach founded on the actual use of law, not on the text.[2]

The existence of a single functional method is controversial; more likely a plurality of functional approaches dwell in the comparative landscape. Platsas argues that there is a paradox between 'functional principle', the term used in other sciences, and the 'functional method' of comparative law.[3] While function understood as *tertium comparationis* is the core of the functional method, it is not clear how exactly one should define function and pursue its deeper understanding.

Many misunderstand the function as the intent of the legislator, while most laws have unintended consequences – likely to be important in the

---

[1] Ronald H. Coase, *The Problem of Social Cost*, 3 J.L. & ECON. 1 (1960).

[2] Ralf Michaels, *The Functional Method of Comparative Law*, SSRN ELIBRARY, 3 (2005), http://ssrn.com/abstract=839826 (last visited Jan 9, 2012).

[3] Antonios Emmanuel Platsas, *The Functional and the Dysfunctional in the Comparative Method of Law: Some Critical Remarks*, 12 ELECTRONIC JOURNAL OF COMPARATIVE LAW, 2 (2008), http://www.ejcl.org/123/art123-3.pdf.

assessment of law's influence on human behaviour. Function is commonly understood by those comparing it as the effect that law has on the given society. This meaning is more appealing, as it clearly enables comparisons wherever law has an influence, but does not answer the second part of the question: how one should conceptualize and research functions of law.

The proposition of this article is that the field of law and economics is a toolbox for the functional method. Economics is a field of social sciences oriented towards researching incentives (and the functional approach fundamentally concentrates on the effects[4] of law, which translate into incentives). The question is whether law provides incentive that can be analysed by economics. Possible answers are 'yes', 'no', and 'yes and no'. 'Yes and no' is a short answer to the majority of the complex questions in social sciences, and applies in this case. Law and economics is undoubtedly a field of legal science in its own right. It can also lend its services to the functional method of comparative law.

Definition of Pure Economic Loss

The definitions of pure economic loss may be divided into dogmatic definitions, i.e. those formed on the ground of legal rules, judicial decision and the doctrine of a particular legal system, and the economic definition, formulated by scholars influenced by the explanation provided by Bishop.[5]

The differences in defining pure economic losses in various legal systems are based not only on the doctrinal differences. The main reason for the discrepancy is the emphasis on the kind of harm in common law and the emphasis on the kind of infringed right in civil law. Legal systems such as the French, Spanish or Polish make use of the concept of absolute rights, obligations and economic interests. Common Law, on the other hand, puts the nature of the harm at the centre of the definition.

Feldthusen defines pure economic loss as an "economic harm not consequential upon a physical harm to the victim or his rights."[6] This definition excludes losses that arose in contract. A more precise definition is formulated by Gómez Pomar, by pointing out a group of important factors:

1) sufficient degree of proximity, which allows the attribution of liability,

---

[4] Michaels, *supra* note 2 at 5.

[5] William Bishop, *Economic Loss in Tort*, 2 OXFORD J. LEGAL STUD. 1, 1 (1982).

[6] Willem H. van Boom, *Pure Economic Loss: A Comparative Perspective*, *in* PURE ECONOMIC LOSS, 1 (Willem H. van Boom, Helmut Koziol, & Christian A. Witting eds., 2004).

2) causation between the behaviour of the tortfeasor and the victim,

3) purely economic character of the loss.[7]

Polish literature also provides definitions of pure economic loss. Pajor defines pure economic loss as an exclusively financial extra-contractual loss, not consequential to any harm to a person or property.[8] Kaliński defines pure economic loss as a loss occurring independently of the infringement of a subjective right of the victim.[9]

In von Bar's opinion there are two definitions of pure economic loss: 1) harm oriented, 2) and interest oriented. In the harm oriented definitions, pure economic loss is defined as an injury, which arises independently of harm to a person or a thing. In the interest oriented definitions, pure economic loss is defined as an injury to the economic interests, which is not causally connected to an infringement of an absolute right, or a contract.[10] Both approaches imply that the victim cannot base his claim on the loss of health or harm to his possessions.[11] It could happen that a pure economic loss is a consequence of an aforementioned harm. In these situations one subject's absolute right is infringed and that causes a pure economic loss for another subject, whose subjective rights are not infringed. The word 'harm' and 'loss' are used here in the meaning pertaining to the politics of private law, and not to any particular dogmatism.

The number and variety of situations in which pure economic loss might occur is particularly great. Many divisions between the classes of cases are possible. Popular examples of pure economic loss are the so-called "cable cases", i.e. cases concerned with a cutting of an electric cable or an oil pipe, or other kind of transmission lines. If an excavator negligently cuts an electric cable, which carries energy to a factory, then the machines in the factory might or might not be damaged as a result of power outage (traditionally, such damage would be called *damnum*

---

[7] Fernando Gómez Pomar & Juan Antonio Ruiz García, *La noción de daño puramente economico: Una visión crítica desde el análisis económico del derecho*, 4/2002 INDRET, 2 (2002).

[8] Tomasz Pajor, *Pure Economic Loss. Polish Report*, *in* RAPPORTS POLONAIS PRESENTES AU XVIIE CONGRES INTERNATIONAL DE DROIT COMPARE 37, 37 (2006).

[9] MACIEJ KALIŃSKI, SZKODA NA MIENIU I JEJ NAPRAWIENIE 255 (2008).

[10] CHRISTIAN VON BAR, 2 THE COMMON EUROPEAN LAW OF TORTS: DAMAGE AND DAMAGES, LIABILITY FOR AND WITHOUT PERSONAL MISCONDUCT, CAUSALITY, AND DEFENCES 29 (2000).

[11] Por. Christian Witting, *Distinguishing between Property Damage and Pure Economic Loss in Negligence: A Personality Thesis*, 21 LEGAL STUD. 481, 481 (2001).

emergens on the ground of civil law legal family). Independent of the material harm, production is halted, which worsens the economic situation of the factory. The results of the cable cut may be divided as following:

1) consequential economic loss, when the production is halted and there is a material damage to property of the factory,

2) pure economic loss, when the production is halted, but no damage has been done to property of the factory, or the damaged property has been repaired before the occurrence of electricity outage.[12]

Creation of a perfect working definition for the needs of comparative research, but grounded on the existing legal rules is not possible. Even the definition proposed by Pajor, although very broad, leaves room for the interpretation of the expressions such as "harm to property". The definition of harm to property becomes necessary in cases where use of a thing is prevented by the tortfeasor, but the victim has only a contractual interest in it. This definition seems to exclude cases, in which property was damaged, but the economic loss is suffered by a third party. According to these difficulties, a functional, case-based approach is more feasible for comparative research.

In the economic analysis of law, the concept of pure economic loss is defined from a different point of view. The division of absolute rights, obligations and economic interests does not find a clear confirmation in the economic analysis.[13] Those are just resources, and the division seems artificial.

Bishop proposed that pure economic loss is an economic loss incurred by the victim and an economic gain to a third party. In other words, pure economic losses are simply transfers of wealth between various persons, and do not constitute a loss for society. In cases where property is damaged or destroyed, pure economic loss is therefore a part of total harm, characterized by the nature of being a purely financial transfer. From the economic perspective, pure economic losses are not a social cost; they are mere financial transfers between people and do not influence the amount of wealth in the economy as a whole.[14] The lack of physical harm makes the subject easily treatable with economic analysis, as there are fewer moral questions, and emotions involved.

The economic approach to the definition of pure economic loss is more useful for comparative purposes than the dogmatic approach; however, the

---

[12] van Boom, *supra* note 6 at 4.

[13] Guiseppe Dari Mattiacci, *The Economics of Comparative Law and the Internalisation of Multiple Externalities*, *in* PURE ECONOMIC LOSS, 169 (Willem H. van Boom, Helmut Koziol, & Christian A. Witting eds., 2004).

[14] Cf. Bishop, *supra* note 5 at 1.

classic case-based functional approach is equally useful.[15] The case-based approach does provide a method which enables one to compare the institutions of the law of delict related to liability for pure economic losses, and the comparisons are made with high resolution. What the case-based approach lacks is the ability to answer the questions about the effect of the norms on the incentives of its addressees (or the incentives of the economic actors – as one might prefer to say).

Social cost and private loss

When we depart from the economic definition of pure economic loss, a number of questions arise: 1) Is it possible that allowing claims for pure economic losses would create incentives for the potential tortfeasor, which would produce a net loss for society? This question has its roots in the Learned Hand formula[16] and is particularly valid as there are no costs to society. 2) What incentives are created by various institutional configurations regarding pure economic losses? 3) What rules are the most beneficial to society? 4) Should law exclude remedies for exclusively private losses? The answers to those questions point to the actual function of compared laws.

The first economic analysis of pure economic loss was made by Bishop, who revealed the economic reasons for the exclusionary rule that is a principle which excludes damages for pure economic losses. His main argument envisages pure economic loss as an involuntary transfer of wealth between two or more parties.[17]

Differentiating between private loss and social cost gives a conceptual framework to the economic analysis of pure economic loss. The assumption being that there is a class of cases in which the victim suffers economic harm, while society as a whole does not incur any cost. It follows that there is a class of cases where the economic harm to the victim is greater than the cost to the society; in these cases pure economic loss consists of the difference between the social cost and the economic

[15] For an example of pure economic loss cases classification please refer to: Guiseppe Dari Mattiacci & Hans-Bernd Schaefer, *The Core of Pure Economic Loss*, 27 International Review of Law and Economics 8, 12 (2007).

[16] The Hand formula states that the tortfeasor was negligent if $B < pL$, where 'B' is the cost incurred by the tortfeasor, 'p' is the probability of loss, and 'L' is the gravity of loss. In a case where $B > pL$, the tortfeasor is wasteful. Some legal rules may encourage taking excessive precautions and produce a negative economic result.

[17] Cf. Bishop, *supra* note 5 at 1.

harm to the victim. The distinction between social cost and private loss has inspired the view that only social harm should be compensated, while private losses should be regulated outside the realm of tort.[18] The proposed base for the exclusionary rule is not sufficient.[19] For example, if a will is drafted by a professional in a negligent manner resulting in succession by another person other than the one intended by the testator, there is no economic harm to the society. Yet no lawyer would agree that law should 'drive by' such a case, ignoring it. It might be argued that such cases should be dealt with by the law of succession or law of contract, but in this case tort constitutes the last line of defense if the former branches of law fail to provide a remedy. The distinction is useful for assessing cases of pure economic loss resulting from businesses' activity, but loses its usefulness when we enter the realm of values other than money.

Pure Economic Loss as Internalization of Positive Externalities

Dari Mattiaci proposed that the main problem of regulating pure economic losses in tort law derives from the fact that tort law is a mechanism designed for dealing with negative externalities, and pure economic losses are seen as both negative and positive externalities.[20] Negative externalities are imposed by the tortfeasor on the victim. Positive externalities arose from the fact that pure economic losses are monetary transfers from the victim to some third party (usually called a "gainer"). Thus the negative and positive externalities might be said to be their own mirror images.

Introduction of the gainer into the model makes it possible to have a more detailed picture of incentives in model pure economic loss cases. Dari Mattiaci distinguishes four types of cases: 1) unilateral, where only the tortfeasor is able to take precautions, 2) bilateral (I), where only the tortfeasor and the victim can take precautions, 3) bilateral (II), where only the tortfeasor and the gainer can take precautions, and 4) trilateral, where all the parties can influence the final outcome.[21]

---

[18] See generally George P Fletcher, *Fairness and Utility in Tort Theory*, 85 HARV. L. REV. 537 (1971).

[19] Accord Mario J Rizzo, *Economic Loss Problem: A Comment on Bishop, The*, 2 OXFORD J. LEGAL STUD. 197, 200 (1982).

[20] Dari Mattiacci, *supra* note 13 at 167.

[21] *Id.* at 176–177.

In the unilateral model,[22] the socially optimal level of precautions is $min_x\{p(x)(h-g)+x\}$; in other words, we should seek to find a point in $f(x)=p(x)(h-g)+x$ which represents a minimum of the sum of precautionary spending and the social cost $\hat{x}$. He then argues, that the tortfeasor's best level of precaution is represented by $min_x\{p(x)d+x\}$. It follows, that under strict liability, the behaviour of the tortfeasor is socially optimal if $h-g=d$.[23] It is hard to imagine that this could be the case. Usually law would admit damages equal to h , or exclude the damages altogether. The cases which fall under the unilateral model can be exemplified by the so-called, transferred loss incurred by an insurer, as well as by the case of negligent notary cited above.

In cases described by the unilateral model, but falling under the negligence rule, the situation is different. The problem of the tortfeasor is described by Dari Mattiaci as:

$$min_x\begin{cases} x & if x \geq \hat{x} \\ p(x)d + x & if x < \hat{x} \end{cases}.$$ [24]

The Author argues, that for $d \geq h-g$ the tortfeasor will spend $\hat{x}$.[25] There is, however, one assumption that has not been explicitly stated, that $\hat{x}$ is considered by the law as a level of precaution separating negligent behaviour from the non-negligent; this is not necessarily the case. Law might set the required amount of precaution in order to exclude negligence at a lower or higher level, let's call it $\mathring{x}$. It is then difficult to assess the relationship between the minimization which is socially optimal, and the minimization which represents the optimal level of precaution for the tortfeasor. The minimization problem for the tortfeasor becomes:

$$min_x\begin{cases} x & if x \geq x \\ p(x)d + x & if x < x \end{cases}$$ and it does not necessarily equal $\hat{x}$ $if\ d \geq h-g$.

[22] The variables signify the following: x – cost of precaution; p(x) – function of probability with respect to x; h – magnitude of harm; g – gain of the third party; d – damages paid by the tortfeasor.

[23] Dari Mattiacci, *supra* note 13 at 178.

[24] *Id.* at 178–179.

[25] *Id.* at 179.

The application of the above formulae to real life cases may be undertaken using the example of careless notary, whose drafting of a will results in transmission of the legacy to a person who was not intended by the testator. This type of case is usually characterized by the objectification of liability, i.e. even if a legal system is directly saying that the rule of liability is negligence, the notary is considered such a highly skilled professional that a mere occurrence of harm almost always indicates negligence. Thus, for the sake of argument, I will treat the model case as a strict liability case. The socially optimal solution in this case is given by $min_x\{p(x)(h-g)+x\}$, but if $h=g$ then we can simplify it to $min_x\{x\}$. The minimization problem for the notary is represented by $min_x\{p(x)d+x\}$; therefore, if we agree with the Dari Mattiaci model, then any $d>0$ will produce a socially inefficient outcome.

The inability to shape legal norms by economic analysis does not prevent them from being useful in comparative perspective. While it might be the case, that the socially optimal level of spending is wrongly represented, the method enables much clearer thinking about the incentives the law provides to its subjects. The example of a careless notary is often given as a difficult case, which supposedly breaks the theory. But it does not; it only diminishes the scope of the theory. There are insights given by the formal treatment of the problem that cannot be denied. Firstly, the model shows the necessity to compare the socially optimal level of precaution and the level of precaution required by the negligence rules. It is the case that different standards of negligence in various countries cause the discrepancy at the level of incentives given to the tortfeasor.

Conclusions

The law and economics methodology is a valuable tool for comparative research. It is a dynamically developing field of inquiry and often its criticism is not well-deserved, rather it is built on a foundation of some model, which later proves faulty or too general. The truth is that all models are wrong, even the laws of physics; some models are wrong by a mile, while others by a nanometer. Criticism of the economic analysis should not be based on the fallacies one can find in a certain model. Economic analysis of law allows us to think about the legal rules in a manner different from that taught at the university. The norms can be viewed as something to be treated in a special manner, which is a certain sense of piety. The same norms can be treated as rules of a game played between the tortfeasor, the victim, and the gainer. I think it would be insufficient to think about the law solely from one perspective. Lawyers treat norms in manners which differ not only from lawyer to lawyer, but from situation to situation.

On the other hand, it is evident that the economic analysis of law is to be assessed in the present moment. Even if it is theoretically possible to create a model of pure economic loss from which would follow a way to set the norms up in order to reach a perfect outcome, the economic analysis of law is not there yet. The models do not incorporate some of the dogmatics, yet the dogmatics are well-founded. Of course, it is possible to assign value to reconstruct the model to, for example, acknowledge the harm caused by a careless notary to be a social cost. If we do that, the model is no longer teaching us about reality; it is no longer taking us from assumptions to conclusions. Rather, we would take conclusions that we expect and modify the model to suit expectations. For that, no economic analysis is necessary; we already know what we expect from the mere fact that we expect it. The economic analysis should be used as a tool in comparative research, but it would undoubtedly be a mistake to think about it as an ultimate solution to the problems of comparative methodology.

UNIFICATION OF THE HUMAN RIGHTS IN EUROPE

MARINA BORKOVECA

UNIVERSITY OF LATVIA IN RIGA, LATVIA

Abstract

The creation of the European Communities, later transformed into the European Union, necessarily led to the unification of a considerable part of the laws of the Member States of this organisation. The area of human rights was not the main one to be harmonized and indeed was not even mentioned in the founding treaties. However, partly under the pressure from the constitutional courts of the Member States (especially the German Constitutional Court) the European Court of Justice recognised in its judgements that human rights were a fundamental principle of the European Communities. The European Court of Justice in its case law referred to the common constitutional traditions of the Member States and the international human rights treaties as a source of the identification and interpretation of particular human rights.

Even after this principle was explicitly accepted in the Maastricht Treaty, the European Court of Justice continued to further develop its statement that human rights play an important role in the legal system of the European Union, recognising that they could even limit the fundamental freedoms of the European Union. The Lisbon Treaty took the next step in the field of the protection of human rights. The Charter of Fundamental Rights of the European Union has become an integral part of the founding treaty itself (Article 6 (1) of the Treaty on European Union) and the European Union is proceeding towards accession to the European Convention of Human Rights. This will definitely ensure a higher level of protection for individuals.

At the moment, the European Union is trying to unify the level of protection of the human rights, which stem from three different sources – the national constitutional law, the European Convention for the Protection of Human Rights, Fundamental Freedoms and the Charter of Fundamental Rights of the European Union – thus trying to create a unified understanding and standard of the human rights in all the Member States. Nevertheless, three different actors responsible for ensuring this standard still exist – the national constitutional courts, the Court of Justice of the European Union and the European Court of Human Rights. It will be very important to ensure conformity also at the procedural level.

Introduction

The principle of protection of human rights was not even mentioned in the founding treaties of the European Communities. This may be explained by the aims of the original Communities, mostly if not exclusively economic in nature. The first time that human (fundamental) rights were directly addressed in the Community's primary law was in the Single European Act,[1] signed at Luxembourg in 1986 and becoming valid on July 1st, 1987. The will of the Member States 'to work together to promote democracy on the bases of the fundamental rights recognized in the constitutions and laws of the Member States, in the Convention for the Protection of Human Rights and Fundamental Freedoms and the European Social Charter, notably freedom, equality and social justice' is stated in the preamble of this Act. This declaration on recognition of the fundamental rights by the European Communities at Treaty level was followed by Article F (after 6(2)) of the Treaty on European Union,[2] then by the Treaty of Amsterdam,[3] Article 9 of the Treaty Establishing a Constitution of Europe[4] and the Charter of Fundamental Rights.[5]

After the amendments made by the Lisbon Treaty, the first sentence of Article 6 (1) of the Treaty on European Union now states explicitly that: 'The Union recognizes the rights, freedoms and principles set out in the Charter of Fundamental Rights of the European Union of 7th of December 2000, as adapted at Strasbourg, on December 12th, 2007, which shall have the same legal value as the Treaties.' In its turn, part 3 of the same article provides that: 'Fundamental rights, as guaranteed by the European Convention for the Protection of Human Rights and Fundamental Freedoms and as they result from the constitutional traditions common to the Member States, shall constitute general principles of the Union's law.' However, this does not mean that the protection of fundamental rights did not exist before the principle of the protection of the human rights was

---

[1] OJ L 169, 29.6.1987.

[2] OJ C191, 29.7.1992.

[3] OJ C 340, 10.11.1997.

[4] OJ C310, 16.12.2004.

[5] Takis Tridimas, *The General Principles of EU Law* 304 (2nd ed. 2007).

recognized at the legislative level. The next sections will explore the judicial contribution to the recognition of human and fundamental rights in the European Community and Union legal order and the substantive and procedural challenges that the regime is likely to face in the future.

The recognition of fundamental rights in the case law of the European Court of Justice.

The European Court of Justice (hereinafter the 'Court' or the 'Court of Justice') already in the year 1969 referred to the fundamental rights in the judgement in the case No. 29/69 *Stauder*, stating that: 'The provision at issue contains nothing capable of prejudging the fundamental rights enshrined in the general principle of Community law and protected by the Court'.[6] One of the most important judgements of the Court of Justice concerning the issue of human rights was the case of International *Handelsgesellschaft* where it stipulated that: 'Respect for fundamental rights forms an integral part of the general principles of law protected by the Court of Justice. The protection of such rights, whilst inspired by the constitutional traditions common to the Member States, must be ensured within the framework of the structure and objectives of the Community'.[7] In the judgement in the *Nold* case,[8] the Court of Justice extended the scope of protection of human rights in the Community by drawing upon the international treaties for the protection of human rights, on which the Member States have collaborated, or of which they are signatories. It held that these treaties 'can supply guidelines which should be followed within the framework of Community law'. In some cases, for example, the *Schmidberger* case,[9] the Court of Justice has even ruled that human rights could serve as the limitations of the fundamental freedoms recognized in the Community. However, the explicit acknowledgement of the respect for fundamental rights in the case law of the Court of Justice was not enough

---

[6] Judgment of the Court of November 12th, 1969 in the case 29-69 *Erich Stauder v City of Ulm - Sozialam*t. European Court reports 1969 Page 00419, para.7.

[7] Judgment of the Court of December 17th, 1970 in the case 11-70 *Internationale Handelsgesellschaft mbH v Einfuhr- und Vorratsstelle für Getreide und Futtermittel*. European Court reports 1970 Page 01125, para.4.

[8] Judgment of May 14th, 1974 in the case 4-73 *J. Nold, Kohlen- und Baustoffgroßhandlung v Commission of the European Communities*. European Court reports 1974 Page 00491, para.13.

[9] Judgment of the Court of June 12th, 2003 in the case C-112/00 Eugen Schmidberger, Internationale Transporte und Planzüge v Republik Österreich.. European Court reports 2003 Page I-05659.

for the constitutional courts of the Member States as the guardians of their national constitutions.

The judgments of the constitutional courts of the Member States concerning the Community (European Union) law and human rights

When one considers the case law and position of the constitutional courts of the Member States, it is necessary to start with the German Constitutional Court. Its contribution in the recognition and development of the principle of protection of the fundamental rights in the European Communities is very important. The German Constitutional Court in its judgement in the so-called *Solange I* case limited the supremacy of the Community law. It stated that in the case of a conflict arising between Community law and the fundamental rights guaranteed by the Constitution, the guarantee of fundamental rights prevailed as long as the competent organs of the Community had not removed the conflict of norms in accordance with the mechanism prescribed in the founding treaty. The German Constitutional Court based its judgement on the fact that the Community lacked a bill of rights enacted by a parliament, with substance that would be comparable to the catalogue of fundamental rights contained in the Basic Law (Constitution of the Federal Republic of Germany) and would be reliably fixed for the future. The Constitutional Court admitted that developments of the Court of Justice, however favourable to fundamental rights they might be, were insufficient in this regard. So the German Constitutional Court concluded that it had the right to review the compatibility of the secondary acts of the Community with the Basic Law.[10]

After some period of time in 1986, the German Constitutional Court in the judgement in the so-called *Solange II* case changed its position in favour of the Community stating that, after *Solange I,* a mechanism of protection of fundamental rights comparable with the standards provided in the Basic Law had been established within the jurisdiction of the Community. According to the German Constitutional Court, the acknowledgement of the respect and protection of human rights by the institutions of the Community was contained in a Joint Declaration of the Council, Commission and Parliament of the Community of April 5th, 1977

[10] Judgment of the German Constitutional Court of May 29th, 1974 in the case *Solange I.* Available in English: Andrew Oppenheinmer, *The Relationship between European Community Law and National Law: The Cases* 440-452 (1994).

and a subsequent Declaration of the Council adopted on April 7th, 1978. The German Constitutional Court ruled that the requirements set by its judgement in *Solange I* were satisfied by the Community. As long as the Community law and, in particular, the case law of the Court of Justice ensured an effective protection of fundamental rights, the Constitutional Court would no longer decide on the applicability of the secondary law of the Community or review such legislation by the standard of the protection of fundamental rights contained in the Basic Law.[11] In its judgement in the so-called *Banana* case, the German Constitutional Court went even further, stating that it would monitor the conformity of the Community acts with the standards of the fundamental rights only if the necessary control at the level of Community law would no longer be available.[12]

The position of the German Constitutional Court has been supported by several constitutional courts both of the 'old' and 'new' Member States of the European Union. For example, the Italian Constitutional Court referred to the doctrine of counter-limits to limitations of sovereignty – fundamental constitutional principles and rules – and stated that it would rule against the norms of the Community law only if they did not comply with the fundamental principles of the constitutional system.[13] In *Frontini,* the Italian Constitutional Court held that: 'Article 11 of the Italian Constitution permitted those limitations of sovereignty, which were necessary for the international organization concerned to achieve its purpose. (..) If Article 189 of the Treaty were ever interpreted so as to give the institutions of EEC the power to violate the fundamental principles of the Constitution or the inalienable rights of man, the Court reserved the right to review the continuing compatibility of the Treaty with the Constitution'.[14]

The Czech Constitutional Court has also used the doctrine of counter-limits in its judgements. In the decision on the compatibility of the Lisbon

---

[11] Judgment of the German Constituional Court of October 22nd, 1986 in the case *Solange II*. Available in English: Andrew Oppenheinmer, *The Relationship between European Community Law and National Law: The Cases* 466-495 (1994).
[12] Judgment of the German Constituional Court of June 7th, 2000 in the case *Banana,* no. 2 BvL 1/97, EuZW, (2000) 702.
[13] Marta Cartabia, *The Italian Constitutional Court and the Relationship between the Italian Legal System and the European Community*. 12 (173) Mich. J. Int'l L. 183 (1990-1991).
[14] Judgment of the Italian Constitutional Court of December, 27th 1973 in the case Frontini v. Ministero delle Finanze, Case No.183/73. Available in English: Andrew Oppenheinmer, *The Relationship between European Community Law and National Law: The Cases* 630 (1994).

Treaty with the Constitution of the Czech Republic, [15] the Czech Constitutional Court noted that, according to the Constitution, not all, but only certain powers can be transferred by treaty to an international organization. Thus, the transfer of powers of Czech Republic bodies cannot go so far as to violate the very essence of the republic as a sovereign and democratic state governed by the rule of law, founded on respect for the rights and freedoms of the human being and of citizens, or to establish a change in the essential requirements for a democratic state governed by the rule of law.[16] At the same time, already by 2006 the Constitutional Court had recognized that the current standard within the Community for the protection of fundamental rights could justify the assumption that, through the assertion of principles arising therefrom, such as otherwise follows from the above-cited case-law of the Court of Justice, it was of a lower quality than the protection accorded in the Czech Republic, or that the standard of protection markedly diverged from the standard till now provided in the domestic setting by the Constitutional Court.[17] In the Lisbon Treaty decision, the Court reaffirmed this, noting in addition that the content of the catalogue of human rights expressed in the EU Charter was fully comparable with the content protected in the Czech Republic on the basis of the Czech Charter of Fundamental Rights and Freedoms, as well as the Convention for the Protection of Human Rights and Fundamental Freedoms. Moreover, the Constitutional Court recognized that the EU Charter was in harmony not only with the material core of the Constitution, but also with all provisions of the constitutional order.[18]

The Polish Constitutional Court also did not impugn the level of protection of human rights in the European Union. In its judgement in the case on Poland's membership of the European Union (the Accession Treaty), the Constitutional Court made a reference to the common constitutional traditions as formulated in Article 6 (2) of the European

---

[15] The analysis of the decision is available in Petr Bříza, *The Czech Republic. The Constitutional Court on the Lisbon Treaty. Decision of 26 November 2008.* 5 EuConst 143-164 (2009).

[16] Decision of the Czech Constitutional Court of November 26th, 2008, para. 97. Available in English at http://tinyurl.com/3gqdqhm [April 11th, 2011].

[17] Judgment of the Czech Constitutional Court of March 8th, 2006 in the case Pl. US 50/04, 28.-29. lpp. Available in English at http://tinyurl.com/3s4o6l5 [April 11th, 2011]. See also the analysis of the judgment in Anneli Albi, Supremacy of EC Law in the New Member States 3, EuConst 53-54 (2007).

[18] Decision of the Czech Constitutional Court of November 26th, 2008, para. 197. Available in English at http://tinyurl.com/3gqdqhm [April 11th, 2011].

Union Treaty and the Constitutional Court concluded that 'it would be unfounded to reduce the notion of common 'constitutional traditions' to the constitutional system of a single Member State.'[19] An interesting point was determined in response to a request by the Spanish government, asking for the ruling of the Constitutional Court of Spain concerning the Constitutional Treaty. The difficulty pointed out by the government was the coexistence of three systems for the protection of fundamental rights (the Constitution of Spain, the European Convention of Human Rights and Charter of Fundamental Rights of the European Union), which necessarily suggested a process of mutual influences not exempt from difficulties. The Constitutional Court of Spain replied to this concern of the government in the following manner: 'The specific constitutional problems, which may arise from the integration of the Treaty may not be the object of an anticipated and abstract opinion. As happens with those being proposed from the beginning by the integration of the Agreement of Rome, the solution may only be sought within the framework of the constitutional procedures attributed to the knowledge of this Court, i.e. weighting for each specific right and in the specific circumstances thereof the more relevant formulae for constitution and definition, in constant dialogue with authorized jurisdictional instances, where applicable, for the authentic interpretation of the international agreements that contain declarations of rights that coincide with those set forth by the Spanish Constitution.'.[20]

From the judgments and decisions of the Constitutional Courts of the Member States it is possible to conclude that they have mostly recognized that the standard of protection of the human rights provided in the European Union is not lower but sometimes even higher than one guaranteed by the national constitutions.

The accession of the European Union to the European Convention for the Protection of Human Rights and Fundamental Freedoms

In its opinion of March 28th, 1996, the Court of Justice ruled that accession of the Community to the European Convention for the Protection of Human Rights and Fundamental Freedoms (the Convention)

---

[19] Judgment of May 11th, 2005 in the case K 18/04. Available at http://tinyurl.com/3dwz62h [April 11th, 2011].

[20] Opinion of the Spanish Constitutional Court of December 13th, 2004 in the case DTC 1/2004, FJ 2. Available in English at http://tinyurl.com/3glfje3 [April 11th, 2011].

was not possible without making amendments in the Treaties, as the Community – at that time – did not have the competence to do this.[21] So the amendments took place via the Lisbon Treaty in such a way to make the accession real. Article 6 (2) of the Treaty on the European Union now directly stipulates: 'The Union shall accede to the European Convention for the Protection of Human Rights and Fundamental Freedoms. Such accession shall not affect the Union's competences as defined in the Treaties.' Protocol No.8 relating to Article 6 (2) of the Treaty on the European Union on the accession of the Union to the European Convention on the Protection of Human Rights and Fundamental Freedoms (Protocol No.8) specifies the conditions of the accession.

Already before the process of accession of the European Union to the Convention had become possible, the European Court of Human Rights had the possibility to rule on the relations between the law of the European Union (Community law) and the human rights' protection provided in the Convention. In the *Bosphorus* case, the Strasbourg Court ruled that the impugned interference was not the result of an exercise of discretion by the Irish authorities, either under Community or Irish law, but rather amounted to compliance by the Irish State with its legal obligations flowing from Community law. The European Court of Human Rights, in assessing the level of the protection of human rights in the Community, concluded that the protection of fundamental rights by Community law could be considered to be, and to have been at the relevant time, 'equivalent' to that of the Convention system.[22]

After the Lisbon Treaty came into effect, the European Court of Human Rights on the 21st January 2011 delivered its judgement in the *M.S.S.* case.[23] This case is interesting from the perspective of the accession of the European Union to the Convention. In this case, one of the respondent states – Belgium – submitted that, in application of the Council Regulation No. 343/2003 of 18 February 2003 establishing the criteria and mechanisms for determining the Member State responsible for examining an asylum application lodged in one of the Member States by a third-country national (the Dublin Regulation), it was not responsible for

---

[21] Avis de la Cour du 28 mars 1996. - Adhésion de la Communauté à la convention de sauvegarde des droits de l'homme et des libertés fondamentales. - Avis 2/94. Recueil de jurisprudence 1996 page I-01759.

[22] Judgment of June 30th, 2005 Bosphorus Hava Yolları Turizm ve Ticaret Anonim Şirketi v. Ireland para.165. Available at http://tinyurl.com/6m8fhez [April 11th, 2011].

[23] Judgment of January 21st, 2011 M.S.S. v. Belgium and Greece. Available at http://tinyurl.com/83wxuk7 [April 11th, 2011].

examining the applicant's request for asylum, and it was therefore not the task of Belgium's authorities to examine the applicant's fears for his life and his physical safety in his country of origin (Afghanistan). The European Court of Human Rights concluded that, under the Regulation, the Belgian authorities could have refrained from transferring the applicant if they had considered that the receiving country, namely Greece, was not fulfilling its obligations under the Convention. Consequently, the Court considered that the impugned measure taken by the Belgian authorities did not strictly fall within Belgium's international legal obligations. It is interesting that the European Union was not participating in the *M.S.S.* case and did not give its opinion on the interpretation of the Dublin Regulation and of the other relevant law of the European Union applied in this case. Participation of the European Union as a third party before the Strasbourg Court is therefore not consistent at the moment. The situation will definitely become clearer after the European Union's accession to the Convention and will have the possibility to participate as a party of the case before the European Court of the Human Rights.

Because of the features specific to the European Union legal system, the Convention will possibly be amended and some new mechanisms will be introduced. First, because of the special place and role of the Court of Justice in the legal system of the European Union, it must be given the possibility to rule on the validity and interpretation of the law enacted by the institutions of the European Union. As is stated in the discussion document of the Court of Justice: 'On the basis of that principle of subsidiarity and in order to ensure that it is put into practice in the context of preparing for accession, the Union must make sure, as regards acts of the Union which are susceptible to being the subject of applications to the European Court of Human Rights, that external review by the Convention institutions can be preceded by effective internal review by the courts of the Member States and/or of the Union'.[24] *Tobias Lock* argues that the prior involvement of the Court of Justice is not recommended since this would lead to further delay of procedure in the Strasbourg Court; in addition it would lead to a privilege of the legal order of the European Union.[25] However, taking into account the length of proceedings in Strasbourg (sometimes even 10 years), it is possible to obtain a Court of Justice ruling without the suspension of the proceedings of the European

---

[24] Discussion document is available at: http://tinyurl.com/3bxyaoa [April 11th, 2011].

[25] Tobias Lock, *EU Accession to the ECHR: Implications for the Judicial Review in Strasbourg* 35 (6) E.L.Rev. 789 (2010).

Court of Human Rights. For example, an accelerated or urgent procedure[26] could be used by the Court of Justice for adjudicating such a case. The possibility to rule on the compatibility of the legal act (or its part) of the European Union with human rights also does not seem to be a privilege for the court of the European Union. Actually every national court has a right to evaluate the contested measure of national law before it comes before the Strasbourg Court.

The second aspect peculiar to the accession of the European Union is the introduction of the co-respondent mechanism in the Convention. Here one is tempted to agree with *Tobias Lock* that the existing third party intervention is not an adequate substitute for the introduction of the co-respondent mechanism. The most important argument concerning this question is that a third party intervener is not bound by the judgement of the Strasbourg Court.[27]

Conclusion

Both the constitutional courts of the Member States as well as the European Court of Human Rights have accepted the level of protection of human rights in the European Union as acceptable and even sufficient. The accession of the European Union to the Convention will definitely have a positive effect on the development of the protection of human rights in Europe. At the same time, the accession is quite a complicated process and many questions and problems are likely to arise in this context. The most important is the possible concurrence between two jurisdictions – the Strasbourg Court and the Luxembourg Court. It remains to be seen whether and how the two European courts shall interrelate in practice, and what doctrinal, judicial or legislative innovations shall be employed to ensure the harmonious nature of this relationship. One can only hope that the shared teleology of providing the highest possible level of protection of human rights will lead to cooperation rather than friction between the different judicial bodies.

---

[26] Article 104 and 104b of the Rules of procedure of the Court of Justice. OJ C 177/1, 2.7.2010.

[27] Tobias Lock, *EU Accession to the ECHR*... 783-784 (2010).

POLISH LAW AS AN OBJECT OF A COMPARATIVE LAW ANALYSIS (SOME PERSONAL REFLECTIONS)

JAN A. PISZCZEK

UNIVERSITY OF WARMIA AND MAZURY IN OLSZTYN, POLAND

During several decades of my scientific work, I have had the opportunity to read numerous publications written in Polish or foreign languages, primarily concerning broadly defined civil law. This enabled me to shape an opinion on the comparative law studies, the results of which were presented in the literature concerning this branch of law. Generally speaking, my opinion of them is not the best. First of all, the disproportion between the matter relating to foreign legal solutions, which can be found in the writings of Polish lawyers, and what the researchers from other countries have to say about Polish Law, is striking.

It is difficult to find a reliable Polish publication in which the author does not refer to solutions/regulations existing in foreign legal orders, supporting his/her arguments with literature and judicial decisions, sometimes even with clockwork precision. However, even in the highest rated works of foreign researchers, references to Polish Law can be found only occasionally.[1] The reasons for this state of affairs are numerous. I think the first reason is the tightness of the Polish language, going hand in hand with a lack of publications on Polish Law in foreign languages.

If we do not overcome this obstacle, we will not be able to count on changing the existing disproportions. Probably, the level of legislation in Poland is equally important. Its crushing evaluation was presented by W. Skrzydło, who pointed out a number of premises justifying such a diagnosis, such as 'the quality of departmental services preparing government draft laws, weak government control over the legislative process, legislation instability, parliamentary procedures, overproduction

[1] Compare e.g. A. Dietz.

of legal acts leading to surplus legislation etc.'[2] The poor quality of laws is demonstrated by the decisions of the Constitutional Tribunal, which resolves not only matters relating to the acts already in force, but also to those purposed. Therefore, a foreigner studying the Polish legal system encounters a challenge, which usually cannot be overcome. We may take one of many examples. The Press Law Act enacted in 1984,[3] has been amended several times already after the political changes in Poland, most recently in 2007.[4] Analysing its current text, some odd provisions can be found already in the first two rules. The provision of Article 1 is that 'the Press, in accordance with the Polish Constitution, has the right to freedom of expression and realises the right of citizens to reliable information, openness of public life and social criticism'. Whereas, a further adjustment, contained in Art. 2, imposes on public authorities a duty to create the necessary conditions for the press to perform its functions and duties, and it is to be done… in accordance with the Constitution of Polish People's Republic…!

A correction of this phrase would not require the efforts of a great legislator, but it still remains to be done so far. A rigorous legalist might rightly claim that since such a provision exists in the law in force, it should be respected.[5]

The cited example concerns a trivial matter. If they are numerous, however, it should be worrying. For many of them may be difficult to diagnose, which undermines confidence in the applicable law, with the conceptual confusion introduced to legislative and juridical languages especially by tax law provisions and fiscal administration (e.g. a private partnership recognized for the legal needs as 'an organizational unit', a lending agreement as a payable agreement, even though its essence is i.a. gratuitousness etc.). If a competent Polish lawyer cannot always find a proper solution in such cases, then what result may we expect in the case of comparative studies conducted by a foreigner?

---

[2] Wiesław Skrzydło, *Problem doskonalenia legislacji w Polsce* in Władysław Czapliński (ed.), *Prawo w XXI wieku. Księga pamiątkowa 50-lecia Instytutu Nauk Prawnych Polskiej Akademii Nauk* 793ff. (2006).

[3] The Act of January 26th, 1984, Journal of Laws No. 5, item 24, as amended.

[4] Journal of Laws No. 89, item 590.

[5] J. Sobczak correctly indicates that 'although the Act of January 1984 – Press Law was established under the rule of Constitution of 1952, but the provisions of Art. 2 of Press Law requires a reference to the applicable provisions of the RP Constitution'. See Jacek Sobczak, *Prawo prasowe. Komentarz* 173 (2008), it still does not justify a lack of appropriate, small but significant correction in its text.

On February 4th, 2011, Polish Parliament passed the Private International Law Act, which was approved without amendments by the Senate on March 3rd,[6] therefore we should expect its approval and signing by the President. Although the Private International Law Act,[7] in force since 1965, was considered a good act, a need to change it, strongly emphasized in the literature,[8] for more than ten years has become a

---

[6] The draft act caused almost no response except for a narrow circle of specialists; therefore it can be assumed that during the final stages of preparing the draft, the Members of Parliament did not refer to or not know at all the charges against the Act both in the context of Polish and European regulations; the only problem which 'transpired to the media and generated discussions on matrimonial matters concerned the regulations included in chapter XI of the draft act; during the discussions on the draft, it was indicated that the legislator's proposal opens a back door for marriages between persons of the same-sex, Michał Szułdrzyński & Katarzyna Borowska, *Kwiatkowski pisze list do biskupów*, Rzeczpospolita February 25, 2011, at A7; see Marek Domagalski, *Związki partnerskie: Senat nie rozwiał wątpliwości*, Rzeczpospolita March 3, 2011, at C3, which resulted in the submission of an amendment, which intended to clearly indicate that the foreign regulations, which recognize same-sex relationships have legal effect in Poland, or 'the foreign laws regulating same-sex relationships shall not apply', the amendments were not considered by the Senate, which approved without amendments the Act passed by Parliament. It may be surprising that there is no reference to the doubts raised in the doctrine concerning the regulations on the legal status of a legal person, as well as on the statements generally questioning the need to enact the law when the European Parliament is working intensively on the unification of the European Private International Law. For it is known that at the time when the Council of Europe and the European Parliament enact subsequent regulations, they will be applied in the Polish legal order and the solutions of the Act being currently approved will cease to be current at least within the European Economic Area. It may be assumed as well that the EC will also engage into the problem of the relationship between the Community law and the legal orders of non-members of the Community. For the existence of such solutions would entirely eliminate the Polish act, compare Andrzej Mączyński, *Europejski kontekst rekodyfikacji polskiego prawa prywatnego międzynarodowego* in 2 *Finis legis christis. Księga pamiątkowa dedykowana ks. Prof. Wojciechowi Góralskiemu z okazji 70-tej rocznicy urodzin* 1173-1191 (2009).

[7] Act of November, 12th 1965, Journal of Laws No. 46 item 290.

[8] From very numerous publications, the same. *Kodyfikacyjne zagadnienia części ogólnej prawa prywatnego międzynarodowego* in Andrzej Janik (ed.), *Księga jubileuszowa dedykowana prof. Andrzejowi Całusowi* 409-445 (2010); Mariusz Piotr Wójcik, *Tradycja i postęp w nowelizacji prawa prywatnego międzynarodowego,* Teka Kom. Praw., OL PAN, 217-225 (2008); compare Maksymilian Pazdan, *O potrzebie reformy polskiego prawa prywatnego międzynarodowego i niektórych proponowanych rozwiązaniach*, 3 Kwartalnik

necessity in view of the changes taking place in Poland, Europe and the world.[9]

First of all, a trend towards harmonizing legal solutions is noticeable in the European Community actions towards convergence of the Private International Law within the European Economic Area,[10] as well as an intensifying trend towards cross-border economic activities of large corporate entities. [11] An increase in the number and importance of international agreements, especially multilateral, is of great importance. The literature indicates first and foremost numerous conventions elaborated by the Private International Law conferences in The Hague and the Convention on the Law Applicable to Contractual Obligations in Rome on 19th June 1980.[12]

An inquisitive researcher, who deals with the personal status of legal entities in the applicable law finds very modest regulations contained in Art. 9, which only mention that the capacity of legal entities shall be assessed according to the law of their place of residence. Thus, the doctrine expounded that the law of residence defined the legal position of legal person in all aspects of their existence and functioning. It also signalled the difficulties arising in the case of a transfer of a legal person

---

Prawa Prywatnego 501ff. (2000); Jerzy Poczobut, *Osoby prawne w polskim prawie prywatnym międzynarodowym. Projekt nowelizacji ustawy*, 3 Kwartalnik Prawa Prywatnego 529ff. (2000); compare also Jadwiga Pazdan, Pełnomocnictwo w prawie prywatnym międzynarodowym. Stan aktualny – uwagi de lege ferenda, 3 Kwartalnik Prawa Prywatnego 533ff. (2000); Andrzej Mączyński, *Statut personalny osób fizycznych. Refleksje de lege lata i de lege ferenda* in Wacław Uruszczak et al., *Leges sepere i Studia i prace dedykowane prof. Januszowi Sądlowi w 50-tą rocznicę pracy naukowej* 309-327 (2008); in the footnote I indicate only a few examples, which will enable a researcher to understand the general issues concerning changes in P.I.L.

[9] The literature reveals that the P.I.L. Act of 1965, although completely ignoring the issues of the procedural issues, its application did not cause serious problems in the judicature, nor did it cause doctrinal disputes, compare Andrzej Mączyński, *Polskie prawo prywatne międzynarodowe u progu XXI w.* in Władysław Czapliński (ed.), *Prawo w XXI wieku...* 564-565 (2006).

[10] See e.g. The Hague Programme Adopted by the Council of Europe in Brussels on 4-5 November 2004, Official Journal of the European Union 2005, C 53/01; compare also Andrzej Mączyński, *Europejski kontekst rekodyfikacji...* 1173-1191 (2009).

[11] Widely on this topic Adam Opalski, *Prawo właściwe dla osób prawnych w świetle projektu ustawy – prawo prywatne międzynarodowe* in Józef Okolski et al. (eds.), *Księga pamiątkowa 60-lecia Sądu Arbitrażowego przy Krajowej Izbie Gospodarczej* 812-844 (2010).

[12] Andrzej Mączyński, *Polskie prawo prywatne...* 565 (2006).

from one country to another due to the differences between the residence (of a legal person) concept and its foundation. There were attempts to solve these difficulties by means of the Hague Convention of 31.10.1951, however, this convention has no legal validity. Calling for changes in the Polish Private International Law, J. Poczobut pointed out that 'assessing the overall usefulness of the foundation theory and the residence theory of a legal person revealed conflict of legislated laws', a choice of one of them 'mainly depends on answers to the questions how to evaluate economic and political influences and the need for supervision of large enterprises, as well as to what extent autonomy of will in the private international law should be granted'.[13] Therefore, the cited author suggests a change of the content of Art. 9 sec. 2 PIL by 'extending the scope of this standard and defining clearly the essential properties of the law applicable in the location of the registered office of a legal entity, as well as adding additional sections', so that the final shape of the provision is:

'§ 1. a legal person is governed by the law of the state where its seat or registered office is located, as determined in the foundation charter. In the absence of such a seat or registered office, the law of the state where a legal person is registered shall apply, and in the absence of a registration, the law of the state where the governing body of the legal person is acting shall apply.

§ 2. if the law applicable to a legal person refers to another law, this law is to apply.

§3. however, if a legal person performs legal transactions through its enterprise, the capacity of that person shall be governed by the laws of the state where the seat of this enterprise is located.

§4. on the basis of the law applicable to a legal person, the following, in particular, shall be determined:

- foundation, transformation and termination,
- the legal nature
- the name or business name,
- the legal capacity,
- internal structure and rules of operation,
- the representation
- acquisition and loss of membership and the rights and obligations attached thereto
- responsibility of members for the liabilities of the legal person
- amendment of the foundation charter'.[14]

---

[13] Jerzy Poczobut, *Osoby prawne w polskim prawie...* 549 (2000).

[14] Jerzy Poczobut, *Osoby prawne w polskim prawie...* 551-552 (2000).

The presented proposals date from 2000; since then significant achievements of the doctrine have been recorded, which broadly expanded the issues of the personal status of a legal entity based creatively on the interpretation of Art. 9 § 2 P.I.L.[15] Since 2002, the Private International Law Team in the Civil Law Codification Commission also began its work. In December 2005, this Commission approved a new draft law modified in 2006.[16] This draft has not received a positive assessment in the literature. First of all, it was indicated that the justification of the draft refers to the need for enacting a new law caused by the change of the political and socio-economic system, increasing international passenger traffic, movement of capital, etc.[17] Similarly, the authors of the draft were seen as pointlessly referring to the need for changes due to the coming into force in the near future of the Rome Convention while ignoring the Hague Programme.[18] Eventually, the draft of 2006[19] was not passed, and the Private International Law Team prepared another draft law of December 16th, 2008, and then the draft, modified in May 2009, in the shape from 2008, was justified by its objective, i.e. harmonization of Polish Law with European Union standards. This argument has been severely criticized as completely pointless. The reasons for this assessment included ignoring the Hague Programme in the draft previously mentioned.[20] Although it was mentioned twice, the references were not significant enough to meet with approval, particularly that the Hague Programme dealt with only some issues, and their solution might be found insufficient in an unforeseeable future.[21]

---

[15] Compare especially Maksymilian Pazdan, *Prawo prywatne międzynarodowe*, 97-105 (3rd ed. 2009).

[16] Mariusz Piotr Wójcik, *Tradycja i postęp w nowelizacji...* 221 (2008), see the text of the draft in 3 Kwartalnik Prawa Prywatnego 825-846 (2006).

[17] Andrzej Mączyński, *Polskie prawo prywatne...* 568 (2006)., rightly indicated that referring to the circumstances, banal in their essence, does not explain the problem.

[18] *Ibid.*, 568, 581; the cited author rightly indicated a number of reasons justifying the critical opinion about the draft act of 2006, concluding that 'a significant reason of defects of the proposed new regulation was a lack of a clear position towards the efforts undertaken in the European Union or the unification of the private international law'.

[19] The draft was not approved by the Council of Ministers, compare Andrzej Mączyński, *Europejski kontekst rekodyfikacji...* 1175 (2009).

[20] Andrzej Mączyński, *Europejski kontekst rekodyfikacji...* 1182-1183 (2009).

[21] *Ibid.*, 1185 the cited author states that 'contrary to what was written in support of the government bill, the scope of issues covered by the Hague Programme is very broad, since it covers contractual and non-contractual obligations, alimony issues,

In the draft of 2008, the personal status of a legal entity was governed by the provisions of Art. 19 and 20 in the chapter titled 'Legal entities and other organizational units'. It differs little from the proposal *de lege ferenda* submitted by J. Poczobut. According to the provisions of Art. 19 sec. 1 of the draft of 2008, a legal person is governed by the law of the state where its seat or registered office is located. Therefore, as a principle, this provision indicates the seat of a legal person as its personal status indicator. However, if the law indicated in the provisions of sec. 1 provides the governing law of the state, under which a legal person is established, this country's law is to apply. As may be seen, the Polish legislature refers here to the state of incorporation, thus withdrawing from the seat or registered office theory. Therefore, depending on the indicator mentioned in sec. 1 Art. 19 (seat) and referring to the state of establishment, the indicated law shall be applied, in particular, to the following:

1. foundation, conjunction, division, transformation or termination of a legal person,
2. the legal nature of a legal person,
3. the name or business name of a legal person,
4. the capacity of a legal person,
5. competencies and principles of operation and appointing and dismissing members of its bodies,
6. the representation,
7. acquisition and loss of a partner status or membership and the rights and obligations attached thereto,
8. responsibility of partners or members for the liabilities of the legal person,
9. consequences of the breach of the Act, the foundation charter or the statute, by a legal person's representative.

---

matrimonial property law, divorce and inheritance cases, while from the matters governed by the Polish law, there remains only the issues of personal law, non-property matrimonial law, parental rights and property rights'; in conclusion the author expresses a negative evaluation of justifications of legislative intents within the scope of private international law, indicating the need for Polish activity in the preparation of Community legislation in place of introduction into our legislation 'the regulations which, in the coming years, following the entry into force of EU regulations, will lose their significance regardless of whether they are consistent with Community rules or not', the more so as it seems that the Hague Programme may be regarded only as the first step of activities leading ultimately to the unification of private international law of the EU Member States; *Ibid.* 1187-1188.

According to sec. 4 Art. 19 of the draft, if a legal person performs legal transactions through its enterprise, it is enough that the person has a capacity to perform the action under the law of the state where the business is conducted. In relation to another party, a legal person may refer to the limitations concerning its capacity or representation resulting from the law indicated in the provisions of sec. 1 or sec. 2, if the limitations are not provided by the law of the state where the legal action was performed, only if the other party was aware of them or was not aware due to negligence (sec. 5 Art. 19). This rule does not apply to the asset disposal actions related to real estate in a country other than the one where the legal transaction was performed. The consistent dominance of the registered office theory in the draft of 2008 is also expressed by the fact that, at the moment when the registration is transferred to another country, the legal person is governed by the law of that state. However, the legal personality obtained in the previous country of registration is maintained if it is provided by the law of each of the states concerned. Transferring the registered office within the European Economic Area does not lead to a loss of legal personality (sec. 6 Art. 19). In the case of a merger of legal persons with the registered office in different countries, it would be possible if they comply with the requirements of the laws of these countries (sec. 7). The draft law also refers to organizational units without legal personality in respect to which it provides a proper application of its provisions concerning legal persons. However, the protection of the personal interests of legal entities or organizational units without legal personality is included in the relevant provisions of Art. 18 of the draft, which refers, as a principle, to the native law of the legal person. The draft, in the form from October 30th, 2008, was analysed in the literature. Especially extensive are the considerations presented by A. Opalski in the already quoted study.[22] He put forward his arguments in the context of the national laws (including Polish) allowing a broad use of arbitration over corporate disputes (from the company status).[23] Lack of P.I.L. legislation in this field therefore causes the need to regulate the Polish P.I.L. in respect to the matter of arbitration in Poland. After a regulatory review of legal theories and legal solutions concerning the choice of indicator for the regulation of the personal status of legal entities, the cited author indicates that the draft law formulated a combined concept using the registered office indicators, i.e. Art. 19 sec. 1 of the draft (Art. 17 sec. 1 of the Act), and the foundation theory, Art. 19 sec. 2 of the draft (Art. 17 sec. 2 of the

[22] Adam Opalski, *Prawo właściwe dla osób prawnych...* 820ff. (2010).
[23] *Ibid.*, 812.

Act). A. Opalski denounces the authors of the draft because the adopted solution does not solve the question of how the concept of a legal person's registered office should be understood, for it can mean both the actual premises, and the registered office as well.[24]

For a comparative lawyer familiar with the literature, which arose against the background of existing regulations included in provisions of Art. 9 § 2 P.I.L., the defect indicated by A. Opalski creates a danger of adopting aan incorrect position, according to which the registered office of a legal person is considered the actual office of the governing body of the legal person.[25] According to A. Opalski, the actual office indicator constitutes a threat to the security of trade. Justifying the use of this indicator, it is pointed out that it is to restrain foreign legal persons from choosing a registered office of legal order with lower standards than their national law.[26] Meanwhile, the Court of Justice of the European Union considered that this solution achieved a protectionist objective to defend its own territory against infiltration by foreign entities. A. Opalski sees the threats to the security of trade in the fact that the registered office theory enables questioning the legal personality of a legal entity because it moved the centre of its business outside the home state, which puts its creditors in an unfavourable position, while favouring debtors. Questioning the legal personality because of changing the registered office leads to loss of legal capacity on the new territory, therefore the legal person cannot be a party in litigation. An unclear personal status is not insignificant to potential business partners of such a legal person. In addition, A. Opalski indicates the lack of obstacles in concentrating management activities of a legal person in a convenient location abroad, which, using the concept of registered office as the actual office, in practice may prevent determination of the registered office at all.[27] The resulting danger concerns not only the 'external' relations: a legal person – its creditors and debtors, and business partners, but also it threatens the intra-corporate order, e.g. by the termination of a company without the consent, or even knowledge of the

[24] *Ibid.*, 817.

[25] compare the literature quoted in the footnote 20 of A. Opalski's study, the footnote which also indicates that the authors of the draft act omitted the ETS settlements recognising the real registered office theory to be incompatible with EU law; *Ibid.*, 818-821.

[26] *Ibid.*, 821.

[27] Adam Opalski, *Prawo właściwe dla osób prawnych...* 823 (2010); A. Opalski underlines that the difficulties in determining the registered office would also result from the fact that the National Court Register does not disclose the office of the body that manages the corporate legal person.

partners, while as a result of changing the applicable law, it will not have a legal capacity. If we refer to the national law, in this case to the Polish law, the adopted solutions provide a subordination of a legal person's corporate structure to informing its business partners or shareholders, however having no impact on the everyday activities of such a person's bodies. A. Opalski also indicates that the actual registered office theory is in conflict with secondary European Community law, which demands the Member States refrain from dissolution of a capital company in any way other than through liquidation proceedings.[28] Some of A. Opalski's remarks were considered by the legislature, but it did not comply with the actual 'lenient' registered office theory, allowing the conversion of a foreign company into a domestic trading partnership company or a private partnership. Under the current law, the Polish courts deciding the cases of corporate persons referred to their registered offices determined in their foundation charters, thus a solution consistent with European law and safe for the market. This is because it protects the termination of a company, or its reincorporation, on the basis of arbitrary actions of managers undertaken without the approval of their business partners.[29]

The Act of February 4th, 2011, approved by Parliament and accepted by the Senate, in the provision of Art. 17 sec. 3, contains an open list of issues concerning personal status (Art. 19 sec. 3 of the draft). Point 4 of this catalogue takes into account the capacity of a legal person as a part of its personal statute. This solution is questioned in the cited publication by A. Opalski, who indicates that it is controversial in the literature of the theory of private international law, because it determines the problem of the recognition of a legal person identifying it with a personal statute and subordinating it to this statute.[30] In practice, this problem, although not yet clearly determined in either European or Polish law, is of increasing importance. It results from a very dynamic process of shaping cross-border economic relations, both within the European Economic Area and beyond it. Predicting contracts of business delegations etc. is based on economic objectives possible to achieve in a legal order different from that which regulates the legal status of a corporate legal person. Doubts about the capacity of a legal person appearing as a consequence of the provisions of the new Polish act are significant. They pose a serious threat of

---

[28] *Ibid.,* 824.

[29] Adam Opalski, *Prawo właściwe dla osób prawnych...* 827 (2010); the author rightfully indicates that the essential significance is therefore attached to the choice of the ultimate corporate indicator to the legal system under which a legal person was founded; such a solution remains consistent with the jurisdiction of ETS.

[30] *Ibid.*, 832.

ineffectiveness of measures, invalidity of concluded contracts, and therefore they are destructive to the security of trade. Thus, we can share A. Opalski's view that the issue of acquiring legal capacity should be excluded from the scope of the personal statute, for it should regulate the range of legal capacity of a legal person and the principles for its representation, but not the issue of acquisition and loss of the capacity.[31] A. Opalski also questions the solution included in the provisions of Art. 19 sec. 6 of the draft, finally placed in the provisions of Art. 19 sec. 1, concerning the cross-border transfer of the registered office and conjunctions of legal persons. The Act, passed in February 2011, maintained the solution unchanged, including it only in a separate regulation. It provides that upon the transfer of the registered office to another country, the legal person is governed by the law of this state. The legal personality obtained in the previous registration country is maintained if it is provided by the law of each concerned state. The transfer of the registration within the European Economic Area does not lead to a loss of legal personality. A. Opalski also indicates that in this solution the most defective is the lack of legislative clarification of the registered office concept, for the transfer of the registered office, the head office or the main production plant are completely different processes from the perspective of the legal person system.[32] A. Opalski also indicates that included in the draft (but not changed in the provisions of the Act – J.A.P.'s note) solution concerning a merger of legal persons according to which a merger of legal persons with the registered offices in different countries requires meeting the regulations specified in the law of each country, which raises doubts about the internal consistency and is also incompatible with European law.[33]

Presented widely, A. Opalski's critical opinions to the draft law pose obstacles difficult to overcome by a researcher comparing the current

---

[31] *Ibid.*, 836-837.

[32] Adam Opalski, *Prawo właściwe dla osób prawnych...* 837ff. (2010)

[33] *Ibid.*, 840ff., generally A. Opalski considers the draft act and the included solutions concerning the personal status of a legal entity as insufficiently pursuant to the demands of adjusting the Polish conflict of law to the European law and difficult to reconcile with the modern tendencies in private international law; in addition, the draft is inconsistent with the binding interpretation of Art. 49 and 54 of the Treaty on the Functioning of the European Union, approved in the jurisdiction of the ECJ and completely ignores the conflict of laws rules resulting from the 10 Directive on cross-border merges of companies, *Ibid.*, 843-844; the observations are still valid in relation to the provisions of the Act of February 4th, 2011.

solutions included in the act actually being passed. These difficulties cannot be overcome by the justification of this act, which relates to the solutions concerning the personal status of a legal entity and also indicates that the conflict of laws of regulation of legal persons is more extensive in the draft (Art. 19-20) than in the provisions of the Act of 1965. The registered office indicator was maintained as fundamental (Art. 19 sec. 1). However, a reference to the law of the state under which a legal person was established is permitted. For if the conflict of laws applicable in the country where a legal person has a registered office leaves the evaluation of the capacity and other issues covered by the personal statute of a legal entity to the law of the country under which the legal person was established, there is no reason to persist in Poland in applying, as a personal statute, the law of the country with the registered office of a legal person as a personal statute.

The regulations of Art. 19 sec. 3 determine the scope of application of the personal statute of a legal entity. This was necessary due to the practical significance of this issue and endless doctrinal disputes as to the extent of this statute. The disputes should have been cut and the existing doubts removed.

Art. 19 sec. 3 pt. d contains a mention of the capacity of a legal person as a part of its personal statute. Therefore, according to the statute, it should be evaluated whether a legal person may use its general or special legal capacity and its so-called active capacity (in particular the capacity to legal actions and within the sphere of other actions).

Deviations from the general rule are provided in the following sections of Art. 19.

They use the indicator of the business registered office in determining the applicable law to assess the legal actions undertaken by a legal person within the scope of its business (Art. 19 sec. 4). A possibility was also excluded to inform the other party of the limitations of the representation capacity resulting from the provisions of the personal statute of a legal entity, if such limitations are not provided by the law of the state where the legal action was taken, unless the other party was aware of those limitations (Art. 19 sec. 5). The further provisions regulated conflict of law issues, related to the transfer of a legal person's registered office to another country (Art. 19 sec. 6) and the merger of legal persons with the registered office in different countries (Art. 19 sec. 7). The provisions include the specific relations within the European Economic Area (Art. 19 sec. 6 sentence 3).

They are new regulations in our law.

A new regulation is also Art. 19 sec. 8, which relates to so-called temporary (imperfect) legal entities. It requires the respective application of the regulations (included in Art. 19 sec. 1-7) related to legal persons to organizational units which are not corporations. Therefore, if an organizational unit is a corporation, or it only has a legal capacity, it does not really matter while inquiring into its personal statute. This reduces the difficulties resulting from a considerable variation in different jurisdictions in the scope of incorporated organizational units.

The discussed provision does not define the concept of an organizational unit, leaving the task to judicature and doctrine.

As may be seen, the legislature did not treat the critical opinions regarding the draft very rationally; therefore the resulting legal act is far from expectations. From the comparatist's point of view, private international law is deemed to be the most difficult area among the branches of law. This is because it requires a perfect knowledge of not only conflict of laws rules contained in the legal acts, but also a very extensive and competent knowledge of substantive laws to which the conflict of laws rules refer, whereas the scope of the substantive laws is incredibly vast and diverse. In my opinion, undertaking comparative law studies which would promise an achievement of good and accurate results, requires 'balancing' the comparatist's techniques. The higher the language skills and the more profound the legal knowledge, the more promising the results of their work. However, with quite modest competencies, it is better to be satisfied with not very complicated matters, such as the press law I referred to in the beginning of these considerations. The recorded observations carry a conviction that comparative studies should not be treated in the literature as a categorical imperative, and undertaking comparative law studies would require a specific self-examination of the researcher's own competence.

Mutual Transition, Spiral and Evolutionary Development of Single Positive Law and Plural Normative Order Related to the New Comparative Normative Order Study in the Context of Global Conflicts Resolution

Bizina Savaneli

St. Grigol Peradze University. Georgia

Abstract

I distinguish two types of single positive law: positive law of the nation state (internal law) and positive law of nation states (international law). Both represent legal monism.

I distinguish two types of plural normative order: normative orders of the nation state (internal normative orders) and normative orders of nation states (international normative orders). Both represent normative pluralism.

In my statement I discuss single internal positive law of the nation state and plural normative orders of the nation state, and their mutual transition, spiral and evolutionary development through the lens of Universal Human Rights Law. Simultaneously, I discuss single international positive law and plural international normative order, and their mutual transition, spiral and evolutionary development related to new comparative normative order study in the context of global conflicts resolution with regard to Universal Human Rights Law.

I. **Legal Monism** (Public Positive Law and Private Positive Law) indicates how natural and legal persons ought to act **ideally**. **Normative Pluralism** (Public Normative Order and Private Normative Order) shows how public bodies, and natural and legal persons acts **really**. Legal

Monism (what ought to be) and Normative Pluralism (what is) never coincide.

II. The theory is about mutual transition, spiral and evolutionary development of positive law and normative order removing any contradiction between them and making possible peaceful coexistence of positivism and sociological directions in jurisprudence, and creates **balance between public law and private law**, and public normative order and private normative order on the global, regional, national and local levels.

III. The 'legal families' theory or Comparative Law ignores the phenomenon of normative order. Almost all scientists operating in comparative law and legal theory ignore any role of practice of individual normative acts of public bodies and private persons in formation of normative order. However, the state and certain combinations of practice of individual normative acts of public bodies and private persons construct the individual attributes of normative order of the country, which are always different from another country, disregarding that both could be even be in the same legal family. So it is necessary to introduce a new branch of legal science: **Comparative Normative Orders Study**, which should not initially investigate within the frameworks of Comparative Law Study.

IV. **The Idea of Just Law** suggests the sort and kind of law legislators (in Roman-Germanic i.e. 'civilianist' legal space) or judges (in Anglo-American, i.e. common law legal space) should make, so that any laws would be **just** in regard to Universal Human Rights.

V. The Mutual-Transition of Legal Monism, Normative Pluralism and the Idea of Just Law must be based on the **Universal Human Rights Law as the Entity of Basic Norms'**, and this process must be repeated **dialectically, i.e. spirally, constantly, evolutionary and endlessly**.

Therefore we the people of the world need a **New Human Philosophy under the auspice of the Universal Human Rights Law**, which links the East and West, North and South, ethics and religions, public and private life, technologies and environmental protection, and the myriad problems which have never previously existed ubiquitously in the history of mankind.

Humankind has one type of law - **Universal Law of Human Rights as the peak of World Law**, which rises above internal positive law and normative order, as well above international positive law and normative order.

My scientific position warns us never to absolutely accept any theory and/or philosophy of law. It gives us the universal key to open the door in the world, which might be equally acceptable for different cultures. It is not a new intercultural theory and/or philosophy of law. It is a new cross-cultural meta- and common language for humanity based on the **Universality of Human Rights and Freedoms.**

'To make just law, makes a dry tree green' – Shota Rustaveli (12th Century)

I. **Globalization in the modern world** reflects such transnational problems that have never previously existed widely in the history of mankind: Islamophobia and Judaeophobia, European Union and NATO, World Bank, IMF and Developing Countries, International Drugs Network and Terrorism, Internet and E-mail, Global Warming and Ozone Depletion, Deforestation and Marine Pollution, Israel, USA, UK and Muslims, Monopolization of World Economics and Extreme Poverty, Contraband Armaments Traffic and Unregulated Financial Transfers, Amnesty International and Greenpeace, Coca-Cola and McDonald's, Exhaustion of Non-renewable Natural Resources and Neo-colonialism, Corruption and Illegal Human Trade, International Trade Union Organizations and Transnational Woman's networks, 'Black Africa' and 'Yellow Asia', Catholic Church and Russo-phobia, Ethnic Conflicts and the vast masses of Displaced Persons, Growth of Racism and Ethnic separatism, and a cross-synthesis of the above mentioned realities in combination with other factors.

In 1994 I had warned about the Islamic fundamentalists attack on the 38th parallel. (By the way, Washington and New York are near the area of the 38th parallel (!))... Madrid is located on the 38th parallel... New danger is evident from the 38th parallel between North and South Korea.[1] The tsunami in Japan unfortunately fell upon the 38th parallel.

Scientists of legal theory throughout the centuries and scientists on comparative law for about 60 years are still oriented exclusively toward the municipal law of nation states and/or international (inter-states) law, while the normative order (established practice of normative acts of public bodies and private persons) of each country and the world has remained in the shade.

However, the long prevailing notions of international law do not appear ill suited to finding adequate solutions for the myriad problems that are transnational in scope. Modern international law seeks to subsume the individual interests of the states under the general interests of common

[1] Bizina Savaneli, *Kampf ums Recht. Rechtsreform in Georgien* 23 (1994).

good. That is good. But the common good of governments means nothing if the citizens of the state have remained in extreme poverty, and/or if their civil and political rights are systematically and seriously violated. Most people in most countries, except for the European Union, the USA, Canada and a few others, live under such conditions.

In the framework of international law a comic situation has been established: the fact is that the principles of Human Rights are created by the states being the potential violators of Human Rights. States mainly act, not only out of respect of law, but also and very often, primarily in their 'best' political interests. Recent actions of the UK and US are the best examples of such a situation, to say nothing about the 50 years occupation of Arab territories by Israel. Annual reports of Amnesty International and Human Rights Watch clearly indicate this comic situation. In the region of Asia and Australia, where meaningful political organizations such as the Council of Europe, the Organization of American states and the African Union organization are failing, and there is a conspicuous lack of corresponding human rights conventions and charters. If a state is not fulfilling responsibilities or is actually violating Human Rights, a curious situation arises as to the standing of the other contracting parties in securing from the transgressing party the observation of its obligations. The principle of state immunity, non-intervention in domestic jurisdiction of state, freedom of contract and the consensual nature of proceedings before international tribunals, weaken protection of Human Rights.

According to Epping, the individual has no legal capacity in international law because he/she does not participate in the norm-setting process. He/she enjoys their partial legal capacity through his/her state of nationality.[2] Legal capacity to participate in the norm-setting process is possessed partly and by only some international NGOs, as their legal capacity is constrained by consultative status.

The fact is that only Europe could partly achieve progress in this field, especially after the adoption of Protocol 11 ECHR. The rest of the world remained without any efficient mechanism of responsibility of states regarding individuals. ICC for Rwanda and Yugoslavia was an exemption, not a rule.

Lack of a World Court of Human Rights comparable to the European Court of Human Rights completely prevents any international mechanism of protection of Human Rights in the rest of the World and endangers Peace as a whole. Thus most of the population of the world, especially in developing countries, has remained without efficient protection of their

---

[2] Volker Epping & Knut Ipsen, *Völkerrecht* 75 (4th ed., 1990).

fundamental rights and freedoms. In such a situation, the populations of developing countries are forced to use popular action like revolution, rebellion, terrorism and other criminal actions. Despite greater homogeneity in regional human rights arrangements, states still show some reluctance to litigating against each other. However, that the individual can have both the procedural capacity to exercise those rights and legal capacity to possess the same in international law, has been affirmed by prominent scientists like H. Kelsen and I. Brownly.[3] Some authors interpret such a position as an argument for the recognition of the individual as a subject of international law. But those authors ignore that the above mentioned scientists emphasize that: '...the individual can have procedural and legal capacity', not 'has'.

Actually, if we remain the individuals in the framework of international law (exactly inter-states law), an individual may be exclusively considered as an object not a subject of international law, because in any case state and individual are not and may not be equal subjects of international law. But if we consider the individual and state in the framework of Universal Human Rights Law, they may be considered as equal subjects of Law such as exists at the level of European Court of Human Rights. Universal Human Rights Law consists of inter-state agreements, which are unilateral and not dependent on other initially corresponding rights and obligations among states under international law. At the same time, Universal Human Rights Law is itself obligated to the state character relations of any individual (not just the citizens) inside of territories of the appropriate states. The Natural Law heritage means that the International Human Rights instruments do not create the Human Rights of individuals and respectively obligation of states, they merely recognize them. But that does not mean that if human rights are inherent in nature, they should enjoy inviolable status. Declarative recognition of Natural Human Rights and respectively the obligation of states in the Human Rights instruments are nothing without adequate mechanisms of their protection.

I state that the problem which humankind really faces today is the following: Human Rights are **de facto** not Universal. For the resolution of that problem, I invite a fundamental rethinking of our modern state and our modern concepts of Law. In 1993 I indicated on Anthropological Catastrophe underlining the following: 'Our planet is sick, and its symptomatic treatment will not give us any results. It is necessary to seek

---

[3] Hans Kelsen, *Principles of International Law* 143 (1952); Ian Brownlie, *Principles of Public International Law* 57 (4th ed., 1997).

the deep-remote reasons for the sickness that are settled in unconscious layers of brain as a result of the development of mankind's barely-controllable aggressive inclinations into the social stereotype. We are speaking about anthropological catastrophe, about the circumstance that the human being is still not formed as a 'human being'. The progressive representatives of humanity tried to embellish the facade of human society with ideological myths to change the vampire's face at least outwardly. But without substantial results'.[4]

I distinguish two types of single positive law: positive law of the nation state (internal law) and international positive law of nation states. Both represent legal monism.

I distinguish two types of plural normative order: normative orders of nation state (internal normative orders) and normative orders of nation states (international normative orders). Both represent normative pluralism.

In this statement I refer to single internal positive law of the nation state and plural normative orders of the nation state, and their mutual transition, spiral and evolutionary development, as seen through the lens of Universal Human Rights Law. At the same time, I discuss single international positive law and plural international normative order, and their mutual transition, spiral and evolutionary development Related to the New Comparative Normative Order Study in the Context of Global Conflicts Resolution also through the lens of Universal Human Rights Law.

Therefore, at the worldwide level there is a single positive (public and private) international law and plural (public and private) transnational normative orders. Plural (public and private) transnational normative orders need their coexistence, convergence and harmonization, and after that, creation of a new positive world law, which would be beyond the existing positive (public and private) international law and would be oriented on the resolution of above mentioned problems. (What kind of new positive world law might be preferable, I will indicate below). The final aim of the creation of a new positive world law for humankind is **'to be able to join the supernal order of orders'** (see below, paragraph VI).

---

[4] Bizina Savaneli, *Legal Theory. Manual* 207 (1993). More narrow see also: Bizina Savaneli (Pkhaladze), *Correlation between Universal Human Rights and Legal Capacity of Citizens* in Moscow State University, *Candidate's Dissertation Essays* 4-5 (1969). (Since 1970 'Savaneli' is my pseudonym, which connected with the village 'Savane', a birthplace of my ancestors in Sachkhere region of Georgia).

Following Kant's idea in 'Perpetual Peace' (1795) we must reject a centralized regime of world government on the grounds that it would either be a global despotism or else an unstable and fragile empire torn by civil strife. This is a quite different point of cosmopolitan argument than any dominant political order needs to be established in a wider, transnational or global context. The world without borders is a new fascism.

On the other hand, I cannot agree with Bonaventura de Sousa Santos, who attempts to argue that: 'In jurisprudence modernity is associated with legal positivism, liberal legalism and the equation of legal science with legal dogma. Under this paradigm law has had an important, but secondary place, as the main instrument of technocratic management of society.' [5] For me the position of Santos, who considers law as the main instrument of technocratic management of society, is a slighting, careless and scornful treatment of law and legal professionals. In particular, on the contrary, laws never distort reality and never reflect it, because 'ought to be' as a hypothetical judgment cannot distort reality and never reflects it. Distortion of reality and misrepresentation are basically the activities of public bodies and/or private persons, especially politicians at the top. As he justly criticized Santos, William Twinning underlines: 'All of this looks like a nutshell of vaguely familiar post-Marxist interpretation of the ‘paradigm liberal legal ideology. …Like many commentators, I find the more general parts of *Toward a New Common Sense* obscure, jargon-ridden and, in some instances, wrong. I resisted the temptation simply to dismiss Santos’ philosophy as ‘bosh’, because this kind of ‘post-modern’ writing is both fashionable in academic law and too important to be ignored. …Santos presents an utopian sociological theory of law as part of a grand politico-social theory. I am a more orthodox jurist, an insider, concerned with the health of my discipline in the next 10 to 20 years'.[6] Moreover, analyzing Santos’ position, which was exposed in detail by W. Twinning, I come to the conclusion that in his work Santos has weakened a regulatory function of law (including human rights law) over state, eroding its contents and dissolving institutions of law in the meta-juridical phenomenon. Substantially, the position of Santos is a modernized Marxism, while the embodiment of Marxism in practice – USSR (empire of evil) - destroyed, left behind it the totalitarian Russian empire and

[5] Bonaventura de Sousa Santos, *Toward a New Common Sense: Law, Science and Politics in Paradigmatic Transition* 2 (1995). Moreover, according Santos: 'Laws, like maps, distort reality rather than merely reflect it'. (See *Ibid.*, 464).

[6] William Twinning, *Globalization and Legal Theory* 201, 243 (2000).

metastasis as former soviet republics with some paranoid and/or sadist heads of state...

Past and contemporary problems of civilization are connected namely with devaluation of stable principles of rule of law and enlarging of unstable rules of politics. Politics without legal frameworks is a precondition of disorder at the global, international, transnational, internal and local levels.

Alternatively, can rule of law serve the resolution of global conflicts?

In his famous lecture given in Vienna in 1888, **Ernst Zitelmann**, professor in Bonn, exhaustively discussed the possibility of **World Law**.

This lecture was published the next year under the title of 'Die Möglichkeit eines Weltrechts'. (Vortrag, Gehalten in der Vollversammlung des juristischen Gesellschaft zu Wien am 20. März 1888). It is interesting to note that in the same year, **Julius Ofner** gave another lecture entitled 'Der Grundgedanke des Weltrechts', later published under the same title by Alfred Holder (Wien, 1889). Ofner did not discuss the question of a World Law as Zeitelmann did, but discussed the fundamental issue of World Law.

I remember that **R. Jehring** lamented the fact that traditional jurisprudence did not go beyond the framework of *Landesjurisprudenz* and did not study the problem of law in the light of its universal character. I may also mention the names of eminent jurists who discussed the universal character of law, such as **Kohler, Saleilles, Lambert, Vinogradoff, Pound, Wigmore** from the point of Sociology of law or comparative law; **Kohler, Berolzheimer, del Vacchio** from the point of the history of law or the legal doctrine; **Carthrein, Mausbach, Schillind, Petrazhitsky, Rommen** from the point of natural law. These scholars certainly contributed to the idea of World Law from their respective legal expertise.

But Law as such is not a universal phenomenon, as demonstrated by S. P. Sinha in his 'thesis of non-universality of law'. For Sinha, 'Law' cannot be equated to social organization but is only one particular form of it, developed by western civilization and largely ignored by other civilizations such as China, India, Japan or Africa's animist societies.[7] Therefore negotiation demands dialogue that cannot be reduced to chatting or a mere exchange of points of view, but has to be understood as a real

[7] Sinha Surya Prakash, *Legal Polycentricity* 32 (1995).

journey through different cultural logic, which may enable the emergence of a new inter cultural approach.

At the top of the pyramid of legal pluralism is situated a single world human rights law. A single world human rights law does not mean the necessity of the existence of world government. Mikhacko Tsereteli, founder of international law in Georgia, in his famous work 'Nation and Humankind' (1910) followed Kant (Perpetual Peace, 1795) and rejected a centralized regime of world government on the ground that it would either be a global despotism or else an unstable and fragile empire torn by civil strife. This is a quite different point from the very cosmopolitan argument that any domestic political order needs to be set in a wider, transnational or global context. The existence of single world human rights law means only an existence of a Code of Universally Recognized Human Rights and an appropriate legal mechanism of their protection by the World Supreme Court of Human Rights, such as the European Court of Human Rights and Freedoms in Strasbourg.

The fact is that at the beginning of the twenty first century we are forced to recognize that the authority of law should be based on meta-norms named by us as Universal Human Rights Law, which should be hierarchically superior to the International and Domestic laws.

But politicians have polluted the Positive Law and Normative Order. Thus it is necessary to purify them.

What is the general and theoretical model of 'purification' of Positive Law and Normative Order from the meta-juridical notions and categories?

The fact is that almost all post-modern scientists in legal theory became entirely alienated from the substance of law and legal rights and obligations, and flitted to philosophy, anthropology, hermeneutics, sociology, ethnology, economics, and more over to geography etc. They attempt to analyze the juridical notions and categories through the above mentioned spheres of science, while none are specialized in the appropriate fields, and they were attracted by width but not by depth. They disembowel law from law. In jurisprudence came a smell of dampness without the perspective of light to the end of the tunnel. And as a result societies really do remain without law and people without human rights. Societies and people remain in 'stark nakedness'. On the planet rages a tornado of amorphous and often inadequate rules of politics without any borders of rule of law. Globalization of such politics turned human beings into slaves with invisible fetters.

What is the matter?

Let us begin with the certification of fact that Plato, Aristotle, Kant and Hegel were preoccupied with the question of: **not what the law is, but what the law ought to be**.

According to Kelsen's Pure Theory of Law, every legal norm is in accord with another 'higher' legal norm that authorizes its creation. The 'higher' legal norm, in turn, is valid only if it has been created in accord with yet another, even 'higher' legal norm that authorizes its enactment. More concretely, the constitution is the basic authorizing norm of the rest of the legal system, and the Basic Norm is the presupposition of the validity of the constitution. Furthermore, Kelsen argued that every pair of norms which derive their validity from a single Basic Norm necessarily belongs to the same legal system and, *vice versa*, so that all legal norms of a given legal systems derive their validity from one Basic Norm. It is widely acknowledged that Kelsen erred in these assumptions about the unity of legal systems. However, the role of the Basic Norm in explaining the normativity of law is crucially important. The presupposition of the Basic Norm as the condition of validity of legal norms marks Kelsen's theory as 'pure', which distinguishes it from other theories in the legal positivist tradition. Kelsen was convinced that any attempt to ground law's normativity - on the 'ought' aspect - is doomed to failure if it is only based on facts, whether those facts are natural or social.

Once again, to account for an 'ought' conclusion, one needs some 'ought' in the premises. Therefore, Kelsen thought, normativity of law, as a genuine 'ought', ultimately, be presupposed. Kelsen's pure theory of law as an attempt to find a middle way between natural law's dogmatism, and positivism's reduction of law to the social sciences. Kelsen does not claim that the presupposition of the basic norm is a necessary feature, or category, of rational cognition. The Basic Norm is an 'ought' presumption and, as such, is optional. It is not necessary for anyone to accept the basic norm. The basic norm is necessarily presupposed only by those who accept the 'ought'; namely, the normativity of the law. The validity of a legal system partly, but crucially, depends on its actual practice: a legal order is regarded as valid if its norms are by and large effective. Furthermore, the actual content of the basic norm depends on its effectiveness. However, actual legal practice is characterized by normative pluralism, and the effectiveness of the legal system depends on the normative order, which is free from sharp subordination to the single legal system.

However, making a sharp distinction between 'to be' and 'ought to be' is very disputable, which has characterized the English analytical tradition from Bentham through Austin, Holland, Pollock, Buckland, Hart and Raz.

Therefore, to reply to all of the above mentioned, unprecedented events so comprehensibly as to sufficiently reconcile two contradicting theories: Natural Theory of Law and Pure Theory of Law, I suggested a new theory named by me as '**Normative Anthropology**', and I argued the idea of the **Jus Cogens character of Universal Human Rights Law.**

Canonical jurists – Bentham, Austin, Kelsen, Dworkin, Hart, Habermas – tended to assume that a theory of law is only concerned with two types of law: state law and public international law. For the most part, their theories of law do not purport to give an account of non-state law. Moreover, classical and contemporary scientists traditionally identify 'Law' and 'Order'. Such identification is mistaken. I consider 'Law' as Positive law, and 'Order' as Normative Order. Positive Law and Normative Order compose the Normative System of each nation state. Accordingly, Positive Law as part of the Normative System has a single form, while a Normative Order has plural form.

At the same time it is necessary to make the distinction between legal pluralism and normative pluralism.

Legal pluralism is connected to the plurality and differences of legal systems of nation states.

Legal pluralism in developing countries involves different sources, but it does not mean that different positive laws are operating in these countries. For example, in the middle of the 20th century Tanzania, it seems, had hybrid positive law, which involved customary, Islamic, Hindu laws and legislation, but it does not means that in this country there was not a single law but rather four positive laws operating. All these sources simply coexist, but one of them was preferable on the whole than others and this source was recognized as positive law. An analogical situation may be seen in other developing countries. For example, before the colonization of Georgia by Russia (1801) two sources of law coexisted in Georgia – legislation (mainly in the lowland) and customary law (in the uplands), but legislation had mainly prevailed over customary law. By the way, the term 'sources of law' clearly, shortly and directly indicates that we have one positive law (but not positive laws), which could involve different sources when one of them is preferable.

Contrary to positive law, normative pluralism is connected to the plurality of normative orders within each country.

More broadly, on the level of each nation state a single legislator ***in abstracto*** distributes mutual rights and obligations among natural and legal persons as potential participants of possible normative relations. That is Positive Law. On the level of each nation state different natural and legal persons themselves, as individual participants of the real normative relations, distributed mutual rights and obligations ***in concreto***. That is Normative Order or normative pluralism.

Normative pluralism or normative order in each country refers to the co-existence of multiple normative orders in the frameworks of normative order (order of orders) in parallel with a single legal system such as positive law. In other words, in each country there is a **single legal system** (legal monism) and a **plural normative system** (normative pluralism).

Normative order and normative pluralism are synonyms. Normative order or normative pluralism divides into two parts: legal pluralism and 'non-legal' pluralism. Legal pluralism is a summary of normative acts of public bodies. (Separate are the normative acts of courts, which in summary consist of judge-made law). 'Non-legal' pluralism is a summary of normative acts of private persons (private persons include individuals and their groups).

Normative pluralism or normative order is used sometimes to apply to those who advocate plural orders in contrast to state centralism. Positive law is a system of legal rules which indicate how public bodies or private persons ought to conduct themselves **ideally**, regardless of the functioning of such rules in reality. The normative order is a system of established rules which show how public bodies or private persons **really** act, regardless of what the rules of positive law point to ideally.

The normative order generally comprises both public and non-public orders. So, there are two fields in the space of normative order in general: official normative order, which includes normative acts of public bodies, and unofficial normative order, which includes normative acts of private persons. More clearly, normative order includes two spaces: individual normative acts of public bodies and individual normative acts of private persons. Individual normative acts of public bodies in their entity may be in the figurative term described as **Positive Law** (public law and private law) **in action**. Individual normative acts of private persons in their entity could be described as **Individual Law** (normative facts) **in action**.

An official normative order comprises individual decisions of public (official) bodies. An official normative order has a **vertical character**. An unofficial normative order comprises individual acts of private (unofficial) persons. Unofficial normative order has a **horizontal character**. Both also include cross-sectional fields, which reflect a result of the coexistence and interaction of an official normative order and unofficial normative order, and the feasibility of normative acts and normative facts. So, the normative order has legal and non-legal contexts.

In other words, I am distinguishing legal (official) order and non-legal (unofficial) order as two forms of normative order.

As a whole, normative order is the existence of positive law in action and existence of individual law or non-state law in action, as well as of their coexistence.

Therefore, single positive law is the state established entity of general legal rules, which regulate civil, political, economic, social and cultural relations among potential natural and legal official or unofficial persons through the distribution among them of mutual rights and obligations ***in abstracto***.

Therefore, normative order is that entity of individual normative rules (normative acts) established by the individual natural and legal official or unofficial persons, which really regulate different civil, political, social and cultural relations through the distribution among and by them mutual rights and obligations ***in concreto***. (For assessment and clarification of normative order in the official context we may use the official reviews of authoritative bodies and competent organizations.)

Normative order in the official context could be considered as a whole or as an entity of different sections (orders) of normative order in the official context.

An attempt has been found of subsequent development of the theory of normative order by W. Twinning, who underlines: 'A healthy global general jurisprudence should be able to give a total picture (descriptive/explanatory/ normative/analytical) of the phenomena of law in the modern world. Such accounts can be constructed from multiple perspectives. For most purposes, they need to include not only municipal legal systems and traditional public international law, but also global, regional, transnational, and local orderings that deserve to be treated as 'legal' for given purposes and the and the relations between them. This will involve addressing the phenomena of legal pluralism, both within and beyond municipal legal systems and different cultures and traditions. The facts of interdependence cast doubt on any 'black box' descriptive or normative theories, which treat legal or other normative orders as self-contained and in particular those, which purport to limit the sphere of their application to notionally self-contained nation states, societies or other impervious units'.[8]

---

[8] William Twinning, *Globalization...* 88 (2000); But the author could not differentiate substantially not only positive law and normative order, but legal order and non-legal order in the framework of normative order. (See *Ibid.,* 228-

Normative pluralism or normative orders in the framework of normative order on the whole ('order of orders' – see below) is the **empirical reality** in the Kantian sense, which can become a subject of scientific or other research and investigation through the method of transcendental idealism in the Kantian sense.[9]

II. The notion and functioning of the normative order in the official context i.e. the individual normative acts of public bodies, traditionally have been explored more carefully than the normative order in the unofficial context i.e. the individual normative acts of private persons. **The notion of normative order in non-legal contexts** refers to certain social facts, which have been named by Prof. George Naneishvili as 'normative facts' i.e. facts which have normative power. Sometimes G. Naneishvili uses the notion of 'autonomous normative facts'. 'Autonomous normative facts' in the space of social life nicely catches the imprecision and porosity of the juridical context of normative order.[10] After 40 years, Sally Falk

235). On the page 172 he writes: Legal orders are made up complexes of social relations, ideas, ideologies, norms, concepts, institutions, people, techniques and traditions. On the page 147 he identifies legal system and legal order. Moreover, he basically on the declarative level distinguishes: normative pluralism and legal pluralism as a species of normative pluralism, and pluralistic state legal systems and non-state legal orders as sub-species of legal pluralism, and legal order and non-legal orders and other phenomena, and state and non-state law, and legal orders, systems, traditions, cultures. For him distinctions between them are context-dependent, which depends on one's vantage-point, perspectives and goals. (See *Ibid.*, 228, 229, 231-233). But 'one's vantage-point, perspectives and goals' remained very abstract and unclear. Normative pluralism, legal pluralism, pluralistic state legal systems, non-state legal orders, legal order, non-legal orders, state law and non-state law are the bulk of terms only.

[9] Transcendental idealism is a doctrine founded by great German philosopher Immanuel Kant in the eighteenth century. Kant's doctrine maintains that human experience of things is similar to the way they appear to us - implying a fundamentally subject-based component, rather than being an activity that directly (and therefore without any obvious causal link) comprehends the things as they are in and of themselves. The best way to approach transcendental idealism is by looking at Kant's account of how we intuit objects, and that task demands looking at his accounts of space and of time. (See 'Transcendental idealism' by Wikipedia). Normative character of positive law and normative character of language are coincides as Kelsen saw. (See Hans Kelsen, *Eine Grundlegung der Rechtssoziologie* in Archiv für Sozialwissenschaft und Sozialpolitik 40 (1946); Id., *General Theory of Law and State* 175 (1934).

[10] George Naneishvili, *Positive Law and Normative Facts* (1930). G. Naneishvili graduated from Freiburg University in 1924. He was an assistant of the founder of Psychological Theory of Law - Prof. Leon Petrazhitsky and follower of Edmund

Moore is talking about a semi-autonomous social field instead of subgroups. A semi-autonomous social field is defined and its limits identified not by its type of organization but a character of a procedural type residing in the fact that it gives birth to norms, and, by constraints or incentives, ensures their application. The space, within which a certain number of corporate groups are in relation one to another, constitutes a semi-autonomous social field. A large number of fields of this type may be connected one to another in such a way that they form complex chains, in the same way as the network of social relations which link individuals may be compared to chains, which have no ends. The interdependent connection of a large number of semi-autonomous social fields constitutes one of the fundamental characteristics of complex societies.

Normative facts are the coexistence of different norms in the form of mutual individual rights and obligations within different every-day social relations of private natural and legal persons' lives.[11]

More precisely, for the clear illustration of the formation of normative facts in the private space I would like to cite a simple example. Let us assume that any private person publicly expressed the free will of readiness to undertake an obligation to act in the specific private space. The readiness to undertake an obligation to act in the specific private space has the normative effect, but that is not a normative fact until the other person or persons will not express its or their counter free will of readiness to undertake an obligation to act in that specific private space. In the favourable case, the **expression** (fact) of readiness by one or both parts to act in specific space and distribution of **mutual obligations** and **corresponding rights** (norm) by both parts is the end of formation of normative fact. If we consider such normative facts and analogous and other normative facts in the private space in totality we shall receive the unity, which could be named as non(out)-normative order simultaneously with legal normative order.

G. Naneishvili's position, which is also mine, may be set forth in the summary:

1. The normative facts do not depend on the positive law or its sources.

Husserl in Jurisprudence. Prof. George Nanaeishvili is only one scientist, who on a high creative level develops Reinach's theory about Social Facts. (See Adolf Reinach, *The A Priori Foundations of Civil Law* (1983).

[11] Bizina Savaneli (Pkhaladze), *Correlation between Universal...* 4-5 (1969); See also Id., *Juridical Forms of the Citizens Position in Soviet Society* (1969). Reviews on monography see Sergei Sergeyevich Alekseev, 5 Jurisprudence 106-107 (1970); Michel Fridieff, Revue International de Droit Compare 272-273 (1971); Anna Michalska, 3 Ruch Prawniczy, Ekonomiczny i Socjologiczny 305-307 (1971).

2. Normative facts are always prior to positive law.

3. We can always imagine normative facts in a space, which is not subject to the regulation of positive law.

4. Positive law cannot increase or decrease the number of normative facts.

5. The notion of normative facts excludes the idea of the free creation of rules of law. Positive law has an artificial, man-made character.

6. Concerning positive law: because the specific character of positive law depends on the specific character of external transitional factors we can say that this (but not other) positive laws appeared. Therefore, each instance of positive law is but one of several possible (un-instantiated) positive law alternatives.

7. Concerning normative facts: because the specific character of normative facts does not depend on the specific character of external transitionally factors, we cannot say that this (but not other) normative facts have appeared. Each normative fact is not a possible normative fact, because a normative fact is the fact.

8. Normative facts can only be used by positive law for its aims or can institute constraints over the result, which, according to its value, should occur, but positive law can never annul normative facts.

9. In contradiction to the positive law, which always has an authoritative legal source, normative facts have no authoritative source. We can always say that positive law 'happens', but we cannot say this about normative facts, because any fact is history.

10. Normative facts should be investigated irrespective of positive law.[12]

Normative facts (***Seinsregel***), i.e. the individual normative acts of private persons, reflect the normative pluralism in the day to day lives of individuals and their groups, and, partially by the ‘production’ of individual social rules by individual private persons. For example: 'You ought to keep your promise' is a normative fact. More clearly: normative fact = 'promise' + 'ought to keep', where 'promise' is the individual fact and 'ought to keep' is the individual norm, disregarding: positive law contains or not a claim to act. Positive law can claim to act or not claim to act depending on the different character of normative relations. Positive law can use or not use normative facts, and that is all. The normative lives of private individuals and groups always form the independent normative life

[12] George Naneishvili, *Positive Law...* 55 (1930). Radical position concerning legal force of contracts was expressed by Jerome Frank. For him not only legislator, but also private persons create positive law. See Jerome Frank, *Courts on Trial* 308 (1949).

of society based on the distribution of mutual individual rights and obligations by private persons.[13] Private normative order (normative facts in private space) also refer to the norms of a given group, community, or society or they may refer more broadly to any norm that guides or governs social relations. But private normative order out of mutual rights and obligations among participants of social relations is not the subject of the science of law.

The theory of normative facts, i.e. the individual normative acts of private persons, is based on the principles of contract, treaty, and so on. These include, in particular, private civil contracts, mutual contractual aid, trade and collective commercial agreements, as well as the vast range of internal institutional rules, rules of private different units, etc. but not property rights. Property rights have a static, not a dynamic character. Normative facts, i.e. the individual normative acts of private persons, have a dynamic and not a static character; they reflect factual relations between two or more private natural and legal persons. Mutual rights and obligations among participants of social relations always precede positive law.

On the level of sociology, I am talking about the normative coexistence of private persons. The normative coexistence of private persons is the essence of the human being. More precisely, normative coexistence is a supreme product of the social life, as it is that which comes to the self-consciousness and conscious increase of interpersonal relations. Searching for the meaning of social life results in the necessity of self-knowledge, essence of being. The normative cognition of potential participants of social relations is vertical in the process of the elaboration of mutually acceptable rights and obligations, whereas all others are distributed on the horizontal plane. In other words, potential participants of social relations attempt to discover a common and mutually adopted model of action, which would be higher than their individual 'wills', a third imperative power situated above their individual 'wills'. This vertical of meaning of the social life is nothing else but self-cognition as a result of which the essence of the persons is developed and created, showing the normative archetype of humanity in total disregard of different cultural symbols. Based on the normative coexistence, the private persons with a greater depth are capable of comprehending their potential position in the social area with the others. In the process of normative coexistence, minimally, two regular methods are organized, which are realized in 'logos' and 'theos'. The third method is situated at the junction of 'logos' and 'theos',

---

[13] Bizina Savaneli (Pkhaladze), *Correlation between Universal...* 14 (1969).

the comprehension to which the participants of social relations strive. The result of such striving, i.e. normative coexistence, is a distribution of mutual rights and obligations by the participants of social relations. Moreover, the normative coexistence appears in the form an option. The option, which brought humanity through the spiral and evolutionary development, is crucial, because it is a matter of life, and choosing life is possible through the normative coexistence.

The voluntary actions of individuals and their groups (normative facts) create normative relations, and this is not an idealized illusion. That is the space of '**is**'. Only after that, the legislator makes the choice of what normative relations are needed in regulation. Then the legislator creates a model of regulation passing into the space of '**ought**'. Passing into the space of '**ought**' the legislator obeys the rules of linguistics, and in doing so, fills a theoretical gap between normative relations and the positive law, etc. spirally, evolutionary and endlessly. However positive law through legal language cannot directly construct a reality. The positive law through legal language attempts to construct a reality only through the voluntary actions of individuals and their groups (normative facts). Can the positive law achieve its aim? But again there is the question of **fact**. Moreover, even the judges are semiotic objects, but positive law cannot exactly predetermine judges' decisions even in analogized cases because they take into consideration **factual** consequences and their unrepeated combinations. Can the positive law achieve its aim? But again it is the question of **fact**.

On the level of philosophy, I underline that the idea that normative facts, i.e. the individual acts of private persons, do not depend on the positive law or its sources based on the **Giant Goethe's** formula: '**Im Anfang war die Tat**'. Instead of '**How to Do Things with Words**', I support the formula: '**How to Do Words with Things**'. Human beings do things without words. The things do words, the words do new things, new things do the new words, the new words do new things, and so on.

As correctly underlined by J. Calamari and J. Perillo: 'When the parties manifest their agreement by words the contract is said to be expressed. When it is manifested by conduct it is said to be implied in fact. For example, if 'A' telephones a plumber to come to 'A's' house to fix a broken pipe (the pipe is the result of act but not word – B. S), it may be inferred that 'A' has agreed to pay the plumber a reasonable fee for his services although nothing is said of this. The contract is partly express and partly implied in fact. There are cases of contracts wholly implied in fact. A contract implied in law is not contract at all but a general, impersonal obligation imposed by law to do justice even though it is clear that no promise was ever made or intended. . . Words are notoriously slippery symbols and there may be a wide divergence between the meaning a person intended to convey with his expression and reasonably or unreasonably understood by the person to whom he was communicated'.[14]

Permanent and cyclical interaction between things and words, inter-substitution of things and words, and permanent and cyclical inter-transition of things and words at global, regional, national and local levels, has a trend to comprehend a sense of law of Humankind that must be based on the Universally Recognized Human Rights. The aim and goal of such interaction, inter-substitution and inter-transition is to achieve sustainable development of Humankind. The formula '**New things produce new words**' means that new facts produce new mutual rights and obligations. The entity of new facts and new mutual rights and obligations creates new normative space, which causes the necessity to establish new positive law etc. Generally speaking: to claim 'ought to be' means that such 'ought to be' is practically possible. In other words, it is nonsense to claim human action, which is not practically possible. 'Ought to be' should be based on the individual human capacity.

Developing G. Naneishvili's theory, I underline that mutual rights and obligations of private persons are neither psychological entities nor are they mental. The bearers of rights and obligations are related to each other psychologically or mentally but their mutual rights and obligations are related to each other - **logically**. In other words, normative facts, i.e. the individual acts of private persons, using P. Winch's term could be described as 'rule-governed behaviours'.[15] Such rules have been naturally implanted into human behaviours and issued from human knowledge, skills, habits, experience, interdictions, permeations, traditions, ethics, customs, dispositions, etc. Indivisible connection between individual human rights rules and individual behaviours and their transitions is the vital connection ('**Lebenszusammenhang**', using the Dillteis term) and transition. The participants of such vital connections and transitions disseminate mutual rights and obligations among themselves by which they govern their behaviours. Therefore mutual rights and obligations are the rules through which, and together with participants' behaviours, 'rule-governed behaviours' have been created, which in legal theory are known as 'normative facts', i.e. the individual normative acts of private persons. Theoretically, normative facts are divided into facts (behaviours) and norms (mutual rights and obligations).

---

[14] John Calamari & Joseph Perillo, *The Law of Contracts* 19, 23 (2nd ed., 1977).
[15] Peter Winch, *The Idea of Social Science* (1958).

The theory of normative facts departs from questions about the effect of law toward conceptualizing official and unofficial forms of normative order. Only 50 years after George Naneishvili, Sally Falk Moore introduced the term 'semi-autonomous social fields', which, as W. Twinning correctly perceived, 'nicely catches the imprecision and porosity of the social contexts of most normative orders'.[16] At the same time 'Many normative orders do not have discrete boundaries, they tend to be dynamic rather than static, and relations between them are extremely complex'.[17] The positive law and the normative order coexist and interact in complex ways. 'Sometimes they compete or conflict; sometimes they sustain or reinforce each other through interaction, imposition, imitation and transplantation'.[18]

My position concerning normative facts, i.e. the individual normative acts of private persons, is based on the logical investigations of Edmund Husserl. As is generally known, Husserl developed a thesis advanced by his teacher Brentano to the effect that all mental acts are intentional, that is, that they are directed towards an object. The existence of man is the existence of another existence of permanent choice. Husserl maintained that all intentional experiences are in this sense 'objectifying acts'. Husserl's account of meaning builds upon this theory. All uses of language are, he says, referential. Accordingly, Husserl viewed acts such as questions or commands as masked assertions. The command 'sit down on the chair' he interpreted as a statement to the effect that 'your sitting down on the chair is my current request.' The man is what he is not yet, but what he ought to be.

The range of objectifying acts for **Husserl** includes:

1) Acts directed towards individual things, events, processes, etc., and towards the parts and moments of these;

---

[16] William Twinning, *Globalization...* 85 (2000). As W. Twiningcorrectly noted: 'We all experience normative pluralism – that is to say the coexistence of different bodies of norms within the same social space – every day of our lives'. (See *Id.*, 83). Such norms every day of humans' lives were named by G. Naneishvili (1930) as normative facts. See George Naneishvili, *Positive Law...* 53 (1930).

[17] William Twinning, *Globalization...* 88 (2000).

[18] *Ibid.*; At the same time, Twining distinguishes two types of legal order: municipal state law and public international law (see p. 51). It means that he identifies positive law and legal order, which substantially contradicted his above mentioned positions. I have to repeat again that municipal state law and public international law are two types of positive law. Legal (official) order and non-legal (unofficial) order are two types of normative order.

2) Acts directed towards species or essences, and towards ideal objects such as numbers;

3) Acts, above all acts of judgment, directed towards 'Sachverhalte' or states of affairs.

At the same time the radicalism of Husserl's phenomenological reduction pushes him to bring the transcendental ego to the forefront but posing the problem of alter ego. Husserl solves the problem by claiming the transcendental ego constitute other egos as equal partners in an inter-subjective community, which in turn form the objective, i.e. the inter-subjective world. Maurice Merieau-Ponty, after studying unpublished manuscripts of Husserl, brings out the notion of '**Lebenswelt**'. Succeeding Husserl, Martin Heidegger investigates the study of '**Dasein**' (lit. being-there), which includes the being-with. The inter-subjective nature of subjectivity is emphasized in the philosophies of Gabriel Marsel and Martin Buber in notions of participation and dialogue. We can find a similar term in the Eastern philosophies. For example, in Confucianism self-cultivation entails relating rightly with others in the family, community and society. A deeper study of Taoism may reveal that self-cultivation also involves relating with others, not only with the Tao in humility. In Hinduism, there is a movement of the self's finding of adornment from the Brahman to the Atman. In Buddhism, the extinction of desires entails the attitude of compassionate love. All of that is a philosophical foundation of the theory of normative facts which consist of mutual rights and obligations of participants of social relations.

On the other hand, plural forms of normative facts, i.e. the individual normative acts of private persons, are based on the idea that there are many real spaces, which are largely independent of the individual's knowledge of a given world, furthermore, including knowledge in the positive law. First of all, normative facts, i.e. the individual normative acts of private persons, are mainly associated with 'non-state law'. As is generally known, E. Ehrlich, the pioneer of sociology of law, argued that a realistic depiction of the law in action had to account for 'the living law' of sub-groups as well as 'the official law' of the state. He saw that these could diverge significantly and that sometimes one, sometimes the other would prevail. This was an important step not only in the direction of 'realism', but also in deliverance from the idea that the state has a monopoly of law-creation. These ideas were developed in a number of directions. For example, K. Llewellyn saw clearly that within a major group such as a nation-state, society or tribe, the basic functions of law, such as conflict-prevention and dispute-resolution, could be performed at different levels by a variety of mechanisms in addition to rules by education or the threat or use of brute force, and that different bodies of rules could coexist without necessarily being ranked in a clear hierarchical order.[19]

Concerning notions of Positive Law and Normative Order it is necessary to underline the following: K. Llewelyn's 'law-jobs theory' has no deal with the positive law, particularly public law, because the function of the legislator (the positive law-maker) is a **general** distribution of mutual rights and obligation among the participants of 'normal' political, social, economic, cultural and civil relations.

K. Llewelyn's 'law-jobs theory' has a deal with the normative order, particularly legal order, because function of public bodies (legal order-makers) is the **individual** distribution of mutual rights and obligation among the participants of 'abnormal' (dispute or conflict) political, social, economic, cultural and civil relations.

In other words, K. Llewelyn's 'law-jobs theory' does not relate to the general jurisprudence, but with particular jurisprudence.

Normative order is a summary of personal rules, which specifically regulate factual economic, social, cultural, civil and political relations in the country through distribution of mutual rights and obligations among or by the individual participants of these relations. Normative order or normative pluralism is the outcome of public normative acts and private normative acts.

In a broad sense I am talking about the normative life of civil society. The life of civil society has been influenced not only by the normative coexistence of private persons (private normative order) but also by other elements of culture: language, local customs, statehood traditions, religious rites, public normative order of state bodies, folklore, etiquette, art, social and family ceremonies, music, cooking, dress, agricultural and industrial practice and so on.

At the same time it is necessary to take into consideration the following abnormal situation: due to the tremendous pressure of 'big' cultures in the age of globalization, many small cultures step by step have lost their identities, thus degrading the culture of humankind. Although the preservation of cultural identity of small nation-states is very difficult, national (not corrupted, mercenary and venal) governments must permanently explore some way out and they can show some new techniques to achieve balance between national and universal cultures. But it does not mean that dialogue between nation-states cultures excludes.

---

[19] Karl Llewelyn, *The Normative. The Legal and the Law-Jobs: The Problem of Juristic Method*, 49 Yale Law Journal 1355-1360 (1940). Shortened version was reprinted in K. Llewelyn, *Jurisprudence: Realism in Theory and Practice* 233-262 (1962).

Not at all! Dialogue between national cultures serves mutual enrichment and enrichment of the culture of Humankind.

To talk about the global society today means a dictatorship of representatives of God's 'minions'. To talk about the global society, i.e. world society without borders, is too early because it means degradation of nation-states. Each nation-state has the natural right to self-determination. The exception is the situation when a nation decides that it has exhausted its own political, social, civil, economic, cultural and other potential. Only after that it can merge with another state-nation. That should be exclusively of its own free will.

Assertion that the European model has spread all over the world is illusionism.

Contemporary western tradition differentiates between the West and East. It is mistaken. Differences between the West and East are not substantial, because the origination of Western Culture is historically and basically connected with the Eastern Culture (India, China, South-East Asian countries, and Japan are clear examples). The people from the Northern space (I mean the people of the Council of Europe's Member States, USA and Canada) are oriented toward modernity. For these people modernity is associated with currency and relevance, and focuses on the future in Darwin's evolutionary spirit.

The gap between North and South is substantial. I would like to argue that the gap between North and South is deeper than we can imagine. Contrary to the people of Northern space, the people from the Southern space are oriented toward the past (I mean Muslim and African cultures). The golden era of Islam stretches from the 7th century. Since that time the Muslim community has been perceived to be in decline. Various reformists have called for a return to the lifestyle of the ancestors. African thought is not different from this perception of life. What is valuable in African culture is not what is yet to come but what has already passed. The concept of 'Development' and 'Progress' are absent from Afro-Islamic culture. If 'Development' and 'Progress' mean movement to a changed mode of system in general, Muslims and Africans have no willingness for such movement. The Koran depicts life as a worthless enterprise compared to spiritual life, because it ignores the importance of spirituality. Science and technology do emphasize causality, something that Muslim theology denies, and replaces it with atom-ism and 'occasional-ism'. Although Africans believe in causality, this causality however is not material but rather is spiritual. When an African goes out to hunt, the motive is mainly not to get food but to reveal his manly attributes.

Some philosophers from the East underline the contradiction between two - Eastern and Western - philosophies, issuing from two questions: one is – **what is**, and the other – **how that is**. Such a contradiction is superficial. Both are engaged in comprehension of these two questions but with different intensity. From my point of view, more important meter, which should consolidate not only East and West, but mainly North and South, is the following: **what and how ought to be in reality?** That is a third dimension, which removes any distinction between, and occupies, the place above them, despite what is and how that is. **That is the normative i.e. pure dimensional space**.

A traditional thesis distinguishes 'Law in the books' and 'Law in the action'

Law in the books or positive law in the books includes a state law. The state law or State in the legal sense as the part of positive law is the system of **general** rules, by which the functions of legislative, executive and judicial powers have been defined. Such general rules are usually set forth in constitutions.

Law in the action or positive law in the action includes public normative order. Public normative order, or order in the legal sense, as the part of normative order is the established system or practice of individual legal acts of legislative, executive and judicial powers, by which individual public and/or private relations among public and/or private persons are authoritatively regulated.

Therefore I distinguish 'state law in the books' and 'state law in action'.

My position concerning single positive law is partially based on H. Kelsen's pure theory of law; partially because individual normative acts of public bodies and individual normative acts of private persons are '***Seinfeld***', but not '***Solenoidal***' which is connected with rules of positive law, but not rules of normative order. Taking out 'Pure theory of law' and simultaneously 'Stepped theory of law' means taking out the State's (***Pollen***) frameworks, which is fraught with complete destruction of the purity of positive law and stepped structure of positive law. Moreover, that means endangering statehood which is the main guarantee of stability of contemporary society.

Law in the books, i.e. Single Positive Law (public law and private law), is investigated and explored more broadly and deeper than law in the actions and normative acts of public bodies.

The hierarchy of the state's bodies and the officials in it, is a result of lawmakers' activities, i.e. a general legal model of organization of the state's power. Accordingly, the hierarchy of state's bodies and the officials in it, is a reflection of the hierarchy of sources of positive law; in other words - 'Law in the books'.

On the level of positive law, '**San**' and '**Pollen**' are not mutually contradictory; they coexisted **logically** in the framework of two parts of the structure of each legal rule: hypothesis and disposition. On the level of normative order, '**San**' and '**Pollen**' are not mutually contradictory; they coexist **empirically** in the framework of two parts of the structure of each normative fact: fact and rule (for example, a treaty as normative fact consists of two parts: a fact of conclusion of the treaty and mutual rights and obligations between participants of the treaty). In other words, normative order embraces factually settled order (practice) of application of general legal rules by individual public bodies (precedent in broad sense) and factually settled order (practice) of application of mutual rights and obligations by private persons. On the level of normative order, '**San**' and '**Pollen**' coexist not logically, but factually, and they are indivisible.

Moreover, all societies have different normative spaces, in which positive law does not exist in isolation, and moreover is not necessarily the most powerful element thereof. The state has no monopoly of lawful power within a given country, except criminal law and administrative law, because the normative order does not have discrete boundaries. The normative order is dynamic rather than static, and social relations in each normative order are extremely complex.

'Law in the action' expresses one part of normative order, which is only connected with the official normative acts of public bodies. By normative acts of public bodies mutual rights and obligations are distributed officially. The comparably independent part of the normative order is unofficial normative acts of private persons (normative facts). By normative acts of private bodies, mutual rights and obligations are distributed unofficially. Common for both acts is that both are established mutual rights and obligations of participants of relations.

Normative acts of public bodies and normative acts of private persons (normative order) accordingly have their several forms i.e. normative orders, etc. Normative order is divided into normative orders, etc.

Normative order (public normative acts and private normative acts) includes speech acts of public bodies and private persons too. What I said about normative acts of private persons (normative facts) concerning speech acts in section III I repeat about normative acts of public bodies (legal normative acts). But as far as I would like to consider both together concerning speech acts, I have decided to analyze the problem more broadly.

Speech act theory will forever be associated with the great **John L. Austin.** One of Austin's core insights is reflected in the title of his William James lectures, delivered at Harvard in 1955, '**How to Do Things with Words**'. When we use language, we usually don't say what the world **is** like; when we use language, we **do** things. We command, request, apologize, contract, convey, and admonish. Speech act theory focuses on the ways in which oral language is used for the performance of actions.

Speech act theory begins with the idea that language can be used to perform actions.

Here are the following forms of speech acts:

Constants: affirming, alleging, announcing, answering, attributing, claiming, classifying, concurring, confirming, conjecturing, denying, disagreeing, disclosing, disputing, identifying, informing, insisting, predicting, ranking, reporting, stating, stipulating.

Directives: advising, admonishing, asking, begging, dismissing, excusing, forbidding, instructing, ordering, permitting, requesting, requiring, suggesting, urging, warning.

Commissions: agreeing, guaranteeing, inviting, offering, promising, swearing, and volunteering.

Acknowledgments: apologizing, condoling, congratulating, greeting, thanking, accepting.

Legal theorists are interested in speech act theory for a variety of reasons, but one of the most important is that speech act theory helps to explain the way that the law uses language. Constitution, Statutes and other normative acts are not like 'the cat is on the mat.' That is, a statute does not tell us how the world is in the same way that a declaratory sentence does. Legal language is full of speech acts.

Reinach maintains that such truths are not merely necessary and universal, but also informative, thus they are examples of truths that are both a priori and synthetic. Adolph Reinach mentions many social acts in his treatise on 'The A Priori Foundations of the Civil Law' (1913): commanding, requesting, warning, questioning and answering, informing, enacting, revoking, transferring, granting, and waiving of claims, but he devotes the most attention to the act of promising. Drawing on the theory of essences or intrinsically intelligible structures referred to above, Reinach offers the following examples of a priori truths about what he sees as the intrinsically intelligible structure instantiated through the performance of a promising act:

- through promising, one incurs an obligation;

- by receiving a promise, one has a claim to what was promised;
- such claims are extinguished when the promise is fulfilled;
- such claims may also be extinguished if the claim holder waives the **claim;**
- promising is subject to a range of variations or modifications, including conditional promising, promising on behalf of or as a representative of someone else, promising to a group, promising by a group, and so forth.

I am sure that one of the most fundamental distinctions in legal theory is the distinction between 'positive law theory' and 'normative order theory.' The core idea of the distinction between positive law theory and normative order theory is simple: positive law theory seeks to explain what the law **is**, in other words, **what the law says**, whereas normative order theory tells us what the positive law **ought to say**, in other words, **what the law should be.**

A bridge between **what the law says and what the law should be or should say** lies through the normative order. Investigation of normative order gives us an opportunity to assess how positive law (Sollen) is really implemented in legal order (Sein). In the process of investigation of normative order an idea of justice arises, in other words, an idea of what the law should be saying. To reconcile H. Kelsens' and G. Naneishvili's contradictory theories, I have suggested a new 'Spirally and cyclically developing theory of interaction and mutual-transition of Positive Law and Normative Order'. This is based on human rights' permanent and cyclical interaction between positive law and normative order, and permanent and cyclical inter-transition of positive law and normative order at global and local levels as a trend to comprehend permanently an **Idea of Justice**. The aim and goal of such interaction and inter-transition is to achieve sustainable development of Humankind based on Universal Human Rights.

Instead of '**How to Do Things with Words**', I suggest the formula: '**How to Do Words with Things**' in the sense of **Giant Goethe: 'Im Anfang war die Tat'**, because '**New things produce new words**', which means that in normative space new facts produce new mutual rights and obligations. Human beings do things without words, the things do words, the words do new things, new things do the new words, the new words do new things etc. Similarly the entity of new facts and new mutual rights and obligations creates new normative space, which causes necessity to establish new positive law, etc.

Permanent and cyclical interaction between things and words and permanent and cyclical inter-transition of things and words at global, regional, national and local levels as a trend to comprehend a sense of existence of Humankind based on the Universal Human Rights. The aim and goal of such interaction and inter-transition is to achieve sustainable development of Humankind.

The positive law and normative order in civilized countries are not strictly mutually contradictory; they exist in parallel regimes, because they are entirely different levels of life of the nation state and civil society as a whole. Functional asymmetry between them is a normal process and that process indicates the perspective of evolutionary development of society as a whole. Particularly, positive law is the unempirical space of the life of civil society, while normative order is the empirical space of the life of the civil society. Exposition of contradiction between positive law and normative order is possible only **theoretically** in the process of investigation of their dynamics, using comparative and other methods.

As a whole, normative order is 1) the established and stable order or practice of realization of abstract legal acts by public bodies that particularly and specifically regulate real interpersonal relations through the official distribution of mutual rights and obligations among the individual participants of normative relations, and 2) the established and stable order or practice of realization of free individual will of private persons that particularly and specifically regulate real interpersonal relations through the unofficial distribution and realization of mutual rights and obligation among the individual participants of private normative relations, and in the case of their violations they have been guaranteed by the application of legal force by the appropriate judiciary. Moreover, individual public normative acts and individual private normative acts coexist and interact in complex ways. Sometimes they also compete or conflict, sometimes they sustain or reinforce each other and often they influence each other through interaction, imposition and transplantation. Frequently such influence is reciprocal.

In legal space, the state of positive law does not directly influence the state of legal order i.e. on the state of established legal practice of public bodies. Analyzing human rights records of authoritative and competent organizations such as UN agencies, Amnesty international, Human Rights Watch, Charles Humana, Freedom House, Transparency International and numerous of other bodies concerned with observation of universal human rights law by different nation states and regimes, directly underlines the distinction (sometimes huge distinction) between 'Law in the Books' and 'Law in Action', i.e. between Single Positive Law and Plural Normative Order.

The necessity of eradication of contradiction between positive law and normative order arises when 'anti-entropic' (self-regulatory and/or self-governing) autonomous mechanisms exhaust their means and resources, and the level of disorder in normative order reaches a critical stage. The necessity of eradication of contradiction between individual acts of public bodies and individual acts of private persons inside the normative order arises when 'anti-entropic' (self-regulatory and/or self-governing) autonomous mechanisms exhaust their means and resources, and level of disorder in normative order reaches a critical stage.

When entropy in any space of normative order reaches the stage at which the legal system is threatened, an idea of legal reconstruction of appropriate space of positive law appears. More clearly, when the process reaches an evident theoretical contradiction between positive law (ought to be) and normative order (to be), and between individual acts of public bodies and individual acts of private persons inside normative orders, which indicates that positive law inadequately and unjustly regulates relations between natural and/or legal persons, any legislator must begin the process of thoughtful investigation of normative order for the elaboration of new positive law, which adequately and justly resolves such contradiction between positive law (ought to be) and normative order (to be) generally, and between individual acts of public bodies and individual acts of private persons inside legal orders particularly. In other words, the aim and goal of such investigation is to discover the normative disorders inside normative orders, and then elaboration of new positive laws for eradication of normative disorders. Achievement of such an aim and goal is the main function of any legislator on the local, internal, regional or global levels.

The purpose of investigation of normative order i.e. investigation of individual acts of public bodies (public normative order) and individual acts of private persons (private normative order) are to decrease entropy through the improvement of appropriate fields of positive law. First of all, it means generalization of normative practice of normative acts of public bodies in the process of distribution of mutual rights and obligation among participants of normative relations and generalization of normative practice of private persons in the process of distribution of mutual rights and obligation by them, which first of all is the obligation not of sociologists but professional jurists with the sociological bias.

After that, adequate and just resolution of contradiction between positive law (ought to be) and normative order (to be) normative system of the country as a whole, and between individual normative acts of public bodies and individual acts of private persons inside the normative order through the creation of new positive law, using P. Ricoeur's general model, generally consists of three stages: pre-figuration (anticipation), con-figuration (formalization) and re-figuration (reorganization).[20] Particularly, the process of thoughtful investigation of normative order for the elaboration of new positive law should be based on the normative pyramid of reasoning. In the normative pyramid of reasoning the core meaning variants concentrate in the centre and move from the bottom up to the top, while all the marginal ones after checking and filtering remain on the lower levels or strata of the model to form background knowledge to influence the cognitive normative concepts. Every previous phase is a preparatory stage to proceed on to the follow-up phase until finally the investigator hierarchically achieves the top phase to elicit the conceptual information. The process of making predictions includes a certain adaptation. The degree of adaptation depends on the amount of frustrated expectations or justified predictabilities. So that in the case of regular goal-oriented movement of the above mentioned methods and adaptation, the investigator may benefit, elucidating the maximum information at expense of minimum time and effort.

Simultaneous with the movement upward to the top of the cognitive-normative pyramid, there is top-down sensor checking process as well, which sets up loose associations condensed in our concept. It offers the knowledge and experience of all the previous phases. Alternatively this self-regulated system shows how to achieve the non-finalized decisions made in every phase. Any element that occurs in this system has its own normative structure. Giving attention to the most important one, the investigator reluctantly receives information about other parameters, i.e. we observe a constantly changing process of analysis and synthesis.

To the end, the cognitive normative concepts assist us to cognize the world, both visible and/or invisible, organizing the surrounding chaos of normative disorder into the 'order of orders' (see below). The process of permanent taking of the contradiction between individual normative acts of public bodies and/or individual normative acts of private persons inside legal orders, and the process of taking the contradiction between positive law and/or normative order in the frameworks of their permanent inter-transition, creates a spiral, sustainable and evolutionary tendency through which any legislator comprehends a sense of law.[21] In philosophical terms: mutual transition, spiral and evolutionary development of positive law and

[20] Paul Ricœur, *Temps et recit* 59 (1983).

[21] Bizina Savaneli, *General Theory of Law. Manual* 201-205 (1993).

normative order based on the 'principle of causality through freedom', but not the 'principle of causality of the nature'.

The aim and goal of such mutual transition, spiral and evolutionary development of positive law and normative order is to achieve the sustainable development of humankind.

Therefore, normative order is the system of normative orders ('order of orders' using Rustaveli's term – see below). Normative orders interact with each other in the frameworks of normative order. Normative order and normative orders interact wholly and partially, but not generally and singly.

More precisely, the normative order of each country is a gamma of normative orders of individuals and/or groups bound by mutual rights and obligations. Developing A. Reinach's and G. Naneishvili's theories, I underline that the bearers of mutual rights and obligations are related to each other psychologically or mentally, but mutual rights and obligations are themselves related - **logically**. Mutual rights and obligations of individuals and groups are neither psychological nor mental entities. Mutual rights and obligations are exclusively normative entities like norms of positive law. Moreover they are always prior to the positive law.[22]

Different levels of normative order are not neatly arranged in hierarchies; they are neither impervious, nor static. They interact in complex ways. Moreover, to understand the normative order, the study of norms is almost never enough. One also has to take account of values, facts, meanings, processes, structures, power relations, personnel, and technologies.

On the other hand the only way to make sense of the overlapping normative orders in the modern world is to take refuge in picturing all states' legal systems, international order, and other orders in a single monist or pluralist system. Monism and Pluralism are the entire process, which establishes a new synthetic system of law building globally. Assertion that the European model has spread all over the world is an illusion.

Single positive law (Sollen) and normative order (Sein) are different spaces of the life of Humankind.

Single positive law is a summary of impersonal rules, which generally regulates potential economic, social, cultural, civil and political relations in the country through distribution of mutual rights and obligations among the possible participants of these relations.

---

[22] George Naneishvili, *Positive Law...* 58 (1930)

At the international level we have a single positive law – international (public and private) law and plural normative order which includes public normative acts of sovereign states and their united bodies (official normative order), and private normative acts of sovereign persons and their unions (non-official normative order).

At the regional level we have a single positive law, for example, EU (public and private) law and plural normative order which includes public normative acts of EU and their united bodies (official normative order), and private normative acts of sovereign persons and their unions in EU space (non-official normative order).

At all levels, international, regional and internal, the normative order censors how positive law favours the observation of human rights and freedoms by public bodies and how it favours the development of human rights and freedoms of private persons.

Using the great J. Bentham's term **'Censorial Jurisprudence'** concerning my theory I ascribe to this term the following sense:

'Censorial Jurisprudence' should explore the positive law regarding its conformity to the jus cogens principles of law and international law.

'Censorial Jurisprudence' should explore the normative order examining its conformity to the positive law.

'Censorial Jurisprudence' should explore any contradiction between positive law and normative order relating to their conformity to social justice based on the principles enshrined in the International Bill of Human Rights.

III. Comparative analyses of Positive Laws of different countries traditionally have been carefully made by scientists, but comparative investigation of Normative Orders of different countries have not been made.

The 'legal families' theory or Comparative Law ignores the phenomenon of normative order. Almost all scientists operating in comparative law and legal theory ignore any role of practice of individual normative acts of public bodies and private persons in the formation of normative order. However, the state and a certain combination of practice of individual normative acts of public bodies and private persons construct the individual external traits of normative order of the country, which is always different to that of other countries, disregarding that both could be even entered in the same legal family. So it is necessary to introduce a new branch of legal science: **Comparative Normative Orders Study**, which should not be distinct from the framework of Comparative Law Study.

If we compare Positive Laws of different countries inside and/or outside the contemporary legal systems, we will find much more commonality than difference. Principles of Roman Law permeate the global legal system. 'Law in books' has a cosmopolitan character. Differences between Anglo-Saxon and French legal systems are largely superficial and not substantial. For example, the distinction between written and unwritten law is principally superficial, because each is composed of Norms. 'Written law' however is technically precise.

To counterbalance the above mentioned, if we compare legal orders of different countries inside and/or outside of the globalizing ***ius commune*** we shall find many more differences then commonalities. The 'comparative legal families' theory ignores phenomena of normative order as well as different normative orders of and in countries, separating jurisprudence from reality. In this respect, it is necessary to restore in transformative form a particular jurisprudence, which will explore the normative order of each country and then compare the normative orders of different countries.

Our construction is based on the following strong foundation.

Positive law, as the system of sustainable general norms of each country, includes sustainable Public Law and Private Law. Accordingly, Comparative Law, as the part of legal science, compares sustainable Public Laws and Private Laws of different countries.

Normative Order, as the system of sustainable individual norms of each country, includes sustainable practice of execution of Public Law and Private Law by public bodies and sustainable practice of distribution of mutual rights and obligation by individual natural and legal persons. Accordingly, Comparative Normative Order, as the part of legal science, compares sustainable practice of execution of Public Laws and Private Laws by public bodies of different countries and sustainable practice of distribution of mutual rights and obligation by individual natural and legal persons of different countries.

Thereto it is methodologically helpful to introduce a new branch of the legal science – '**comparative normative order**'. Such a point of view is necessary for the strengthening of the European house and the distribution of Democracy in Post-Soviet and developing countries. Our early position (1978) has been strengthened independently by W. Twining in his fundamental scientific work, in which he correctly underlines: 'I have suggested that normative ordering reflects all levels of human relations (including legal persons, groups etc)... It has the advantage of drawing attention to various levels of non-state ordering and emphasizing the point that these different levels are not arranged in a single vertical hierarchy'.[23]

[23] William Twinning, *Globalization*... 223-224, 253 (2000).

Accordingly, the duty of scientific research is not only to comment on and analyze laws but also to describe and analyze the normative order in its several forms. The plurality of the normative orders includes the normative order of countries, regions, cities, villages etc, as well as of different macro and micro groups in these spaces.

Through investigation of normative order on any level, the legislative powers receive information about the justice and/or injustice of appropriate segments of the positive law. Such information must be scrupulously presented and then 'translated' into the language of positive law.

I believe that the above-mentioned differences should serve as a starting point for the continuing dialogue among different cultures of West and East (for example, between Christians and Muslims). The constant coexistence of constant positive law and inconstant normative orders is a historical fact. Historically, positive law and normative order never coincided - fortunately, because such differences are a precondition of progress and prosperity. But, for sustainable development, it is necessary to create permanent checks and balances between them. If positive law supersedes the normative order, dictatorship results in the national system. If the normative order supersedes positive law, the result is anarchy in the international system. Positive law, as a monistic phenomenon, consolidates. Yet normative order, as a pluralistic phenomenon, disperses humankind. This is a good balance, such as the balance between public law and private law. The goal is to strengthen positive law and to bring normative orders of different cultures closer together, into greater harmony. Looking for isolated differences from the whole is a dangerous mistake. A function of the legislator and of the administration of justice is to create permanent checks and balances between them on both levels.

The interaction between positive law and normative orders today needs an adequate conceptual framework and meta-language that can transcend national legal culture. Such a function could be undertaken by **Universal Human Rights** as a coordinator of peaceful and cyclical inter-transitions of positive law and normative order.

Once one has recognized both the natural and positive character of human rights (1993) and rejected the theory that bases the whole international law on the agreement of the will of states (1997), one finds no special reason to deny that human rights have the character of ***ius cogens***. The universal recognition of human rights signifies that no state may freely dispose of the rights of its own nationals, and that other states are equally responsible for the protection of the rights of those who are not their own nationals. So far as the respect and protection of human rights are concerned, a World Law dealing with human rights and having a universal character limits the sovereignty of each Member State of the United Nations.

H. Kelsen found that 'freedoms are Human Rights'.[24] Professor van Boven emphasizes the 'supra-positive' character of Fundamental Human Rights, and urges they are based on Natural Law.[25] The Positive Human Rights Law is based on the Natural Human Rights Law, from which it originated. Moreover, the legal relationship between the individuals and the state is based on the natural law principle – ***pacta sunt servanda***, which originated from the latent Social Contract (or quasi contract) between society as a whole and representatives of that society, who are employed for the fulfillment of legislative, executive and judicial functions as guarantors of sustainable development.

On the other hand, ***pacta sunt servanda*** has received the positive character of law as a result of constitutional recognition and notification of Human Rights by the States, which means that the legislative, executive and judicial bodies take responsibility in the effective implementation of that social contract.

The end the process has gone to the recognition of the ***ius cogens*** character of Universal Human Rights Law. The concept of *ius cogens* according to Rozakis was 'conceived as a minimum legal standard of world order, which may give an air of social consideration to the otherwise unstable and extremely individualistic family of nations'.[26] The evolution historically may have been from a deity, but is now seen as a product of human actions.

Therefore, *ius cogens* restricted the scope of treaties. States are bound by these *ius cogens* limitations when entering Human Rights treaties regardless of present or past views of the state. While states must voluntarily assume treaty obligations, these obligations are regulated by the rules of Universal Human Rights Law independently of the present views of international states.

Universal Human Rights Law as a junction of Natural Law and Positive Law rose above them and expressed the Universality of Human Being. The Bill of Human Rights is a normative confirmation of such Universality, leaving no state-party, particularly legislative, executive or judicial bodies without choice, but only with the absolute and unilaterally binding obligation (derogation is an exception but not a rule). This leads

---

[24] Hans Kelsen, *The Law of the United Nations* 29 (1966).

[25] Theodoor Van Boven, *Distinguishing Criteria of Human Rights*, The International Dimensions of Human Rights 44 (1982).

[26] Christos Rozakis, *The Concept of Jus Cogens in the Law of Treaties* 11 (1976).

me to the hierarchy of World Law headed by Universal Human Rights Law as a ***Grundnorm***, which is the peak of the Pyramid of World Law.

Moreover, the Public International Law can no more also answer problems which face Humanity today: globalization and pluralisation of conflicts. The main theme that links the emergence of this new kind of World legal order is **disengagement of Law and State**. I aspire to make law and jurisprudence more relevant to contemporary politico-economic realities. Unlike Natural Law or Positivism, I do not rely upon theological or other abstract sources such as an 'ultimate rule' for its validity. Instead, it criticizes Positivism's 'disastrous neglect of how rules are made, as well as other important aspects of the comprehensive process of authoritative decision'. Likewise, it finds Natural Law theories deficient in failing to relate decisions to events in the social process to which they are a response and, in turn an effect.

The benefit of the methodology of Anthropology of Law, which is based on the idea of personal experience and indisputably, leads us from a dialectical method of understanding reality to a dialogical one. But what is the purpose of the dialectical method of understanding reality, if not the construction of any law for the subsequent 'social reproduction and conflict management?' Construction of law is the further stage after understanding 'Reality', after which the cycle will be repeated again, and so the imperfect process proceeds.

Why, in the capacity of the grand theory of law, which 'puts normative forms and puts into normative forms the reproduction of humanity', could the Pure Theory of Law not be used, which is a very normative, perfect and paramount form for building the hierarchy of Human Rights Law? From that point of view, Human Rights Law removes any principle distinctions between state - and non-state law, between state - and international law. Only Human Rights Law could be Universal. Is this not so? Using recognized words: only Universal Human Rights Law 'underlying social reproduction and conflict management though legal normativity'.

But I would like to go farther. The second level of the process of interculturality must be exchange of information on legal experience among people which removes some negative outcomes of pluralism, as well as globalism, and lead us to crystallization of new principles of Law through dialogue. If we stop at the stage of description of diversity and/or common legal values, we cannot reach the substance of Law.

Allow me begin from the last problem. Obviously cultural diversity has an influence on the legal systems and life style appropriate to countries, but 'Human Rights as the Common Language of Humanity' is able to resolve global problems of Humanity through improvement of Human Rights machinery on the international level initially, like the European Human Rights Protection system. The Human Community paradigm is not simply a natural concept but intends to provide a theoretical framework permitting the rethinking of Human Rights in plurality though a united and praxis oriented method on the global level.

What is at the core of the debate is rethinking a 'Human Rights Community' enabling a 'Rule of Human Rights Law' on the local and global levels. For the possibility of such a Rule of Human Rights Law it is not enough to build on the different cultural theories of Human Rights to permit the emergence of a 'universal' one. If we want a working 'Human Rights Community' we must also build on the practices, and not only on the representations of those who are concerned (and who are not only the national states). 'Therefore Human Rights Law is Universal, because Human Rights are an indivisible and inherent virtue of Human Beings to which Human beings refer normatively (logically). That is the non-ethnocentric approach to Human Rights Law. Contrary to Human Rights, which always is universal for all, disregarding race etc., Law practically is linked to statehood and other public institutions on the international, national and/or local levels. Only the Human Being is a natural entity, all others in society are man-made creations, including laws, but not Human Rights Law, because Human Rights Law is identical to the Human Being. Only one Reality is a Human Being and other creatures of God'.[27]

Universal Human Rights Law is not linked by its nature to the existence of a state, nor to the formulation of rules, and nor to the recognition of its rationality. What makes human rights the foundation of the new state is their status as law, more correctly - as positive law. The expansion of positive human rights law as supranational World-Citizens' Law today constitutes the essential preconditions for generality and reciprocity of granting fundamental rights to citizens. I speak of the new State decentralized by the Fundamental Human Rights, or - to be more prudent – creation of the new state, named by us as the **Human Rights State**.

Europe seems to offer a hybridized version of the state in the **human rights** context. In the case of *Refah Partisi v. Turkey*, the Grand Chamber of the European Court of Human Rights acknowledged democracy as the

---

[27] Bizina Savaneli, *Jus Cogens Character of International Human Rights Law* in David Agmashenebeli (ed.), *Philosophy and Legal Theory for 21st Century* 13-14 (2003). (This work is dedicated to the Memory of the Giant of Law and International Law – Hans Kelsen). See also Bizina Savaneli, *Law, Religion, Ecology* in id., *Theory of Law...* 307 (1993).

relevant constituent element of statehood. The case involved a human rights challenge to the decision of the Turkish Constitutional Court to have the Refah political party dissolved on the basis that it was a 'centre' of activities contrary to the principles of secularism. The Refah party, among other things, supported a system based on sharia law. The Grand Chamber reiterated its view that democracy is a fundamental feature of the 'European public order'. It considered that that 'there could be no democracy without pluralism' and viewed the state's role as the 'neutral and impartial organizer of the exercise of various religions, faiths, and beliefs.' Most clearly, the Court said that the freedoms guaranteed in the convention 'cannot deprive the authorities of a State in which an association, through its activities, jeopardizes that State's institutions, of the right to protect those institutions'. Human rights protection then, is subject to the state's ability to survive as a democratic institution.[28]

Universal Human Rights Law has a non-ethnocentric character, while positive law and normative order basically have an ethnocentric character. Universal Human Rights Law is a new and the highest level of rule of law. Universal Human Rights Law as *Grundnorm* closes a World Law system at the top. Using Kelsen's term about international legal constitution, I consider Universal Human Rights Law as the **World Legal Constitution**.

IV. My theory of normative order is based on the justice of equality in general human rights and inequality in individual private rights. My opinion is as follows: 'Justice based on two pillars: the fundamental human rights and legal capacity of each person. Fundamental human rights concerning justice mean that **all persons have equal fundamental human rights**. Individual legal capacity concerning justice means that **all persons have equal right to possess unequal private rights**. Fundamental human rights and legal capacity in their entity characterize each person as a subject of law, which defines their general position in society. More broadly legal capacity is a summary expression of those different private (social and economic) rights, which each person could possess concerning his/her different interests. In other words legal capacity is an abstract opportunity to possess individual human rights. Legal capacity includes its own equal right to possess unequal private (social and economic) rights, because human beings are different in individual signs such as: physical and mental strength, manual labour, clearness of purpose, resourcefulness, enterprise and other individual

[28] *Case of Refah Partisi (The Welfare Party) and Others v. Turkey*, European Court of Human Rights Grand Chamber, hearing June 19th, 2002; Application numbers 41340/98, 41342/98, and 41344/98.

characteristics concerning which the law has no ability to equalize across the individuals. The law can provide only one: recognition for all of the equal chance to satisfy different social, economic, cultural and political interests, in other words equal capacity to possess unequal private rights. As a result all natural and legal persons are distinguished by the particular positions in society, by the different extents of private rights to different social and economic benefits. And that is justifiable. In other words inequality in private (social and economic) rights is a condition of justice. Fundamental Human rights is an objective category, but legal capacity is subjective one. Legal capacity is a 'right to rights'.

For example, related to the ICESC the State parties recognize that every capable individual has the right to work, which includes the right to the opportunity to gain his/her living by work, which he/she freely chooses or accepts. Such a right is an equal public right that is a fundamental right. The State parties to the ICESC also recognize the right of everyone to the enjoyment of just and favourable conditions of work, which includes the right to ensure fair wages and equal remuneration for work of equal value. Such a right is a public/private right that is a legal capacity, because the realization of the right to the enjoyment of just and favourable conditions of work is equally possessed by workers (public right), but the results of realization of the right to ensure fair wages and equal remuneration for work of equal value would always be unequal, because results depend on individual capacities (private right). Insofar as the individual states (statuses) of private persons in society are different so far as these states (statuses) are the parts of private normative order, but not positive law'.[29]

It is generally known that Rawls analyzed justice in the frameworks of diversity of social, political and economic life of the society. But scientific investigation of social, political and economic aspects of justice is the object not of legal, but of social, political and economical sciences. If we operate by the normative correlation between human rights of the individual and obligation of states concerning justice, Rawls considers justice as a basis to provide cooperation in conditions where there are opposing religious, philosophical and moral convictions and this basis is to be found in the idea of overlapping consensus.

If we correctly compare Rawlsian and my own theories, we discover that Rawlsian theory is not strictly connected with the legal theory of justice, but is linked with the political, economic and social theory of justice, which defines moral obligations of political, economic and social

---

[29] Bizina Savaneli (Pkhaladze), *Correlation between Universal...* 11-12 (1969); See also Id., *Legal Personality and Legal Capacity,* Soviet Law 31 (1965).

institutions before the principles of justice. Contrary to J. Rawls, I am sure that the justice of human rights is nothing other than ideology because the criteria of justice have multiple aspects, which depend on the different political, social, economic and cultural positions of very different groups of society. Special danger issues from the official authorities because historically they have, under the flag of justice, excused any inhuman acts. Any theory of justice, including those highly localized ones within families, societies, regional groupings, transnational associations and so on, has to be set in a much broader context, which prescribes background rules for more localized spheres of justice. Such a broader context is the future Code of Universal Human Rights. Civilized humanity created the legislative, executive and judiciary powers and separated them not for the state but for Human Beings. Consequently, for the future of humanity I suggest a possible structure of World Positive Law. World Positive Law should be constructed in layers (using Kelsen-Merkl's term - '**Stufentheorie**'). At the top of the structure has been placed the Code of Universally Recognized Human Rights, followed by the not-contradictory regional positive law, then not-contradictory constitution of each country etc. down to the local level. On the global, regional, national and local levels, regional, national and local human rights codes and the related human rights courts should be created.

Therefore, **I suggest a spirally, evolutionary and endlessly sustainable developing theory of interaction and mutual-transition of Positive Law and Normative Order at global, regional, national and local levels**. Permanent and spiral interaction between positive law and normative order on the local, national, regional and global levels presents a trend to comprehend permanently an idea of **Just Law**, which must be based on Universal Human Rights.

It is a deep mistake to consider positive law as a decisive factor of conflict prevention and resolution, because unjust law of legislative power could be a factor of conflicts. The important factor of conflict prevention and resolution is: '**To make just law, which makes a dry tree green**', as Shota Rustaveli - the famous Georgian philosopher and poet of the 12th Century and one of the founders of Neo-Platonism - proclaimed. In other words, clearly, 'To make just law, makes a stagnant society evolutionary'. On the contrary, 'To make unjust law, makes a green tree dry'. In other words, 'To make unjust law, makes an evolutionary society stagnant.'

Moreover, although legislative power can make just law, executive power can 'make' unjust acts and much more, judicial power can 'make' more unjust acts in both situations from the point of Universally Recognized Human Rights Law.

Accordingly, judicial power, particularly the Constitutional Court, can 'make' just acts in the direction of correction of unjust laws of legislative power, but legislative power can continue to make unjust law from the point of view of Universally Recognized Human Rights Law.

Therefore, the decisive factor of conflict prevention and resolution is the Universal Human Rights Law and creation of the World Court of Human Rights and Freedoms.

So, a final conclusion in this direction is the following: **the criterion of Just Positive Law and Normative Order is the Universal Human Rights Law**. The Universal Human Rights Law is the ultimate unit of justice.

More than 50 years before Rustaveli, the Georgian King David the Builder (11-12th century) in the seminal work 'Canon of Repentance' in the form of lyrical poetry described a just court's decision-making process.

When on doomsday the Code is opened
And I shall stand to be condemned,
When the ire of the angels shall be roused,
O judge, pass the sentence as just as the Lord.
After the blessed rejoice,
The sinners are cast into the flames,
After which will began the triumph of justice,
Then have mercy upon me, o Jesus.'

The aim and goal of interaction between positive law and normative order is to achieve a sustainable normative order of Humanity. The moral foundation of Global Order expressed Shota Rustaveli in the following couplet:

'Since deception is the source of all humankind's misfortunes,
Why I should betray the congenial soul dearer to me than brothers?
Not at all! What avails me knowledge of philosophizing of philosophers?
That's why we are taught to be able to join the supernal order of orders.'

L. Jokhadze proposed the following interpretation of Shota Rustaveli's epigrammatic concept's - **join the supernal order of orders** - meaning: '(1) mystical joining the Lord posthumously; (2) the road to super cognition; (3) personification of super nature which prophesies human's Godly nature; (4) to share super principles of order; (5) to join in living liturgy partaking God's Eucharist; (6) to join the cosmic order through organized behaviour and righteous way of earthly life'.[30]

I think that if we are not taught to be able to join the supernal order of orders, we shall have disorder in the sense of '**paranoid society**', which is described by the great **Thomas Pynchon** in his novel 'Gravity of Rainbow'. 'If we consult English concise dictionaries we read that **paranoia** is defined as 'mental disorder characterized by systematized delusions as of grandeur or persecution'. As 'social language' it characterizes society with all the attendant vices: 1. any abnormal mental state; 2. mental case; 3. satanic evil power of distraction and degradation; 4. aimless and false propaganda to 'improve' the situation; 5. the atmosphere of fraud and deception created by officials in the state establishments; 6. injustice, corruption and immorality disguised under the mask of kindness and nobleness; 7. devalued virtues of degraded society; 8. an exclamation of surprise or wonder etc. and a euphemism for God, like Gosh or nonsense that has a kernel of truth; 9. any wrath poured out due to fair or just claim'.[31]

Prevailing notions of public international law do not appear ill suited to finding adequate solutions for the myriad problems that are transnational in scope. Among these are global warming, ozone depletion, over-fishing, deforestation, marine pollution, corruption, and terrorism, narcotics and contraband armaments traffic, illegal trade in endangered species of flora and fauna, and unregulated financial transfers. These problems exceed the capacities of any individual state or even any block of states to control effectively. To respond to such historically unprecedented events comprehensively as is necessary to reconcile two contradictory theories: Pure Theory of Law and Sociology of Law. We suggest a new theory named by me as '**Anthropological Normativizm**' and attempt to argue the idea of the **ius cogens character of the Bill of Human Rights**. The Bill of Human Rights removes any distinction between Pure Theory of Law and Sociology of Law. In this respect transformation of International Law into Universal Human Rights Law is a decisive challenge of our time, especially after the events of September the 11th. Politics has polluted the Positive Law and Normative Order. Thus it is necessary to purify them. My device in 2001 was the following: 'Save the Planet after September the 11th through ideological war against several forms of racism based on

---

[30] Lali Jokhadze, *Intercultural Communication and Didactics of Foreign Word Concepts* in Aktuel Pädagogik und Kulturdidaktik 14 (2000); Id., *Literary Text as a Stylistic-Conceptual System* 219 (2008).

[31] Id., *Social Entropy for Thomas Pynchon's Literary Criticism* in Journal for Phenomenological Inquiry 17 (2010).

religion. Terrorism is not a cause, but outcome of such racism. Accordingly we must fight not only against terrorism, but also and basically fight against the cause of it. **The cause of terrorism is the tendency toward the formation of Global Government.**

Paradoxical statistics approving this process are given by the well-known researcher Q. Wright: the number of armed conflicts on the European continent in the 15th century was 9, in the 16th century - 87, in the 17th century - 239, in the 18th century - 651, in the 19th century - 781, in the 20th century - 892.[32] Such alarming statistics are corroborated by another scientist and are considered to be indubitable. So, the higher the level of civilization the greater the number of conflicts and vice versa. It is strange and very perplexing relationship. After September the 11th Humanity has entered into a new, initially more dangerous, transition era, in the seventh dimension. Religious separatism is today's tragic reality and the real 'chance' of perdition of humanity.

The only escape from such a dangerous situation is the following. A Hierarchy of norms in the World Legal System has to issue from Universal Human Rights as the peak of the pyramid (***Grundnorm***) of World law and order. Excessive passion for 'Universalization' (excepting Human Rights) is as dangerous as excessive passion with endless fragmentation (except the ***rule of law state***). The method must be based on the investigation of the correlation between 'a pluralist approach to positive law' (legal families) and 'a pluralist approach to normative orders' (inside legal families). We base our study on the well established normative methods of synthesis and analysis and present this process in a pyramidal chart, where normative variants are step by step concentrated on multi-hierarchical levels. Each stage should be a theoretical rethinking of the above mentioned 'approaches' and the elaboration of recommendations towards their rapprochement. In other words, these variants interact and strive to make a more complete decision in every phase to gain access to the top of the pyramid, which is the effective stratum to form a final normative concept – a new sense of law. Therefore the pluralist approach also means a scientific and legislative investigation of the diversity of normative orders, but that is only the start. The task of such an investigation is to discover common and distinctive elements in positive law and the normative order, and then the elaboration of 'consensus laws' and means of rapprochement through 'an intercultural approach to law and

[32] Quincy Wright, A Study of the War with a Commentary of War since 1942 221 (2nd ed., 1965);

order' based on universal human rights. **Universal Human Rights should be the sense and spirit of any Positive Law and Normative Order.**

In such a sense the Universal Human Rights Law should be the apex of the Pyramid of the Positive World Law, which is based on Natural Human Rights, and which obliges the member-states, particularly in the light of the necessity of reconstruction of the UN's functions in peacekeeping operations in transition periods for the World. In that sense it is necessary to abolish the Security Council of the UN, because three permanent members of the Council are permanent aggressors in the world. In the modern 'globalistics' it is ascertained that today the world is in such a complicated situation that we do not have the possibility of using one system or other of values, ideology or culture as a model in order to preserve its existence.

In my opinion the Universal Human Rights Law as the result of the convergence of Natural and Pure theories of Law shall have a large and dominant part in the development of whole branches of modern law, as for example in the efforts of legislatures and courts to restrict unfair methods of competition and unfair restraints of trade. In short we are talking about morality substitution by Universal Human Rights.

Another real problem is that the greatest immorality first and foremost is the fact that the human being is the only creature that produces rubbish. Yet everyone is entitled to a sustainable environment, in which the Rights and Freedoms set forth in the Bill of Universal Human Rights could be fully realized. The religious dogma of mankind's ascendancy over nature was instilled into the human mode of life as the directing norm of their activity and it has directed humanity to ecological catastrophe.

The human being is ambivalent. On the one hand, he feels the evident advantage in comparison of all beings or events known by him; on the other hand, during the process of becoming acquainted with surrounding nature, he becomes sure that he is infinite and in-cognizable, and the deeper he encroaches upon the essence of events (phenomena) of the universe the more he is seized with the feeling of vanity. Besides these, the unlimited free will in the 20th century has led humanity to the brink of planetary catastrophe twice. At the beginning of this century the global ecological crisis became still more dangerous, and this crisis grows deeper and deeper progressively. Free will has transformed into global self-will!

One of the universally recognized means of rendering the above-mentioned dangerous situation harmless is the peremptory subordination of Governments to the human rights and freedoms of mankind recognized everywhere. This implies the global 'ecologization' of the thought and mode of life of humanity. Beyond orthodox politics there are many hopeful symptoms of break-through in this direction, but really there are only grounds to make an insecure prognosis. One of the reasons for the unprecedented Tsunami (2004, 2011) and floods (2010-2011) is uncontrolled and global output of oil and other non-renewable natural resources.

Energetically our planetary ecosystem is an open and dynamic system. There is a rather delicate balance between incoming solar energy, internal energy from radioactive decay, and radiated 'blackbody' energy. There exists a balance because ecosystem processes are organized cyclically and the non-entropic processes in them are indissoluble with energy degradation. At the same time, the system is not static, it is dynamic in a spiralled sense, as long as the forces creating the equilibrium are entrained themselves into the stream of changes. Thus the natural search for equilibrium is accompanied by deviations from it because of the participation of oppositional forces in the transactions. The infinite natural combination of forces leading to equilibrium and as such deflecting from it is the very moving force of the evolution process. Renewable energy is regarded more and more as a profitable and rational investment in the light of dramatic and continuing reductions in capital costs, reliability improvements, the volatility of fossil fuel prices, and the environmental compliance costs of generating electricity from fossil and nuclear fuel sources.

If we sincerely wish to solve the global environmental crisis, we must make a revolutionary break and establish new, Earth-friendly legal and social institutions oriented on Daylight-power generation. Actually it means a global substitution of very expensive and dangerous exploitation of the Earth's non-renewable resources by using, at the beginning, inexpensive and safety Day-light, including Solar and Wind energy, as a stable guarantee of the sustainable development of humankind. **The above mentioned should be an evolutionary and endlessly spiral process of civilization.** This will certainly necessitate a fundamental change in philosophy, beliefs, norms, values and lifestyle for many people, based on the doctrine of **Saint Francisco d'Assisi**, finding common propositions in fundamental religious systems and acting in concert towards the creation of new and united **Environmental Religion,** because **God is one and unique for all Nations**!

I am sure that one of the practical means of extrication from the above-mentioned dangerous situations is the 'aphroditization' of men's minds, or the 'hermaphroditization' of the whole of society. In the works of Aristotle, Aquanaut, Rustaveli and Dante the consideration is developed that the harmonious consensus of manhood and womanhood is the necessary condition for making the picture of reality without distortion, which creates the grounds for the adequate behaviour of the human being and excludes social catastrophes. In the works of famous scholars of the 20th century, especially in the fundamental investigations of K. Stern, it is argued with sufficient depth that in the thought of Dante, Shakespeare and Goethe, and also of several well-known current prominent persons, we may find the ideal harmony of the two trends. Woman is not the surrogate of man, but the global patriarchal manner of thinking and mode of life allege the opposite. However the history of Civilization numbers only about some millennia, while the history of Humanity is significantly longer. During the history of humanity were established the stereotypes of man as a hunter, i.e. killer, and of woman as a family person, i.e. thoughtful.

Another way is the method of establishing prudence and moderation in public and private life. The theory of 'Comparative normative Orders' is an important one in order to plot an alternative course to the present approaches to the 'Contemporary Comparative Law' and 'Rule of Law', which seem less and less satisfying. My scientific position warns us never to adopt any absolute theory of law. It gives us the universal key to open the wide door in the real world, which could be equally acceptable for different cultures. It is not a new intercultural theory of law. It is a new human philosophy based on the **Universality of Human Rights and Freedoms.**

Conclusions

The fact is that almost all post-modern scientists in legal theory are entirely alienated from the substance of law and legal rights and obligations, and have flitted to philosophy, anthropology, hermeneutics, sociology, ethnology, economics, and more over in geography etc. They attempt to analyze the juridical notions and categories through the above mentioned spheres of science, while none are specialized in the appropriate fields, and they have attained width but not depth. They disembowel law from law. In jurisprudence a smell of dampness has risen, without the perspective of light at the end of the dark subway. As a result, societies have really remained without law and people without human rights. Societies and people remained in 'stark nakedness'. On the planet is a raging tornado of amorphous and inadequate rules of politics without any borders of rule of law. Globalization of such politics worldwide has turned the human being into a slave with invisible fetters.

Therefore we, the people of the world, need a **New Human Philosophy of Law under the auspice of Universal Human Rights**, which links the East and West, North and South, ethics and religions, public and private life, technologies and environmental protection, and the myriad problems which have never previously existed in the history of mankind in the broad aspect.

Based on **Human Rights Law** values, the paper tries to show the methodological perspectives that can stimulate us to establish the universal elements in different cultures and the ways of harmonizing them for the purpose of recovering human freedom and human creativity as the basis of sustainable development of humanity and building of egalitarian peace on the Planet.

I. The positive law exposes how subjects of law **ought to act**. Positive law is an entity of 'ideal' legal rules, which regulate civil, political, economic, social and cultural relations among persons ***in abstracto*** through the recognition, separation and/or protection of mutual rights and obligations by the application of judicial force in the case of their violation. Public Law and Private Law are the two branches of Positive law. Public Law regulates public relations between public persons. Private Law regulates private relations between private persons. Public Law and Private Law have fields of conjunction. Positive law includes a cross-sectional field, which reflects a result of some congruence of public law and private law. Positive law has a vertical hierarchy. Legal theory refers to phenomena of positive law. In short, Positive Law is '**law in the books**'.

The Normative Order is 1) the established and stable order or practice of realization of abstract legal acts by public bodies that particularly and specifically regulate real interpersonal relations through the official distribution of mutual rights and obligations among the individual participants of normative relations; and 2) the established and stable order or practice of realization of individual free wills of private persons that particularly and specifically regulate real interpersonal relations through the unofficial distribution and realization of mutual rights and obligation among the individual participants of normative relations, and in the case of their violations they have been guaranteed by the application of legal force by the just judiciary. In short, the normative order (normative pluralism) is '**law in action**'.

The normative order censors how positive law favours the observation of human rights and freedoms by public bodies and how it favours the development of human rights and freedoms of private persons.

II. The notion of normative order is based on the philosophical thesis that there are 'multiple realities'. The normative order is an entity of '**real**' individual legal acts of public bodies and normative acts of private persons, who regulate civil, political, economic, social and cultural relations among public and/or private persons ***in concreto*** through the recognition, separation and/or protection of mutual rights and obligations by the application of judicial force in the case of their violation. The normative order also includes a cross-sectional field, which reflects the coexistence of feasibility of legal acts and normative facts. The normative order has a horizontal character.

Legal acts constitute the legal order, which shows the **real** state of public and private relations in society. The legal order can be directly described, because it has documentary forms, is transparent and easily accessible. The analysis of the legal order is not problematic for the legislator. The legal order is an official form of the normative order. Normative facts constitute the non-legal order, which shows the **real** state of private relations in the society. The non-legal order cannot be directly described, mainly because it has no documentary forms, is latent and often difficult to access. To analyze normative facts is problematic for the legislator: it needs scientific investigation. Normative facts relate to the category of 'non-state law'. Normative facts are an unofficial form of normative order. The theory of normative facts is an important step not only in the direction of 'realism' but also away from the idea that the state has a monopoly of law-creation.[33]

III. I distinguish positive law on the global, regional, national and local levels, and normative order on the global level from the regional, national and local levels.

Positive law on the global level refers to Human Rights Law, Environmental Law, Public International Law, Humanitarian Law, Private International Law, Trade Law, Trans-national Law, Regional Law, Inter-Communal Law etc., worldwide. Positive law on the local level refers to the single legal system of each state, which should be compatible with the Universal Human Rights Law, Environmental Law, Public International Law, Humanitarian Law, Private International Law, Trade Law, Transnational Law, Inter-communal Law etc.

Normative order on the global level refers to the state of realization of universal human rights law, environmental law, public international

---

[33] 'Normative pluralism is generally marginalized and viewed with skepticism in legal discourse. Perhaps the main reason for this is that for over 200 years Western legal theory has been dominated by conceptions of law that tend to the monist (one internally coherent legal system), static (the state has monopoly of law within its territory), and positivist (what is not created or recognized as law by the state)'. See William Twinning, *Globalization...* 232 (2000).

law, humanitarian law, private international law, trade law, trans-national law, regional law, inter-communal law etc, which form legal orders and a large space of normative facts worldwide. Normative order on the local level refers to the state of realization of Universal Human Rights Law, Environmental Law, Public International Law, Humanitarian Law, Private International Law, Trade Law, Trans-national Law, Regional Law, Inter-communal Law, etc., which form legal orders and a large space of normative facts within each country's boundaries. Description and analysis of normative order on the global and on the local levels along with description and analysis of single positive law on the global and on the local levels enables description and analysis of the normative system of each country as a whole and of the world also in its entirety.

IV. One of the most fundamental distinctions in legal theory is the interaction and mutual transition between 'the theory of positive law' and 'the theory of normative order'. **The core idea** of the distinction between the theory of positive law and the theory of normative order is simply this: **the theory of positive law seeks to explain what the law is, in other words, what the law claims, whereas theory of normative order tells us what the positive law ought to be, in other words, what the law should claim.**

If we use the great J. Bentham's terms, from my point of view: the positive law is the subject of explanatory jurisprudence, while the normative order is the subject of censorial jurisprudence.

A bridge between **what the law claims and what the law should claim** is a space of idea of law. Investigation of the legal order in the framework of the normative order gives us an opportunity to assess how positive law (**Sollen**) is implemented in practice (**Sein**). In the process of investigation of the legal order in the framework of normative order, an **idea of law** arises; in other words, claims to what the law should be from the point of view of the Just Law.

In philosophical terms: mutual transition, spiral and evolutionary development of positive law and normative order is based on the 'principle of causality through freedom', but not the 'principle of causality of the nature'.

V. I suggest a spiral, evolutionary and endless development of theory of interaction and mutual-transition of Positive Law and Normative Order on the global, regional, national and local levels. Permanent, evolutionary and spiral interaction between positive law and normative order on the local, national and global scale presents a trend to permanently comprehend the idea of **Just Law**, which must be based on Universal Human Rights, because: 'To do just law, makes a dry tree green', as Shota Rustaveli - the famous Georgian philosopher and poet of the XII Century and one of the founders of Neo-Platonism - proclaimed. The aim and goal of interaction between positive law and normative order is to achieve a sustainable normative order of Humankind. The moral foundation of Global Order is related to **'the supernal order of orders'** expressed by great Shota Rustaveli.

My theory about mutual transition, spiral and evolutionary development of positive law and normative order removes any contradiction between them, making possible peaceful coexistence of positivism and sociological directions in jurisprudence, and creating balance between public law and private law on the global, regional, national and local levels.

VI. The 'legal families' theory of Comparative Law ignores the phenomenon of the normative order, because it does not explore and compare normative orders of different countries, which are in the same 'legal family'. Almost all scientists operating in comparative law and legal theory ignore any role of the practice of individual normative acts of public bodies and private persons in the formation of normative order. However, the state and a certain combination of practice of individual normative acts of public bodies and private persons construct an individual persona of the normative order of the country, which is always different from another country, disregard that both could even be entered in the same legal family, such as Germanic, Roman, Common Law, Islamic, Post-Soviet, or Far Eastern legal families. So it is necessary to introduce a new branch of legal science: **Comparative Normative Orders Study**, which at the beginning should not be within the framework of Comparative Law Study.

VII. My core argument is that post-modernity is in crisis. It has exhausted its political potential and is in the process of being replaced by a new post-positivist paradigm, which could be built on the emancipation possibilities of the **Rule of Just Law based on the Universal of Human Rights.**[34]

Particularly, in the modern 'globalistics' it is ascertained that today the world is in such a complicated situation that we cannot use one or other system of values, ideology, or culture, as a model in order to preserve its existence. The first step that humanity must take is the integration of basic religious trends, because **God is one and unique**. We consider this trend as acceptable, even to act in concert towards the creation of a **new and united environmental religion**. Actually it means a global substitution of

---

[34] Bizina Savaneli, *Jus Cogens Character...* (2003).

very expensive and dangerous exploitation of Earth's non-renewable resources by using inexpensive and safe Day-light including Solar and Wind energy, as a stable guarantee for the sustainable development of humankind.

THE INFLUENCE OF THE TRADITION OF BRITISH LAW ON THE AMERICAN LEGAL SYSTEM (SOME HISTORICAL ASPECTS)

EDYTA SOKALSKA

UNIVERSITY OF WARMIA AND MAZURY IN OLSZTYN, POLAND

Abstract

The law of the United States was originally largely derived from the *common law* system of English Law, which was in force at the time of the Revolutionary War. The colonists, who moved to the New World, brought with them the legal traditions of their homelands. The vestiges of each system – Dutch, English, French and Spanish – can be found in the laws of the various states. The history of a system of law is largely a history of borrowings of legal materials from other legal systems and of assimilation of materials from outside the law. The supreme law of the land under the Constitution's Supremacy Clause is the United States Constitution, as well as laws enacted by the U.S. Congress. The Constitution forms the basis for federal laws. At the beginning, federal law traditionally focused on areas where there was an express grant of power to the federal government, such as military, money, foreign affairs (especially international treaties), tariffs, intellectual property and mail. Everybody would agree that since the beginning of the 20th century federal law has expanded into such areas as aviation, telecommunications, railroads, pharmaceuticals, antitrust and trademarks. The states delegate lawmaking powers to thousands of agencies, counties, cities and special districts.

The law in the United States is derived from four sources. These four sources are: constitutional law, statutory law, administrative regulations and common law. The most important source of law is the United States Constitution. All other law falls under and is subordinate to that document. No law may contradict the Constitution. If Congress enacts a statute that conflicts with the Constitution, the Supreme Court may find that law unconstitutional and declare it invalid.

It seems that the court organization is complicated by the form of American government – federalism. Instead of a single, unified court system such as exists in Great Britain or France, the United States actually has fifty one court systems. The courts of the United States include both: the Unites States federal courts comprising the judicial branch of the federal government of the United States, and state and territorial courts of individual U.S. states and territories. This situation results in two different consequences for the American legal system. Firstly, the U.S. Congress and the state legislatures are free to organize their respective court systems to meet their own needs. The result is that not only is the federal court structure different from that of the states, but there is also tremendous diversity among the individual states. A trial court may be called a district court in one state, a superior or supreme court in another. The second consequence of the federal form of government is its impact on substantive and procedural law. Each state is free to determinate for itself what behaviour is forbidden, and each is free to establish reasonable punishment for defined crimes. But it is noticeable that state courts have their jurisdiction limited in some way. The jurisdiction of any court comes from the state constitution or from statutes passed by the state legislature or both.

American federalism emerged as a product of the deteriorating relationship between the colonists and the British in the New World. Several European countries laid claims to parts of North America but the British quickly emerged as the dominant power. Initially, most of the authoritative capabilities in the new political arrangement were left with the colonists, who were awarded limited self-government as a part of the benefits associated with their settlement. Boundaries between the British and colonists became loose and the colonists slowly began to consider alternative arrangements, particularly with respect to more comprehensive self-government.

History of the federal government of the United States

The governmental structure in the United States was established by the Constitution of 1789. The two characteristics of that structure that most directly affect the legal system of the United States are separation of powers and federalism. The separation of powers principle ensures that none of the three branches of federal government - legislative, executive or judicial – oversteps the boundaries of its proper constitutional role and assumes power belonging to the others. American federalism means that there are two levels of government in the country: federal and state. The fifty states of the U.S. have a great deal of independence and power. Actually, in the version of the American federalism there are fifty-one governments in the U.S.: fifty states and the federal government. As some authors suggest, the governmental system in the United States owes much to English institutions and philosophies of government. The idea of popular sovereignty, separation of powers, rule of law, natural rights and natural law were well developed but not always in effect in England, and were transported by the early settlers in the colonies.[1]

The country started out as thirteen colonies of Great Britain. During the period between 1760 and 1775 there were many violent clashes between British colonial authorities and the dissatisfied American colonists over a variety of taxation measures and other grievances against colonial rulers. The dissident colonists identified strongly with their own colony and concentrated on resistance to British authority at the local level. However, they made an effort in 1774 to take collective action in Philadelphia at the First Continental Congress. In response to measures adopted at that Congress, King George III sent soldiers and the American War of Independence began in 1775. At the beginning of the American Revolution, each colony organized a government without any constitution and sent representatives to the Second Continental Congress, which first met in May 1775 after the Battle of Lexington in Massachusetts.

It is impossible to understand the legal system of the United States without understanding its structure of government. The governmental structure was established by the Constitution of 1789. The two characteristics of that structure which most directly affect the legal system are 'separation of powers' and 'federalism'. The separation of powers principle ensures that the three branches of federal government – legislative, executive or judicial – are not able to overstep the boundaries of their proper constitutional role and take powers belonging to the others. It will be shown that the separation of powers significantly influences the legal system, especially, the role of the federal courts.

The American legal system is complicated by the form of government-federalism. The law of the United States was originally largely derived from the common law system of the English law. The colonists who moved to the New World brought with them the legal traditions of their homelands. The supreme law of the land under the Constitution's Supremacy Clause is the United States Constitution, as well as laws

---

[1] See, e.g., Joseph F. Zimmerman, *Contemporary American Federalism. The Growth of National Power* 14 (1992).

enacted by the U.S. Congress. The U.S. Constitution forms the basis for federal laws.

English influences

The American legal system and all others that have grown from English roots are characterized as Common Law, in contrast to the systems of continental Europe which are derived from Roman Law and are called Civil Law systems. England never absorbed Roman principles and methodology, but developed its law from unique native sources. The spread of English social culture has become the foundation of the law in most English speaking countries.

It is claimed that the earliest idea of common law was advanced by the English kings' judges abut 900 years ago in an attempt to create a national legal system and to consolidate royal power through the centralization of the administration of justice. The national royal courts were very attractive to litigants because of their relative freedom from corruption and their ability to enforce judgments on a national basis through the executive power of the royal officials. In contrast to rules applied only locally, they applied the law known as 'common', because it represented customs common to the whole kingdom. In other words, the common law had a unifying, state-building aspect which had both an ideological and a practical appeal, as Graham Hughes remarks.[2]

The first royal courts developed from the King's Council in Britain after the Norman invasion in 1066. The king's closest advisers were the first royal judges. They travelled through the country controlling local administration and deciding disputes. Later their tasks became primarily judicial. They separated from the council and began to acquire their own jurisdiction as royal courts. Local courts controlled by local nobles continued to resolve most disputes. But it should be stressed that more important cases were reserved for the King's courts.[3]

Anglo-Saxon England, by the early twelfth century, differed from other European realms in having an organized system of justice. The country was divided into special divisions. The administration of justice was local at the beginning. There were public courts at hundred and shire levels. There were courts under the auspicious of the lord of the manor, who resolved disputes among his tenants. Court procedure was uniform. Parties

---

[2] Alan B. Morrison, *Fundamentals of American Law* 9 (2004).

[3] William Burnham, *Introduction to the Law and Legal Systems of the United States* 14 (3rd ed. 2002).

appeared in the court. 'The plaintiff would allege improper activity in the form of an oath, and the defendant would enter a denial in the form of an oath. Generally, the defendant would then present a requisite number of character witnesses (frequently twelve) who would swear that the defendant was telling the truth; the witnesses did not testify on the facts of the case but merely on the veracity of the defendant. The communities were small, and all the trial participants were known to each other. Those who swore falsely were subject not only to distrust from their peers, but also to punishment imposed by God'.[4]

As for criminal cases, a dozen freemen were accusers before the court. They revealed the names of those who committed the crime. Guilt or innocence would then been proven by ordeal or by compurgation.[5] Anglo-Saxons also employed fines or a system of reparation for those who were found guilty. The Normans added the possibility of trial by combat, where one could compete for oneself or hire a champion to engage in a battle.[6]

The Normans strengthened and tightened the administrative organization of the country and brought close control of the government in the hands of the monarch. They introduced a different kind of feudalism that existed in continental Europe at that time[7]. William the Conqueror appointed his own tribunal, the king's Court for the protection of royal interests and as an appellate court for those litigants who were able to travel to the royal court. The king and his successors did not overturn the laws that they found but instead supplemented them with a strong centralized judiciary and uniformity of decisions. Much of the Anglo-Saxon law and customs continued relatively unchanged.[8]

It should not be forgotten that Henry II (1154-1189) heavily influenced the development of English law and the centralization of the judicial system. He ensured that fees paid by litigants enriched the royal treasury, not the barons, and consolidated royal control. The king bolstered his

---

[4] James V. Calvi & Suzan Coleman, *American Law and Legal Systems* 28 (6th ed. 2009).

[5] 'Ordeal' was in Middle Ages used to prove if someone was innocent or guilty not only in England. Trial by ordeal often involved burning a person's arm or hand and examining it after a short period. If the arm was clean, the accused was cleared of the crime. 'Compurgation' was the process of clearing the person by oaths of others as to his veracity.

[6] Gordon C. Post, *An Introduction to the Law* 20 (1963).

[7] More about history of British law, see, e.g., J.H. Baker, *An Introduction to English Legal History* 3-9 (1979); Andrzej Bryk, *The Origins of the Constitutional Government. Higher law and the sources of judicial review* 87-108 (1999).

[8] Stefan F. Milsom, *Historical Foundations of the Common Law* 82-80 (1981).

control over local courts by applying the royal executive writ. A writ might very well order judges of the shire, hundred, or seigniorial courts to find for a particular plaintiff, a usurpation of authority, which contributed to the demise of the local courts. He also sent judges from Curia Regis into the countryside to settle disputes, although their primary task was revenue collection. By the Statute of Westminster in 1285 he institutionalized the practice of sending itinerant judges on circuits to render justice.[9]

By the end of the thirteenth century, there were three law courts in the secular realm. They were distinguished by their function: the Court of Common Pleas (in London), the Court of the King's Bench (mobile), and the Exchequer. The Catholic Church enforced canon law and had jurisdiction over marital relationship and inheritance. Canon law was strongly rooted in the traditions of the Roman Law. The domination of the ecclesiastical courts over marriages lasted until the middle of the nineteenth century, despite the fact that the Catholic Church was replaced by the Church of England.

Rejection of the civil law tradition in England and the substitution of the common law was strongly connected with the kings' centralization of the judicial system. Strong kings consolidated judicial power and imposed a uniform system of tribunals over the country. Because of the paucity of statutes, the judges formalized the customs and mores of the times into court decisions and applied the same rules. Judicial decisions were written as reports and kept by the king's courts. Henry Bracton was one of the first who collected them. They were used as authority or precedent by subsequent judges.[10]

It is noticeable that with the evolution of common law the development of the equity system can be observed.[11] In the thirteen century in England there were two governmental departments: the Exchequer (fiscal matters) and the Chancery (secretarial department). The Chancery was managed by the chancellor who was responsible for handling the government's paperwork, including the writs for courts. The writs served three purposes: as a method of designating which court would decide the case; as the document giving the plaintiff access to the courts in exchange for the payment of a fee: as a tool for directing the sheriff to summon the defendant for the court appearance. Despite being initially creative and flexible, the common law courts soon started to adopt harsh and rigid

[9] Gordon C. Post, *An Introduction…* 22 (1963).

[10] James V. Calvi & Suzan Coleman, *American Law and...* 31 (2009).

[11] Different cases connected with common law and equity system are developed in George P. Flecher & Steve Sheppard, *American Law in a Global Context* 15-28 (2005).

procedures. The Chancery achieved fame in jurisprudence.[12] The result of the chancellors' activities was to forge parallel court systems, each with different remedies. Then, England had two types of courts: the historic common law courts and more flexible courts of equity. In the late eleventh century these two merged and all courts started to apply the rules of both, with the equity dominance in case of conflict.[13]

Looking at the origins of emerging common law, the primary sources were not only legislative (royal statues). The common law was declared by judges but it was not wholly invented by them. The truth is that much of it consisted of a blending of Anglo-Saxon customary rules and principles with northern French practices and procedures familiar to the governing Anglo-Norman elite. In the process of selecting customary rules and practices from two cultures, the judges displayed the practical genius of common law culture in building a structure of acceptable and efficient principles and rules.[14]

One must acknowledge that the early centuries also exhibited an important phenomenon that characterizes common law systems. Early England developed a powerful group of learned lawyers - the Bar - who had a high status and who were regarded as virtual equals by the judges. The arguments these barristers addressed to the courts are preserved in law reports. They relied on appeals to the authority from particular earlier decisions of the courts (precedent), which are treated as worthy of the greatest respect. At the same time there were vigorous arguments among the lawyers and the judges about the best way of understanding earlier decisions in the light of general considerations of efficiency and justice. In that way, the law developed through the dialogue between justices and lawyers, with the courts often adopting the reasoning and language urged upon them by members of the bar.[15]

Through the action of judges and lawyers, common law in its early centuries laid the foundations of the modern Anglo-American law of contracts, torts (civil wrongs), criminal law and the law of real property (interests in land). While there has been later statutory intervention in all these areas, the underlying governing principles and style of argument and

---

[12] About historical jurisprudence, see Anthony Chase, *Law and History: The Evolution of the American Legal System* 11-50 (1999).

[13] Stefan F. Milsom, *Historical Foundations…* 85 (1981).

[14] Andrzej Bryk, *The Origins of the Constitutional…*97-100 (1999).

[15] An influential figure of Renaissance England and a great jurist, *Sir Edward Coke* bravely fought for the supremacy of the common law over the monarchy, for more see Andrzej Bryk, *The Limits of Arbitrary Government: Edward Coke and the Search for Fundamental Law* 1-205 (1995).

decision-making are still those that were worked out long ago in the emerging years of Common Law. When large sections of commercial law were codified, as in the English sale of goods Act of 1893 and the twentieth century American Uniform Commercial Code, although some reforms were introduced, much of the statutory content represented a restatement of common law principles.[16]

It is noticeable that while common law evolved in the royal courts and was enforced by royal officials, its fundamental justification from the beginning was the idea of the tradition of customs of the English people. The common law theory rejected doctrines of absolute royal sovereignty that were part of the continental European tradition. The early declarations of the liberty of the subject and restrictions on royal power of Magna Charta in 1215 started to be seen as part of the common law tradition. That strengthened the view that the common law was an embodiment of fundamental liberties and human rights. The American colonies were greatly influenced by this ideological aspect, especially during the war of independence against England. The Americans invoked their rights under the common law as against royal prerogatives and saw themselves not as rebels, but as exercising the best traditions of their English heritage.

English common law was well-developed when the North American colonies were being settled, at the beginning by English colonists. Colonists who moved to the new World brought with them the legal traditions of their homelands. Vestiges of each system can be found in the laws of various states: Dutch, English, French and Spanish. When the English colonized North America, among various customs and goods, they imported the common law. Since the common law was used as an ideological weapon in the American struggle for independence, cutting off the links with England brought some changes in the basic structure of the legal system but the content and method of Common Law were absorbed into American culture and have never been replaced.[17]

The reception of common law in the United States was stimulated by the very popular and influential treatise *Commentaries on the Laws of England* by Sir William Blackstone, published in the late eighteen century.[18] 'Blackstone combined great talent as a systematizer and expounder of the common law with a great literary grace and style. His treatise gave the common law a modern presentation in an orderly and

---

[16] Alan B. Morrison, *Fundamentals of American*... 11 (2004).

[17] About differences and connections between English and American legal system, see Richard A. Posner, *Law and Legal Theory in England and America* 1-152 (1997).

[18] George P. Flecher &Steve Sheppard, *American Law*... 15 (2005).

attractive manner, whereas before it had been accessible only in thousands of cases in the law reports and in ancient and out-of-date institutional works. The development of the law also brilliantly linked by Blackstone with the constitutional and political history of England'.[19] The work of Blackstone strengthened the continued reception of the common law from the American colonies into the constituent states. Because of the large measure of sovereignty of the states, common law has not exactly developed in the same way in every state. Despite the fact that a single common law was originally exported from England to America, a great variety of factors has led to the development of different common law rules in different states.[20]

American society moderated the system and imposed new rules of law that more accurately reflected economic and social realities of the newly created country.[21] 'One hallmark of the new system was the merger of law and equity, and the power of a single judge to render both types of remedies in the appropriate cases (as opposed to English scheme of parallel systems). A second characteristic of the new system was the abolition of the common law power of judges to define crimes, and the substitution of the legislature as the body to identify criminal activity and to determine the appropriate range of punishment'.[22] Colonists modified as well as adopted some aspects of common law that were appropriate.

Indisputably, judges remain the most powerful element of the American legal system. The reliance of judges on precedent and the doctrine of 'stare decisis' remains very powerful to this day. Stare decisis refers to the policy of courts to follow the rules laid down in previous judicial decisions and to refrain from disturbing established points of law; the purpose being to ensure certainty and stability in the legal system.

The influence of American administrative division on the American legal system

Most people assume that there are two great families of legal systems in the world. The common law applies in all the countries that speak English. The civil law applies everywhere else, with a few important

[19] Alan B. Morrison, *Fundamentals of American...* 12 (2004).
[20] Lawrence M. Friedman, *American Law in the Twentieth Century* 4-5 (2005).
[21] More about American perception of law, see Dudley Odell McGovney, *The British Origin of Judicial Review of Legislation*, 93/1 University of Pensylvania Law Review 1- 49 (1944). Nature of law and its impact on the society, see Roscoe Pound, *Social Control through Law* 10-100 (1997).
[22] James V. Calvi & Suzan Coleman, *American Law and...*33 (2009).

exceptions, such as Chinese or Islamic law. Of course, that sort of classification is an oversimplification. The American legal system, despite having roots in English law, has also its own specific features.

The distribution and limitation of legal authority in the United States is complex. The complexity is the result of federal structure that distinguishes the government of the United States from most of world's national legal systems. The United States remains a federal legal system, with each of the fifty states of the national union seised of largely independent legal authority, and the federal government, in turn, possessed of a sprawling legal authority overlapping that of the states. This feature of law in the U.S. is complicated still by the tradition of localism within the respective states, pursuant to which important legal authority is often delegated to a diverse structure of local governmental entities. It is significant that, to the essentially hierarchical or vertical questions of legal authority posed by federalism in the United States, there are the horizontal questions of the distribution of authority among the different branches of government at any level.

The federal government is understood to be a government of 'enumerated powers', which enjoys only that authority specifically granted to it by various provisions of the federal Constitution. Indisputably, all federal legislation is open to question on the grounds that exceeds the enumerated and apparently rather narrow domain of federal legislative authority. Realities of a national economy and overwhelming sense of national authority and responsibility have dominated American constitutional law, and have had the effect of removing most of the legal barriers to the exercise of federal legislative authority.[23]

American law is basically state law. Federal law as a national law is reserved for certain well-defined areas. The private law of torts, contracts and property, family law, criminal law, corporation and commercial law-all are rooted in state codes and interpretative decisions. There are fifty-one jurisdictions among the states, where statutes and cases differentiate. Federal law controls certain limited areas, such as immigration, patents and copyright, international affairs, and the marketing of corporate securities, in a uniform, national set of laws.[24]

The important point of the American court structure is that in a typical state there are two tiers of appellate decisions. The federal system has a parallel structure. Appeals come from the federal district court to the circuit court of appeals for one of the twelve regional circuits and then to

---

[23] Lawrence G. Sager, *The Sources and Limits of Legal Authority* in Alan B. Morrison (ed.), *Fundamentals of American Law* 28-29 (2004).
[24] George P. Flecher &Steve Sheppard, *American Law...* 5-6 (2005).

the Supreme Court. These are two parallel systems: state court for state law and federal courts for federal law. State courts represent the last word on matters of state law, including the state constitution. For a federal court to intervene in a case initiated in a state court is to raise a federal question[25] or to consider a dispute between citizens of different states. The later dispute may be held in a federal district court and be subject to federal appeal, but all of the federal courts apply state law.[26]

It might be surprising to civil law countries, but there is only a single unified system of courts in state or federal jurisdiction. A single court with the same judge hears and decides private law disputes, criminal cases, constitutional issues and administrative complaints. In contrast with American judges, civil law judges are specialized in some areas. Naturally, there are some state or federal specialized courts in the United States, such as federal courts for bankruptcy and taxes, but it is not as striking as in civil law systems.[27]

Some legal system experts argue that these days the federal government under its commercial powers can probably regulate most subject matters everywhere in the country that can be shown to have some economic impact. At the same time states have retained their traditional sovereign power to make laws for people and transactions within their borders. This situation results in a situation where state and federal governments have overlapping or concurrent power in making law governing transactions and events taking place on the same geographical territory.[28]

Where Congress has the right to legislate, state law that is conflicting must be changed under the supremacy clause. Undeniably, some areas of federal law have little occasion to conflict with state law. For example, Congress has created a whole body of new law, such as federal tax law or laws dealing with administration of the federal government. But at the same time there are many other areas of federal legislative activity that are more general and have the potential of displacing state law.

There are many areas of law that remain predominantly state law. Congress has the power to pass a national commercial code for the whole country but is not interested in it. Consequently, most of the law that governs ordinary transactions among private citizens or companies remains state law. Corporations and other business enterprises are regulated at first by state law. Contract, property, tort, family and

---

[25] An issue under the U.S. Constitution, a federal statute, or treaty.

[26] Lawrence G. Sager, *supra* 30.

[27] John T. Noonan, *Persons and Masks of the Law* 11 (1976).

[28] William Burnham, *Introduction to the Law…* 28 (2002).

commercial law, public utilities and professions, as well as most ordinary crimes, such as robbery, rape, and murder are also regulated in accordance with the state law.

When Congress chooses to intervene in an area usually governed by a state, the result might be a mix of federal and state law on the same theme. The coexistence of both state and federal law on the same matter is made all the more likely by the Supreme Court's doctrine on 'preemption' of state by federal law. When the supremacy clause invalidates state law that conflicts with federal law, there is a presumption against federal preemption. State law will be displaced only if there is a direct conflict between state and federal law or Congress has clearly expressed intent to 'occupy' an entire 'field' of law.[29]

It is significant that law can vary from state to state. There is no uniform body of federal choice-of-law rules to mediate between the competing state interests involved. Instead, the choice-of-law rules of the state where the case is pending apply to determine the question. One difficulty with this is that state choice-of-law rules are in a great flux, so it is very difficult to predict what law will be applied to a given dispute. Interstate cases governed by state law can present the lawyer with a wide variety of courts and bodies of law to choose from. Also decisions of where to file suit is often a complicated one.

Summary

In the United States, the relationship between federal and state laws is extremely complex and confusing as a result of the unique nature of American federalism. The American law derives from a few sources, such as constitutional law, statutory law, administrative regulations and the common law (including case law). The most important source of law is the United States Constitution. All other law falls under and is subordinate to that document. Indisputably, the federal Constitution is the highest source of law. The lower are: federal statutes, treaties and court rules, federal administrative agency rules, federal common law, state constitutions, states statutes and court rules, state agency rules and state common law. Each level of enacted law includes the case law interpreting that enacted law. If two sources of law on the same level of the hierarchy conflict, then the later in time will govern.[30]

---

[29] William Burnham, *Introduction to the Law…* 28 (2002).

[30] Lief H. Carter, *Administrative Law and Politics: Cases and Comments* 38 (1983).

It seems that the court organization is complicated by the form of American government – federalism. Instead of a single, unified court system such as it exists in Great Britain or France, the United States actually has fifty one court systems. The courts of the United States include both the Unites States federal courts comprising the judicial branch of the federal government of the United States; and state and territorial courts of individual U.S. states and territories. This situation results in two different consequences for the American legal system. Firstly, the U.S. Congress and the state legislatures are free to organize their respective court systems to meet their own needs. The result is that not only is the federal court structure different from that of the states, but there is also tremendous diversity among the individual states. A trial court may be called a district court in one state, a superior or supreme court in another. The second consequence of the federal form of government is its impact on substantive and procedural law. Each state is free to determinate for itself what behaviour is forbidden, and each is free to establish reasonable punishment for defined crimes. But it is noticeable that state courts have their jurisdiction limited in some way. The jurisdiction of any court comes from the state constitution or from statues passed by the state legislature or both.

PRIVATE LAW

CONSUMERS' BANKRUPTCY IN COMPARATIVE APPROACH

ALEKSANDER JAKOWLEW

JAGIELLONIAN UNIVERSITY CRACOW, POLAND

Introduction

The law permitting consumers to file petition for insolvency was adopted in Poland in the year 2008[1] and came into force on the 1st April 2009. Although the authors claimed to base themselves on foreign experiences, the regulation was criticized as ineffective and ill-fitted ever since its very adoption. After nearly two years of legal validity, only about one thousand five hundred petitions have been filed and the courts have declared only 22 persons insolvent on the basis of the rules on consumers' bankruptcy.[2]

The aim of the paper is to propose possible solutions to change the current, unsatisfactory state of affairs; solutions as adopted in foreign legal systems. Firstly the objectives and values specific for this kind of proceeding are discussed. The current Polish regulation is then outlined. Furthermore the principles of American, French and German regulations on consumers bankruptcy with their most notable traits are presented. The summary shall present the modifications with which the Polish mode might be modified on the basis of foreign law regulations.

Objectives of consumers' bankruptcy

By insolvency proceedings opened against business-active entity, the purpose is either liquidation or reorganization of the insolvent entity. The economically ill entity is either removed from the economic system or cured. In many legal systems, the principle goal of the insolvency proceedings is to satisfy the claims of the bankrupt person's creditors to

[1] The Act of December 5th, 2008, Journal of Laws No.234, item 1572.
[2] Cf. Tomasz Kurowski, *Tak trudno upaść*, Gazeta Wyborcza (February 28th, 2011).

the maximal possible extent. The second often emphasized purpose of the insolvency proceedings is to maintain the enterprise of the debtor.

The insolvency of a consumer differs widely from the above presented model. A consumer cannot be liquidated, being a natural person, a consumer cannot be declared nonexistent by a court judgment. The insolvency proceedings are understood as a form of assistance provided for those consumers who have found themselves in a vicious circle of debts. Often such bankruptcy is perceived as a form of rehabilitation of the insolvent consumer, rendering him a productive member of society.[3] The debtor's estate cannot be completely liquidated; the debtors shall be allowed to keep the necessities of life.[4] Those peculiar traits raise the question whether the rehabilitation of a consumer, returning him to society, is or is not more important than satisfying his creditors.

Weighting the interest in favour of the consumer leads to the breach of the fundamental civil law principle of *pacta sunt servanda* (lat. the contracts shall be abided by). Cancelling all or most of consumer's debts and providing him with the fresh-start opportunity can create moral hazard.[5]

On the other hand, weighting the goals in favour of creditors can render the rehabilitation of the debtor virtually impossible. In most instances the insolvent debtor is so heavily indebted that he ceases pay his debts, exposing himself to the augmenting interest charges, and thus becoming even more insolvent than beforehand. Furthermore the consumer is not an equal in the relation with most of his creditors. The consumer's creditors are in most instances professionals. Some people can be lured into incurring excessive debts due to the advertisements of the future creditors. The contracts between consumer and a professional are frequently strongly weighted in favour of the creditor.

Consumer bankruptcy is an area of law equally related to the branch of law regulating insolvency proceedings and to the branch of law

---

[3] Richard E. Flint, *Bankruptcy Policy: Toward a Moral Justification for Financial Rehabilitation of the Consumer Debtor*, 48 Wash.&Lee L. Rev. 515, 515-516,529 (1991); Karen Gross, *Preserving a Fresh Start for the Individual Debtor: The Case for Narrow Construction of the Consumer Credit Amendments*, 135 U.Pa.L.Rev. 59, 60 (1986).

[4] Richard E. Flint *supra* 3, 515-517.

[5] Jason J. Kilborn, *Behavioural Economics, Overindebtedness and Comparative Consumer Bankruptcy: Searching for Causes and Evaluating Solutions*, 22 Emory Bankr. Dev. J. 13, 28 (2005).

concerning the protection of consumers and party equality of the consumer-professional contracts.[6]

The two interests, that of the consumer and that of his creditors, have to be balanced properly by creating the rules on consumers bankruptcy.

Polish law on consumers' bankruptcy

Description

Special provisions regulating the bankruptcy of consumers were introduced in Polish Law in the year 2009. The title V of Polish Insolvency and Reorganization Act (*Prawo Upadłościowe i Naprawcze*)[7] containing the regulation of consumer bankruptcy is titled: Insolvency proceedings against natural persons not engaged in business activity.[8] Consequently the law applies to all those natural persons that cannot be declared insolvent in normal insolvency proceedings,[9] proceedings that are suited for the active business entities whenever they are natural persons, legal persons, or other types of entities.

However it does not suffice to be a consumer to successfully file for consumer insolvency proceedings, there are specific conditions that must be met by the consumer seeking to be declared insolvent.

First of all the debtor must be insolvent; that means unable to pay his due debts.[10] During the legislation process there were attempts to also provide for debt restructuring proceedings against solvent customers threatened with insolvency, but finally the law is addressed only to those customers that are insolvent.[11]

---

[6] Although in most instances the insolvency of the consumer is regulated in the acts or codes regulating insolvency proceedings e.g. Polish Insolvency and Reorganization Act (*Prawo upadłościowe i naprawcze*); German Insolvency Act (*Insolvenzordnung*) or American Bankruptcy Code; in French law for example the consumer bankruptcy is regulated in the law regulating protection of consumers Consumption code (*Code de la consommation).*

[7] The Polish Insolvency and Reorganization Act (Ustawa Prawo Upadłościowe i Naprawcze, hereinafter referred to as PrUpNapr) of 2003, Journal of Laws No.60, item 535 with changes,.

[8] Michał Kosiarski & Paweł Wrześniewski, *Upadłość konsumencka tylko dla nielicznych*, Rzeczpospolita (November 17th, 2008).

[9] Art. 491^1 PrUpNapr.

[10] Cf. art 10 in relation to art. 11§1 PrUpNapr.

[11] Project of December 22th, 2003 – art. 48-58, project of Mai 9th, 2006 – art. 53-63.

The insolvency of the debtor must be caused by exceptional and unpredictable circumstances.[12] Therefore the debtor cannot successfully apply for insolvency proceedings if he was incurring further debts while already being insolvent, also the insolvency proceedings shall not be opened against a customer who willingly gave up a job and therefore became insolvent. The predictability of the occurrence of a specific circumstance shall be verified from the objective point of view.[13]

Insolvency proceedings cannot be opened against a debtor who does not have sufficient assets to cover the costs of the proceedings. In such a case the debtor's petition to declare him insolvent shall be denied.[14]

Polish Law does not follow the 'fresh-start' principle, the discharge of the debtor's debts does not occur automatically. All of the debtors assets are to be given to the creditors, including the debtor's apartment, then the court decides on a five year plan determining to what extent the debtor is bound to pay the rest of his debts in the due five years. Only if the plan is executed properly shall the court grant the discharge of the rest of the debts.

Criticism of the Polish regulation

Since its adoption the new procedure has been criticized as impractical. The condition of debtor insolvency being caused by exceptional and unpredictable circumstances is considered both too restrictive and at the same time too vague.[15] There is no clear rule or judgment how to understand those conditions; different courts understand them differently.[16]

It is also pointed that the law is harsh on the debtor. The discharge of his debts is by no means automatic, such discharge shall be granted only after the execution of the five year payment plan.

Further the debtor is bound to move out of his apartment; without that, the debtor's petition for insolvency shall be denied.[17] The appointed liquidator has to provide the debtor with enough money to pay the twelve month lease for another lodging,[18] however the amount of that money and

---

[12] Art. 491[3] PrUpNapr.

[13] Aleksander J. Witosz in Rafał Adamus & Aleksander J. Witosz (ed.), *Upadłość konsumencka. Komentarz praktyczny* at 62 (2009).

[14] Art. 18 PrUpNapr.

[15] Cf. Michał Kosiarski & Paweł Wrześniewski, *Upadłość konsumencka...* (2008).

[16] Tomasz Kurowski, *Tak trudno...* (2011).

[17] Cf. art. 491[6] and art. 491[7] PrUpNapr.

[18] Art. 491[6] (1) PrUpNapr.

the lodging requirements are decided by the bankruptcy judge[19] and the debtor cannot be sure how much would be granted to him.

It is to be noted that in the case of ordinary execution from a debtor's estate there are various protections prohibiting the creditors from expelling debtors and their relatives from their apartment. Therefore after filing for insolvency the debtor has to abide by rules that are harsher and more restrictive than the rules of normal execution of debts as provided for in the civil procedure.

Summing up, the Polish regulation on consumers' bankruptcy is creditor-oriented, the provisions are intend to favour the creditor, little comfort or help is offered to debtors, hence the relatively few petitions to open consumer insolvency proceedings and very few actually declared insolvencies.[20]

American regulation

Introduction

The American law is frequently perceived as the most debtor friendly system of consumers' bankruptcy law,[21] especially with the procedure providing for the immediate discharge of debts and 'fresh-start' for a debtor. However the most recent amendments seek to prevent abuse of the law, and implement harsher rules on the reckless or opportunistic debtors.

The American law provides for various procedures for insolvency procedures, however two procedures are most commonly applied for by insolvent consumers. The first procedure is provided for in Chapter 7 BC, the procedure in which all of the debtor's debts are discharged, the second procedure is provided for in Chapter 13 BC and is specially suited for restructuring of the debts of the consumers.

The important feature of both procedures is the fact that a debtor seeking relief under both Chapter 7 and Chapter 13 should, prior to filing the petition, seek and obtain counselling on budget and credit planning. The certificate that such counselling was received within the 180 days prior to filing the petition, shall be attached to that petition.

---

19 Art. 491^6 (2) PrUpNapr.

20 Only 22 persons were declared insolvent in the consumer insolvency proceedings since the adoption of the law (Tomasz Kurowski, *Tak trudno...* (2011).

21 Jason J. Kilborn, *The innovative German approach to consumer debt relief: revolutionary changes in German law, and surprising lessons for the United States*, 24 Nw. J. Int'lL&Bus. 257, 281 (2004).

Chapter 7 – 'Fresh start' procedure

The proceedings as provided for in Chapter 7 offer the debtor the possibility of a so-called 'fresh start'. The estate of the debtor at the moment of filing the petition for bankruptcy,[22] with the exception of the exempt property,[23] becomes the bankruptcy estate and is liquidated or sold by the trustee[24] in order to pay the creditors and cover the costs and expenses of bankruptcy proceedings.[25] After the court issues a discharge under Chapter 7, the debtor is relieved of personal liability and can retain the exempt property.[26]

Not every debtor can receive the discharge under Chapter 7. First of all, the debtor cannot receive a second discharge if a prior discharge was granted to him within the period of eight or six years prior to the second filing.[27] Secondly the bankruptcy judge or trustee can challenge a debtor's petition and request the court to dismiss that petition on the ground of 'substantial abuse'. The notion of 'substantial abuse' is not defined in the law;[28] the courts found that such abuse occurs when the debtor is capable of funding a payment plan under Chapter 13,[29] or when the debtor abuses any of rules as provided for in the Chapter 7;[30] or when the granting of the relief to the debtor is unnecessarily prejudicial to the creditors.[31]

There is a number of debts that cannot be discharged under the Chapter 7 proceedings under any circumstances: certain taxes, debts to creditors to whom the debtor failed to give notice of the bankruptcy petition, alimony and child support, certain fines, student loans, and claims that were not discharged in prior proceeding.[32]

---

[22] 11 U.S.C. § 541 (a)(1).

[23] 11 U.S.C. § 726.

[24] Robert L. Jordan et al. *Bankruptcy* 23-24 (5th ed. 1999).

[25] *Ibid.*, 21.

[26] 11 U.S.C. § 727 (b); however the court must deny the discharge if the debtor has acted improperly or has been granted a discharge within 6 years prior to the filing for the insolvency; see Robert L. Jordan et al. *Bankruptcy* 26 (1999). 26; see also 11 U.S.C. § 727 (a).

[27] See 11 U.S.C. § 727 (a)(8) and 11 U.S.C. § 727 (a)(9).

[28] Charles J. Magee, *The Bankruptcy Reform Act of 1999*, 25 Seton Hall Legis J. 167, 172 (2001).

[29] *United States Trustee v. Harris*, 960 F.2d 74 (8th Cir. 1992).

[30] In re Keniston, 85 BR 202 (Bankr D.N.H. 1988).

[31] In re Higginbotham, 111 B.R. 955 bankr. N.D. Okla. 1990); In re Goodson, 130 B.R. 87 (Bankr. N.D. Okla. 1991); In re Dickerson, 193 B.R. 67 (Bankr. M.D. Fla. 1996).

[32] 11 U.S.C. § 532 (a).

Chapter 13 – Consumers' reorganization procedure

The debtor seeking relief under Chapter 13 must be 'an individual with regular income' who holds, on the date of the petition, less than $250,000 of unsecured debt and $750,000 of secured debt.[33] The debtor has to pay at least part of his debts, over the period of three years. The payments are made either from the liquidation of the debtor's assets or the incomes obtained by the debtor during the three year period. After all of the payments are received, he obtains the discharge of all debts that were included in the payment plan.

The discharge as provided for in Chapter 13 has a much broader range than the discharge under Chapter 7.[34] Only alimony, maintenance and support, student loans and DUI debts are exempt.[35]

The reform as introduced in the BAPCPA

The Bankruptcy Abuse Prevention and Consumer Protection Act of 2005 (BAPCPA) was intended to prevent abusive filling, consumers filling for discharge under Chapter 7 who were capable of making payments under Chapter 13, and also filling by consumers who incur debt intending to discharge it in future bankruptcy proceedings.[36]

The principal change aimed at the abuser is the 'means test' of § 707 (b). The test uses a formula based on incomes and expenses that compares consumers' income with state median incomes and evaluates consumers' disposable incomes after allowance for secured debt and hypothetical expenses.[37] The means test supplements the substantial abuse principle by preventing the debtors able to pay the payments under Chapter 13, from obtaining the discharge under Chapter 7, without paying the payments.

The second important amendment introduced by the BAPCPA is the credit counselling requirement; a device intended to reduce filings by educating debtors about alternatives to bankruptcy prior to filing.[38]

It should be noted that the BAPCPA has significantly reduced the number of consumers' bankruptcy filings.[39] The American consumers

---

[33] 11 U.S.C. § 109 (e).

[34] Cf. Michael J. Herbert, *Understanding Bankruptcy* §12.05 (C)(1) (1997).

[35] 11 U.S.C. § 1328 (a)(2).

[36] Douglas W. Kassebaum, *BAPCPA's Effects on Consumer Bankruptcy Fillings* 6/15/07/NwFinRev S2.

[37] *Ibid.*

[38] *Ibid.*

[39] *Ibid.*

bankruptcy law no longer favours the reckless and opportunistic debtor, who incurs debts only to discharge them in the bankruptcy proceedings.

French regulation

Introduction

French law provides for two procedures available for insolvent consumers, firstly the procedure of personal over-indebtedness (*surendettement personel*) and the discharge procedure (*retablissement personel*). The important trait of French law is that the consumer bankruptcy procedures are not regulated in the insolvency law, but rather in the consumers law, in this case the Code of the Consumption (*code de la consommation*).

Unlike many legal systems, in French law the consumers' insolvency proceedings are conducted mainly not before a court or bankruptcy judge, but before the special administrative body of the commission on insolvency (*commission de surendettement*).

The other characteristic feature of the French system of consumer bankruptcy law is also the condition of good faith (*bonne foi*) of the debtor filing the petition for insolvency. That general clause aims to protect the system from abuse by reckless debtors. No other measures are provided for in the law. However the law declares the debtor to be in bad faith and therefore excluded from insolvency proceedings (*déchéance du débiteur*) when he:

1. committed fraud while filing the petition; or
2. attempted or committed fraud by the declaration of the state of his assets; or
3. aggravated his own state of insolvency.[40]

The law contains general presumption of good faith,[41] so the debtor does not have to prove that he was in good faith, rather those who oppose the debtors petition have to prove that he was in bad faith.[42] The court's decision states that the presumption of debtor's good faith is rebutted

[40] Art. L333-2 Code de la consommation.

[41] Art. 2268 Code civil.

[42] Cass. 1 chambre civile, 4.04.1991, Bull.civ. 1991, I, n° 124; Cass. 1chambre civil, 4.04.1991, Bull.civ. 1991, I, n° 123; Cass. 1 chambre civile, 24.02.1993, I, n° 8.

when debtor, aware of his own bad financial condition, incurred new debts;[43] or when the debtor intends to cheat his creditors.[44]

Procedure of personal over-indebtedness

The procedure is provided for insolvent consumers. The state of insolvency (*surendettement*) is defined in the law as the state in which a debtor is unable to pay his due debts as well as those debts that will become due in a short period of time.[45] It should be noted that, because of its character, the procedure is not provided for those debtors who have incurred debts because of their business activity.

The procedure starts with a debtor filing the petition with the proper commission. The commission urges the debtor and creditors to work out a solution, and agree on the payment plan (*plan conventionnel de redressement*). In case the sides do not agree on the plan, the commission recommends the special measures to be adopted, measures leading to repair the financial situation of the debtor (*recommandations*).[46] The measures recommended by the commission are then subject to approval of the bankruptcy judge (*juge de l'exécution*).

The measures as provided for in the law contain:

- the changes in the payment of the debts (*rééchelonnement de paiement de dettes*);[47]
- reversal of the rule that payment is considered to be the payment of the interests rather than debt if both are due;[48]
- in exceptional circumstances the commission can recommend the reduction of interest rates;[49]

---

[43] Tribunal d'Instance Angoulême, 26.04.1990, Bulletin rapide de droit des affaires Francis Lefebvre 30.06.1990; Tribunal d'Insance Brest, 20.11.1990, Institut national de la consommation nº 716, at 9.

[44] Cass. 1 chambre civile, 31.03.1992, Bull.civ. 1992, I, nº 109; Cass. 1 chambre civile,10.02.2005, Juris-Data nº 2005-026890.

[45] Art. L330-1 al. 1 Code de la consommation.

[46] Katarzyna Michalak, *Przesłanki wszczęcia konsumenckiego postępowania niewypłacalnościowego (surendettement personel) i postępowania prowadzącego do uwolnienia z reszty długów (retablissement personel) we Francji*, 1 Transformacje Prawa Prywatnego 33, 42 (2008).

[47] Art. L331-7, nº 1 Code de la consommation.

[48] Art. L331-7, nº 2 Code de la consommation.

[49] Art. L331-7, nº 3 Code de la consommation; see also Cass. 1 chambre civile 27.10.1992, D. 1992 at 278; Cass. 1 chambre civile, 01.06.1994 Contrats, conc.consom. 1994, commentary 185.

- reduction of the debt incurred to buy real estate to the amount of the debt that remains after the sale of that real estate;[50]
- suspension of payments (*moratoire*) for the period of at most two years;[51]
- partial discharge of debts (*effacement partiel de créances*).[52]

Discharge procedure

The discharge procedure was implemented in French law in the year 2003.[53] The problem of excessive debts of consumers was becoming more urgent and it occurred that the procedure of personal over-indebtedness did not suffice to deal with that problem. Therefore the procedure providing for swift discharge of debts of consumers was adopted.[54]

The discharge procedure is provided for those consumers who are so in debt that their situation has became beyond repair (*la situation irrémédiablement comprise*).[55] The debtor's situation is beyond repair when it is obvious that the means as provided for in the procedure of personal over-indebtedness (*recommandations*) will not suffice.

The procedure starts the same way as the procedure of personal over-indebtedness does, however should no plan be agreed on, and should the commission not find any measures to be sufficient to repair the situation of the debtor, then the bankruptcy judge can declare the opening of the discharge procedure.[56]

The bankruptcy judge appoints a provisional liquidator (*mandataire*) and orders that social research on the debtor's status and situation be conducted (*enquête social* or *suivi social*).[57]

There are three possible outcomes of the discharge procedure. Firstly the judge can decide on the payment plan, including in the plan some of

---

[50] Art. L331-7, nº 4 Code de la consommation.

[51] Art. L331-7-1 Code de la consommation.

[52] Art. L331-7-1 Code de la consommation.

[53] Act of 01.08.2003 nº 2003-710 d'orientation et de programmation pour la ville et la rénovation urbaine.

[54] Katarzyna Michalak, *Przebieg konsumenckiego postępowania upadłościowego (surendettement personnel) i postępowania prowadzącego do uwolnienia osoby fizycznej z reszty długów (retablissement personnel) we Francji*, 2 Transformacje Prawa Prywatnego 49, 74 (2008).

[55] Art. L330-1 al. 3 Code de la consommation.

[56] Katarzyna Michalak, *Przesłanki wszczęcia konsumenckiego postępowania...* 43 (2008).

[57] Art. L332-6 Code de la consommation.

the measures (*recommendations*) as provided for in the procedure of over-indebtedness.

Secondly the judge can declare the proceedings closed due to the insufficient amount of bankruptcy estate (*clôture pour insuffisance d'actif*), the decision that ensues an instant discharge of all of the debtor's debts.

Thirdly the liquidation of the bankruptcy estate can be opened and the appointed liquidator (*liquidateur*); should some amount of debts rest unpaid after the liquidation, the debtor shall be granted relief by the bankruptcy judge.

German regulation

Introduction

In German law consumer bankruptcy is regulated in the Insolvency Act (Insolvenzordnung)[58] in sections § 286 to § 310.

There are four phases of the procedure, firstly the out-of-court debt arrangement plan negotiations;[59] should the plan be not agreed on, then the second phase occurs, which means court-directed negotiations. Should the parties not achieve agreement in the court, the court adopts the plan on its own, then the third phase starts, the period during which the debtor is bound to abide by that plan (*Wohlverhaltensperiode*). The fourth phase occurs after the plan is executed; the court grants the debtor the discharge of the unpaid debts (*Restschuldbefreiung*).

The procedure is available for insolvent consumers being natural persons who do not and did not conduct independent business activity (*selbständige wirtschaftliche Tätigkeit*) and also for small businessmen with no debts arising from labour law with transparent economic situation (*überschaubar*),[60] the debtor's situation is transparent, and when debtor has no more than 20 creditors.[61]

The regulation contains the list of persons excluded from the benefits of consumer bankruptcy:

10. the person convicted of committing the insolvency crimes as regulated in the §§ 283-283c German Penal Code [62] (*Strafgesetzbuch*);[63]

---

[58] Act of 5.10.1994, (BGBl. I 2866) hereinafter referred to as InsO.
[59] § 305 (1)(1).
[60] § 304 (1) InsO.
[61] § 304 (2) InsO.
[62] § 290 (1)(a) InsO.

11. the person who within three years before filing for insolvency or afterwards intentionally committed fraud by declaring in writing unclear or untrue financial status in order to be granted credit or obtain exemption from some payment;[64]
12. the person who obtained discharge of debts within the period of ten years before filing for insolvency;[65]
13. the person who within the year before filing for insolvency or afterwards intentionally undertook actions that reduced the possibility of satisfying the creditors.[66]

Rehabilitation of the debtor – the important feature of the German regulation

German bankruptcy consumer procedure does not vary greatly from the Polish one; in fact the Polish regulation is to some extent based on the rules of the Insolvency Act. Howcvcr thc important fcaturc of thc Gcrman law is the condition of debtors receiving debt counselling, a feature that is absent in Polish law, and also the duties imposed on the debtor during the six-year period of realization of the plan. Both differences were implemented in order to rehabilitate the debtor, make him conscious of his duties vis-à-vis creditors, and ensure that he will not become excessively indebted in the future.

During the very first phase of the proceedings, the out-of-court negotiations of a debt arrangement plan, the debtor must be supported by a 'suitable person or office'.[67] In most circumstance the suitable person or office is a state-financed debt counselling centre (*Schuldnerberatungsstelle*).[68]

In debt counselling centres, the debtors are sure to receive counselling on how to develop a manageable budget, enabling some offer of compromise to the creditors.[69] Furthermore the debtors are reminded of their duty to pay the debts, by the obligation to attempt to negotiate with creditors, and also by the six-year payment plan during, which certain duties are imposed on them.

---

[63] German Penal Code (*Strafgesetzbuch*) of 1.01.1871 (BGBL. I S. 3322).
[64] § 290 (1)(b) InsO.
[65] § 290 (1)(c) InsO.
[66] § 290 (1)(d) InsO.
[67] § 305(1)(1) InsO.
[68] See Gerhard Pape, *Ein Jahr Verbraucherinsolvenz - Eine Zwischenbilanz*, 20 Zeitschrift für Wirtschaftsrecht 2037, 2040 (1999).
[69] Jason J. Kilborn, *The innovatice German approach...* 295 (2004).

The most important duty is that during the six-year period the debtor is bound to hold or actively seek any suitable employment[70] in order to be able to pay a part of his income to the creditors. Although the debtor's income during the six-year period rarely exceeds the exempt amount and therefore is of little use to the creditors, the obligation of working and earning is an important psychological device impressing on the debtor the importance of trying to pay the unpaid debts in order to earn the privilege of discharge.[71]

The very name of that six-year period – *Wohlverhaltensperiode*, can be translated as 'good behaviour period'; a fact that is quite telling. The whole proceedings are intended to educate the debtor, enable his resocialization and his re-entry into the open economy.[72]

Conclusion

Too harsh on the debtor and of no practical importance – the Polish regulation on consumer bankruptcy could be so described. The foreign solution can offer assistance in amending that law.

The American law, especially the reform as introduced in BAPCPA, shows that consumers' bankruptcy law shall contain some protection against abuse from reckless or opportunistic debtors. However such protection can be achieved by various means, not all as harsh as the current Polish regulation.

Firstly the important feature shall be providing the debtor with some kind of debt counselling and helping him create some manageable budget for the future, thus preventing him from becoming over-indebted again. Such a solution exists in the German law and to some extent also in the American law.

Secondly it seems reasonable to create a procedure for over-indebted consumers, who are not yet insolvent, for example the procedure of personal over-indebtedness as provided for in French law. A heavily indebted consumer has virtually no possibilities or hopes for a better economic situation; therefore he should be able to take some action before his situation becomes even worse, and not be forced to wait till he becomes completely insolvent.

---

[70] § 295 (1)(1) InsO.

[71] Jason J. Kilborn, *The innovatice German approach...* 291 (2004).

[72] Cf. Margaret Howard, *A Theory of Discharge in Consumer Bankruptcy*, 48 Ohio St. L. J. 1047 (1987) stating that the resocialization of the debtor is the most important goal of consumer bankruptcy.

Thirdly the solution leading to out-of-court agreement between debtor and creditors shall be encouraged in the form of direct negotiation between debtor and creditors, or in the form of a special administrative body acting as a arbiter or mediator between parties. Such measures can greatly reduce the costs of insolvency proceedings while also leading to hastening the proceedings.

Finally by imposing the duties on the debtor, his interests shall be balanced with those of the creditors, and the debtor shall not be stripped of all his property in order to satisfy the creditors. It is primarily a question of determining the extent of the exempt property. However the Polish solution forcing the debtor to move out of the apartment in order to be declared insolvent seems too harsh. The possible solution could be based on German law. Rather than being severe on the debtor's assets as existing in the day of filing for bankruptcy, the law shall force the debtor to work hard in order to pay the biggest possible part of debts in the future. Such a solution is not the vengeance of society and creditors on the insolvent debtor on the one hand, but it also does not encourage reckless or opportunistic incurring of debt on the other hand.

BACK TO THE CONTINENTAL LEGAL FAMILY? TRANSPLANTATION OF WESTERN LAW IN CIS

IRINA KHUZHOKOVA[1]

It is the aim of this paper to research general characteristics of the process of law modernization of the ex-USSR countries. The process of modernization by means of borrowing from western law is normal for post-socialist countries. New practices required the changing of not only Soviet ideology but new legislation also. So transplantation of some institutions of western law into the Russian legal system was the main reason for the developing of comparative law studies in Russia and other CIS countries. The area of my research is CIS countries' legislation between the Soviet political heritage and the influence of western laws: main models, general tracks, and analysis of the main sources for legislative borrowing, the reasons for it, the effect of borrowing, and legal results of this practice. The article asks the question why the borrowing of western law did not change the reality of Russia in many aspects, and why many western law norms were ineffective in Russia and were of no use in practice. Part 1 applies to some public law formulae (constitutional and human rights law) vested in constitutions of post-socialist countries with comparison of their meaning in western law constitutions. Part 2 applies to some institutions of private law vested in Russian Civil Code and civil legislation of CIS countries in the context of the Concept of the development of civil legislation of the Russian Federation and civil law reform.

Introduction

Soviet legal tradition in the USSR and Soviet Russia had no predecessors; the basis of Soviet tradition was only socialist ideology: the creators of Soviet law in the USSR and revolutionary Russia tried to make

[1] PhD in constitutional law, LLM in comparative law, senior researcher of the department of foreign countries civil legislation of the Institute of legislation and comparative law under the Russian Government, advocate of Moscow Bar 'Delcredere', khuzhokova@gmail.com.

something extra new, such law that has nothing in common with previous law. Perhaps the new objectives of Soviet law were constructed on the Roman-German legal system basis and by such means.

From the point of view of communist ideology, law must disappear in the developed communist society, so law was regarded as a temporary phenomenon, which is necessary for the transition period on the way of state development from the bourgeois state to communism. The goal of Soviet legislators was to be quite different from western law models in constitutional law and civil law as well. The Soviet Republic moved away from old Russian law and from all western models also. It was the first attempt to create Soviet Law over the world.

If before 1917 Russian law was, as was universally recognized, part of the Roman-German system, after 1917 some legal scholars decided that such a kinship was more than doubtful. The question was, is it possible to associate Soviet Law with the Roman-German legal system or must it be an independent legal system?

David René in his famous book[2] noted the difference between the principles of the Roman-German legal system and the principles of Soviet Law. It was the reason for regarding Soviet Russian Law as independent and breaking the ice of the Soviet legal system. In the world of western scholarship the estimation of Soviet Law was predominantly negative and the work of David René was no exception. Anyway, negative or positive, the verdict was that the 'new Soviet Russian Law has nothing in common with the Roman-German legal system'.

Now Russian official legal scholarship repudiate the 'Soviet Law family' and is trying to be in keeping with the Roman-German legal system. Western authors write about 'the death of the Soviet legal family' and socialist law[3] besides the fact that the 'Socialist legal family' never existed as the 'Bourgeois legal family'.

If in the USSR legal science the trend was 'how to combat the bourgeois nature of law and legal ideology in the Soviet republic' (the first step of V. Lenin was to abolish all old laws), nowadays the trend in Russia is comparative law[4] and the question is 'why post-socialist law very often

---

[2] David René & Camille Jauffret-Spinosi, *Les grands systèmes de droit contemporains* (10th ed. 1992).

[3] Inga Markovits, *The Death of Socialist Law?*, 3 Annual Review of Law and Social Science 233-53 (2007).

[4] In modern Russia the amount of 'comparative law centres' is comparable with the amount of such centres in the USA, and now some academics approve of the idea to include the subject 'comparative law' into the first category of law scholar specialty of the current nomenclature of scholastic specialties 'law theory and law

has no effect on real social relations'. During the last ten years many new laws, including the Constitution of Russian Federation, were enacted in Russia and the same in other CIS countries. In modern Russia we have just a few Soviet period laws;[5] some of them are partially valid still but none of them is of principal significance. Other Soviet laws were not invalided but are now forgotten and have no real force. At the same time the Soviet legal heritage is with us still because the legal tradition and legal ideology are more powerful than they usually appear.

Nowadays Russian legal scholars write about new democratic law, which is totally different from Soviet legislation. Perhaps, the effectiveness of it is very doubtful. So the only permanent characteristic of Russian law is that it is always new and 'totally different from the previous one'. Having such a short history of new law, Russian society already has experience of modernization of several legal reforms including amendments of the Constitution and reviewing of the biggest modern codification – the Russian Civil Code. I wish to note in this article only several of them which more obviously demonstrate how the previous legal ideology might manipulate the legal norms' construction and their issue.

Public Law

From the point of view of very many western lawyers, human rights did not exist in the USSR because individuals had no right to be defended against the state. As some western commentators noted, the Soviet people had no opportunity to defend themselves from the state and from the Communist party. This seems to be true. Now the Communist party has receded into the background, and nobody regards it as a serious political power. But the problem with the interpretation of human rights norms still exists.

First the Soviet Constitution contained no provisions about personal rights such as the right of personal integrity, presumption of innocence, right to privacy, etc. Basic human rights constructions were adopted by Russian constitutional law in accordance with international law models, strange as it may appear in the Stalin Constitution. Perhaps the Soviet law tradition was so powerful that some misunderstanding of western law norms still exists, not only in legal science, but in laws also. Fundamental

---

history'. In comparison to the USA, in Russia 'comparative law centres' simply have no great history and tradition, or an adequate basis for such a great ambitions.

[5] E.g., RSFSR Law About Defence and Usage of Relicts of History and Culture 1978, USSR Law About Cooperation in USSR 1988, RSFSR Law About Securing of Economic Basis of Independence of RSFSR 1990 (Consultant Plus) etc.

Law is no exception. Inorganic interpretations together with inorganic elements of norm construction were added to the norm in the Russian legal field. It was the main reason for the change of the real meaning of norm.

Wrong Interpretation

Some of the human rights in post-socialist countries, having been transplanted, were interpreted wrongly. The best example is the norm containing the right to privacy.

The Russian Federation Constitution provides that 'Everyone shall have the right to privacy, personal and family secrets, the protection of honour and good name. Everyone shall have the right to privacy of correspondence, of telephone conversations, postal, telegraph and other messages. Limitations of this right shall be allowed only by court decision'.[6] This norm is the translation of the norm of several international treaties such as the UN Convention of human rights which was ratified by the USSR. In such a way this norm was transplanted to the last USSR Constitution and to the Constitution of Russia 1993. Singly it is a classic norm that provided the right to privacy.

At the same time, the other element of this norm connected to its limitation is provided by article 56 of the Russian Federation Constitution.

Article 56 of the Russian Federation Constitution provides ‘In conditions of a state of emergency in order to ensure the safety of citizens and the protection of the constitutional system and in accordance with the federal constitutional law certain limitations may be placed on human rights and freedoms with the establishment of their framework and time period (part 1). A state of emergency may be introduced in the whole territory of the Russian Federation and in its certain parts in case there are circumstances and according to the rules fixed by the federal constitutional law (part 2). The rights and freedoms envisaged in Articles 20, 21, 23 (the first part), 24, 28, 34 (the first part), 40 (the first part), 46-54 of the Constitution of the Russian Federation, shall not be liable to limitations (part 3)’.

In context with article 56 the norm of part 1 article 23 brings new meaning in the term ‘privacy’, because according to part 3 of article 56 the right envisaged in Article 23 (part one) shall not be liable to limitations.

---

6 Constitution of Russian Federation art. 23 (1993).

At the same time the Russian Federation Constitutional Law Concerning National Emergency[7] provides that freedom of movement, freedom of enterprise, inviolability of home and private property and a wide range of other personal rights and freedoms may be limited in the case of national emergency. In this situation the legislator sees no limitation of the right to privacy. Following this logic the right to privacy is so deep inside a person that any bodies and officials have no real instruments to violate it. Quite the contrary from the original western norm's point of view, it is logical to assume that the right to privacy will be limited in the case of legal permission to search a personal automobile or conduct a body search.

Roman-German or Anglo-Saxon doctrine deals with the right to privacy as with the right which includes such a wide range of behavior[8] that the absence of its legal limitation seems to be something extraordinary. At first glance this norm of the Russian Federation may be seem as more liberal than parallel norms of international treaties. From the other side it seems to be very hard to envisage the right to privacy as an absolute right. In a nutshell it is impossible.

Obviously the main reasons for creating such a legal construction in the Russian Federation Constitution were a misunderstanding of the right to privacy that cannot be unlimited with or without the will of the state, and the desire to humanize the human rights block of the Russian Federation Constitution. Like other attempts to create something additional from western democracy, this 'reform' of the right to privacy became just idle rhetoric, having no real force. The only effect of such provision is the limitation of interpretation of the right to privacy and legal nihilism because the norm relevant to unlimited privacy cannot be realized.

The same problem occurs in the other CIS countries. The Ukrainian Constitution[9] provides limitation of judicial protection of the right to privacy that is also nonsense. The meaning of this proposal does not take into account that limitation of judicial protection cannot exist in a democratic society.

---

[7] Constitutional Law of Russian Federation About the National Emergency 30/05/2001, art. 11, 12, 13.

[8] Samuel Warren & Lois Brandeis, *The Right To Privacy*, 4 Harvard Law Review 193 (1890); Allan Westin, *Privacy and freedom* 50-67 (5th ed. 1968).

[9] Constitution of the Republic of Ukraine Art. 32, art. 64.

Amendments

The main source material for constitutional norms in Russia was the US Constitution. As usual, Russian legislators added some 'Russian specifics' to the western proposals. Changing of western originals was direct and indirect.

Regarding direct changes, the Russian Constitution was amended twice, firstly to prolong the term of office for the Russian President (from 4 years to 6) and the Duma (from 4 years to 5), and secondly to impose the obligation of the Federal Government to present a report of its work before the Duma annually.[10] The American original (4 years) was transformed into post-socialist familiarity (six years). The same tendency is evident in Belarus[11] and other CIS countries.

By the referendum of 2002 in Uzbekistan the term of office of the President was extended to seven years. In Kazakhstan the President has no limits to prevent running for the presidency several times consecutively. In such a situation the extension of this period from five to seven years is irrelevant.

Indirectly changing of constitutional norms was reached by creation of new administrative bodies and officials and concentrating more power in the President's hands.

I have assumed that indirectly, transformation of legal norms and its ignorance, is more likely to violate human rights than the direct changing of laws. Now 'Corruption has become our Constitution, and irresponsibility for it is our every day practice'.[12]

Transformation of civil norms

The Civil Code tradition is a principal element of the Roman-German legal system, and codification is the most important process in continental

[10] Russian Law About Amendment to the Russian Federation Constitution 'About Changing ot the Term of Office of Russian President and State Duma' 2008, Russian Law About Amendment to Russian Federal Constitution 'About State Duma Power to Control Federal Government' 2008 (Consultant Plus).

[11] By Referendum in Belorussia the term of office of Belorussian President was changed from 4 years to 5 years. In 2004 in Belarus the norm about the impossibility to hold the office of President twice was removed from the Constitution.

[12] Victor V. Luneev, Questions of criminal legal science, 5 State and Law 41.

law.[13] Continental countries had Corpus Juris Civilis to start with. The Code of Napoleon was a very important step. The Civil Code of Napoleon was transplanted to many countries including not only such European countries as Luxemburg and Belgium, but also Quebec and Louisiana in North America, Chad and the other ex-colonies of France in Africa. Despite the sameness of the Code's text, even in European countries the interpretation of this text is different. Judges of France, Luxemburg, and Belgium also interpret the norms of Code Napoleon differently.[14] Inside the Roman-German legal system interpretation of the Code is not uniform.

Soviet codes willingly or not, partly borrowed the norms of western civil codes, and in part constructed their own legal phenomenon. Some of them were somewhat extraordinary in the Roman-German law tradition.

From the early '90s the legislative machine was activated and several books of the new Code of Russia were soon enacted.

Now all the independent countries of ex-USSR have their own civil codes. Because of the status of modern economic relationships all codes were adopted extremely soon after the destruction of the USSR. Legislators of the CIS countries had a very limited choice at that moment; the issue of this choice was transplantation of western law (first choice) or transplantation of western law with Soviet law elements (second choice).

In the sphere of civil law the opinion about the 'very special Russian way' became the basis for choosing a second round of Russian legal development. Not surprisingly the norms of the Russian Civil Code were transplanted to the other CIS countries.

Transplantation of civil codes is the most popular kind of transplantation of law the world over. As previously noted, the best example of this is the story of the French Civil Code[15] and its acceptance by countries of Europe and Africa as well. The French Civil Code being the first modern civil code in world legal history still applies in Luxemburg and Belgium in Europe and was the model for the application of civil law in very many others (e.g. Germany and The Netherlands). The track of transplantation was from French Civil Code to Bürgerliches Gesetzbuch (BGB) and from BGB to Nederlands Burgerlijk Wetboek[16]

---

[13] John Henry Merryman, *The Civil Law Tradition. An Introduction to the Legal Systems of Western Europe and Latin America*, 58-59 (2nd ed. 1996).

[14] About transformation of civil codes as a result of borrowing, see Rémy Cabrilla, *Les codifications* (2002).

[15] See *Code civil. Version consolidée au 6 février* (2011).

[16] See *Niew Nederlands Burgerlijk Wetboek Het Vermogensrecht (Zahenrecht, Verbintenissenrecht en bijzondere overeenkomsten* 5 – 15 (1990).

(BW). It is no news that BW became a model for the creation of the Civil Code of the Russian Federation.

The reason of transplantation of BW in Russia was simple and subjective as well. In the '90s the Russian Government needed to create a new civil code to engage the new economic environment of the country, so they asked for help from western countries and (I suppose with connection to art. 90 of The Netherland's Constitution)[17] The Netherlands was first to answer.

That is why Russian reformers decided to elaborate the civil norms of the Dutch Civil Code to adopt new civil norms for Russian reality. No surprise that the main source of norms relating to 'Russian reality' was the norms of Soviet civil legislation.

The result of such creative work was not efficient law. In the period of enforcement of the Russian Civil Code from 1994 till now, 46 federal laws were enacted to correct some norms of the Code.[18] Some of these amendments contain several norms connected to general provisions and also other principle norms.

Now the revision of Russian Civil Code is starting again. The concept of Development of Civil Legislation[19] was prepared to remove faulty norms. This Concept, perhaps, includes some corrections to repair legislators' mistakes and to return to the original Dutch text.

Bringing to light the differences between the original Dutch version of the Civil Code, Russian Civil Code text and provisions of the Concept will reveal the issue of the legislation framework of Russian reformers. Let us examine several of the most principal provisions to determine what was newly added to the Dutch Code in its Russian version. They are public policy and contra bona mores doctrine, legal customs, and bona fides doctrine.

Public policy and contra bones mores doctrine

Public policy and bona mores doctrine is a traditional institution of the Continental legal system beginning from Ancient Rome.

---

[17] See Grondwet voor het Koninkrijk der Nederlanden art. 90 'De regering bevordert de ontwikkeling van de internationale rechtsorde' (The Government shall promote the development of international legal order).

[18] Federal Laws of Russian Federation 20.02.1996, 12.08.1996, 08.07.1999, 16.04.2001, 15.05.2001 etc. (Comsultant Plus).

[19] *Conception of Development of Civil Legislation*, 11 Vestnik Visshego Arbitrajnogo Suda RF (2009).

Article 169 of the Russian Civil Code provides that a transaction concluded for a purpose knowingly contrary to the fundamental principles of legal order or morality shall be void. When both parties to such transaction have intent – in the event of performance of the transaction by both parties – everything received by them under the transaction shall be forfeit to the revenue of the Russian Federation, and in the event of the performance of the transaction by one party, everything received shall be forfeit to the revenue of Russian Federation from the other party and everything due from it to the first party in compensation of that received. When only one party of such a transaction has intent, everything received by it under the transaction must be returned to the other party, and everything received by the last or due to it in compensation of that performed shall be forfeit to the revenue of the Russian Federation.[20]

The rule has been much criticized as being divorced from commercial reality. Generally speaking, the state has no right to take citizens' property, and delict is not a criminal case in which to do it. Russian judges were confused by this norm, and tried to apply it in tax litigation.

Law custom

Article 5 of the Russian Civil Code provides that a custom of business turnover shall be deemed to be a rule of behaviour, which has been formed and extensively applied in any domain of entrepreneurial activity and is not provided for the legislation irrespective of whether it has been fixed in any document. In any words legal custom is recognized as the source of law only in commercial practice.

Now matters have changed. The Concept of Development of Civil Legislation proposes changes via recognition of not only commercial customs as a source of law. This idea also is not new, and existed 20 years ago in western codes. Why was it renounced by the Russian legislator 20 years ago? The odds are that in post-USSR reality customs did not exist. But the goal of the post-USSR legislator was not to state what legal institution exists or does not exist: the legislator had the obligation to create things which were needed, but did not exist.

---

[20] See William E. Butler (ed.), *Civil Code of the Russian Federation. Parts 1, 2 and 3. Parallel Russian and English Texts status juris: 10 Novenber 2007* 151, 152 (2008).

Bona fides doctrine

In contradiction to so many European codes, the Russian Civil Code does not contain any general provision requiring parties to act in good faith. On the date of transplantation of Dutch civil norms in Russia, the good faith doctrine of course was provided by the Dutch legislator. As it seems, the reason to rule out this provision is in fact that good faith is the simplest of notions in the abstract but more difficult to apply in reality. In other words the main reason, as it seems, was to discredit Russian judges from the point of view of the Russian legislator.

The Concept of Development of Civil Legislation provides the necessity of including good faith. This step to appreciate proposals about good faith in other western codes, was possible almost 20 years ago.

Movable and immovable things

In accordance with Article 130 of the Russian Civil Code, to immovable things shall be relegated land plots, subsoil plots, and all that is firmly connected with the land. To immovable things also shall be relegated aircraft and sea-going vessels subject to State registration, vessels of internal navigation, and space objects.[21]

The Concept of Developing Civil Legislation proposes the exclusion of aircraft and sea-going vessels subject to State registration, vessels of internal navigation, and space objects from the category 'immovable things'. It is assumed that the current position of the Russian Civil Code will be reversed via legislative procedure. Perhaps it was a great opportunity to create the right rule in the '90s because the Dutch Civil Code contained these 'new' provisions about immovability from its birth. Article 3.33 of Book 3 provides that 'immovable' are the land, the not yet mined minerals, the plants connected with the land, and the buildings and constructions permanently attached to the land, either directly or through a connection with other buildings or constructions.

Amendments to the Russian Civil Code should be in force in the near future, but obviously Russian civil law is going to be under construction for a long season.

All these examples show attempts firstly (1) to fit western norms to 'Russian reality' taking part in a legislative experiment, and secondly (2) to return to the original meaning of civil norms. I would like to doubt the expedience of such kind of attempts. Nobody can determine what 'Russian

---

[21] See William E. Butler (ed.), *Civil Code...* 129, 130 (2008).

reality' is and whether it is this reality that the legislator suggests. Judicial practice shows that our judges are out of step with 'Russian reality': they have no idea how to apply art. 169 of the Russian Civil Code. Could it sometimes be better to change some reality instead of changing a classic civil norm via including in it detrimental or out-to-date constructions? Especially in the case if 'reality' is the violation of civil law principles, and is not in the interest of the population and market players.

Socialistic/Post-socialistic Legal System?

In spite of differences between Russian and German, Russian and Dutch, Russian and French law there is no reason to single out the Socialist or post-Socialistic legal system as independent. Only one principal argument was posited, this argument is that Socialist and post-socialist law have an addition of Marxist ideology. However most authors confirm that Socialist law is primarily based on the Roman-German system.[22]

Really, with such a context, it is hardly possible to imagine Socialist law based on the Anglo-Saxon legal system, too many elements of which are principally different from Socialist law and its normative structure. It also seems simply to prove that all the achievements of Socialist law were ignored by the Anglo-Saxon law system. The best example is the story of non-recognition of collective rights in USA. The fact of negation of such collective rights as cultural rights and others does not mean that in the USA people have no ability to protect themselves, it means that they have no ability to do it by such a method as using 'collective rights'. Many aspects of continental 'collective rights' in USA are protected as a right to privacy and by other legal means.

A different portion for collective rights was written on the Continent. Collective rights were adopted by public international law through implementation by international agreements and by national constitutional law of European countries. This concept was not wholly un-European.

It must be recognized that, despite all reasonable criticism, the endowments of legal rethinking were useful upon a fair balance. The output of this rethinking was a new generation of human rights, and afterwards the development of European law.

---

[22] John Quigley, *Socialist Law and the Civil Law Tradition*, 7 American Journal of Comparative Law 787 (1989).

To determine what is Socialist law and whether the Socialist legal system exists is it necessary to determine what law is, and what a legal system is.

To my way of thinking the most important components of a legal system are legal style, character of sources of law, instrumentation of legal construction and legal philosophy.

In questions of law sources, legal style, code systems as legal style Socialist law looks totally closed to the Roman-German legal system and quite different from the Anglo-Saxon legal system.

The legal philosophy of Socialist law also is primarily based on a branch of German positivism philosophy. The main methodology of all national Socialist legal systems and Socialist legal science is ultra positivism.

Being a militant atheist Socialistic legislator was more closed to Canon Law in the methodology of law construction than to the Anglo-Saxon law system law-makers.

Atheistic legal constructions are wholly based on the direct effect of laws without any possibility of recognition or non-recognition of this law by courts.

Socialist law is just law used in Socialist states including the CIS countries. Some of them have had a Traditional legal system (such as several Caucasus republics became members of the USSR), some of them have used the Roman-German legal system (such as Russia) before they were incorporated into one legal system following Roman-German formal criteria. In the case of legal system, the term 'formal criteria' is demonstrable more than formal. Formality of law, legal philosophy and legal style is an issue of legal system that may be determined via formal characteristics.

The phrase 'death of Socialist law' is the equivalent of the phrase 'death of Roman law'. This kind of death never happened and never will happen because every legal phenomenon of such scale never disappeared but transformed because law includes social relations and influence. States may fragment, and regimes or ideologies may change, but legal tradition is something that exists and has more or less influence irrespective of these facts.

Conclusion

At this time comparative law is the trend in Russia and other CIS countries. But the fact of the matter is that the role of most CIS countries in the world process of law elaboration is within the field of mechanical transplantation of western law or creation of new legal constructions via the association of Socialist law elements with western law elements without any true understanding of the issue.

Dissonance between Russian norms and western law cannot be comprehensible through the disengagement of Soviet and post Socialist law from the Roman-German legal system. This problem is a problem of law culture and efficiency of law transplantation. In the Soviet system basic principles of western law were reversed. But it does not mean that Russian law moved from the Roman-German legal system in 1917.

The best examples of membership of Socialist law in the Roman-German legal family are the characters of legal sources and connections between the law of the USSR and the Continent in the Soviet period. By now proposals of modern international and European law about social rights are based on revolutionary history of the Soviet state.

Modern Russian law has a multitude of problems, inside and outside of law. They include corruption, legal nihilism, undeveloped democratic institutions, languorous condition of legal scholarship, etc. But none of them are reasons to exclude Russia and the other CIS countries from the Roman-German legal system. Connections between the law of Socialist Russia and the development of European law prove that rethinking of human rights has nothing in common with a change of legal system.

The main difference between Socialist Russia and modern Russian law is that if Socialist law brought new elements to international public law and national laws of continental countries (such as social rights, development of labour law, etc.) the contribution of post-socialist legal science in world legal development is feeble.

NON-TRANSFERABILITY AND NON-HERITABILITY OF A SERVITUDE OF HABITATION: DE LEGE FERENDA POSTULATES

ADAM BIERANOWSKI

UNIVERSITY OF WARMIA AND MAZURY IN OLSZTYN, POLAND

Introduction

The importance of habitation reveals itself in many facets. Not only does a habitation satisfy basic human needs but it also facilitates an intellectual, family as well as social and cultural development. Simultaneously, it caters for an individual's right to privacy.

The legislator gives a great variety of legal tools to fulfil such needs. A right of habitation may take the form of a servitude of habitation.

The institution of a servitude of habitation is often underestimated. Milzer depicts it in the following way: "Der Gedanke an dinglich gesicherte Wohnrechte mag bei manchem Juristen Assoziationen mit Filzpantoffeln und Gelsenkirchener Barock hervorrufen. Wohnrechte stehen daher nicht im Brennpunkt der rechtswissenschaftlichen Diskussion. Die jüngste, im neuesten Palandt zu der Bestimmung des § 1093 BGB nachgewiesene Entscheidung des BGH datiert aus dem Jahre 1968 Dessen ungeachtet hat die Bestellung von Wohnrechten in der täglichen Beurkundungspraxis eine nicht zu unterschätzende quantitative Bedeutung".[1] Expressing a standpoint that the issue of a servitude of habitation is also of great importance in Polish law, it must be stressed that from the perspective of observing legal transactions, this institution is widely used in practice, not only in the countryside, but in cities too (due to the popularization of ownership of premises).

---

[1] Lutz Milzer, *Varianten von dinglichen Wohnrechten*, 7 Zeitschrift für das Notariat in Baden - Württemberg 136 (2005).

The issue of a servitude of habitation is multi-threaded and wide.[2] The aim of this study is to look for an optimal normative shape of a servitude of habitation from the perspective of two features: non-transferability and non-heritability.

Comparative outline

German law

Within the territory of the German Reich a property right of habitation (*das dingliche Wohnrecht*), as a result of adopting a Roman and German institution by particular national laws, existed in various forms. Apart from those originating from Roman Law, in Bavarian landrecht a right of habitation existed, which was an example of a real burden, for instance in a situation in which a noble clerk was granted a free dwelling as part of remuneration.[3] Moreover, as an institution of a right to build up a plot, a property right of habitation was created within the territory where Prussian landrecht was in force. It was debatable whether *superficies* should be regarded as *ius in re aliena*, or if a holder under *superficies* is vested with *dominium utile* on the foreign land.[4]

The basis for regulating a right of habitation in the BGB was the assumption that it had to be an essence of a restricted personal servitude. It corresponds more or less to *habitatio* of subsequent Roman law.[5]

As a restricted personal servitude, a property right of habitation is not transferable (§ 1092.1, § 1093.1.1 of the BGB). Consequently, a servitude of habitation, as a matter of principle, may not be seised (§§ 851, 857.3 of the ZPO).[6] Pursuant to § 1093.2 of the BGB, in their dwelling a holder is entitled to admit into their residence their family and the people required for service befitting his attendance and for care. The notion of family in this provision was used in the way it operates in colloquial language. Therefore, one should not refer to a narrow juridical definition of a

---

[2] More information Adam Bieranowski, *Służebność mieszkania* (2011).

[3] Paul von Roth, *Bayrisches Zivilrecht* 155 (2nd ed., 1881) cited by Wolfgang Fricke, *Über das dingliche Wohnrecht* 8 (1998).

[4] Wolfgang Fricke, *Über das dingliche...* 11 (1998).

[5] *Ibid.*, 13; cf. Albert Rainer, *Das dingliche Wohnungsrecht, Unterhaltungspflicht und Aufwendungsersatz* 6,7 (1996).

[6] Hartmut Schöner et al., *Grundbuchrecht* 462 (1989).

family.[7] The Federal Court of Justice of Germany (BGH) in the judgement of 07.05.1982, V ZR 58/81 decided that the notion of family used in § 1093.2 of the BGB may be extended to cohabitations.[8]

Use of a dwelling by third parties not included in § 1093.2 of the BGB is possible only when an owner gives permission in accordance with § 1092.2 of the BGB. Such permission does not require a special form. It may even be expressed in an implicit way.[9] For the permission to be effective for a subsequent owner, an entry in the Land and Mortgage Register is indispensable.

Since a right of habitation is not heritable, it ends with the death of the holder (see § 1090.2 and § 1061 of the BGB). If it is established for jointly entitled spouses, the right terminates upon the death of the surviving spouse.[10]

---

[7] Claus Ahrens, *Dingliche Nutzungsrechte. Niessbrauch. Dienstbarkeiten. Wohnungsrechte* 209 (2004); Hartmut Schöner et al., *Grundbuchrecht* 460 (1989); Peter Bassenge in *Palandt Bürgerliches Gesetzbuch* 1233 (1996).

[8] Bundesgerichtshof, *Entscheidungen in Zivilsachen* 84, 36. Such a standpoint was earlier expressed (without an extensive justification) by AG Ahrensburg in the decision of December 19th, 1979, MDR (936) 1980. As Karl Eckhart Heinz notices, Ist der Inhaber eines dinglichen Wohnungsrecht befugt, die Partnerin einer nichtehelichen Lebensgemeinschaft in die Wohnung aufzunehmen, Zeitschrift für das gesamte Familienrecht 763ff. (1982) a commented point of view of the BGH reveals a drastic misunderstanding of the meaning and purpose of the provision of § 1093.2 of the BGB and shows engagement in abolishing differences between marriage and cohabitation, the latter being perceived as a 'more progressive' form of a sexual partnership. According to the author it is often forgotten that marriage as a legal institution is one of the greatest cultural achievements. In this context he considers the BGH judgement to be a fatal contribution to legal policy. A critical approach towards the said decision was also taken by Rolf Stürner, *Anmerkung zu BGH, Urteil vom Mai 7th, 1982, V ZR 58/81*, Zeitschrift für das gesamte Familienrecht 775 (1982). Compare the Life Partnership Act of December 16th, 2001 (Lebenpartnerschaftsgesetz) BGB1.IS.266.

[9] The issue is more widely discussed by Wolfgang Schmidt-Futterer, *Die Ausübung eines dinglichen Wohnrechts durch Dritte*, Zeitschrift für Miet- und Raumrecht 163-164 (1967); see also Heike Kroll, *Das dingliche Wohnungsrecht im Verhältnis zum Mietrecht* 31 (2004); Peter Bassenge in *Palandt Bürgerliches Gesetzbuch* 1233 (1996). Judicial decisions express a standpoint that such permission – in the context of a supplementary interpretation of a contract – does not reflect a hypothetical will of the parties, see the judgement of the BGH of January 9th, 2009- V ZR 168/ 07, 4 Zeitschrift für NotarPraxis 147-149 (2009).

[10] Hermann J. Fassbender, *Das dingliche Wohnungsrecht für mehrere als Gesamtberechtigte nach § 428 BGB* 671, Deutsche Notar-Zeitschrift (1965);

Swiss law

Swiss doctrine distinguishes real servitudes and personal servitudes. Personal servitudes are divided into regular (*Eigentliche*) and irregular (*Irreguläre*). Regular servitudes are non-transferable, whereas irregular ones are heritable and transferable.[11] A right of habitation can only exist in the form of a regular personal servitude.[12]

Basic features of a servitude of habitation were normatively expressed in Section 776.2 of the ZGB. The said provision excludes *expressis verbis* transferability and heritability of this right ('Es ist unübertragbar und unvererblich'). The relationship between these two features was highlighted by M. Heinz. He emphasized that if a servitude of habitation were transferable, the provision of its being non-heritable would become ineffective. It would be annulled by every transfer of this right.[13] Such 'perpetual burdens' would result in a servitude of habitation not being established at all.[14]

A servitude of habitation cannot be seised and cannot be encumbered with usufruct or a pledge. According to doctrine and judicial decisions it is impermissible to circumvent the prohibition on transferability by establishing an irregular servitude under Article 781 of the ZGB.[15]

Prima facie a violation of a nonheritability principle may seem to be a so-called successive exercise of the right. The nature of this figure lies in establishing a servitude of habitation to the benefit of two or more people in such a way that one of them holds this right until their death, then the

---

Johann Bader, *Zum dinglichen Wohnungsrecht gemäß § 1093 BGB an denselben Räumen für mehrere Personen*, Deutsche Notar-Zeitschrift (1965).

[11] Hans Michael Riemer, *Die beschränkten dinglichen Rechte. Grundriss des schweizerischen Sachenrechts* 43, 46 (1986); Heinz Marx, *Das dingliche Wohnrecht* 11 (1970); Peter Tuor et al. in Id. et al., *Das schweizerische Zivilgesetzbuch* 937 (2002).

[12] Hans Michael Riemer, *Die beschränkten dinglichen Rechte...* 46 (1986); Manfred Zobl, *Der zulässige Inhalt von Dienstbarkeiten* 21 (1976).

[13] *Ibid.*, 16.

[14] *Ibid.*

[15] Heinz Rey, *Funktionen des Dienstbarkeitsvertrages*, 5 Schweizerische Zeitschrift für Beurkundungs-und Grundbuchrecht (hereinafter ZBGR) 262-263 (1983); Peter Tuor et al. in Id. et al., *Das schweizerische...* 959 (2002).; see also judgements of the Federal Supreme Court of Switzerland of September 29th, 1977, *Entscheidungen des Schweizerischen Bundesgerichts* (hereinafter BGE) 103 II 176 and of September 20th, 1990, BGE 116 II 281; Adam Bieranowski, *Służebność mieszkania w prawie szwajcarskim*, 3 Kwartalnik Prawa Prywatnego 685 (2011).

second, then the third, etc.[16] In this case it is required that all the persons entitled be already born and that a basic legal transaction defines all of them as entitled.[17] It has been stated accurately in the Swiss doctrine that a successive exercise of this right does not violate the non-heritability principle since the right of the second person entitled does not come from the first holder, but directly from the person who established a servitude. A servitude can never last longer than until the death of the longest-lived holder.[18]

In contrast to cantonal acts, no explicit prohibition on transferring the exercise of a servitude of habitation has been included in the ZGB. The analysis of codificational materials does not reveal which motives the legislator took into consideration while introducing such a provision. It can be only assumed that the legislator considered an explicit regulation to be necessary.[19] This gives rise to certain ambiguities. Although both doctrine and jurisprudence are of the opinion that a servitude of habitation is absolutely nontransferable, even in its exercise, significant differences regarding this standpoint have appeared. E. Huber, C. Wieland and H. Leemann derive the prohibition on transferring the exercise of a servitude of habitation from Article 777 of the ZGB. From subsection 1 of this Article reading: 'Das Wohnrecht wird im allgemeinen nach den persönlichen Bedürfnissen des Berechtigten bemessen' they conclude that the holder – subject to Article 777.2 of the ZGB – is allowed to exercise a right of habitation only personally. The above reasoning has attracted criticism. It has been emphasized that Article 777 of the ZGB refers only to the scope of a right of habitation.[20] Neither subsection 1 nor subsection 2 of said Article refers to the issue discussed here. The analysis of Article 776.2 of the ZGB leads to similar observations. The Article contains only the impermissibility of a transfer of the right. An ordinary leaving of the right to be exercised is not a transfer of this right and as such does not undergo the aforementioned regulation.

As M. Heinz relevantly emphasizes, answers to the question of whether a servitude of habitation may be transferred to be exercised

---

[16] Heinz Marx, *Das dingliche...* 65 (1970).

[17] *Ibid.,* 65.

[18] *Ibid.*

[19] *Ibid.,* 15.

[20] Heinz Marx, *Das dingliche...* 15 (1970); The above-mentioned author also pointed out Leemann's inconsistence when he defined non-transferability of a right of habitation (derived from Article 777 of the ZGB) as absolute whereas in a different place he claimed that the norm of Article 777 of the ZGB is of dispositive nature.

should be sought within a broader context by placing deliberations within the system of servitudes.[21] Regular personal servitudes (*Die eingentlichen Personaldienstbarkeiten*) are *ex definitione* inseparably connected with the holder. The legislator rejected this principle in the case of usufruct and allowed transferability of its exercise in the provision of Article 758.1 of the ZGB. Following this principle, regarding specific personal servitudes are used in relation to a right of habitation due to a lack of an explicit regulation. The feature of their inseparable connection with a holder irrevocably decides about non-transferability of the exercise of a servitude of habitation.

As opposed to ordinary usufruct, it is not allowed to transfer, even in the form of an obligation, the exercise of a right of habitation. However, under Article 777.2 of the ZGB it may be extended to family members and people employed in the household.[22]

Other foreign legal systems

A right of habitation has been regulated in Book II, Title III of Usufruct, of Use and Habitation of the French Civil Code in Articles 625 - 635. A right of use and of habitation have been jointly regulated in Chapter II. A right of habitation is, in turn, tightened in comparison with a right of use. It is stated in doctrine that a right of habitation is a right of use which is restricted to a habitation to satisfy needs of a holder and their family and undergoes the same principles as a right of use. [23] Consequently, a right of habitation is a narrowed right of use (*un petit droit d'usage*).[24]

One of the characteristics of use, is transferability. Nonetheless, it disappears upon the death of the first user and not his/her legal successor. Owing to its strictly personal character a right of use is not transferable, it may not be leased, and it does not undergo execution. A holder may live there with his family, even if he was not married at the time when that right was granted to him (see Article 632 of the French Civil Code). Under

---

[21] See *Ibid.*

[22] Hans Michael Riemer, *Die beschränkten dinglichen Rechte...* 67 (1986); Heinz Marx, *Das dingliche...* 50 (1970); BGE 52 II 136.

[23] Under Article 633 of the French Civil Code 'A right of habitation is restricted to what is necessary for the habitation of the person to whom that right is granted, and of his family'. See also Sophie Schiller, *Droit des biens* 149 (2005); Erwin Beysen, *Frankreich* in Christian von Bar (ed.) *Sachenrecht in Europa. Systematische Einführung und Gesetzestexte* 253 (2001).

[24] Philippe Malaurie & Laurent Aynés, *Droit civil. Les biens* 277 (2005).

Article 634 of the French Civil Code a right of habitation may not be transferred or leased. This solution is justified by a strictly personal nature of a right of habitation.[25]

Title V Book III of the Italian Civil Code includes the regulation of usufruct, use and habitation. The major part of this regulation refers to usufruct (Article 978-1020 of the Italian Civil Code). Provisions of Articles 1022 – 1026 of the Italian Civil Code are devoted to a right of use and habitation. The first of these articles indicates the nature of a right of habitation, whereas Article 1022 of the Italian Civil Code deals with a right of habitation. Under this article he who has a right of habitation may live in it within the scope limited to his needs and the needs of his family. In doctrine, discussions are conducted about the issue of whether a right of habitation is created to be a separate property right or whether if is a subtype of a right of use or a right of usufruct.

Pursuant to Article 1024 of the Italian Civil Code, a right of use and habitation are not transferable and they may not be leased. Non-transferability is a specific feature which distinguishes a right of habitation (and a right of use) from usufruct. Some authors (De Martino) justified the mentioned prohibition by referring to a historical and social function 'of a strictly alimony nature' (*strettamente alimentare*) attributed to this right. This reasoning is thought to be unconvincing. It is considered to be inadequate particularly in relation to a right of use (see Article 1021 of the Italian Civil Code), since it is assumed that a holder of a legal title may perform all acts related to using a house for economic purposes as long as he/she does not have it at his/her disposal in a legal sense (Palermo).[26] Apart from transferring and leasing other acts leading to any voluntary or compulsory transfer of a thing (property) for example a mortgage, are forbidden.[27]

Article 3: 226.1 of the Dutch Civil Code refers to a proper application of principles regarding usufruct (vruchtgebruik) to a right of use (recht van gebruik) and a right of habitation (recht van bewoning), excluding provisions defined in subsections 2-4. Subsection 2 of said article contains the characteristics of a right of use. The nature of a right of habitation is expressed in subsection 3. It states that the essence of this right is a holder's entitlement to live with their family in a habitation subordinate to

---

[25] Sophie Schiller, *supra*.

[26] This standpoint is cited by Paolo Cendon, *Commentario al Codice Civile, Volume terzo, artt. 810 – 1172* n. 344 (1999).

[27] More examples in *Ibid.*

their right. A right of habitation has a strictly personal nature.[28] Under Subsection 4 it is impossible to transfer or encumber such a right.[29]

Polish law – key issues

In Polish law a servitude of habitation was formed as a specific type of a personal servitude. It is therefore – in accordance with Article 300.1 of the Civil Code - non-transferable (*quoad ius*). Both a preliminary agreement proceeding the establishment of a transferable servitude of habitation as well as an agreement establishing a transferable servitude of habitation and an agreement obliging to transfer a servitude of habitation and a dispositive agreement for a transfer of this right are null and void.[30] It is also impermissible to reserve legal succession (apart from exceptions stipulated in Article 301 § 2 of the Civil Code). For instance, the establishment of a servitude of habitation for the benefit of person A and their legal successor.[31] As a rule, the nullity of a provision stipulating the succession of a servitude will not extend over the whole agreement.

Nonetheless, there are no obstacles to establish a servitude of habitation: 1) for the benefit of A on condition subsequent, and 2) pending on condition precedent for the benefit of person B. It is stated in German doctrine that a similar outcome may be achieved if an agreement for the benefit of a third party is used (see § 328 of the BGB).[32]

A change of holder may not be achieved in a devious way by transferring a claim to establish a servitude of habitation resulting from, for instance, a bequest or another obligation relationship.[33] If the very servitude of habitation is non-transferable, then the claim to establish this right should suffer the same fate.

---

[28] Henricus J. Snijders & Eline B. Rank-Berenschot, *Goederenrecht* 538 (2007).

[29] To compare, usufruct may be transferred and encumbered without changing a duration of this right and an holder and the first user are jointly and severally liable for all obligations arising from usufruct towards the main holder. (Article 223.1 and 2 of the Dutch Civil Code).

[30] Adam Bieranowski, *Służebność mieszkania* 90, 91 (2011).

[31] The same in German jurisprudence and judicial decisions, see for instance OLG Dűseldorf, RPfleger 297 (2001).

[32] See Klaus Urlich Schmolke, *Der Grundsatz der Nichtübertragbarkeit beschränkter persönlicher Dienstbarkeiten aus rechtsvergleichender und rechtsökonomischer Perspektive*, 208 Archiv für die zivilistische Praxis 518 (2008).

[33] German doctrine presents a firm standpoint against the permissibility of transferring an obligation claim to establish a personal servitude (although the justification is not uniform); see *Ibid.*, 520.

However, a holder of a servitude of habitation is allowed to renounce his right since the concept of non-transferability of a personal servitude does not contain a loss of this right by a unilateral legal act.

A servitude of habitation may not be encumbered by a lien or usufruct.

Unlikely usufruct, the legislator excluded a possibility to transfer the entitlement to exercise personal servitudes (*quoad usum*).[34] Nevertheless, certain people may be admitted into a habitation (Article 301 § 1 of the Civil Code).

Dogmatically, non-heritability of a servitude of habitation arises from the termination of personal servitudes with the holder's death at the latest (compare Article 299 of the Civil Code).

This principle is not violated by a successive exercise of servitude since the right of the second holder does not derive from the first holder, but directly from the person who has created this servitude. Servitude may never last longer than until the death of the longest-lived holder.[35]

The Civil Code allows a possibility to arrange that after the death of a holder of a servitude of habitation the right will be held by his/her children, parents or spouse (Article 301 § 2 of the Civil Code).[36]

De lege ferenda postulates – relaxing the straightjacket of a servitude of habitation

The above observations make one consider if there are some particular reasons for relaxing a ban on transferring a servitude of habitation. Therefore, firstly, it is essential to present arguments against transferability of personal servitudes in general. This will help to examine a justification of a departure from perceiving a servitude of habitation as a non-transferable right.

Jurisprudence mentions three circumstances that contest a departure from the prohibition on transferring personal servitudes. The first crowning argument refers to the nature of personal servitudes. According to a prevailing standpoint they focus on satisfying the holder's personal needs and are based on trust between an owner of an encumbered real property and a holder of servitude. Secondly, what is exposed is a lack of a need to establish personal servitudes as transferable rights. Finally, it is

---

[34] More Adam Bieranowski, *Służebność mieszkania* 101ff. (2011).

[35] Heinz Marx, *Das dingliche...* 65 (1970); Adam Bieranowski, *Służebność mieszkania* 170ff. (2011).

[36] As for this construction, see Adam Bieranowski, *supra* 156ff.

underlined that the permissibility of transferring personal servitudes makes them perpetual.[37]

Let us therefore verify whether non-transferability of personal servitudes is a constitutive element of the relation between an owner and a holder. The first of the arguments mentioned, which speaks for creating a servitude of habitation as a non-transferable right, is considerably easier to refute since the norm of Article 298 of the Civil Code, which requires that the scope of a personal servitude as well as the way it is exercised while taking into account the holder's personal needs be defined, is of dispositive nature.[38] It does not mean that a personal servitude is a right which may be created freely within the autonomy of parties' will. The legislator gives only a certain amount of elbow room to define the scope and way of exercising the right more precisely. However, the conclusion that 'personal needs' of the holder always have to play the most decisive role would be far-reaching. Following this line of thinking the prohibition on transferring personal servitudes should be viewed as an expression of the legislator's positive solution not anchored in the nature of this right.[39] Nonetheless, in view of *de lege ferenda* it is postulated that the point of the argument resting on the nature of the right weakens since the legislator may stipulate it by a certain legislative resolution.

Let us move on to considering whether a lack of a practical need to create this right differently advocates retaining the prohibition on transferring personal servitudes. This argument can be easily rebutted on the grounds of German law. In German judicial decisions there are examples of disclosing in the Land and Mortgage Register a claim to establish a personal servitude for the benefit of the original holder's legal successor.[40] Apart from other reasons, it proves an economic usefulness of establishing a personal servitude as a transferable right. In Polish judicial decisions and notarial practice there are no similar examples, which however does not mean that such a need does not exist (e.g. to maintain priority) or that it may not appear (e.g. in cooperative housing construction). Primacy must be given to the usefulness of a certain legal

---

[37] These arguments are quoted in reference to restricted personal servitudes and polemised with by Klaus Urlich Schmolke, *Der Grundsatz der Nichtübertragbarkeit...* 517 (2008).

[38] In German doctrine see Klaus Urlich Schmolke, *Der Grundsatz der Nichtübertragbarkeit...* 526 (2008).

[39] The same in the case of usufruct Wolfgang Schön, *Der Nießbrauch an Sachen: gesetzliche Struktur und rechtsgeschäftliche Gestaltung* 238-239 (1992).

[40] Referred to by Klaus Urlich Schmolke, *supra* 528.

institution for legal transactions and not to faithfulness to its traditional formulation.

While evaluating the last argument it should be stressed that endowing a personal servitude with a feature of transferability would permanently deprive an owner of entitlements constituting his right. In fact, an owner would be left with a bare right (*ius nudum*). However, such 'perpetual' constructions of real rights are known to Polish law. It is not alien to usufruct established for the benefit of a legal person since its existence is not determinate and in practice this entity may last forever (taking into account transformation of legal persons). Nevertheless, it is fully presented in the case of perpetual usufruct[41] and a cooperative ownership title to residential premises.[42] *De lege ferenda* the construction of rights, which may exist for an indeterminate period of time but from the start should be rejected as one which threatens the essence of ownership and interferes in the broadest property law to the unacceptable degree. These conflicts, however, may be reconciled. A permanent split in the owner's entitlements in the case of establishing personal servitudes as transferable rights may be avoided in various ways. In the first variant a personal servitude would end at the moment of a dissolution of legal subjectivity of the original holder. Nevertheless, a proposed mechanism may cause practical complications connected with the necessity to find whether a predecessor in title, who/which often does not stay in actual relations with a current holder, lives (exists). According to the second approach, personal servitudes would be considered *par excellence* temporary rights. They would end after, for instance, fifty years at the latest. This period should be sufficient, taking into consideration the fact that jurisprudence does not note cases of establishing personal servitudes for the benefit of minors.

There is a characteristic trend noticeable in American Law which distinguishes three types of servitudes. Among them *easement in gross* (in contrast to *easement appurtenant,* a dominant estate does not appear in this construction) shows a similarity to personal servitudes.[43] American

---

[41] A clear indication of the permanence of a split in an owner's entitlements in the above example is granting perpetual usufruct a claim to prolong it (see Article 236 § 2 of the Civil Code). Cf. Zygmunt Truszkiewicz, *Użytkowanie wieczyste. Zagadnienia konstrukcyjne* 214, 215,646 (2006).

[42] See also Adam Bieranowski in *Małżeńskie prawo majątkowe* 428 (2011).

[43] Lewis Mallalieu Simes, *The assignability of easements in gross in American Law*, 6 Michigan Law Review 521 (1924); Giles Morgan, *Easements in gross revisited*, 18 Anglo American Law Review 220 (1999).

Law evolves from a complete negation of transferability of personal servitude towards gradual extension of their transactional capacity.[44]

While searching for a normative scheme in which transferability will be defined, two possibilities come to mind. The first one (liberal) stipulates the transferability of personal servitudes unless otherwise decided by the parties. The second model (moderate) preserves as a principle of non-transferability of these rights, yet at the same time it allows parties to make them transferable. An apt choice is not easy because what clashes is contradictory values and interests, legal tradition and habits of transaction parties and finally making law attractive from an economic perspective. Having considered arguments for and against, I am in favour of the first variant and approve of the primacy of economic qualities of the right, with a possibility of parties granting this right, in the agreement to establish a servitude, a feature of non-transferability depending on particular individual needs of the people concerned. It is also important that personal servitudes other than a servitude of habitation do not occur in practice, not to mention few cases of establishing easement by necessity in favour of a possessor. Not only does this observation strengthen a thesis about the postulated necessity of making these rights attractive among others by endowing them with transferability, but also due to a lack of establishment, facilitates greater freedom and the adoption of a liberal model. It may be assumed (following the experience of the foreign practice) that so established a personal servitude will mainly be used for economic purposes. The proposed solution has to be safeguarded against negative effects for the sake of the clarity of a legal construction of a personal servitude. Accordingly, transferability of a servitude should be made dependent on disclosing this feature in the Land and Mortgage Register. A normative nature of a servitude would be defined more precisely. This would also prevent a violation of reliability of transactions.

An issue of extending the nature of a servitude of habitation by an entitlement to its transferability is more complex. In this aspect the aforementioned observations refuting arguments, which invoke a lack of an economic need or a danger of personal servitudes lasting *ad infinitum,* are valid. A broader consideration should be given to a specific bond between an owner and a holder of a servitude of habitation. It is difficult to deny that an owner does not mind who becomes a holder of a servitude of habitation. Personal qualities of a holder such as his lifestyle, family relationships, and manners play a decisive role in an owner's decision

---

[44] See Klaus Urlich Schmolke, *Der Grundsatz der Nichtübertragbarkeit...* 539 (2008).

about giving a holder the property to use. Thus, in practice the establishment of a servitude of habitation is often accompanied by close family relationships between parties, for example a child as a donee secures a dwelling for his/her parents in this way. An even bigger role is played by personal relations in the case of an owner living in the same residential premise as the holder.

This raises a question of whether it is possible, without distorting a relation of trust between parties concluding an agreement to establish a servitude of habitation, to review the provision of Article 300 of the Civil Code and to relax a ban on this servitude since no other reasons support transferability and this feature arises 'only' from the legislator's decision. Firstly, issues of utmost importance. I am of the opinion that the existence of a relation of trust in the case of a servitude of habitation is not an obstacle to form this right as transferable, because the owner's consent means that *in concreto* personal qualities of the holder of a servitude of habitation cease to have nontrivial importance. This should mean enriching attributes of the holder of a servitude of habitation by an entitlement to transfer his right, which would increase the flexibility of a servitude of habitation. The holder would be able to transfer this right to the third person in return for his using a different dwelling. A roundabout transaction would not be necessary – interrelating the relinquishing of a servitude of habitation with establishing the same right for the benefit of another person.

Establishing such a right as basically transferable would be a significant *novum* in our property law. A servitude of habitation is most often used to secure a dwelling for parents, who have transferred the ownership of a real estate to relatives.[45] It is also crammed into life annuity.[46] In typical situations an attribute of transferability of a servitude of habitation does not correspond to parties' interests. Additionally, taking into consideration habits of participants of legal transactions, a more lenient model should be advocated, which allows the transferability of a servitude of habitation under the parties' explicit reservation (dispositive transferability). The efficiency of such a reservation should be dependent on disclosing in the Land and Mortgage Register. Parties endowing a servitude of habitation with an attribute of transferability would not harm the safety of legal transactions. Simultaneously, a servitude of habitation would obtain a broader adjustability to particular needs, which could be

---

[45] More information Adam Bieranowski, *Służebność mieszkania* 98 (2011).

[46] See *Ibid.*, 82ff.

used in other spheres of life in which transferability of the right may play a significant role, for example in cooperative housing construction.

Non-heritability is a quality of a servitude of habitation emphasised in many legal systems.[47] A lack of this feature would result in an excessive impossibility to exercise ownership. This would lead to a permanent 'split' of entitlements arising from the nature of ownership. Restricting ownership by a servitude would exist for the indeterminate period from start, which, similar to the case of allowing transferability, should be criticized. The Civil Code admits a possibility to make a reservation in the agreement that after the holder's death a servitude of habitation will be vested in specific persons (Article 301 § 2 of the Civil Code). This mechanism is not based on universal succession. A servitude of habitation does not constitute part of an inheritance. It is acquired by designated people, regardless of whether they are inheritors or not.

The scope of protection of close friends' or relatives' interests, particularly in the context of legal mechanisms accompanying other legal and housing institutions, should be considered insufficient. It does not constitute the protection of close friends' or relatives' interests to the same degree as the security they enjoy while living with a tenant or a holder of a cooperative housing tenancy right. In the first case provisions of Article 691 of the Civil Code allow a continuity of tenancy of premises after the tenant's death above inheritance order.[48] Explaining *ratio legis* of such a mechanism, it has been emphasised that it has to provide for those who have permanently lived with the deceased, creating a common family hearth with a roof over his/her head.[49]

In the second example when the right to premises ends due to the holder's death, pursuant to Article 15.2 of Housing Co-operatives Act, a spouse, children and other close friends and relatives are entitled to make a

---

[47] For instance in the German law see Hartmut Schöner et al., *Grundbuchrecht* 462 (1989). See also Heike Kroll, *Das dingliche Wohnungsrecht...* 16 (2004); Claus Ahrens, *Dingliche Nutzungsrechte...* 214 (2004); Hartmut Schöner et al., *Grundbuchrecht* 462 (1989); in Swiss law see 2 Hans Michael Riemer, *Die beschränkten dinglichen Rechte...* 55 (1986).

[48] The same mechanism was stipulated in Article 12.1 of the Tenants Rights Act of April 11th, 1924 (Journal of Laws no. 39 item 406) and Article 391 of the Code of Obligations, see 2 Jan Korzonek & Ignacy Rosenblüth, *Kodeks zobowiązań. Komentarz* 97 (1935); L. Domański, *Instytucje Kodeksu zobowiązań. Komentarz teoretyczno-praktyczny. Część szczegółowa* 260-263 (1938). It was adopted by postwar regulations, see more in Zbigniew Radwański, *Najem mieszkań w świetle publicznej gospodarki lokalami* 49ff. (1961).

[49] See the decision of the Supreme Court of January 15th, 1930, C 1681/29 cited by Jan Korzonek & Ignacy Rosenblüth, *supra* 1524.

claim to be admitted to a housing cooperative and to conclude an agreement on establishing a cooperative occupancy right to residential premises.

Having in mind the above regulations it is difficult to find a justification for an uneven treatment of close friends or relatives dependent upon whether they lived with the tenant, or the holder of a cooperative occupancy right to residential premises, or of a servitude of habitation. From amongst these three rights, the interest of members of a family group of property law is the most weakly protected. The intensity of protection should at least be similar. What should be suggested is a resolution, which would strengthen an axiological coherence of a legal system. The fullest protection of the closest friends and relatives is provided by a system of acquiring a servitude of habitation *ex lege*. Being contented with granting only certain people a claim to establish a servitude of habitation does not seem to be sufficient. Leaving out issues related to the execution of the claim, which prove a weakened position of the holders, it is sufficient to stress here a danger of losing a hitherto existing priority by a terminated servitude of habitation. Accordingly, it may be proposed to introduce in the Civil Code a regulation which would make the continuation of a servitude of habitation above inheritance order dependent upon a cumulative fulfillment of three conditions:

1) the death of the holder of a servitude of habitation,

2) the existence, at the moment of death of a holder of a servitude of habitation, of his/her spouse, descendants, a person over whom he/she exercises protection or a person with whom he/she cohabits,

3) permanent residence of entities mentioned in 2) with the holder of a servitude of habitation until his/her death.

In the case of the above mentioned legal successors, a servitude of habitation would end. In order to remove doubts as to whether the scope of succession comprises also duties accompanying a servitude of habitation (e.g. an obligation to pay remuneration), it is justified to adopt a wording stating that 'Along with a servitude of habitation the purchaser acquires all obligations connected with it as well as a duty to pay remuneration'.

Alternatively, the above mentioned people should be considered to be given *ex lege* a claim to establish a new servitude of habitation (while maintaining their priority). According to a traditional principle, a servitude of habitation would then end with the death of the holder at the latest. However, upon fulfilling all statutory conditions, a new servitude of habitation could be established within the expired right. On the other hand, having established such a servitude, an owner would hold a proper remuneration claim. The model of constitutive acquisition has some advantages. In exceptional cases it protects a holder of a servitude of habitation against the expiration of this right (e.g. when the servitude has been established for the benefit of a minor) since it is not always necessary to create a servitude of habitation as a temporary right.

In both cases the position of an owner can be strengthened by creating ex lege an obligation of a recipient of servitude of habitation to waive the right after the expiry of the fixed period of time.

ORIGIN, DEVELOPMENT AND LEGAL REGULATION OF A SOCIETAS EUROPAEA

KATARÍNA HARAJDOVÁ AND ANNA SCHNEIDEROVÁ

MATEJ BEL UNIVERSITY IN BANSKÁ BYSTRICA, SLOVAKIA

Abstract

The growing number of commercial transactions has created borders that overlap individual states; also ambitions have been born to establish a commercial company having a supranational character. A result of such efforts was the formation of Societas Europaea (European public limited-liability company) as a supranational European analogy of a public limited-liability company. The aim of its existence was to enable the free flow of capital within the whole European Union and unify legal regulations of business companies within the European Union. The European company known under the Latin name as Societas Europaea (SE) is a legal entity with the legal subjectivity of which capital is divided into shares, while each partner's liability is limited up to the amount of their share. Societas Europaea (SE) is governed directly by the Council Regulation (EC) No 2157/2001 of the 8th October 2001 on the Statute for a European company (hereafter referred to as 'SE') that determines issues related to the formation of an SE, basic issues of an SE position, structure of its bodies and several provisions that are related to accounting and winding up of an SE.

The primary legal regulation is subsidiarily complemented by the Directive 2001/86/EC of the 8th October 2001 supplementing the Statute for a European Company with regard to the involvement of employees. Other issues related to the SE are governed by a legal regulation adopted by the Member States in relation to the SE (in the Slovak Republic it is Act No. 562/2004 Coll. on European public limited-liability company, in Poland it is European commercial business grouping and European company Act, Official Gazette No. 62, entry 551, Ustawa o europejskim zgrupowaniu interesów gospodarczych i spółce europejskiej (Dz. U. nr 62, poz. 551) and in the Czech Republic it is Act No. 627/2004 Coll. on European company) or legal regulations of the Member States with regard to public limited-liability companies.

The authors of the article have attempted to introduce the European public limited-liability company through the development of its original idea, functioning, organisational structure, current existence and activity, as well as related pros and cons. The article also points out the results of public consultation that was started in March 2010 by the Directorate General for Internal Market and Services. This public consultation was intended to assure the SE statute application intended to examine external studies results and provide the Commission with issues significant for evaluation of a five-year operation of the SE.

Origin of SE

The issue of formation of a supranational company was first raised in the years immediately after the Second World War. It is surprising that the first to propose a project for 'European companies' was the Council of Europe; an international organisation established predominantly for human rights protection. However, the general remit of the Council of Europe was to seek to harmonise legal practice in the Member States via international conventions, thereby promoting awareness of a European identity. The project for 'European companies' clearly had its place in such efforts. Despite its great success, however, the initial project was presented in 1952 but was soon abandoned.[1]

Another idea of creating a European public limited company was raised in 1959, first of all in France at the Congress of Notaries in Tours (in the lecture given by a notary C. Thibierge). Soon afterwards, a Dutch professor who was to play a decisive part in drawing up the first version of the SE statute – Pieter Sanders, Dean of the Rotterdam Law Faculty – made it the subject of his inaugural lecture to the city's Higher Institute of Economic Sciences. The project then reappeared on the official agenda at the instigation of the French government.[2]

In a memorandum dated March the 15th, 1965, France called on the Commission to set up a group of experts to draw up a preliminary draft of the statute for an SE. Professor Sanders was appointed to chair the group

---

[1] Noëlle Lenoir, *The Societas Europea or SE, The new European Company* (2007).

[2] *Ibid.*

composed of law professors and practitioners. The Sanders report was particularly convincing and ambitious. It contained a complete, detailed draft statute for the SE, covering its formation, incorporation, reductions or increases in capital, governance, accounts, amendments to the articles and even winding up. It was inspired by the German law on public limited companies, deemed at the time to be the most accomplished model, the Sanders report put forward a uniform type of company of which the European legal personality implied the application of uniform law in all the States. The system was based on reforms as follows:

• to allow the mobility of companies by making it possible for them to transfer their registered office from one country to another;

• to facilitate mergers and the creation of subsidiaries by companies in different Member States; and

• to encourage the grouping together of production factors scattered all over the Common Market, joint initiatives and access to the European capital market.[3]

The Commission approved the Sanders report and took up its outline in a draft regulation presented to the Council on the 30th June 1970. However, several misgivings and reservations were expressed by certain states, such as the Netherlands, the United Kingdom, and Ireland.[4]

A new text was presented by the Commission in 1975 but was not given an official acceptance.[5] It was only with the Single European Act of 1987 that the reform was given a fresh start. In a memorandum of the 15th July 1988 on the 'Internal Market White Paper', the European Commission took up the idea of a statute for a European trans-national company. However, this project failed and was faced with critical commentaries on the basis of which the Commission in October 1989 submitted two new proposals. The first reacted to the critical comments on the length of the texts and contained frequent references to the national law. The other included the text of the directive - establishing the social system for the SE, i.e. the 'the place of workers' in the SE and their involvement in management being the main bones of contention between the States 5. The process of adopting the statute for the SE was still far from complete. On the occasion of the successive proposals presented by the Commission

---

[3] Noëlle Lenoir, The Societas Europea... (2007). The Netherlands did not agree with with the text of the proposal which, according to their opinion was to a significant extent inspired by a 'continental' system of law and was not flexible in its requirement and the United Kingdom and Ireland had reservations towards tax and social provisions of the Statute.

[4] *Ibid.*

[5] *Ibid.*

from 1991 onwards, the statute for the SE was gradually 'streamlined'.[6] Finally, the conference in Nice on October the 8th, 2001 adopted the Council Regulation (EC) No. 2157/2001 on the Statute for a European company (SE) (hereinafter referred to as the 'Regulation'), and the Council Directive 2001/86/EC of October the 8th, 2001 on the Involvement of Employees in Management.

Basic Characteristics of the SE

The European company is a trans-national European analogy of a public limited-liability company that shall be registered in the Member State in which it has its registered office, in a register designated by the law of that Member State.

An SE has a legal personality and its capital shall be divided into shares. No shareholder shall be liable for more that the amount he has subscribed.[7] The SE must have a minimum subscribed capital of at least €120,000 EUR and it must be expressed in euros.[8] However, the law does not require the capital to be actually paid up in this currency. Notice of an SE's registration and of the deletion of such a registration shall be published in both the registration office (Companies' House) and the Official Journal of the European Communities.

The abbreviation of the European company, SE, i.e. Societas Europaea, must be provided before or after its name.[9] Selection of the Latin expression resulted from the fact that this company shall be identical in all Member States and therefore it should adopt a common name different from any of the Member States' languages. However, translation of the Latin name SE – European company has a little expressive value regarding the fact that an SE is not the only form of a European company.[10] The Regulation as well as foreign literature (mainly the German - "Europäische Aktiengesellschaft") often uses the name European public limited-liability company. National laws of the Member States (for instance Austria, Slovak Republic, Poland, Czech Republic) refer to the "European company".[11]

The SE registered office (the address that has been lodged with the Companies' House as a company headquarters) must, pursuant to the

---

[6] *Ibid.*

[7] Article Nr. 1 Subarticle 2,3 Council Regulation (EC) No. 2157/2001.

[8] Article Nr. 4 Council Regulation (EC) No. 2157/2001.

[9] Article Nr. 11 Council Regulation (EC) No. 2157/2001.

[10] European Economic Interest Grouping, Societas cooperativa europaea.

[11] Jan Dedič & Petr Čech, *Evropské právo společností* (2004).

Regulation, be located within the territory of the EEC in the state in which the company has its head office (the office from which the company is managed). In a contrary case, a Member State must, under the penalty of the winding up of the company by operation of law, adopt an adequate measure for the remedy.

Legal Framework of the SE

The historical failure of the intended project of a unified 'code' resulted in a multi-layered system of legal regulations related to an SE governed by Article 9 of the Council Regulation (EC) No. 2157/2001 on the Statute for a European company (SE) (hereinafter referred to as the 'Regulation'), and within which the SE is regulated:

1. By Council Regulation (EC) No. 2157/2001 on the Statute for a European company (SE),
2. In the case of matters expressly authorised by this Regulation, by the provisions of its statutes,
3. In the case of matters not regulated by this Regulation or, where matters are partly regulated by it, of those aspects not covered by it, by:

c1) the provisions of laws adopted by Member States in implementation of Community measures relating specifically to SE – in the SR – zákon č. 562/2004 Z.z. o Európskej spoločnosti, Poland – Ustawa o europejskim zgrupowaniu interesów gospodarczych I spółce europejskiej (Dz. U. nr62, poz.551), Czech Republic – zák. č. 627/2004 Sb. o Evropské spoločnosti;

c2) the provisions of Member States' laws which would apply to a public limited-liability company;

c3) the provisions of its statutes, in the same way as for a public limited-liability company formed in accordance with the law of the Member State in which the SE has its registered office.

The primary regulation represented by the Regulation in relation to the Employee Involvement in Management is subsidiarily complemented by the Council Directive 2001/86/EC of the 8th October 2001.

Organisational Structure of the SE

Every company has a general meeting of shareholders. From the point of the organisational structure of other bodies, there are two systems – the one-tier and the two-tier systems.

The basis of a one-tier system is a company with a powerful administrative body – the administrative organ headed by a chairman, consisting of at least three members where employee participation is regulated in accordance with Directive 2001/86/EC. This system is historically the older one and it is applied mostly in France, Italy, Spain, the United Kingdom, etc.

A company based on a two-tier system is built on two powerful bodies, i.e. a management organ and supervisory organ. This historically younger system is known mainly in Germany, Austria, the Slovak Republic, etc.

In the case that the Member State fails to recognize any of the above systems, the Regulation orders adoption of a particular legal regulation of the system in absence. Individual Member States accomplished this task differently, e.g. the United Kingdom, claiming significant flexibility of its Companies Law of 1985, failed to perform any modification; the Slovak Republic as well as other lawmakers adopted a minimalistic approach; German and Austrian legal regulation regulates in detail a new one-tier system; and the Czech lawmaker copies a specific French system.[12]

The system that is recognisable by a particular national law shall be subsidiarily governed by appropriate provisions of a national law without any modification options regarding an SE.

The presented co-existence of the one-tier and the two-tier systems is one of the consequences of a political compromise enabling implementation of the SE. An option to select an organisational system of an SE brought about a variety of views, where on one side the unity of the SE is doubted, however, on the other side such dualism is considered a way to both harmonisation and unification.

A one-tier system organised SE with registered office in the Slovak Republic will basically apply the organisation of the Slovak public limited-liability company except for provisions that are regulated by the Regulation. The Regulation is based on the German concept.

A one-tier system has not been known to the Slovak public limited-liability company law, therefore regarding the European company statute it adopted a minimalistic approach whose advantage rests with its flexibility.

Formation of an SE

An SE may be formed in any of the Member States of the European Union, Island, Norway, and Lichtenstein. An SE formation within Article 15 of the Regulation is in issues which the Regulation fails to regulate

[12] *Loi sur les nouvelles régulation économiques n°2001* 420 (2001).

expressly, governed by the law of the EU Member State in which an intended registered office is to be placed. The process of an SE creation, similar to in other commercial companies, recognises two phases, i.e. formation of an SE followed by registration of an SE on the basis of which the SE acquires legal personality.

The Regulation provides four different ways of forming a European company as follows:

- Merging of two or more public limited-liability companies of which at least two have their registered offices in at least two Member States;
- Formation of a European company as a holding[13] by at least two subsidiary companies (s.r.o. or a.s.) that are governed by the laws of a different Member State, or if they have had a subsidiary company governed by the laws of another Member State for two years. In this type of formation, as different from merging of the companies, the subsidiary companies are not wound up;
- Formation of an SE as a subsidiary company of commercial companies (any type of a company) that are governed by the laws of a different Member State or for 2 years have had a subsidiary company governed by the laws of another Member State;
- Transformation of an existing public limited-liability company (only a PLC!) with both the formal and material registered office within the territory of the European Union into the European company if for 2 years it has had a subsidiary company governed by the laws of another Member State.

Individual ways of an SE formation differ predominantly by the scope and character of participating companies and consequences of an SE formation having an impact on their legal existence. However, they do not result in a different position of an SE in external legal relations.

Positive and negative drivers in formation and existence of an SE

It must be stated that evaluation of the final regulation of an SE will take a few years more, since it requires a longer practice to point out the pros and cons of the presented form of an enterprise.

Pursuant to provision of Article 69 of the Regulation 'Five years at the latest after the entry into force of this Regulation, the Commission shall forward to the Council and the European Parliament a report on the

[13] Holding is a company that owns other companies' outstanding stock.

application of the Regulation and proposals for amendments, where appropriate'.[14]

Based on the above Article, on the 23rd March 2010, the Directorate General for Internal Market and Services launched a public consultation on how the European Company Statute (SE) works in practice. The consultations were aimed at testing of the findings of the external study conducted by Ernst & Young ('E & Y') following a call for tender by the Commission and to provide the Commission with information relevant for the assessment of the SE. The consultation report was conducted in June 2010. The issues raised concern: positive and negative drivers for setting up an SE; main trends in distribution of SEs across the EU/EEA; practical problems that companies encounter in the course of setting up or running an SE; and possible improvements of the current legislative system. Respondents often put an emphasis on reaching a combination of the key positive elements before giving preference to only some of them.

According to the above public consultation report, the following findings were provided: The respondents found the main motivation for the setting up an SE is the option to transfer the registered office and the 'European image' associated with the SE and linked to a uniform corporate identity.[15]

Although the regime of the transfer of the registered office could be improved, the SE Regulation offers a greater legal certainty than the judicature of the European Court (Case Cartesio).[16] The importance of the transfer of registered office in the SE Regulation would decrease if the 14th Company Law Directive ('CLD') on Cross-Border Transfer of

---

[14] Synthesis of the comments on the consultation document of the internal market and services directorate-general on the results of the study on the operation and the impacts of the statute for a European company (SE), European Commission, Directorate General Internal Market and Services, Free movement of capital, Company Law and Corporate Governance, Company Law, Corporate Governance And Financial Crime, júl 2010.

[15] Synthesis of the comments on the consultation document of the internal market and services directorate-general on the results of the study on the operation and the impacts of the statute for a european company (SE), European Commission, Directorate General Internal Market and Services, Free movement of capital, Company Law and Corporate Governance, Company Law, Corporate Governance And Financial Crime, July 2010.

[16] Judgement of the ECJ of December 16th, 2008, Case C-210/06, Cartesio Oktató és Szolgáltató bt.

Registered Office [17] were to be adopted, as was the case when the possibility of cross-border mergers on the basis of the SE Regulation was considered less interesting after the adoption of the Cross- Border Merger Directive.[18]

Further motivation involved flexibility in company administration and management, the potential for corporate simplification and regulatory advantages compared to similar forms of national types of companies. Also, the tax regime played one of the decisive roles when deciding on the SE formation.[19]

A positive factor of the SE is also flexibility in the management structure represented by an option to select between the one-tier and two-tier systems. Both variants are of interest mainly due to lower personnel requirements and administrative costs in comparison to national companies.[20]

On the other hand, most respondents agreed that the most important negative drivers were the cost, complexity and legal uncertainty related to the procedures of setting up and running an SE. In this respect, different issues were raised: the need of a cross-border element; the high minimum capital requirement, in particular in Member States where the minimum capital for national forms is lower; the complicated legal regime, which is sometimes very different from one Member State to another; the existing administrative burdens and language barriers; the uncertainties linked to taxation regimes; and the lack of experience at this stage. According to the respondents, in general terms, the time required and the uncertainty related to the procedures played a key role in the decisions of smaller companies for whom these concerns often outweighed the advantage of a European

[17] Directive 2005/56/EC of the European Parliament and of the Council of 26 October 2005 on crossborder mergers of limited liability companies. OJ L310 of November 25th, 2005.

[18] Synthesis of the comments on the consultation document of the internal market and services directorate-general on the results of the study on the operation and the impacts of the statute for a european company (SE), European Commission, Directorate General Internal Market and Services, Free movement of capital, Company Law and Corporate Governance, Company Law, Corporate Governance And Financial Crime, July 2010.

[19] Synthesis of the comments on the consultation document of the internal market and services directorate-general on the results of the study on the operation and the impacts of the statute for a european company (SE), European Commission, Directorate General Internal Market and Services, Free movement of capital, Company Law and Corporate Governance, Company Law, Corporate Governance And Financial Crime, July 2010.

[20] http://tinyurl.com/7rjc8fc.

image. The impact of these factors was more striking in Member States with a large number of SMEs, such as Italy and Portugal.[21]

The lack of awareness of the SE form, both within and outside the EU, was also mentioned as a negative driver. The same goes for the obligation under the SE Regulation to have the real headquarters and registered office in the same place. The employee involvement regime was considered to be a negative driver in Member States that do not have, or have a lower level of, employee participation in their national legislation (e.g. respondents from Italy, United Kingdom). This would be due to its high complexity and uncertainty about the outcome of negotiations with employees, in particular for listed companies.[22]

In the period after the Regulation adoption, a boom in the setting up of an SE was expected. This did not happen as there are currently about 732 SEs in Europe, of which 367 have been formed in the Czech Republic, which exceeds Germany with 175 SEs.[23] However, not all of the registered companies are actually also running. We do believe that the above provided findings will contribute to the improvement of the future regulation of the SE. Especially as it concerns eliminations of the negative factors.

Summary

The authors focused on introducing the SE through its origin, the ways of formation of the SE, legal regulation and organisation of SE. The article also briefly deals with positive and negative drivers of setting up the SE.

[21] Synthesis of the comments on the consultation document of the internal market and services directorate-general on the results of the study on the operation and the impacts of the statute for a european company (SE), European Commission, Directorate General Internal Market and Services, Free movement of capital, Company Law and Corporate Governance, Company Law, Corporate Governance And Financial Crime, July 2010.

[22] Synthesis of the comments on the consultation document of the internal market and services directorate-general on the results of the study on the operation and the impacts of the statute for a european company (SE), European Commission, Directorate General Internal Market and Services, Free movement of capital, Company Law and Corporate Governance, Company Law, Corporate Governance And Financial Crime, July 2010.

[23] http://tinyurl.com/7rjc8fc.

Cognition of Family Courts in Poland in Cases Regarding Parental Authority

AGNIESZKA GÓRA- BŁASZCZYKOWSKA

UNIVERSITY OF WARMIA AND MAZURY IN OLSZTYN, POLAND

Material basis of adjudicating by a Family Court

The Family Court is obliged to grant assistance to parents if such assistance is necessary for proper exercise of parental authority. In particular, each of the parents is entitled to petition the Family Court for removal of a child from an unauthorised person, as well as petition to the Family Court or other appropriate public authority to provide substitute guardianship (article 100 § 1 of the Polish Family and Guardianship Code, hereinafter also referred to as k.r.o.).

Interference of Family Courts in the exercise of parental authority may be valid in many situations. First of all, when parents exercise this authority, but cannot reach mutual consent as to particular activities in relation to the person or assets of the child. The aforementioned relates to cases of entrusting the exercise, limitation, suspension or deprivation of parental authority. When the child's parents live separately, the regard for the welfare of the child may require a determination of the method of the exercise of such authority by the court (article 107 of the k.r.o.). The Court may entrust the exercise of the parental authority to only one of the parents, limiting the parental authority of the other one to particular obligations and entitlements in regard to the child. The Court may keep the parental authority within both parents if they submitted, consistent with the welfare of the child, an agreement on the method of exercising parental authority and maintaining contact with the child, and the expectation that they will cooperate in regard to the welfare of the child is justified (article 107 § 2 of the k.r.o.). The Family Court also decides on the method of maintaining contact with the child by the parent when the child resides permanently with the other parent and there is no proper consent between the parents in this matter (article 113^1 of the k.r.o.).

Secondly, the cognition of the Family Court is taken into consideration when the parental authority is vested to only one of the parents. In such a case, it may be valid for the Court to adjudicate on the issue of restoration of parental authority, determination, limitation or forbidding contact with the child. Thirdly, the intervention of the Family Court in regard to the exercise of parental authority is valid when the legislator obligates the Family Court to undertake a decision on a particular matter, even if the parents consent to the performance (or deny the performance) of a particular act related to parental authority. In compliance with article 101 § 3 of the k.r.o., the parents cannot, without the Family Court's consent, dispose of the assets of the child within the scope exceeding ordinary management, nor consent to performing such acts by the child.

The Family Court may also interfere with the method of exercising parental authority by minor parents, but only when the welfare of the child requires such interference (article 96 § 2 of the k.r.o.).

The Family Court should interfere in the exercise of the parental authority when the welfare of the child is threatened. The Court may, in particular:

1) obligate the parents and the minor to a particular behaviour or send the parents to institutions or specialists of family therapy, providing counselling or other assistance to the family, with a simultaneous indication of a method of control of the execution of the given order,

2) define what acts may not be performed by the parents without the Court's consent, or subject the parents to other limitations that apply to a custodian,

3) subject the exercise of parental authority to a permanent supervision of a court-appointed guardian,

4) send the minor to an organization or institution appointed to render services regarding vocational preparation or other institution maintaining partial custody over children,

5) order the placement of the minor in a foster family or in an institution of emergency care and education (article 109 § 1 and 2 of the k.r.o.).

In the event of temporary obstacles in exercising parental authority the Family Court may order its suspension. The suspension shall be lifted when its reason is eliminated (article 110 § 1 and 2 of the k.r.o.).

The Family Court may deprive the parents of parental authority if parental authority cannot be exercised due to a permanent obstacle or if the parents abuse parental authority or grossly neglect their obligations related to the child, or if the parents are permanently uninterested in the child (article 111 § 1 and 1 a) of the k.r.o.).

If the welfare of the child requires it, the Family Court may limit or even forbid the parents maintaining contact with the child (article 113^2 § 1 and 2 and also article 113^3 of the k.r.o.). The Family Court may in particular: forbid meeting the child, forbid taking the child away from his place of permanent residence, permit meetings with the child only in the presence of the other parent or a custodian, guardian appointed by court, or other person indicated by the court, limit the contact to particular means of remote communication, forbid remote communication.

As indicated before, Family Courts are also competent in particular matters in which the legislator excluded the independence of assuming decisions by the parents or custodians due to the importance of the case for the minor. The aforementioned regards i.a. the consent to collect bone marrow or haematopoietic cells under the Act of July 1st, 2005 on collecting, storing and transplanting cells, tissues and organs (Journal of Laws 05.169.1411). As stipulated in article 12 sec.2 of the Act, in the event of a direct threat of loss of life, and if such threat cannot be averted any other way than by commencing a marrow or circulatory blood hematopoietic cells transplantation, the donor in favour of the sibling may also be a minor, if it does not cause a foreseeable impairment of the donor's organism efficiency. In such an event, collecting marrow or circulatory blood haematopoietic cells from a minor who does not have full legal capacity, may be performed with the consent of a statutory representative after having obtained the consent of the Family Court, competent in regard to the place of residence of the candidate for donation. If the donor is a minor over the age of thirteen, his consent is also required (article 12 sec.3). The Family Court decides on application of the legal representatives of the candidate for donation, after hearing the minor and consulting an expert psychologist and, in the case of a minor over the age of sixteen - also on his application. A proper medical opinion stating that the collection of marrow shall not cause a foreseeable impairment of the donor's organism efficiency should be enclosed (article 12 sec.4).

The Family Court may also issue a permit to execute a surgical treatment on a child that had a sudden accident when the parents do not consent to such treatment. In such an event, the necessity of removing the child from the parents or other persons by the Family Court may occur, in order to place the child in a hospital to execute such treatment. In such events the Family Court may: order the parents to place the child in a hospital or sanatorium, forbid discharging the child from the hospital, grant consent on behalf of the parents to execute a necessary surgical treatment, order collecting blood from a child under thirteen for treatment purposes.

Also if the parents refuse the surgical treatment of the child, e.g. due to religious reasons (e.g. due to the possibility of blood transfer) and such refusal threatens the child's life or health, the collision of the will of the statutory representative of the child and the physician's standpoint should be decided by the Family Court. Until the decision is reached by the Court, the physician is entitled to keep the child in the hospital.

Emergencies in which Family Court is competent are defined by the Polish legislator as: placing the child in a foster family or institution of emergency care and education by a social worker, without the Family Court's decision, in the event of discovering violence in the family that brings up the child. In such an event the Family Court immediately institutes guardianship proceedings (article 579^1 § 1 of the Polish Civil Proceedings Code). The Court is obliged to issue immediately, no later than within 24 hours, a judgement on placing the child in a foster family or an institution of emergency care and education, or a judgement on the return of the child to the family (article 579^1 § 1a of the Polish Civil Proceedings Code). Therefore, the Court is not bound by the decision of a social worker on the removal of the child from the family.

The Family Court is also competent in cases of removing the child detained by an unauthorised person.[1]

The procedural aspects of the cognition of the Family Court

The Family and Minor Department (family court / guardianship court), established in regional courts (*sąd rejonowy*) - the lowest instance courts - constitutes the Family Court.

The intent of the legislator is that the issues of persons subject to the Family Court were heard and adjudicated, whenever possible, before one (the same) court. Thus the decision of subjecting the aforementioned matters is for regional courts (courts of lowest instance), and therefore is the most available for citizens. Those courts are arranged all over the country.

In regard to article 569 § 2 of the Polish Civil Proceedings Code, exclusive competence lies within the Family Court competent in regard to the place of residence of a person whom the proceedings are to consider, and, in the event of lack of such place, the Family Court of the person's current stay. If the person whom the proceedings are to consider has no

---

[1] Decision of the Polish Supreme Court of Mai 5th, 2000, II CKN 765/2000, LexPolonica no. 380646.

place of residence nor accommodation, the regional court for the capital city of Warsaw is competent.

The place of residence of a child subject to parental authority is the place of residence of parents or the parent who exercises exclusive parental authority or who has been entrusted with exercising parental authority. If parental authority lies equally with both parents having different places of residence, the place of residence of the child is at the parent with whom the child stays permanently. If the child does not stay permanently with either of the parents, his place of residence is determined by the Family Court (article 26 § 1 and 2 of the Polish Civil Code).

Family Courts, due to their territorial and functional competence, usually have full material relating to the particular person subject to parental authority or custody at their disposal. The intention of the legislator is that the decisions related to the child are not accidental in character, but are a continuation of previous judgements and orders. Only this way may the Court fulfil its 'guardianship role' correctly. Therefore, the legislator allows only exceptionally, and in urgent cases, the issue of required orders by a territorially different, in regard to competence, Family Court, restricting the necessity of notification of such fact to the Family Court that is territorially competent (article 569 § 2 of the Polish Civil Proceedings Code).[2]

However, in urgent cases, the Family Court issues all necessary orders ex officio, even in relation to persons not subject to its territorial competence, notifying the territorially competent Family Court (article 569 § 2 Polish Civil Proceedings Code).

If the decision has been issued by a territorially incompetent court, it has to notify the territorially competent Family Court. Urgent cases are situations in which the slightest delay resulting from the necessity of undertaking an action by a competent court, after the transfer of the case, could endanger the person, whom the proceedings are to consider, with injury or harm.

The exceptional extent of the Family Court's entitlements consists also of the fact that this Court may institute proceedings ex officio (article 570 of the Polish Civil Proceedings Code), as the Polish civil proceedings – as a general rule - may be instituted only on application (a complaint in legal proceedings).

Instituting proceedings ex officio is not discretionary, but is obligatory for the Family Court in every event when the Court receives information

---

[2] Justification of a resolution of the Supreme Court of February 21st, 1968, III CZP 105/67, OSNC 1968/10/162).

on circumstances justifying such activity. The obligation of the Court in this matter does not exclude the institution of the guardianship proceedings on application of the person concerned.

The Court has to examine the circumstances of the case, establish how reliable and authentic the obtained information is regarding the grounds to institute proceedings ex officio. Issuing a decision should be preceded by a detailed analysis of the case, to avoid unnecessary and hasty actions. The Family Court is obliged to remain in contact with particular bodies, organizations and persons to be able to react on time to situations threatening the welfare of the child.

Particular entitlements of the Family Court relate to a wider - as compared to courts adjudicating in other cases - possibility of establishing the facts of the case. In compliance with article 570^1 of the Polish Civil Proceedings Code, the Family Court may order the performance, by a court appointed custodian, an environmental inquiry, as well as ask for information from a competent body of social welfare in order to establish information regarding a minor, the social situation of the family, the course of education of the minor and his or her ways of spending free time, the relations towards him of parents or custodians, health conditions.

Polish procedural law grants children over the age of thirteen the possibility of expressing their opinion in the course of proceedings before the Family Court.

Following article 576 § 2 of the Polish Civil Proceedings Code, the Court, in cases relating to the person or assets of the child, shall hear the child if his or her mental development, health condition and degree of maturity allow such hearing, having regard, whenever possible, to the child's rational wishes. The hearing takes place outside the courtroom. Such a course of action is consistent with article 12 of the Convention on the Rights of the Child and articles 573, 574 and 576 § 2 of the Polish Civil Proceedings Code.[3]

According to the content of article 574 § 1 of the Polish Civil Proceedings Code, the Family Court may summon the person subject to parental authority, as well as order compulsory bringing up of such person. If a person subject to parental authority does not have the capacity to undertake legal actions in the proceedings, the Family Court may order the person's compulsory bringing to the Court under pain of a fine to anyone with whom the person stays (article 574 § 2 of the Polish Civil Proceedings Code).

---

[3] Resolution of the Supreme Court of December 15th, 1998, I CKN 1122/98, OSNC 1999/6/119.

The Family Court should keep watch that, due the character of the case, the participation of the child in the proceedings does not have a negative social and educational impact or that such impact is reduced to a minimum. The familiarization with the standpoint of a person subject to parental authority or custody is necessary for the judgement issued in the case to be consistent with the welfare of the person. The Court in every case should consider whether summons of the child is absolutely necessary.

Summoning requires proper preparations from the Court in order to create conditions - during the child's presence in the Court - which do not have a negative impact on his or her psyche.

Before issuing a decision as to the subject matter, the Family Court - following article 576 § 1 of the Polish Civil Proceedings Code - shall hear the legal representative of a person, whom the proceedings concern. In more important cases the Court should, if possible, hear the persons close to this person. The circumstances of the case, family, social and environmental situation shall determine who shall be counted as a close person by the Court adjudicating in the case. Therefore, not only relatives and kin of the child, but first of all persons bringing up the child, permanently staying with the child, as well as tutors, trainers, friends, etc. The Court has to previously determine whether such a person has proper information and his or her participation shall contribute to a correct decision on the case. In any other case, hearing of such person is superfluous.

The legislator, in guardianship cases of minors, stipulates the necessity of conducting the whole sitting or its part on camera, if the welfare of the minor is prejudiced by public adjudication of the case (article 575^1 of the Polish Civil Proceedings Code).

Due to the specific nature of the cases decided by Family Courts and the variability of facts of the case, the Family Court has to be vested with the possibility of reacting to changes occurring in the legal and factual situation of the persons whom the proceedings concern. Of course, the most typical examples are the cases regarding parental authority over a minor. Therefore, the Polish legislator vested the Family Court with the possibility of modification of even valid judgements in this matter, in order to provide the minors with the best possible care and education suitable for the minor's age, health and skills, and conditions (see article 577 of the Polish Civil Proceedings Code).

The supreme purpose that stipulates the scope and method of the Family Court's activity and, first of all, method of adjudicating, is the welfare of the child. The judicial decisions of the Supreme Court stress that the welfare of the child in cases regarding the modification of the decision on parental authority and method of its exercise precedes even the authority of the Court.[4] The prerequisite of the welfare of the child obligates the Family Court to a modification or lifting the decision ex officio, also in a case that may be instituted only on application.

The Supreme Court decided[5] that preventing the maintaining of a proper personal contact between a parent and a child violates, in general, the interest of the minor and may be the reason justifying the modification of a valid decision that regulates the exercise of parental authority (article 577 of the Polish Civil Proceedings Code).

For the realization of the prerequisite of the welfare of the child, the Polish Family Court may, following article 109 § 2 of the Polish Civil Proceedings Code, entrust the exercise of the current custody over a child to citizens of a foreign state living abroad.[6] The Supreme Court stresses that if a minor Polish citizen, who has proper recognition, wishes to remain in Poland, then any actions of a parent intended to realize the will of the child cannot be regarded as an abuse of parental authority.[7]

The Family Court may dismiss a plea of the mother regarding the removal of a child from an unauthorised person if the welfare of the child would be prejudiced by such plea; the Court is obligated, however, to issue a decision as to the limitation of parental authority by keeping the child with the person with whom the child remains.[8]

The content of article 598^1 § 1 of the Polish Civil Proceedings Code cannot be omitted; which the aforementioned provision stipulates that in the cases on removing a person subjected to parental authority or remaining under custody, the public prosecutor is notified of the date of the trial and handed a copy of the motion.

---

[4] See the justification of the decision of the Supreme Court of October, 1st 1998, I CKN 834/98, OSNC 1999, no. 4, pos. 72 and judgement of December 15th, 1998, I CKN 1122/98, OSNC 1999, no. 6, pos. 119.

[5] Decision of August, 30th 1977, III CRN 204/77, LEX no. 7986.

[6] Resolution of the Supreme Court of October, 2nd 1991, III CZP 92/91, OSN 1992, no. 4, pos. 58.

[7] Decision of the Supreme Court of October 1st, 1998, I CKN 834/98, OSNC 1999, no. 4, pos. 72.

[8] Resolution of the Supreme Court of July, 18th 1969, III CZP 44/69, OSN 1970, no. 1, pos. 4.

Due to the welfare of the child, negotiating and executing an agreement on the regulation of personal contacts of the parents with their minor child is acceptable.[9]

Following article 582 of the Polish Civil Proceedings Code, resolving the important matters of the child as to which there is lack of consent of the parents, may take place only after the parents have had the possibility of making declarations, unless hearing them would cause excessive difficulties.

Important matters of the child stipulated in the aforementioned provision consist of, for example, the issues of changing the name or surname of the child, gaining or changing the nationality of the child, departure abroad with an intention of establishing permanent residence,[10] as well as securing, awarded to the child, alimony and the performance of the alimony obligation.[11]

Withdrawal from hearing of the parents is justified only if it would cause excessive difficulties. The legislator does not determine such difficulties: whether health issues, great distance of the Court from the place of stay of one or both parents, or their family status may be included. The Court should obtain the standpoint of the parent whom the Court intends not to hear. Even sickness, disability or staying abroad do not have to be seen by the concerned parent as conditions preventing him or her from appearing in the Court. If the parent wishes to be heard, the Court should enable such action, even if in the Court's opinion this would cause excessive difficulties. Naturally, the Court should counteract extending the time of the proceedings by the parent who would apply for his or her hearing not appearing in the court, with the intent of preventing the Court from delivering a judgement.

The decision of the Court, deciding on the important matters of the child, substitutes the parents' agreement and is dropped when the parents reach a substantially different agreement.

For the determination of the cognition of the Family Court, article 582^1 § 2 of the Polish Civil Proceedings Code is very important. It stipulates

---

[9] Resolution of the Supreme Court of October 21st, 2005, III CZP 75/05, OSNC 2006/9/142.

[10] Resolution of the Supreme Court of November 10th, 1971, III CZP 69/71, OSN 1972, no. 3, pos. 49.

[11] Resolution of the Supreme Court of May 30th, 1985, III CZP 6/85, OSN 1986, no. 4, pos. 45; resolution of the Supreme Court of April 19th, 1988, III CZP 26/88, OSN 1989, no. 9, pos. 140; resolution of the Supreme Court of July 26th, 1990, III CZP 36/90, OSN 1991, no. 2-3, pos. 24.

that the Family Court, in order to have contact with the child may, in particular:

1) obligate the person authorised to have contact with the child or a person, under whose custody the child remains, to cover the costs of travel and stay of the child or also a person accompanying the child, including the costs or return to the place of permanent stay,

2) obligate the person, under whose custody the child remains, to deposit in the court deposit account an appropriate sum in order to cover the expenses of the authorised person and related to the performance of the contact in the event of default or improper performance by the person so obligated resulting from the decision on contacts; the aforementioned does not apply to foster families and institutions of emergency care and education,

3) obligate the person authorised to have contact with the child or a person, under whose custody the child remains, to declare a promise of a particular behaviour.

The Family Court should also use other methods than those stipulated in the provision in order to provide the child with contact with parents, mainly having regard to the welfare of the child.

The legislator has provided the Family Court with the authorisation to decide on the assets of the child. Following article 583 of the Polish Civil Proceedings Code, the permit to perform by the parents an act of law exceeding the scope of ordinary management or to express by the parents' consent to performing such act by the child, is issued by the Family Court on application of one of the parents, after having heard the other parent.

The aforementioned provision should be interpreted with the provision of article 101 § 3 of the k.r.o. which stipulates that parents cannot, without the Family Court's consent, perform acts of law within the scope exceeding ordinary management, nor consent to the performing of such acts by the child.

A trial is not obligatory, yet appointing a hearing shall be justified in order to hear one (or both) parents of the child. The Court may also demand a statement in writing. Without the Family Court's consent, no act of law exceeding the ordinary management of the child's assets may be performed. Such interdiction is intended as protection of the minor's interests. Acts of law performed without such consent are invalid and may not be validated.[12]

---

[12] Resolution of the Supreme Court of June 24th, 1961, I CO 16/61, OSN 1963, pos. 187.

The Family Court should examine whether the intended act of law lies within the scope of acts exceeding ordinary management or whether it violates the law or the principles of social interaction and whether it is favourable or necessary in regard to the minor and whether it is consistent with economic reasons.[13]

The decision on the permit to perform an act of law should include necessary elements and conditions of the particular act of law. Granting consent to perform an act of law, the Court assesses its validity and purposefulness as of the date of adjudication. The Court may grant a permit general in character, encompassing numerous acts repeatable in character, necessary for the proper running of a business. Such a permit has to precisely determine the conditions of undertaking such acts.

After granting a permit, the Court should verify whether the act of law that the permit encompassed has been performed and whether the conditions of the permit were realized. A permit for performing an act does not mean an obligation of performing it, therefore even after having obtained the consent, the parents may withdraw from performing an act for any reason.

The issued decision is effective as of the moment of its validation. It may not be modified or revoked (article 577 of the Polish Civil Proceedings Code) if, on the grounds of an issued permit, legal consequences in relation to third parties occurred.

Summary

Family Courts in Poland play an important role in the process of supervision of the due exercise of parental authority. The Polish legislator regards the welfare of the child as the supreme principle, which should be respected by courts adjudicating on parental authority. For the welfare of the child and providing him or her with complete protection, the Family Court may act ex officio. Every person that possesses information on an event that justifies the institution of proceedings ex officio is obligated to notify the Court of such an event. Family Courts, in order to fulfil their tasks, may use the assistance of, for example, the public prosecutor's office, the Police, educational institutions, social workers or other bodies providing custody over children.

[13] Decision of the Supreme Court of February, 24th 1995, II CRN 155/94, MoP 1995, no. 11, p.338.

THE DIVORCE OF COHABITANTS: THE ECONOMIC CONSEQUENCES OF A RELATIONSHIP BREAKDOWN IN THE LIGHT OF THE FAMILY LAW HARMONIZATION IN EUROPE

EWA KABZA

NICOLAUS COPERNICUS UNIVERSITY IN TORUŃ, POLAND

The late 1980s and early 1990s have begun a new epoch for Central and Eastern Europe. [1] The profound political and economic transformations, as well as a growing interaction with Western Europe, have brought rapid, substantial changes in such areas of family law as: marriage, divorce, family support obligations, cohabitation and childbearing. As a result, the family law systems in Europe have become even more unified. It has been a unique process. Hardly any other branch of law has experienced such serious social and demographic changes. While these transformations have been taking place, what we experienced was a great approximation of peoples in terms of communication and transportation. Consequently, more and more people have shared similar cultural experiences and values (thus, we have experienced an increased cultural homogenization). The transformations have also triggered an intense migration of individuals as well as families followed by the need for a fundamental reform of family law.[2] Going beyond national borders and adopting an international perspective have become indispensable.

A significant increase in the instances of non-marital cohabitation has been recorded. This was caused by both structural (shift from the state socialism to capitalism, the decrease of income) and ideological factors

---

[1] Changes in the family law of Western Europe have started in the 1970s. The phenomenon is called 'the great disruption' (Francis Fukuyama, *The Great Disruption* (1999).

[2] Katharina Boele-Woelki, *What comparative family law should entail*, 4 Utrecht Law Review 5 (2008).

(growing alienation,[3] lack of norms, changing attitudes and values concerning marriage and children).[4] People are no longer treating cohabitation only as a prelude to marriage (so-called 'trying out' period prior to marriage). Reluctance to make serious commitment and to bear legal or symbolic responsibility implied by the 'spouse' status, as well as philosophical concepts of liberalism and individualism, all shape today's attitude towards life.[5] Regardless of different reasons behind the contemporary state of affairs, the cohabitation of unmarried couples has come to be a socially accepted alternative to the institution of marriage. On one hand, legal systems should be responsive to new lifestyles and they should pave the way for a more individualistic approach. The individuals' right to choose their own way of living should be respected. An apt illustration of this is the following quotation: 'marriage is a wonderful institution, but who wants to live in an institution?' What cohabitation without marriage offers is a kind of non-conformist escape route from state control into a 'private life' considered to be more liberal and at the same time less binding for partners who decide upon living together. On the other hand, as marriage has become more open, so attitudes towards it have become less judgmental, more private (what is sometimes called *Le Démariage)*[6] and *de facto* very similar to unmarried cohabitation in its 'terms and conditions'. It is just a 'state into which and from which people choose to enter and exit'.[7] It may be argued that family law is called upon to address situations of injustice resulting from the application of dogmatic philosophy inherited directly from medieval religious law to a changed world – a situation in which current rules of marriage and divorce do not address problems faced by large numbers of people in family relations.[8] Changes in living patterns should be mirrored in legislation. If there is a visible tendency 'from status to contract and

---

[3] After a French jurist Bénabent who wrote in 1973: 'Instead of the individual 'belonging' to the family, it is a family which is coming to be at the service of the individual'.

[4] Arland Thornton & Dimiter Philipov, *Sweeping Changes in Marriage, Cohabitation and Childbearing in Central and Eastern Europe. New Insights from the Developmental Idealism Framework*, 25 European Journal of Population 126 (2009).

[5] 'The marital couple is not an independent entity with a mind and heart of its own, but an association of two individuals each with a separate intellectual and emotional make-up' – *Eisenstadt v. Baird*, 405 U.S. 438, 453 (1972).

[6] Irène Théry, *Le Démariage, justice et vie privée* (1993).

[7] *Bellinger v. Bellinger* [2001] 2 FLR 1046, 1082, *per* ThorpeLJ.

[8] Cynthia G. Bowman, *Unmarried Couples, Law and Public Policy* 4 (2010).

relation', it means that we should also focus on 'caring and sharing'[9] rather that on pure facts, i.e. on the conclusion of marriage.

Nowadays, the important question arises whether changes in domestic relations should be mirrored by legislation, *mutatis mutandis*; should unmarried cohabitation, currently a social phenomenon, develop into a legal institution of its own, or should it, in accordance with the presumed intention of cohabitants, exist outside the law (thus, preserving the *status quo*). In other words, should European legal systems follow the example set by countries which introduced regulations governing non-marital cohabitation, such as Croatia (art. 62 of the Constitution passed in 1990, amended in 2001)?[10] Or, is the existing law flexible enough to deal with a new family model and as a result requires no 'special' provisions for cohabitants? Answers to these questions are particularly vital in the case of cohabitation breakdown. In the majority of legal orders, irrespective of social similarities between spouses and cohabitants in their day-to-day life experience (when compared, unmarried cohabitation and marriage show 'a distinction without a difference'),[11] legal consequences of the relationship breakdown are different. Is it justified? An indispensable tool, which will provide us with lessons from the past and the present is a comparative analysis. To formulate a new perspective is an essential step forward as far as legal and political debates on alternative life-styles are concerned. We can no longer defend the unjustified claims that, due to the embedding of family law in unique national cultures, the attempt to construct European family law with a new European cohabitation model is only a 'hopeless quest' which requires the work 'more of a Sisyphus than a Hercules'. Without doubt, faithfulness to tradition and ideology is a part of a 'cherished cultural heritage' of an individual jurisdiction. However, it is not a barrier to the harmonization of family law. As has been plainly shown by our history, in the field of family ideology and law one may not really talk of unique national cultures, but rather of the pan-European culture. One may talk of the non-homogenous culture which is an amalgamation of the two cultures: the pan-European 'conservative' and the 'progressive' one, a

---

[9] Anne Bottomley & Simone Wong (eds.), *Changing Contours of Domestic Life, Family and Law. Caring and Sharing* 5 (2009).

[10] 'Marriage and legal relations in marriage, common-law marriage and the family shall be regulated by law'.

[11] George Cho, *The De Facto Relationship Act 1984 (NSW): Blurring the distinction between de iure marriages and de facto relationships*, 5 Australian Journal of Family Law 33 (1991).

result of a 'two-speed Europe'.[12] The national family laws are more determined by fluid political factors than relatively consistent cultural factors.[13] Hence, there is a glimmer of hope that either an identification of a 'common core' or an adoption of new solutions will enable the creation of a better family law. 'For all their very real differences, nations around the world find themselves facing fundamentally similar dilemmas in defining and regulating the modern family model. Accordingly, it makes sense to take a close look at what has been tried and how it has – or has not – worked elsewhere'.[14]

First and foremost, the term 'cohabitation' proper should be understood as a union of persons of opposite sexes that has not been solemnized in the legally prescribed manner. The external layer of unmarried cohabitation is an equivalent to marriage. The key element of both marital and non-marital cohabitation is a life cohabitation of a man and a woman which is a result of their willingness to start joint living and continue it for an unlimited time as a formal and informal manifestation of a *consortium vitae* between partners in one heterosexual union.[15] The definition serves to draw the distinction between traditional, certified, heterosexual 'marriage' and 'not marriage', namely, any other heterosexual relationships. Secondly, it is also essential to point out that the *ratio* of the homosexual cohabitation exclusion from this analysis is deeply rooted in the nature of this relation and consequences connected with an institutionalization of same-sex unions and/or non-marital heterosexual cohabitation. It is important to keep in mind that from the very beginning that same-sex couples have struggled for legal recognition and protection of their relationships, whereas in the case of heterosexual cohabitants there is a question about the need for multiplication of marriage-like relations. Furthermore, the regulation of the same-sex partnerships is basically an issue of human rights (the problem of discrimination, the right to marry, the right to establish a family)[16] and an ideological battlefield – a

---

[12] Masha Antokolskaia, *Family Law and national culture – Arguing against the cultural constraints argument*, 2 Utrecht Law Review 25-34 (2008).

[13] Katharina Boele-Woelki, *What comparative family...* 16 (2008).

[14] Mathias Reimann & Reinhard Zimmermann (eds.), *Oxford Handbook on Comparative Law* 1101 (2006).

[15] Olga S. Jovic, *Legal Aspects of Unmarried Cohabitation in Serbian Law – The Alternative Way for Man and Woman to Live Together* in Lynn D. Wardle & A. Scott Loveless (eds.), *Marriage and Quasi-Marital Relationships in Central and Eastern Europe* 212 (2008).

[16] See e.g. The *Schalk and Kopf v. Austria* case, Application no. 30141/04, European Court of Human Rights, June 24th, 2010.

challenge, and even a provocation, for nations and the moral standards they accept. At the same time, the introduction of the opposite-sex-couples' provisions is a matter of tension between protection and autonomy in legal order. Of course, there are legal systems (e.g. France or Spain) which put the same– and opposite–sex couples 'under the same roof'. Despite the possibility to treat homo- and heterosexual cohabitation in the same way, I would personally opt for a separate treatment of both issues due to the above mentioned differences.

The first counterargument that is usually formulated against the institutionalization of cohabitation is based on constitutional grounds. Its provisions ensure protection of marriage and family as social institutions.[17] However, the German Constitutional Court (*Bundesverfassungericht*), in the case decided on July 17th, 2002,[18] found that the constitutional value of marriage, understood as the state-assisted union of a man and a woman in a permanent life partnership based on their voluntary decision (*die Vereinigung eines Mannes mit einer Frau zu einer auf Dauer angelegten Lebensgemeinschaft, begründet auf freiem Entschluss unter Mitwirkung des Staates*) is not diminished by the act on lifetime partnerships (*Lebenspartnerschaftsgesetz*). There are at least two reasons for this. Firstly the Act does not cause any negative consequences for marriage as it is addressed to persons who cannot enter into marriage (to homosexual partners). Secondly and more importantly, the Constitutional Court held that the (constitutional) obligation to support marriage did not contain a prohibition against protection of other forms of personal existence. It is not a 'zero-sum game'. The Constitution, as a 'living' act, should be adapted to the attitudinal changes towards values in social life and so it should be interpreted in accordance with them. The constitution's stance on 'special protection' (*besonderer Schutz*) did not exclude the above interpretation since only the institution of marriage remained a

[17] Art. 110 of the Constitution of the Republic of Latvia of 1922 ('The State shall protect and support marriage, the family, the rights of parents and rights of the child'); art. 29 of the Constitution of the Italian Republic of 1947 ('The Republic recognizes the rights of the family as a natural society founded on marriage'); art. 6 of the Basic Law for the Federal Republic of Germany of 1949 ('Marriage and family shall be under special protection of the laws of the Republic'); art. 18 of the Constitution of the Republic of Poland of 1997 ('Marriage, being a union of a man and a woman, as well as the family, motherhood and parenthood, shall be placed under the protection and care of the Republic of Poland'); art. 53 (2) of the Albanian Constitution of 1998 ('Marriage and family enjoy special protection of the state').

[18] 1 BvF 1/01; available at: http://tinyurl.com/4o5y32l.

constitutionally protected value that cannot be abolished by the legislator.[19] This means that, according to the Federal Constitutional Court, constitutional protection of marriage does not constitute a hurdle in the institutionalization of other personal unions unless an equal level of protection is granted to them.

Given the fact that there are no constitutional barriers against establishing *quasi*-marital relations, it should be reconsidered whether it is only marriage (seen as a primary element of social order) that deserves protection and institutionalization. Perhaps non-marital unions should be provided with statutory protection as well? The comparative perspective on *pros* and *cons* will be presented in the consequent paragraphs. Why the comparative analysis? Truly speaking, today's law-making procedure is the process of choosing which parts of legal inheritance can be usefully developed and which should be reconsidered or rejected. The comparative approach is an indispensable tool if we want to learn lessons from the past and the present.[20] 'For all their very real differences, nations around the world find themselves facing fundamentally similar dilemmas in defining and regulating the modem family. Accordingly, it makes sense to take stock of what has been tried and what has - or has not - worked elsewhere. Comparative family law's days as an unlikely pioneer are over'.[21]

The main problem of the discussed topic is to find a golden mean between the principle of a 'clean-break' and continual responsibility borne by the former cohabitants. The first option is tightly bound to the doctrine of the law-free space ('*Rechtsfreier Raum*') and liberal concern for personal autonomy. It may be argued that 'couples do not choose to cohabit instead of marry; they just cohabit' and they consciously choose to organize their intimate relationships outside marriage ('no claims, no shadow of necessity').[22] If the cohabitation without marriage became a part of positive law, it would lose some of its freedom and consequently the essence of its advantages over marriage. In accordance with a

---

[19] Russell Miller & Volker Röben, *Constitutional Court Upholds Lifetime Partnership Act*, 2 German Law Journal (2001). Available at: http://tinyurl.com/6n5s7kr.

[20] Katharina Boele-Woelki, *What comparative family...* 3 (2008).

[21] Mathias Reimann & Reinhard Zimmermann (eds.), *Oxford Handbook...* 1101 (2006).

[22] Maybe the reason for choosing cohabitation over marriage is a believe 'that the spiritual and sentimental bases of marriage are easily colonized by a base and heartless state machinery, paving the way for invidious, deceitful journeys through marriage as well as divorce' (Melanie L. Williams, *Secrets and laws. Collected essays in law, lives and literature* 120 (2005).

postulated principle of the state non-interference in the private lives of individuals, which entitles them to cooperate with one another and to determine their own most intimate relations, it is not the task of legislator to dictate to individuals how to live their lives.[23] There is no need for a paternalistic approach towards a weaker cohabitant due to the fact that cohabitation is an institution different from marriage also in terms of the universal accessibility of a 'fast and easy divorce track' – i.e. no-fault systems, unilateral divorce, divorce on demand where judicial supervision is decreased or partly eliminated. The participants of non-marital relationships are people who absolutely do not want marriage, reject its 'terms and conditions' and its consequences.[24] That is why the general provisions of obligation and property law apply in the event that cohabitation breaks up (unjust enrichment, *societas*, dissolution of co-ownership or *negotiorum gestio*). Despite the fact that such an attitude towards cohabitation causes legal insecurity because neither the cohabitants nor third parties possess clear knowledge on their rights and obligations, and the final decision is to be made by court; the cohabitants are the ones that choose the insecurity. One may be reminded of Napoleon's famous quotation – *les concubins ignorent la loi, la loi ignore donc les concubins* and claim that it is still in force. Cohabiting partners are fed up with institutionalization. They just want to be with each other – nothing more. Consequently, if they choose not to marry, they also should not become 'the beneficiaries' of what marriage has to offer. Nevertheless, sometimes, particularly in the sphere of public law, in order to provide marriage with protection it is essential to equalize cohabitants with married couples or even to introduce completely neutral provisions. An example of this might be found in tax law regulations where benefits are granted only to those individuals who maintain another family member irrespective of their personal status (moving 'from status to contract and relation').[25] It sounds like an oxymoron, but had there been different rules applicable (on e.g. social subsidies) to married and non-married partners, the latter would have been given an advantage over the former, which would contradict the state's negative obligation not to discriminate marriage.

---

[23] Ingeborg Schwenzer, *Model Family Code from a Global Perspective,* 3-4 (2006).

[24] In this sense STS September 12th, 2005; RJ 2005/7148.

[25] Ingeborg Schwenzer, Model Family Code... 2 (2006).

Nevertheless, there are several arguments for cohabitation regulation. As a rule, cohabitants have no obligation to maintain each other.[26] However, there are quite a lot of typical situations when the need for a legal possibility to submit a maintenance claim against a partner is justified and for a paternalistic approach to be adopted. The need appears in the case of, for example, hardship, being unable to support oneself adequately or just to compensate contributions and sacrifices made in order to take care of children, home, etc. Moreover, it seems that the role of family law is to ensure that no person may escape responsibility for the type of life he or she lives.[27] Marriage can no longer be the sole focal point of establishing the responsibility. Interpersonal obligations should arise from the relationship itself, rather than from an external legislative body.[28] The relationship of trust established between partners gives rise to a legitimate expectation that the relationship will not be abruptly discontinued.[29] The consequence of such an approach, focused on post-partnership solidarity, is the recognition of the maintenance right for the cohabitants. The relations between cohabitants show that the belief about obligations being inherent, and not externally imposed, does not give satisfactory social effects.

The green light for the maintenance obligations may lead to the assimilation of matrimonial and cohabitants' property regimes. It may be asked to what extent regulations of cohabitation should mirror matrimonial property regimes. Do similar rules in the case of marriage and cohabitation breakdown have *ratio legis*? Is it possible to apply the rule 'one fits all' in such a case? Assuming that there is no formal act which acknowledges or establishes non-marital union and the moment of the cohabitation commencement *de facto* depends on the judge (due to the fact that cohabitation relationships 'often congeal more slowly into the day-to-day norms of conjugality')[30] and his discretion of the existence of *animus* (i.e. the commitment to share life at every level characteristic of an intimate,

---

[26] Compare Marvin v. Marvin 18 Cal. 3D 660 (Cal. 1976) case where the US court awarded 'palimony' upon separation.

[27] Ingeborg Schwenzer, *supra* 4 (2006).

[28] '(...) obligation may arise not simply through consent, but from shared experience in relationship with another' - Milton Regan Jr, *Alone Together: Law and the Meanings of Marriage* 12 (1999).

[29] Ingeborg Schwenzer, *Model Family Code...* 34 (2006).

[30] Heather Brook, *Conjugal Rites. Marriage and Marriage-like Relationships before the Law* 154 (2007).

close relationship between a man and woman),[31] is it feasible to stipulate regulations saying that partners *per preasumptionem* share in equal parts any asset acquired during their union unless they have agreed otherwise? Adoption of the paternalistic attitude generates further questions. Which scheme to apply – registration or default? In other words, which one to choose: an 'opt-in' or an 'opt-out' scheme? The first option offers the right of choice whether such a system is properly tailored for the parties' needs. They may accept the 'the state's invitation to become a particular kind of political subject'.[32] However, the efficiency of such a system (as the proverb 'forewarned is forearmed' has it) depends on the social awareness of the alternative solutions and the correlated consequences. By contrast, the 'opt-out' schemes are more concentrated on the protection of parties in a potentially vulnerable situation. Or, maybe we should leave the question on the analogy to marriage and the scope of protection to judges' discretion?

An instructive example of the radical approach towards cohabitation comes from Slovenia and, since the enactment of the Family Law Act of 2005, from Serbia. As early as in 1976, the Slovenian Law on Marital and other Family Relations (still binding), has entirely assimilated durable cohabitation to marriage in almost all personal and material aspects (succession, tax law, social security, civil and criminal procedural law, etc.) on condition that the existence of *de facto* union is established in prejudicial proceedings. When parties are able to prove that mere friendship has already transformed into a stable and legally relevant relationship (which is quite often a gradual process and there is no clear method of ascertaining the commencement of cohabitation) it means that since then cohabitants are also, if there is no other agreement, jointly liable for example for obligations undertaken by one partner for the running needs of the family without paying regard to the will of the parties on institutionalization of their relationship. According to family legislature in Croatia, extramarital unions are factually created and dissolved. Nevertheless, the legal consequences arising from their cohabitation in the sphere of property and maintenance rights are similar to those arising from marriage. Cohabitants who do not sign a contract are presumed to be the equally entitled co-owners of the property acquired during their union and they cannot claim different proportions (*mutatis mutandis* to the matrimonial regime – art. 248, 252, 254(2) of the Family Act 2003). Such provisions allow establishing a kind of 'beneficial (equitable) interest' of a

---

31 Dubravka Hrabar et al. (eds.), *Die Rechtsstellung nichtehelicher Lebensgemeinschaften. The Legal Status of Cohabitants* 405 (2005).

32 Heather Brook, *supra* 165.

non-owning cohabitee in property.[33] The same provisions may be found in the family law of Kosovo. There, the property acquired during factual relationship is considered to be a joint property. Provisions relating to spousal joint property of a legally registered marriage apply analogically to property relations of persons in a factual relationship (art. 58(2) of the Family Law of Kosovo).[34] Although it seems to be a good solution from the perspective of mutual relationship between cohabitants (taking into consideration the fact that a common feature of cohabitation is sharing of common living facilities in order to satisfy certain family functions[35] and that the longer a cohabitation relationship endures, the more likely it is to resemble a marriage in fact – particularly with respect to financial matters), it may bring risk both to cohabitants (in the form of the insecurity about their legal status) and to third parties.

In Eastern Europe, some 'heirs' of Bolshevik's legislation on marriage and family enacted in 1917-18 can still be traced. It is said that the legislation was not only 'an early herald of the pan-European "family law revolution"'[36] but also led to the recognition of *de facto* cohabitation significance, and in the years 1926-1944 the status of cohabitation was equalized with that of marriage concluded in a civil registry office.[37] In Ukraine it is *expressis verbis* obligatory to support another cohabitant if the cohabitation has lasted for a prolonged period of time (s. 91 of the Ukrainian Family Code). Also, the property acquired during cohabitation belongs to cohabitants as a common joint property unless they decide otherwise in a written contract (s. 74). In Lithuania, the existence of rights and duties between cohabitants with regard to assets jointly acquired and used depends on the fact of registration of their partnership and cohabiting at least for a year with the aim of creating family relations (art. 3.229 of the civil code).

It can be argued that a better solution to the problem of non-marital cohabitation institutionalization is to give spouses more freedom in shaping their marital rights and obligations. The followers of this attitude opt for the decrease of state regulations on the formation and dissolution of marriage, more negotiability in marriage itself and less conventionality.

---

[33] Cf. sec. 578/G of the Hungarian Civil Code – 'Cohabitees shall acquire joint property during they cohabitation in proportion to their contribution to acquisition'.
[34] Law Nr. 2004/32 available at: http://tinyurl.com/8aa8c8s.
[35] Michael D.A. Freeman & Christina M. Lyon, *Cohabitation without Marriage. An Essay in Law and Social Policy,* 2 (1983).
[36] Masha Antokolskaia, Harmonisation of Family Law in Europe: A Historical Perspective 238 (2006).
[37] Masha Antokolskaia, Semenoe pravo 69-70 (2002).

If so, the parties would have a real possibility to tailor mutual relations in accordance with their needs and expectations. The reexamination process of what 'marriage' is, and what it does, has already started. This is the case for example in the new Serbian Family Law Act, where the mutual fidelity between spouses has been erased from legal definitions of marital obligations. 'This means that the state interest in marriage as a firm traditional framework for the community of life of two persons of different sex weakens and the center of attention moves to (every) community of life in which certain objectives, which have hitherto been reserved exclusively for the marital community, are pursued'.[38]

As far as I am concerned, concluding a contract which deals with existing and future cohabitants' property and making entries into land registers or public records on the grounds of that contract (so that they are legally effective towards third parties) is the best solution for unmarried couples living together. In its nature, the contractual concept of unmarried cohabitation implies the partners' freedom to sign all kinds of contracts, while the validity of such legal acts is judged in compliance with the general rules. Now, such contracts are no longer considered to be contrary to the public policy;[39] hence, they are no longer unenforceable. In addition to that, in Recommendation No. R(88)3 on the validity of contracts between persons living together as an unmarried couple and their testamentary dispositions[40] the Committee of Ministers of the Council of Europe advises the governments of Member States to undertake necessary measures to ensure that contracts signed by cohabitants, relating to their property both during the cohabitation and after its end, as well as the dispositions unmarried partners make for each other in their wills should not be considered to be invalid solely because they have been concluded under these conditions. On one hand, it is not likely to be expected that a couple who are not ready to conclude a marriage will be prepared to sign a property contract. On the other, one cannot ignore the fact that cohabitation may be a fully conscious, deliberate choice which has a perfectly healthy function from an individual rational perspective. Thus, it

---

[38] Olga Cvejic Jancic, *Summary and analysis of the current law regulating marital and quasi-marital relationships in the new Serbian Family Law* in Lynn D. Wardle & A. Scott Loveless (eds.), *Marriage and Quasi-Marital Relationships...* 95 (2008).

[39] The rationale for the prohibition of contractual cohabitation was that it implied contracting sexual services – i.e. an 'immoral consideration'. Today, contracts between cohabitants are immoral only when the nature of such a contract is assumed to revolve around the provision of sexual services.

[40] Recommendation available at: http://tinyurl.com/7ct7l8w.

is essential for parties to be fully informed on the regulations concerning non-marital unions. They also need to understand their deliberate choice to avoid marital law and to feel that the solution is in their best interest. And the process of increasing legal awareness of all rights and legal solutions seems to be the task for us – lawyers.

PUBLIC LAW

TERRITORIAL SELF-GOVERNMENT IN POLAND AND SELECTED COUNTRIES OF WESTERN EUROPE: BASIC PROBLEMS

STANISŁAW BUŁAJEWSKI

UNIVERSITY OF WARMIA AND MAZURY IN OLSZTYN, POLAND

The essence of territorial self-government in Poland

The three-tier structure of the territorial self-government in Poland was established on January 1st, 1999, which was the date of validity of the Act of July 24th, 1998, on the introduction of a fundamental three-tier territorial division of the state.[1] According to art. 1 of the aforementioned Act, the units of the fundamental territorial division of the state are communes (*gmina*), districts (*powiat*), and provinces (*województwo*). A little earlier, on 5th June 1998, the Lower Chamber of the Parliament of Poland (*Sejm*) adopted two statutes which regulate the form of government at the district[2] and province level.[3]

Irrespective of those statutory changes, the commune remains the most fundamental unit of the territorial self-government. It is the commune which is assumed to hold the principal responsibilities and competences in the system of territorial self-government.[4]

The term 'self-government' (*samorząd*) has numerous meanings. According to the Polish language dictionary, it means 'autonomous and independent performance of certain administrative functions by a specific public body'.[5] There are several types of self-government: business, cooperative, commune, municipal, district, provincial, territorial, student,

---

[1] Journal of Laws of 1998, no. 96, item 603, as amended.

[2] Act of June 5th, 1998 on the district-level self-government (consolidated text: Journal of Laws of 2001, no. 142, item 1592, as amended).

[3] *Ibid.*

[4] Zygmunt Niewiadomski in Id. (ed.), *Samorząd terytorialny ustrój i gospodarka* 90 (2001).

[5] Elżbieta Sobol, *Słownik języka polskiego* 901 (2005).

or attorney self-government.[6] According to legal literature, 'the term self-government comprises the following elements:

1. a selected social group, defined by the law, whose membership is established by law;
2. appointed to perform the duties of state administration, within the limits established by law, in an autonomous manner, in forms that are characteristic of state administration;
3. having its own organization defined by the law, which is of representative type and remains under the control of the social group which elected it;
4. the self-government organization, having a decentralized form, acting under the applicable law, is supervised solely by the state authorities;
5. self-government bodies, while not being state administration bodies, constitute an integral part of the uniform administrative apparatus'.[7]

Territorial self-government is a social group, distinguished in the structure of the state, formed under the law for autonomous performance of public administration and equipped with material means enabling it to perform its duties.[8] During the partitions period, the self-government in Poland existed to varying degrees and in various forms, and in the inter-war period it became the foundation of the form of government on the local level. Only in 1933, with the adoption of the so-called 'integration statute,' the system of territorial self-government units was restructured to correspond to basic territorial division into communes, districts, and provinces. After World War II, this structure was replaced with a system of people's councils (*rada narodowa*) as the so-called uniform bodies of state authorities. From April 1950, practically until March 1990, when the

---

[6] Cf.: Jerzy Oniszczuk, *Samorząd terytorialny w orzecznictwie Trybunału Konstytucyjnego* 19 (2002); Stanisław Bułajewski, *Samorządy zawodowe i gospodarcze jako samorządy specjalne* in Marek Chmaj (ed.), *Wolność zrzeszania się w Polsce* 201-204 (2008).

[7] Teresa Rabska, *Podstawowe pojęcia administracji* in 1 Jerzy Starościak (ed.), *System prawa administracyjnego* 332 (1974); see also Zbigniew Leoński, *Samorząd terytorialny w RP* 6 (4th ed. 2002); Zbigniew Bukowski et. al., *Ustrój samorządu terytorialnego* 32-33 (2nd ed. 2005); Agnieszka Korzeniowska, Struktura samorządu terytorialnego w Polsce in Id. (ed.), *ABC samorządu terytorialnego* 35-36 (2004).

[8] Eugeniusz Ochendowski, *Prawo administracyjne część ogólna* 299 (1999).

Act on territorial self-government was adopted, there was no local self-government in Poland.[9]

Let us go back to the essence of territorial self-government. One must keep in mind that in practically all European democratic states the form of government on the local level is based on the principle of dualism. What this means is that nearly all local tasks are performed by self-government bodies, which are both subordinated to the local community and represent it. Only a small percentage of the tasks is performed by the central government administration bodies. As L. Garlicki is right in observing, 'the essence of territorial self-government is to identify the so-called communal corporation (mostly communes) and to grant it a special status, which enables it to manage its own problems. The nature of territorial self-government is universal because it pertains to the whole territory of the state and covers all of its residents. [...] Of key importance to the definition of the structure of territorial self-government is its autonomy (independence of the central government administration), which enables territorial self-government units (communal corporations) to perform tasks intended to satisfy the needs of the residents'.[10] In L. Garlicki's opinion, independence of territorial self-government consists of:

1. the exclusive right to perform certain tasks (the so-called own tasks);[11]
2. separate organizational structure;[12]
3. legal personality (of communes, districts, and provinces) and ownership of local public property (commune property, district property, and property of the provincial self-government);
4. budgetary and financial autonomy;
5. limitation of interference of the central government solely to supervisory procedures;
6. judicial protection of the rights and interests of self-government entities.[13]

---

[9] Cf. Leszek Garlicki, *Polskie prawo konstytucyjne* 216-217 (2001); Jan Galster, Samorząd terytorialny i prawo wyborcze do rad gmin, rad powiatów i sejmików województw in Zbigniew Witkowski (ed.), *Prawo konstytucyjne* 370 (1998).

[10] Leszek Garlicki, *supra* 316.

[11] See verdict of the Constitutional Tribunal of November 3rd, 1999, K 13/99, OTK ZU 1999, no. 7, item 155.

[12] See verdict of the Constitutional Tribunal of April 19th, 1999, U. 3/98, OTK ZU 1999, no. 4, item 70.

[13] Of course this autonomy may be subject to some limitations, however they can only be imposed by a statute; see the verdict of the Constitutional Tribunal of April

There are many other definitions of and opinions on territorial self-government; however, due to both the scope of this article and the lack of a single universally accepted definition, their presentation would be unnecessary.[14] One must keep in mind that opinions about territorial self-government expressed by representatives of legal sciences reflect the conditions of political and social life as well as the legal solutions adopted in various countries. This is why even a brief presentation of all the theories, models, and opinions regarding territorial self-government in this article is impossible.[15]

4th, 1998, K 38/97, OTK ZU 1998, no. 3, item 3; the verdict of the Constitutional Tribunal of May 13th, 1997, K 20/96, OTK ZU 1997, no. 2, item 18.

[14] Territorial self-government is described and defined, among others, by: Zygmunt Niewiadomski, *Samorząd terytorialny w Konstytucji RP*, 3 Samorząd Terytorialny 5-7 (2000); Wiesław Kisiel, *Ustrój samorządu terytorialnego w Polsce* 17-25 (2003); Zbigniew Bukowski et. al., *Ustrój samorządu...* 38-42 (2005); Mariusz Kotulski, *Pojęcie i istota samorządu terytorialnego*, 1-2 Samorząd Terytorialny 82-90 (2000); Sławomir Fundowicz, *Osoby prawne prawa publicznego w prawie polskim*, 3 Samorząd Terytorialny 6-9 (2000); Antoni Agopszowicz et al., *Prawo samorządu terytorialnego w zarysie* 11-16 (2001); Teresa Rabska, *Pozycja samorządu terytorialnego w Konstytucji*, 2 Ruch Prawniczy, Ekonomiczny i Socjologiczny 42-46 (1995); Maria Jastrzębska, *Nowy model samorządu terytorialnego. Istota, zadania, autonomia, władze, jednostki organizacyjne, finanse, nadzór*, 1-2 Samorząd Terytorialny 12-17 (1999); Teresa Rabska, *Pozycja samorządu terytorialnego w konstytucji*, 5 Samorząd Terytorialny 16-20 (1995); Jerzy Stępień, Samorząd w ustawie zasadniczej, 11 Samorząd Terytorialny 40-43 (1994); Zygmunt Niewiadomski (ed.), *Prawo administracyjne część ogólna* 139-150 (2nd ed. 2002); Stanisław Paczyński, *Techniczno-prawne momenty w organizacji związków komunalnych* 7-26 (1933); Maurycy Jaroszyński, *Rozważania ideologiczne i programowe na temat samorządu*, 20,21,23 Samorząd 3-24 (1936); Konstanty Krzeczkowski, *Gmina jako podmiot polityki komunalnej*, 3 Samorząd Terytorialny 3-17 (1938); Stanisław Wykrętowicz, *Samorząd jako wyraz demokracji obywatelskiej* in Id. (ed.), *Samorząd w Polsce, istota, formy, zadania* 13-77 (2001); Zbigniew Leoński, *Ustrój zadania samorządu terytorialnego* in Ibid., 101-116; Jan Sobczak, *Idee samorządowe w Europie i w Polsce XIX i początku XX w.* 1-5 (1999); Janusz Mordwiłko, *Samorząd terytorialny w tekstach siedmiu projektów konstytucyjnych*, 11 Samorząd Terytorialny 44-49 (1994); Bogdan Dolnicki, *Samorząd terytorialny zagadnienia ustrojowe* 13-15 (1999).

[15] More information can be found in Jan Boć (ed.), *Prawo administracyjne* 188-194 (2005).

The constitutional foundations of territorial self-government in Poland

The concept of a multi-tier territorial self-government is established by art. 164 (2) of the Constitution of the Republic of Poland. In the opinion of Piotr Winczorek, which I fully support, the Constitution not only allows, but requires, establishing self-government units other than the commune by way of a statute, without defining whether those units are to be of regional or also local nature.[16] Regardless of the above, the authors of the Constitution decided that only a regular statute may be a foundation for the functioning of units of territorial self-government other than the commune.

It must be emphasized that the structure of the units of self-government in Poland is based on the basic principles established (mainly) in the first chapter of the current Constitution. Those principles include:

1. Subsidiarity – this is a universal principle, which means that it applies not only to territorial self-government. It is expressly stated in the preamble of the Constitution.[17] Subsidiarity means that the basic needs of the people should be satisfied at the lowest possible level of the government. If a self-governing community is unable to perform such tasks autonomously, then the central government should provide assistance. For the purpose of implementing this principle, the authors of the Constitution in specific provisions established the requirement that the state must decentralize public authorities, transfer the assumed duties to the territorial self-government, and establish the commune as the key element of the territorial self-government system.[18]
2. The principle of a democratic law-abiding state, which means that new structures (units) of territorial self-government are established and, consequently, such structures are charged with specific duties and granted specific competences. This approach leads to full

---

[16] Piotr Winczorek, *Komentarz do Konstytucji Rzeczypospolitej Polskiej z dnia 2 kwietnia 1997 r.* 216 (2000); Also Zygmunt Niewiadomski, *Samorząd terytorialny...* 10 (2000).

[17] '[…] we establish this Constitution of the Republic of Poland as the basic law for the State, based [...] the principle of aiding in the strengthening the powers of citizens and their communities'.

[18] Art. 15 (1), art. 163, art. 164 (1). Also see Zygmunt Niewiadomski, *Samorząd terytorialny...* 35 (2000); Leon Kieres, *Zasady ustrojowe samorządu terytorialnego* in Wiesława Miemiec & Bogdan Cybulski (ed.), Samorządowy poradnik budżetowy na 1997 r. Zagadnienia finansowe i prawno-ustrojowe 13 (1997).

implementation of art. 2 of the Constitution, which defines Poland as a democratic law-abiding state, which implements the principles of social justice. 'Territorial self-government is a necessary component of the structure of a democratic law-abiding state. The changes to the form of government implemented after 1989 were intended to transform a centralized state into a civic state whose foundation was to be formed, in part, by territorial self-government'.[19]

3. Unitary character of the state. This principle, established by art. 3 of the Constitution, means that the Republic of Poland is a unitary state. This does not mean, however, that the territory of Poland cannot be divided into various units, i.e. communes, districts, and provinces. Of course, this is not only possible but necessary. Nevertheless, such units cannot gain the legal status of an independent state.[20]
4. Decentralization of public authorities. This principle is established in art. 15 and 16 of the Constitution. It ensures the participation of territorial self-government in the exercise of public power in areas that are not restricted by a statute for the central government.[21] However, in order to enable an actual exercise of the powers, the units of territorial self-government should receive adequate material means and property.[22]
5. The principle of legalism, established in art. 7 of the Constitution, which provides that 'public authorities act under and within the limits of law.' In the case of territorial self-government, this principle means that it is considered as a public authority.
6. Co-creation of law (acts of local law). Art. 87 (2) of the Constitution expressly provides that 'the sources of the universally

---

[19] Verdict of the Constitutional Tribunal of February 20th, 2002, K 39/00, OTK ZU 2002, no. 1A, item 4; also see Mariusz Kotulski, *Samorząd terytorialny jako instytucja realizująca zasadę demokratycznego państwa prawnego* in Stanisław Michałowski (ed.), *Samorząd terytorialny III Rzeczypospolitej – dziesięć lat doświadczeń* 41-52 (2002).

[20] More information can be found in Dorota Dąbek & Jan Zimmermann, *Decentralizacja poprzez samorząd terytorialny w ustawodawstwie i orzecznictwie pokonstytucyjnym* in Paweł Sarnecki (ed.), *Samorząd terytorialny – zasady ustrojowe i praktyka* 10 (2006).

[21] See verdict of the Constitutional Tribunal of June 28th, 1994, K 14/93, OTK 1994, part 1, item 13.

[22] More information can be found in Mirosław Granat, *Zasada decentralizacji władzy publicznej i samorządu terytorialnego* in Wiesław Skrzydło (ed.), *Polskie prawo konstytucyjne* 146-148 (2005); Adam Jamróz, *Demokracja* 51-53 (1999).

binding law in the Republic of Poland are acts of local law – in the areas of competence of the bodies that adopted them'.

7. The principle of freedom of association. According to art. 172 (2) of the Constitution, not only communes, but also districts and provinces have the right to be members of international associations of local and regional communities and to cooperate with local and regional communities in other countries.
8. The principle of autonomy, which is established in art. 165 (2) of the Constitution. The principle means that in the event of a breach of the autonomy of a unit of territorial self-government, such a unit has the right to enforce its rights before an independent court. Thus, under the substantive civil and procedural law, communes, districts, and provinces – as any other legal persons – have not only the capacity to be a party in court proceedings, but also the capacity to sue. The ability to be a party in court proceedings is unlimited and covers the ability to be a party or a participant of court proceedings in practically any civil case. Thus, units of territorial self-government may sue, be sued, and participate in court proceedings.[23] Judicial protection of the autonomy of communes, districts, and provinces also covers those fields of their activities where self-government bodies are present as public authorities making binding decisions in the process of adoption and application of law.[24]
9. The principle of representative democracy, established in art. 169 (1) of the Constitution, means the priority of indirect democracy in performance of the tasks of the territorial self-government. As far as the bodies are concerned, each unit of the territorial self-government has decision-making and supervisory bodies (commune council, district council, and provincial parliament) and executive bodies (commune head (*wójt*), mayor, city president, district executive body, and provincial executive body). What is important is that the decision-making and supervisory bodies in units of territorial self-government must always be elected in direct, general, and equal elections. On the other hand, the executive bodies can be elected in direct or indirect elections, depending on

[23] Bogdan Dolnicki (ed.), *Ustawa o samorządzie powiatowym-komentarz* 30 (2005).

[24] Piotr Winczorek, *Komentarz do Konstytucji...* 217-218 (2000); Jan Boć (ed.), *Konstytucje Rzeczypospolitej oraz komentarz do Konstytucji RP z 1997 roku* 259-260 (1998).

the legislator's decision. Currently only commune heads, mayors, and city presidents are elected directly by the voters.

10. The principle of indirect application of the Constitution is established by art. 8 (2). The Constitution, being the highest-ranking act of law, may be applied in the creation of law by the bodies of territorial self-government units in situations where a given constitutional norm has not been given a definitive form.
11. The principle of presumption of competence of territorial self-government is established by articles 163 and 164 of the Constitution. Thus, if the Constitution or the relevant statutes do not provide for a requirement that a given task be performed by a public body other than the territorial self-government, then the task must be presumed to be in the area of competence of the territorial self-government. This principle is closely linked with the principle of decentralization of public authorities expressed in art. 15 (1) of the Constitution.[25]

Of great significance to this discussion is the European Charter of Local Self-Government,[26] which regulates the status of territorial self-government units in relation to the central governments in various states and in relation to the governments of other states and their local self-government units. The charter was executed in Strasbourg on October 15th, 1985, and became legally valid on September 1st, 1988. Poland ratified the Charter in its entirety in 1993.[27] The key objective of the Charter is to promote the idea of local self-government as the main element of democracy by stimulating the activity of citizens in their place of residence, which is connected with the duty to hear the opinions of local communities in all matters that directly affect them.

In art. 3, titled 'Concept of local self-government', the Charter states that '[l]ocal self-government denotes the right and the ability of local authorities, within the limits of the law, to regulate and manage a substantial share of public affairs under their own responsibility and in the interests of the local population'. The Charter also emphasizes that '[t]his right shall be exercised by councils or assemblies composed of members freely elected by secret ballot on the basis of direct, equal, universal suffrage and which may possess executive organs responsible to them'. Of

---

[25] See Tadeusz Milczarek, *Samorząd powiatowy,* 14 (1999).

[26] The Charter was previously referred to in Poland as the 'European Charter of Territorial Self-Government'. The title of this act was changed in item 1 of the Announcement of the Minister of Foreign Affairs of August 22nd, 2006 in correction of an error (Journal of Laws no. 154, item 1107).

[27] Consolidated text: Journal of Laws of 1994, no. 124, item 607, as amended.

course, as the Charter emphasizes, this provision does not exclude 'recourse to assemblies of citizens, referendums or any other form of direct citizen participation where it is permitted by statute'.

The constitutional foundations and the structure of territorial self-government in selected countries of Western Europe

As L. Rajca rightly observed, contemporary literature contains several typologies of territorial self-government systems.[28] John Loughlin and B. Guy Peters identified four types of 'state traditions' in Western Europe: Anglo-Saxon, Germanic, Napoleonic, and Scandinavian. According to those authors, in the Anglo-Saxon tradition, decentralization takes the form of local self-government (United Kingdom) and the relations between the state and society are pluralistic. In the Germanic tradition (e.g. Germany, Austria, and the Netherlands), decentralization takes the form of cooperative federalism and the relations between the state and society are fairly limited. In the Napoleonic tradition (e.g. France, Italy, Portugal, and Greece), decentralization takes the form of regionalization of a unitary state and the relations between the state and society are antagonistic. In the Scandinavian tradition (Sweden, Norway, Denmark and Finland), decentralization takes the form of a strong local autonomy/self-government, and the relations between the state and society are limited.

Of note are the differences between federal and unitary states with regards to the tasks performed by territorial self-government units. One must keep in mind that in unitary states each of the self-government bodies derives the basis for its functioning from laws adopted by central state authorities. In unitary states, which are centralized, only a horizontal division of the government is possible and territorial self-government is the principal institution of the horizontal division of the government only with regards to executive power. Unitary states with various degrees of centralization in the European Union include France, the Netherlands, Italy, Spain, and the United Kingdom. On the other hand, in federal states there is a vertical division of the government into the legislative branch, the executive branch, and most commonly the judicial branch. This division is in line with the division of sovereignty between the federation and its components. By definition, federations are non-centralized states and their essence is greater limitation of the role of the central government

[28] Lucyna Rajca, *Modele samorządu terytorialnego* in Id. (ed.), *Samorząd terytorialny w Europie Zachodniej* 14 (2010).

to the benefit of local self-government. Notably, unlike in unitary states, there may be various systems of territorial self-government in each federal state. Examples of federal states are Austria, Belgium, Germany, and Switzerland.[29]

The constitutional foundations and the structure of local self-government in France

The constitutional foundations of the French local self-government are defined in Title XII of the French Constitution, titled 'On Territorial Communities'. [30] Art. 72 of the Constitution reads: 'The territorial communities of the Republic shall be the Communes, the Departments, the Regions, the Special-Status communities and the Overseas Territorial communities to which article 74 applies. Any other territorial community created, if need be, to replace one or more communities provided for by this paragraph shall be created by statute. Territorial communities may make decisions in all matters arising under powers that can best be exercised at their level. In the conditions provided for by statute, these communities shall be self-governing through elected councils and shall have power to make regulations for matters within their jurisdiction. Territorial communities or associations thereof may, in the manner provided for by an Institutional Act, except where the essential conditions for the exercise of public freedoms or of a right guaranteed by the Constitution are affected,, where provision is made by statute or regulation, as the case may be, derogate on an experimental basis for limited purposes and duration from provisions laid down by statute or regulation governing the exercise of their powers. No territorial community may exercise authority over another. However, where the exercising of a power requires the combined action of several territorial communities, one of those communities or one of their associations may be authorized by statute to organize such combined action. In the territorial communities of the Republic, the State representative, representing each of the members of the Government, shall be responsible for national interests, administrative supervision and compliance with the law'.

The territorial structure of France comprises 22 metropolitan regions and 4 overseas regions. The regions consist of departments: 96 metropolitan departments and 4 overseas departments (Guadelupe,

---

[29] Lucyna Rajca, *Modele samorządu...* 17-18 (2010).

[30] Constitution of the French Republic of October 4th, 1958 (as of February 22nd, 1996). See Wiesław Skrzydło, *Konstytucja Francji. Wstęp i tłumaczenie* (2005).

Réunion, French Guiana, and Saint-Pierre-et-Miguelon). Four of the above-mentioned departments are at the same time overseas regions. Departments, in turn, are divided into circuits (*arrondisements*), and further into cantons. The basic territorial units are the communes. One must keep in mind that circuits and cantons do not have their own administration and therefore the proper structure is formed by communes, departments, and regions. [31] There French Republic has 36,783 communes.[32]

The constitutional foundations and the structure of territorial self-government in the Italian Republic

The provisions pertaining to the principles of the territorial form of government in the Italian Republic are found in art. 5 and 115 of the Italian Constitution. Art. 5 provides that: 'The Republic is one and indivisible. It recognizes and promotes local autonomies, and implements the fullest measure of administrative decentralization in those services, which depend on the State. The Republic adapts the principles and methods of its legislation to the requirements of autonomy and decentralization'. On the other hand, art. 114 of the Constitution, which is a part of Title V,[33] Regions, Provinces – Municipalities, provides that: 'The Republic is composed of the Municipalities, the Provinces, the Metropolitan Cities, the Regions and the State. Municipalities, provinces, metropolitan cities and regions are autonomous entities having their own statutes, powers and functions in accordance with the principles laid down in the Constitution. Rome is the capital of the Republic. Its status is regulated by State Law'. The Constitution of the Italian Republic defines the following regions: Piedmont, Aosta Valley, Lombardy, Trentino-Alto Adige, Veneto, Friuli-Venezia Giulia, Liguria, Emilia-Romagna, Tuscany, Umbria, Marches, Lazio, Abruzzo, Molise, Campania, Apulia, Basilicata, Calabria, Sicily, and Sardinia.[34] Executive powers are exercised by the state and the regions in observance of the provisions of the Constitution

---

[31] Jacek Wojnicki, *Samorząd terytorialny we Francji* in Lucyna Rajca (ed.), *Samorząd terytorialny...* 28ff. (2010); see also Michał Mariański, *Samorząd terytorialny we Francji* in Bronisław Sitek et al. (eds.), *Funkcjonowanie samorządu terytorialnego w wybranych krajach UE* 63-64. (2011).

[32] Data as of 2002; see Henri Oberdorff, *Les institutions administratives* 177 (2002).

[33] Title V of the Constitution of Italy was modified by the constitutional statute of October 18th, 2001, no. 3 (GU of October 24th 2001, no. 248).

[34] See art. 131 of the Constitution of the Italian Republic.

and of the conditions established by the European Union law and international obligations. Of note is the fact that regions exercise legislative powers over all matters that are not expressly reserved for the state legislature. The regional bodies are the regional council, the *giunta* (the executive body), and the giunta's president. As far as the intermediate level of the territorial division is concerned, the current number of Italian provinces is 107. As far as the communes are concerned, for 150 years their number has remained fairly constant and now is slightly more than 8,000.[35]

The constitutional foundations and the structure of territorial self-government in the German Federal Republic

The constitutional foundations for functioning of territorial self-government in the German Federal Republic are defined in art. 28 of the German Basic Law, which provides: '(1) The constitutional order in the Länder must conform to the principles of a republican, democratic, and social state governed by the rule of law, within the meaning of this Basic Law. In each Land, county, and municipality the people shall be represented by a body chosen in general, direct, free, equal, and secret elections. In county and municipal elections, persons who possess citizenship in any Member State of the European Community are also eligible to vote and to be elected in accord with European Community Law. In municipalities a local assembly may take the place of an elected body. (2) Municipalities must be guaranteed the right to regulate all local affairs on their own responsibility, within the limits prescribed by the laws. Within the limits of their functions designated by law, associations of municipalities shall also have the right of self-government according to the laws. (3) The Federation shall guarantee that the constitutional order of the Länder conforms to the basic rights and to the provisions of paragraphs (1) and (2) of this Article'.[36]

As K. Miaskowska-Daszkiewicz and J. Kowalik observe correctly, in principle the German Federal Republic has a two-tier territorial self-government. The basic unit of territorial self-government is the municipality which, in turn, constitutes a part of a larger unit, i.e. the

---

[35] More information can be found in Izolda Bokszczanin, *Samorząd terytorialny w Republice Włoskiej* in Lucyna Rajca (ed.), *Samorząd terytorialny...* 55ff. (2010).
[36] The Basic Law of the German Federal Republic of May 23rd, 1949, as of January 1st, 2007; See Bogusław Banaszak, *Konstytucja Niemiec (wstęp),* (2008).

district. However, cities with populations larger than 100,000 are by law excluded from districts and constitute separate so-called urban districts. Of course, there are numerous exceptions to this rule. The bodies of the units are the municipal (or city) council and the mayor (or the *Oberbürgermeister* – over-mayor) in municipalities, district councils and district heads in districts.[37]

The structure of the units of the federation and the territorial self-government in Switzerland

Switzerland is a confederacy of cantons, which enjoy extensive autonomy. As far as territorial self-government is concerned, the only units in Switzerland are communes, which can be divided into municipalities (urban communes) and rural communes.

Municipalities are communes that have a population of over 10,000, or less if the locality had its town status established in the Middle Ages. Of note is the fact that both municipalities and rural communes enjoy the same rights. According to art. 50 of the Federal Constitution of the Swiss Confederation of April 18th, 1999, communes are guaranteed autonomy in relation to cantonal law. Also, the federation must be aware of the possible consequences of its actions to communes. The Constitution also emphasizes the specific situation of municipalities and metropolitan areas, and even mountainous areas. Very interesting is the fact that the Swiss communes have two executive power systems. In some communes the legislative power is held by the commune's parliament and the executive power by the commune's council; while in others there is direct democracy where the citizens gather at least four times a year in a commune assembly to vote on important decisions. In the latter system, the executive power is also exercised by the commune's council.[38]

---

[37] More information can be found in Katarzyna Miaskowska-Daszkiewicz & Janina Kowalik, *Samorząd terytorialny w Republice Federalnej Niemiec* in Lucyna Rajca (ed.), *Samorząd terytorialny...* 130ff. (2010); see also Aleksander W. Bauknecht, *Samorząd terytorialny w Republice Federalnej Niemiec* in Bronisław Sitek et al. (eds.), *Funkcjonowanie samorządu...* 112ff. (2011).

[38] More information can be found in Izabela Rycerska, *Tendencje reform samorządu terytorialnego w Szwajcarii* in Lucyna Rajca (ed.), *Samorząd terytorialny...* 183ff. (2010).

The structure and the constitutional conditions of the territorial self-government in the Kingdom of Sweden

Sweden is a constitutional monarchy. The Constitution of Sweden is not a single act of law, as it comprises several documents, such as the 1974 Instrument of Government Act, the 1948 Freedom of the Press Act (see: abolishment of censorship in Sweden), the 1810 Act of Succession, and the 1991 Fundamental Law on Freedom of Expression. The relevant constitutional provisions on territorial self-government are found in chapter 1 art. 1 of the Constitution of the Kingdom of Sweden; chapter 1 art. 8 provides that the Kingdom is divided into municipalities and counties.[39]

In 2005 Sweden had 290 municipalities, 18 regular regions and 2 temporary regions: Skane and Wästra Götland. Of note is the fact that the act on territorial self-government, which regulates its organization and competences, includes identical provisions for both municipalities and counties. Also, the Swedish municipality constitutes not only a unit of the territorial self-government, but also a unit of the state's administrative division. The municipality and county councils are an obligatory body in the self-government system. The executive, managing, and coordinating body (executive committee) is the executive, which is elected in indirect elections by the councilors.[40]

Conclusions

It may easily be concluded from the information presented herein that territorial self-government, both in Poland and in other contemporary democratic states, has been exposed to significant changes in its external socio-economic and political environment. Unfortunately, globalization has brought about a crisis of representative democracy and the functioning of territorial self-government is no longer so attractive to the local communities. One solution to this problem would be stronger involvement of the citizens in direct decision-making, which would certainly help solve numerous complex problems of public life. It appears that the best solution to this problem is to introduce direct democracy by organizing the largest

---

[39] More information can be found in Beata Słobodzian, *Samorząd terytorialny w Królestwie Szwecji* in Lucyna Rajca (ed.) *supra* 231ff.

[40] An interesting solution in the Swedish electoral law is election of deputy councillors, who perform their duties in the event that the actual councillors are ill or cannot perform their duties for other reasons.

number of referendums to resolve important problems of local communities.

An analysis of the basic issues connected with the functioning of territorial self-government in Poland and in Western European countries confirms that the structures of territorial self-government are quite different in different countries. As an example, Switzerland has only one tier of territorial self-government while Poland has three. Recent decades have demonstrated a slow but obvious trend to make the laws regulating the functioning of territorial self-government in different countries more similar. This has been demonstrated in this article, too. In nearly all democratic European countries, the foundation of territorial self-government is defined in their constitutions. This only confirms how important, albeit unappreciated, the problem of local self-government is.

As an active member of local government,[41] I believe that territorial self-government is a necessary element of public authority, which enables quick, effective, and advantageous resolution of the most important problems of local communities. A state without territorial self-government cannot be considered as a truly democratic state.

[41] The author not only holds a research and teaching post and is a lawyer, but also is the Chairman of the Council of the Mrągowo District and a councillor with 13 years' experience.

ASSESSMENT OF THE QUALITY OF PUBLIC ADMINISTRATION

SEBASTIAN BENTKOWSKI

UNIVERSITY OF WARMIA AND MAZURY IN OLSZTYN, POLAND

Management systems based, among others, on models of assessment of an organizations' activities, are used more and more often to improve the functioning of public administration. As an example, since the early 1990s, Poland has implemented programmes promoting adoption of ISO management systems, and since 2009 the Ministry of Interior and Administration has implemented a systemic project, intended for public administration, in order to popularise the knowledge of and to prepare public administration for adoption of the Common Assessment Framework (CAF). The framework assumes that achievement of desirable results in the activities of an organization depends on the quality of its leadership, which influences the policies and strategies, the employees, the interpersonal relations, the assets, and the processes. The quality of leadership is evaluated by performing a general and a detailed assessment as a part of a comprehensive process of analysis of the results of an organization's activity.[1]

In the science of praxeology, the term assessment is defined as any statement where a given portion of reality is assigned a certain value (positive or negative).[2] Sometimes, assessment is limited to certain aspects. For example, T. Kotarbiński does not discuss any assessments,

---

[1] Marian Moszoro et al. *Efektywne Metody Zarządzania w Administracji Publicznej* 14-18 (2002); Jacek Czaputowicz, *Wspólna Metoda Oceny Administracji Publicznej w państwach UE*, 4 Służba Cywilna (2002). See also Stowarzyszenie Konsultantów, *Powszechny Model Oceny – Doskonalenie zarządzania w urzędach administracji publicznej w Polsce* 2ff.; Public Administration Department of the Ministry of Interior and Administration, *CAF w samorządzie terytorialnym. Przygotowanie jednostek samorządu terytorialnego do stosowania Wspólnej Metody Oceny (CAF) w procesie mierzenia potencjału i dokonań poprzez szkolenia pracowników i pomoc doradczą* 19ff. (2010).

[2] M. Lewandowski, *Analiza struktur zadań oceniających*, 3-4 Prakseologia 55-56 (1975).

but rather the so-called practical assessments, which include assessments that do not express feelings or emotions but rather refer to the usefulness or uselessness of a given factor involved in an action, e.g. the actor, the tool, etc.[3]

An analysis of the above-mentioned definitions of the term assessment in the context of the activities of public administration makes it possible to identify the objectives, the functions, and the criteria of assessments of public administrations. In particular, the objective of assessments of public administration is to determine:

- whether and to what extent public administration bodies perform their duties;
- whether and to what extent public administration is capable of creating a legal and organizational system that would enable control of socio-economic development;
- what its ability to perform tasks is, i.e. what the quality of the staff and the level of technical equipment available to the administration is.[4]

The functions of assessments of the activities of public administration may, in turn, be divided into political, social, economic, and praxeological. The political function is important in shaping the policies of the state intended to change the socio-economic conditions. The social function is important for the satisfaction of social needs by the administration. The third function pertains to the actions of public administration concerning proper financing of the tasks performed by it. The praxeological function makes it possible to identify and apply better organizational solutions.[5]

The basic criteria for assessing the functioning of various institutions are defined in organization and management theory and in praxeology; these include the 'worth' of an effective action, such as effectiveness,

---

[3] Tadeusz Kotarbiński, *Traktat o dobrej robocie* 345 (1975); (the English translation was published as: *Praxeology. An introduction to the science of efficient action* (1965).

[4] More information on the criteria of assessment of public administration is found in Marian Kruk-Ołpiński, *Kryteria oceny działalności administracji państwowej,* 20 PPE series report 39 (1983). The matter of the criteria of quality assessment of public administration discussed herein has also been discussed more broadly in Sebastian Bentkowski & Marian Kruk-Ołpiński, *Jakościowe kryteria ocen administracji publicznej* in *Jakość administracji publicznej* (2004).

[5] Marian Kruk-Ołpiński, *Kryteria oceny działalności...* 39-40 (1983). The topic of qualitative assessment criteria and the determinants of the quality of public administration has been discussed in the doctoral thesis of Sebastian Bentkowski in Sebastian Bentkowski, *Normatywne wyznaczniki jakości administracji publicznej* (2006) (not published).

economy, and advantages, analyzed to determine the value that makes it possible to compare, positively or negatively, the desirable and undesirable effects of actions. J. Zieleniewski distinguishes two types of 'value': that of the costs and of the outcome. The value of the costs is the sum of the value of all the negative effects of an action, while the value of a (useful) outcome is the sum of all the positively assessed effects of an action.[6] Depending on the value of the anticipated and desirable states in the future and the resources needed to achieve the outcome of an action, value can be divided into the value of the objective and the value of the costs.[7] In public administration, the value of the objective is connected with such tasks as fulfillment of the society's needs and assurance of socio-economic development. On the other hand, the worth of the outcome is the result of the actions taken by public administration, i.e. the way an impact is made on society by the legal-organizational system and the style of administration. The last criterion is the value of the costs, which is regarded as the public administration's potential, i.e. properly qualified staff provided with the required equipment, premises, and funds.

When assessing actions based on the above-mentioned criteria, one may conclude that an action is considered as effective if the value of the objective is equal to the worth of the outcome. Achieving effectiveness in the activities of public administration requires such organization of public administration that ensures achieving the legally defined objectives. On the other hand, assessment of administration based on the economic criterion, defined as the ratio of the worth of the useful outcomes to the costs and the advantages, as the difference between the worth of the useful outcomes and the value of the costs, requires taking into account the characteristics of the actions and the environment of public administration. Thus, assessment based on the worth of outcomes and value of costs should depend on the degree of achievement of the desirable values, and any differences should influence the final assessment of specific actions.[8]

The literature includes other proposals concerning the criteria of assessment of actions of public administration to be used in praxeological assessments. According to J. Starościak, such criteria include the ability of public administration to implement existing political programmes, to prepare good plans, to use socially accepted methods, to reduce the

---

[6] Jan Zieleniewski, *Organizacja i Zarządzanie* 197 (1976).
[7] Marian Kruk-Olpiński, *Kryteria oceny działalności...* 42 (1983).
[8] *Ibidem.,* 42ff.

circulation of issues within public administration to a minimum, and to adapt to changing conditions.[9]

In addition to defining the assessment criteria, an analysis of assessments of public administration requires indicating the appropriate assessment methods, which include the critical method and the comparative method (classes of methods). The critical method identifies irregularities in the factual state, is helpful in analyzing the opportunities for improvements in a given organization, and may be used to determine the organizational changes that should be implemented. The comparative method, on the other hand, may be used to determine conformity of the actions of a given organization to a standard that has been designated for the organization. It enables identification of discrepancies between the standard and the actual actions of the organization and facilitates finding possibilities for aligning the activity of the organization with the standard.[10]

The entities conducting assessments may be divided into three groups, two external to the organization and one within the organization's structure. The first group of entities is composed of citizens, who are directly or indirectly affected by the administration's actions. Their assessment usually pertains to the method of resolution of citizens' problems, satisfaction of their social needs, such as access to public services, or legality of public administration's actions. The second group includes institutions that are independent of the entity being assessed, which assess the legality of the activities of public administration (control of administrative courts and the Supreme Chamber of Control). The third group includes any institutions constituting a part of the structure of the administrative apparatus, which perform assessments of other elements of the apparatus (ministerial control and control exercised by internal control and audit departments).[11] Such assessments are similar to those performed by the second group, but the assessment processes take place within the assessed entity.

The above-mentioned criteria and methods of assessment of public administration justify the use of assessments based on praxeological

---

[9] Jerzy Starościak, *Administracja, Zagadnienia teorii i praktyki* 32-48 (1974). A smaller set of criteria is proposed in Henryk Nicki, *Metody i kryteria oceny sprawności funkcjonowania organów i urzędów administracji państwowej* in Materiały i Studia 171-175 (1978).

[10] Cf.: Marcin Jełowicki & Jerzy Zapasiewicz, *Organizacja i kierownictwo w terenowych organach administracji państwowej* 236ff. (1975). Cf. Marian Kruk-Ołpiński, *Kryteria oceny działalności...* 48-49 (1983).

[11] Jacek Jagielski, *Kontrola administracji publicznej* 62ff. (1999).

criteria to make public administration more effective; they also constitute a basis for defining the qualitative assessment criteria to determine the efficiency of public administration's actions.

The importance of assuring quality of public administration's activities is due to the role of public administration in satisfying the needs of society as a whole and of individual citizens. Because the requirements that public administration must meet and the expectations it must satisfy are often different, the extent of fulfilment of the aforementioned role enables assessing the fulfilment of quality criteria by public administration. If the actions taken by public administration in order to meet the aforementioned premises are deemed positive and, at the same time, the requirements defined in the regulations governing the functioning of public administration are met, then it may be concluded that the assessment confirms that public administration has achieved the expected quality.

Quality assessments of public administration are made in two areas:

- from the point of view of the citizen affected by public administration's actions in the area of satisfying his social needs, e.g. by ensuring legality, impartiality, timeliness of, and access to public services – external quality;
- from the point of view of public administration itself (its internal processes), in particular the management system, the supervision, and the personnel policies – internal quality.

External quality is measured as the relation between the citizens' expectations and the degree of their fulfilment; and internal quality as the degree of achievement of the objectives and implementation of the tasks of public administration defined by the applicable law.[12] It must be emphasized that the factors determining such assessments pertain, in essence, to all the activities of public administration.[13]

The factors affecting assessments of public administration are usually defined in legal and non-legal norms. As an example, one factor affecting assessments of external quality of the activities of public administration in European countries is the provisions of the European Code of Good Administrative Behaviour, adopted by the European Parliament on September 6th, 2001. The Code defines the basic principles that must be observed by institutions and officials in their contacts with citizens. Those principles include lawfulness, non-discrimination, proportionality, non-abuse of powers, impartiality and independence, objectivity, transfer of cases to proper organizational units, observance of the right to be heard

[12] Kazimierz Dendura, *Podstawy Zarządzania Jakością* 19 (2000).
[13] More information on factors affecting public administration can be found in: Zbigniew Leoński, *Nauka administracji* 26-45 (1999).

and to submit explanations, deadlines for decisions, the duty to justify decisions and to state arrangement for appeals, protection of data, providing information, and enabling access to public documents.[14]

Assessments of public administration are important for the achievement of both the type of quality and the actual quality. They are intended not only to maintain the quality achieved but also to ensure its continuous improvement by reacting to all changes in the organization's environment. Assessments of external and internal quality include, among others, quality system procedures pertaining to fulfilment of the quality requirements and conformance of the organization's actions with expectations of society.[15]

The qualitative criteria of institutions' assessments pertain to each process taking place in the quality management system. Depending on their scope, assessments may involve audits and reviews of the quality systems or self-assessment. Audits are used to assess the effectiveness of the quality systems and to identify opportunities for their improvement. A review of the system, which is one of the duties of the organization's leaders, consists of assessing the utility, adequacy, and effectiveness of the system in relation to the quality policy and objectives. Self-assessment, on the other hand, consists of a comprehensive and systematic review of the organization to determine its priorities and identify the areas that require improvement. The objective of such assessments is to determine whether processes have been identified and properly described, whether responsibility has been properly assigned, whether procedures have been implemented and maintained, and whether the processes enable effective achievement of the expected outcomes. The answers to such questions determine the results of the assessments.[16]

The criteria that have so far been used in assessments of non-government organizations are being used more and more often to improve the functioning of public administration. For this purpose, the assessment criteria are adjusted to match the characteristics and environment of public administration, thus forming public administration assessment models based on the tenets of management science. The models of public administration quality assessments include the M. Baldrige Model, used as a method to shape quality; the Excellence Model (EQFM), used to assess progress achieved in implementing a total quality management system;

---

[14] Consolidated text Journal of Laws of 2000, no. 98, item 1071, as amended. See *European Code of Good Administrative Behavior*, adopted by the European Parliament on September 6th, 2001.

[15] Denis Lock, *Podręcznik zarządzania jakością* 107 (2002).

[16] PN EN ISO 9000:2001.

and the Common Assessment Framework (CAF), developed in the course of analytic works conducted by the European Foundation for Quality Management (EQFM), the German University of Administrative Sciences, and the European Institute of Public Administration in Maastricht. These models are largely based on the tenets of total quality management (TQM).

The basic elements of the system that are assessed in each of the models differ only slightly. They cover assessment criteria that may be divided into two groups: potential criteria and outcome criteria.[17]

The potential criteria include:

- leadership – involvement of the leadership in the process of design and achievement of quality objectives;
- strategy and planning – conformance of the actions taken to the mission and vision of the institution;
- personnel management – the extent to which the personnel of the institution are employed, to include planning of employee selection and training, monitoring of their effectiveness, and shaping of interpersonal relations;
- external partnership and resources – preparation of the institution to take actions in the external area, in particular to satisfy the needs of society, to shape the socio-economic situation, and to manage funds and information;
- process and change management – the way processes are identified, improved, and monitored in the organization.

The outcome criteria include:

- outcomes in relations to society and to individual citizens – the degree of satisfaction of citizens with the activities of public administration and the access to public services;
- outcomes in relations with employees – the results of the actions taken by the organization aimed to achieve employee satisfaction;
- key results of the activities – the actual achievement of the assumed objectives and expectations, with regard to completion of tasks and to financial performance.[18]

---

[17] Jacek Czaputowicz, *Wspólna Metoda Oceny Administracji...* (2002); Stowarzyszenie Konsultantów, *Powszechny Model Oceny – Doskonalenie zarządzania w urzędach administracji publicznej w Polsce* 2.

[18] Tadeusz Wawak, *Wdrażanie systemów zarządzania jakością w urzędach administracji publicznej*, Zeszyty Naukowe Wyższej Szkoły Administracji Publicznej 69-75 (2001); Cf. Marek Bugdol, *Zarządzanie jakością w administracji samorządowej* 77-88 (2001).

Assuming that it is the leadership of an institution that is responsible for ensuring the high quality of its activities, it might be concluded that self-assessments intended to improve the institution's quality should be performed by persons with the most extensive knowledge of the process taking place in a given entity, e.g. by department managers.

Assignment to public administration, in particular local government administration, of the duty to perform services to the local community highlights the importance of service quality assessment criteria. According to the ISO 8402:1996 standard (replaced by the ISO 9000:2001 standard and then by the 9000:2006 standard), quality of a service is defined as the entirety of the properties of the service, which determine its capacity to satisfy the needs that have been identified and that are anticipated.[19] The predominant view in the doctrine is that service quality assessment criteria depend on the feelings, experiences, and education of the individual customers; the list of such criteria and measures of service quality assessments includes:

- access to the service, measured based on the location of the provider's points of service, their business hours, and the waiting time;
- information on the services provided, measured based on the accuracy, availability, and understandability of such information;
- professional conduct and politeness of the employees providing the service;
- trust and reliability, measured based on the credibility of the service provider's staff, their care for the interests of the customers, as well as the thoroughness and precision in their performance of the services;
- responsibility for conformance of the services to the customers' expectations;
- security, which consists of eliminating disturbances in the provision of the services;
- the material infrastructure of the service provider intended to ensure effective performance of the service;
- recognition of the customers' needs due to the service provider's deep knowledge of the current and future requirements and expectations of the customers.[20]

The Polish scientists who have studied the matter of service quality assessments are R. Kolman and T. Tkaczyk. They proposed a 'universal

[19] PN EN ISO 8402:1996, PN EN ISO 9000:2001, PN EN ISO 9000:2006 (U).

[20] Jerzy Łańcucki, *Jakość usług*, 8 Problemy Jakości 6-7 (1997).

service quality standard,' developed separately for customers and for service providers. The customer's standard includes 13 criteria, such as politeness, thoroughness, timeliness, and reliability, which are graded on a 1 to 10 scale. The service provider's standard includes 15 criteria, such as customer's satisfaction, effectiveness, economy with regards to costs and use of materials, and complexity of processes involved, which are graded on a 1 to 15 scale. The ratio of the average value obtained in the two groups of assessment criteria defines the final overall quality of the services. [21] Besides the above-mentioned concepts of assessment of activities of public administration, other models were formulated in the practice of public administration management to facilitate such assessments. For instance, in the United Kingdom, a set of principles of quality achievement was developed and recommended to be used by the local authorities (the so-called Best Value); also, the Charter Mark award is given to public administration entities meeting certain quality criteria.[22]

The information presented herein leads to the following conclusions regarding qualitative criteria used to assess public administration: Assessments, being the final stage of every organized activity, are intended to select the objectives of public administration and to define the methods and outcomes of their implementation; thus, they facilitate the decision-making process. Also, assessments enable the entity assessing public administration to gain knowledge about the possibility to implement a formal system to ensure socio-economic development and to define the extent to which public administration performs its duties. Consequently, assessments constitute an important factor in achieving quality (both type quality and actual quality) in public administration's external and internal activities. Assessments should be based on the praxeological worth of actions and the resulting qualitative requirements and may take the form of audits, system reviews, and self-assessments.

It is worth noting the fact that the aforementioned catalogue of qualitative criteria of potential and outcome assessments may be used to increase the efficiency of public administration. Assessment of such elements of the public administration system as involvement of the leadership in the process of designing and achieving the quality objectives, conformance of the tasks to the needs and expectations of the environment and effectiveness of their performance, the level of training of the staff, as well as relations between society and the public administration, makes it possible to identify and then to eliminate any disturbances to the proper

---

[21] Romuald Kolman & Tadeusz Tkaczyk, *Jakość usług* 213 (1996).

[22] Piotr Rogala, *Podstawowe narzędzia zarządzania jakością w jednostce samorządu terytorialnego*', 2 Problemy Jakości (2002).

functioning of the system. The aforementioned processes may be assessed by external entities to guarantee impartiality of the assessments, or by entities within the system (due to their better knowledge of the processes).

Due to the fact that public administration provides a number of services to society, it is reasonable to implement, using general legal norms and detailed non-legal standards, certain criteria of assessment of those services and to elaborate certain measures that will enable verifying whether the methods of provision and the scope of the services meet the expectations of the customers and whether the current and future requirements of the customers have been thoroughly analyzed.

Although the proposed assessment criteria do not exhaust the subject, they indicate ways quality may be achieved through assessment of certain elements of the public administration system. The assessment criteria are used in specific quality assessment models, but their effective use in public administration requires giving those models a formal and legal status to define the structure and activity of public administration in the area of achievement and improvement of quality.

TAX PROCEDURES IN POLAND AND FRANCE

BOGUMIŁ PAHL AND MICHAŁ MARIAŃSKI

UNIVERSITY OF WARMIA AND MAZURY IN OLSZTYN, POLAND

General comments

Tax matters in Poland and France are not settled by public administration authorities solely in the course of one procedure. The legislators of tax systems in these countries established several distinguishable procedures, which serve to ensure a proper realization of tax obligations. Procedures, which are applied in tax matters are of a complex and not of a homogenous structure. Each of them is typified by certain differences, and consequently serves different functions and purposes. It needs to be emphasised that not all measures of the public administration authorities, which are directed towards a specific subject (an addressee), are taken within the scope of tax procedures. Due to all of these reasons it seems vital to distinguish those procedures, which might be considered as 'tax procedures'.

This article treats tax procedures as those procedures, the object of which is to verify the correctness of a declared tax obligation amount or to define its amount. A particular feature of this kind of tax procedures is the fact that they shape legal relationships, i.e. they grant, limit or deny rights. They may also impose, limit or remove new obligations. Therefore, these tax procedures decide on the rights and obligations and they may form a new legal situation. Not every organized sequence of measures of public administration authorities may be defined as 'tax procedure'.

The purpose of this study is to familiarize the reader with tax procedures, which are in force in the Polish and French tax systems. Due to the framework of this study the main focus will be put on specific features of each tax procedure, which is in force in particular legal systems.

Tax procedures in Poland

General comments

The Polish tax system distinguishes four tax procedures: tax proceedings, checking measures, tax control, and fiscal control. What they have in common is the fact that their main purpose is to ensure a correct fulfilment of tax obligations.[1] Nevertheless, they need to be separated. The above mentioned tax procedures may be divided into two basic categories: jurisdictional tax procedure (tax proceedings) and monitoring tax procedures (checking measures, tax control, fiscal control). The main criterion of the division is the purpose of a given procedure. Tax proceedings involve the measures of tax authorities intending to introduce an administrative deed. Therefore, its principle is to hear and adjudicate a particular case by way of an administrative (tax) decision, which defines rights or imposes obligations. Its purpose is also to verify those decisions in the course of appeal or emergency procedure. As for monitoring procedures, they are intended to verify and assess a particular activity. They do not involve the possibility of legally binding and compulsory influence on subjects, against which the procedures are conducted. Monitoring procedures enables making observations and, subsequently, the definition of the actual present situation and what it should be.[2]

Tax proceedings

The term 'tax proceedings' has been introduced to legal terminology by virtue of the decree of May 16th, 1946, regarding tax proceedings.[3] The Act of March 15th, 1934, known as the Tax Ordinance Act,[4] which was previously in force, was the first legal act thoroughly regulating proceedings in tax cases that did not use the term 'tax proceedings'.[5] The tax procedure regulated by this act was called 'proceedings with tax

---

[1] The notion of tax obligations realization is described in details in Krzysztof Teszner, *Pojęcie oraz zakres i formy realizacji zobowiązań podatkowych* in 3 Leonard Etel (ed.) *System prawa finansowego. Prawo daninowe* 641ff. (2010).

[2] Jacek Jagielski, *Kontrola administracji publicznej* 7ff. (1999).

[3] Journal of Laws No. 27, item 174.

[4] Journal of U. R. P. No. 39 item 346.

[5] In literature of the interwar period a term of 'tax lawsuit' was also used - Władysław Runcewicz, *Ordynacja podatkowa. Szkic systemu ordynacji podatkowej, ustawa, rozporządzenia wykonawcze. Komentarz* 23ff. (1935).

assessment'.[6] In 1981 the approach towards tax proceedings was changed and those regulations were included in the Administrative Code.[7] When a new legal act, known as the Tax Ordinance Act,[8] was passed in 1997, the term 'tax proceedings' returned to legal terminology. This act became effective at the beginning of 1998. Legislators devoted the whole of Section IV, entitled Tax Proceedings, to describe tax proceedings in detail. The term itself, however, remains undefined by the legislator. It led to decodification of administrative proceedings.[9] Procedural regulations included in Section IV of the Tax Ordinance do not constitute a regulation by law, which was introduced in a new field – not previously included in any legal normalization. Inversely, the regulations of the Tax Ordinance were introduced to the legal order as a regulation by law of a field, which for over ten years has had a stabilized legal normalization together with a wide range of legal institutions, a system of basic rules and a guarantee of their application.[10]

As for tax proceedings, it is important to focus only on jurisdiction proceedings regulated in Section IV of the Tax Ordinance.[11] In this sense, tax proceedings correspond to a normative meaning of its definition. Tax proceedings undoubtedly constitute a kind of particular administrative proceedings.[12] They have fixed features, which makes it possible to include them in the category of administrative procedures.[13] Tax proceedings are not of a contradictory nature, which would assume equality of the parties involved in the course of proceedings. A model of tax proceedings shaped in this way brings about consequences to its subject matters. In particular, it makes the tax authorities, rather than the

---

[6] Marian Masternak, *Rodzaje postępowań w sprawach podatkowych* in *Księga pamiątkowa ku czci docenta Eligiusza Drgasa* 102 (1998).

[7] Katarzyna Michałowska, *Postępowanie podatkowe* in Aneta Kaźmierczyk (ed.), *Ordynacja podatkowa. Źródła i wykładnia prawa podatkowego* 181 (2010).

[8] The Act of August 29th, 1997 Ordynacja podatkowa (Journal of Laws 2005 No.8, item 60 with subsequent changes) – later addressed as the Tax Ordinance.

[9] Janusz Borkowski, P*rzepisy postępowania podatkowego na tle kodeksu postępowania administracyjnego*, 3 Przegląd Podatkowy 4 (1999).

[10] Id., *Postępowanie administracyjne ogólne i szczególne* in *Księga pamiątkowa profesora Eugeniusza Ochendowskiego* 73 (1999).

[11] Jan Głuchowski, *Polskie prawo podatkowe* 77 (2004).

[12] Barbara Adamiak & Janusz Borkowski, *Postępowanie administracyjne i sądowo-administracyjne* 89 (2009).

[13] Ryszard Mastalski, *Projekt ordynacji podatkowej. Postępowanie podatkowe*, 5 Przegląd Podatkowy 5 (1996); see Barbara Adamiak, *Zagadnienia ogólne procesowego prawa administracyjnego* in 9 Roman Hauser et al. (ed.) *System prawa administracyjnego. Prawo procesowe administracyjne* 7 (2010).

parties, responsible for producing evidence in the case.[14] The tax case is the subject matter of tax proceedings interpreted in this way.[15] The term 'tax case' shall be understood as the facts of the case, which should be settled after trial proceedings specified by law. Resolution of a tax case requires establishment of two states – statutory factual state specified by legal norms regulating particular kinds of taxes, and actual state, which may be found with a specific subject. Comparing the actual state with the tax-legal factual state may answer a question if, and to what extent, the actual state includes statutory traits of tax-legal factual state. Furthermore, on that basis, resolution of a tax case may be affected.[16]

It is accurately emphasized in the related literature that the subject of tax proceedings is not of a homogeneous nature as the notion of a tax case is in reality broad. It includes, in particular, issues regarding the definition and description of tax obligation and its amount. Moreover, tax cases may concern other issues, such as the amount of tax refund or a surplus of tax calculated on due tax from goods and services, the amount of losses incurred by the taxpayer, the agreement made on fixing transactional prices, exempting the taxpayer from the obligation of tax payment, postponing the dates provided in the regulations of tax law, postponing the date of tax payment, spreading the tax payment out over instalments, stating overpayment or stating the range of responsibility of particular heirs, defining the amount of overpayment or tax refund to heirs, making a ruling on the responsibility of a third party, ensuring the execution of tax obligations. The above mentioned examples clearly indicate that the range of cases settled by means of tax proceedings is quite broad. The regulations of jurisdictional tax proceedings are of a universal nature – they may be applied regardless of a subject of proceedings. Procedures distinct in their kinds and appropriate to a particular case category are not taken into consideration by the legislative body on the level of tax proceeding. It is vital to add that in tax proceedings two modes may be distinguished, i.e. principal proceedings and emergency proceedings. The first one involves adjudicature and decision on tax case in accordance with substantive law regulations. The subject matter of emergency proceedings

---

[14] Antoni Hanusz, *Podmiotowy charakter zasady zupełności postępowania podatkowego*, 10 Przegląd Sądowy 12ff. (2004).

[15] A tax case in a substantive view is defined as a tax obligation resulting from the norms of substantive law – see Krzysztof J. Musiał, *Sprawa a postępowanie podatkowe*, 9 Przegląd Podatkowy 12 (2010).

[16] Ryszard Mastalski, *Ustalenie podstawy wymiaru w polskim postępowaniu podatkowym* (1973).

is verification of a final tax decision issued in principal proceedings. The purpose of this kind of proceedings is making a final tax decision.[17]

Checking Measures

Checking measures are regulated in Section V of the Tax Ordinance Act.[18] It constitutes a distinct procedure in relation to tax control and tax proceedings.[19] Moreover, it plays an important role in measuring activity of tax authorities.[20] Therefore, it is a kind of proceedings of a controlling nature.[21] As a result of article 272 of the Tax Ordinance Act, its purpose is to check the promptness of: submission of declarations, deposit of declared taxes including those charged by taxpayers and collectors; confirmation of a formal correctness of the above mentioned documents and establishing a factual state in the scope vital to confirm the conformity with documents provided. Hence, the purpose of its introduction was mainly a deformalization of proceedings in those situations when conducting complete tax proceedings may be avoided without any loss to creditor and process entitlements of a party. Originally, checking measures were intended to remove minor mistakes.[22] A need to complement a legal regulation of this kind of normalization appeared because tax obligations under the law in tax substantive law became more common. As a result, it led to a widespread introduction of self-calculation of those obligations or calculating them through the payer.[23] One of the effects of introduction of

---

[17] Ryszard Mastalski, *Ustalenie podstawy wymiaru...* 724 (1973).

[18] In reference books it is emphasized that on the basis of Code of Administrative Procedure checking measures were normalized only in article 168, which entitled tax authority to control statements, declarations or register – in case of doubts towards submitted statements. This right was extended in the Tax Ordinance Act - see Ryszard Kubacki, *Postępowanie podatkowe w ordynacji*, 12 Przegląd Podatkowy 31 (1997).

[19] In doctrine, checking measures are defined as a part of tax control differing from it in a technique of proceedings conducted by tax authorities-vide Ryszard Mastalski & Janusz Zubrzycki, *Ordynacja podatkowa. Comment* 316 (2002).

[20] Iwona Kowalska, *Czynności sprawdzające w prawie podatkowym*, 11 Przegląd Podatkowy 51 (2003).

[21] Dobrosława Antonów, *Czynności sprawdzające* in Ryszard Mastalski & Eugenia Fojcik-Mastalska (ed.), *Prawo finansowe* 234 (2011).

[22] Henryk Dzwonkowski, *Czynności sprawdzające* in Id. (ed.), *Ordynacja podatkowa. Komentarz* 1435 (2011).

[23] Checking measures enable one to limit the risk connected with tax self-calculation and with calculation of the amount of payers' tax obligations. They bring the possibility to correct tax declarations and prevent the application of

this procedure was that tax authorities became equipped with the instruments which enabled them to easily and peacefully verify if the taxpayers had fulfilled their obligations correctly, and also enabled assessment of the related measures taken by payers and collectors.[24]

Only tax authorities of first instance are entitled to conduct checking measures. These measures involve only three kinds of circumstances: promptness; formal correctness of documents; and establishing a factual state in order to state the conformity to the documents provided.[25]

This means that in relation to the needs connected with the payers' payments and their control, checking measures are of a formal and introductory nature. They are described as quasi-controlling measures.[26] Their essence is the establishment and confrontation of the executions with the outlines and explanation of the causes of possible inconsistency between them, without the possibility of shaping a taxpayer's, payer's or collector's legal position. Checking measures involve controls, which due to their scope and form of activities taken, fundamentally differ from tax control and tax inspection. Checking measures do not constitute any obstacle to undertaking tax control or tax inspection by tax authorities.[27] As an element of initial control of a formally legal nature, checking measures do not end the activities of tax authorities, which verify if tax law regulations are applied correctly.[28] Legal regulations do not define the period of time during which checking measures may be conducted.[29] As a consequence, tax or execution proceedings may be commenced. Hence, checking measures are not only material-technical measures, but they also

---

criminal fiscal sanctions. However, they do not protect against the occurance of other problems (e.g. an obligation to pay delay interests) - see Cezary Kosikowski, *Czynności sprawdzające* in Id. et al., *Ordynacja podatkowa. Komentarz* 1190 (2011).

[24] Małgorzata Niezgódka-Medek, *Czynności sprawdzające* in Stefan Babiarz et al. (ed.) *Ordynacja podatkowa. Komentarz* 900 (2009).

[25] Since 2005 the scope of checking measures is extended and it covers the examination of documents submitted within exchange of information on tax on goods and services between the EU member countries. This examination is conducted by a Minister in charge of public finances or authorities entitled by the competent Minister.

[26] Bogumił Brzeziński et. al., *Ordynacja podatkowa. Komentarz* 867 (2002).

[27] In details Cezary Kosikowski, *Ustawa podatkowa* 287 (2006).

[28] Bernard Zięba, *Czynności sprawdzające w świetle ustawy ordynacja podatkowa* in Beata Kucia – Guściora et al. (ed.), *Ordynacja podatkowa w teorii i praktyce* 222 (2008).

[29] A verdict of the Supreme Administrative Court of December 3rd, 2003 (I SA/Wr 2889/01), Gazeta Prawna 2 (December 30th, 2003).

make it possible to apply the procedures in order to make certain evidence findings.[30] They are taken officially and selectively. Tax authorities are not obliged to apply those measures towards every taxpayer or payer.[31]

In the scope of checking measures, tax authorities are mainly entitled to perform inspection activities. However, they may also take certain measures leading to the removal of confirmed irregularities. Moreover, tax authorities may take measures which are intended to state a factual state within the scope essential to confirm a conformity with documents provided. A tax authority conducting checking measures does not issue any deed, which would formally constitute a conclusion of a subject procedure. Checking measures may be undertaken repeatedly. The legislative body does not introduce any limits in this matter.

Tax control

Regulations, which standardize tax control included in Section VI o.p. 'Control' signify, in general, the process of verification by authorities entitled if a factual state is in conformity with a standardized state. The latter may be defined as commonly binding legal norms.[32] Hence, both factual state (verifying if it actually is taxable) and legal state (verifying if a taxpayer applied an appropriate legal norm to a given factual state) are subject to tax inspection.[33] This includes measures defined by law, whose purpose is to verify taxpayer's activity through examination of lands, buildings, objects related to the performed business activity, as well as inspection of any kinds of documents and registers.[34] Tax control is an autonomous procedure conducted by tax authorities of first instance, beyond tax proceedings.[35] It is not affected by the fact that in cases not

---

[30] Adam Mariański, *Rodzaje postępowań w ordynacji podatkowej: czynności sprawdzające, kontrola oraz postępowanie podatkowe*, 4 PP 37 (2010).

[31] Henryk Dzwonkowski, *Czynności...* 1434 (2011).

[32] Andrzej Baczyński, *Kontrola skarbowa i kontrola podatkowa. Komentarz* 16 (2001). In administrative law doctrine 'control is defined as a set of activities consisting of: observation, establishing or detecting a factual state, comparing reality with intentions, acting against unfavourable phenomenon and informing competent units about the observations' – see J. Starościak, *Zarys nauki administracji* 212 (1961).

[33] Ryszard Kubacki, *Kontrola podatkowa*, 5 Przegląd Podatkowy 31 (1998).

[34] Ryszard Mastalski, *Prawo podatkowe* 319 (2009).

[35] Tax control is also conducted by the Minister of Finance. Its purpose is to validate if the subjects related apply a transactional price approved by the Minister of Finance - art. 281§3 Tax Ordinance Act.

regulated in Section VI o.p. regulations provided in article 292 o.p. may be applied in tax control. Tax ordinance regulations treat tax inspection as an autonomous activity of tax authority, which is a separate kind of proceedings.[36] It proceeds solely ex officio. Taxpayer or other subject under the scope of inspection may not present a motion of its performance.[37]

Placing the regulations of tax control beyond a section describing tax proceedings indicates that tax inspection may be conducted spontaneously and without instituting tax proceedings. It may also constitute a stage of an instituted tax proceedings.[38] It is emphasized in a doctrine that tax control has an ancillary role in regards to tax proceedings since its effects are judicial consequences.[39] Tax inspection does not aim at settling an individual case in decision but at examining a factual state and stating if it is in concordance with tax law regulations. It is not ended by issuing a conclusion in an individual case but by drawing up a protocol, which reflects its course and a confirmed factual state.[40] Hence, it is a legal procedure for tax authorities to obtain information if a process of tax obligations realization proceeds correctly. One of the consequences of this procedure may be instituting of tax proceedings, during which a tax case is settled. Tax control cannot be attributed with supervisory features because of the nature of relations between an inspector and an inspectee (there is no structural relation of superiority – submission) nor due to a lack of legal possibilities of applying means of an imperious nature by control authorities.[41]

In subjective terms tax inspection may concern solely taxpayers, payers, collectors, and legal successors. It is worth mentioning that in provisions of the tax ordinance, which regulate tax inspection the legislative body does not use the notion of a party in proceedings but instead of that it uses the notions of a controlled or a person representing a

[36] Dobrosława Antonów, *Czynności...* 237 (2011).

[37] Małgorzata Szustek-Janowska, *Kontrola podatkowa* in Wanda Wójtowicz (ed.), *Prawo podatkowe – część ogólna i szczegółowa* 179 (2009).

[38] Cezary Kosikowski, *Kontrola podatkowa* in Id. et al., *Ordynacja podatkowa. Komentarz* 876 (2006); see Jan Zdanowicz, *Kontrola podatkowa w świetle ordynacji podatkowej*, 10 Monitor Podatkowy 315 (1998).

[39] Henryk Dzwonkowski, *Procedury kontroli podatkowej* in Andrzej Buczek et al. (ed.), *Prawo podatkowe* 408 (2006).

[40] According to the article 290§1 of tax control course, the controlling provides documentation in a protocol. Factual state may be consolidated with the equipment recording picture and sound or on a computer data carrier.

[41] Stanisław Jędrzejewski, *Kontrola podatkowa* in *Księga pamiątkowa ku czci...* 65 (1998).

controlled. It also does not refer to the whole of chapter 3 (page) of Section IV of tax ordinance but only to the provisions of articles 135-138, which regulate the issues of legal capacity and capability to take legal actions, an attorney, and a guardian. The number of subjects included in inspection is of an enumerative nature, which signifies that other subjects such as third parties cannot be involved.

Fiscal control

Law defines fiscal inspection as the body of authorities and organizational units appointed to protect the interests and property rights of the Treasury with its entitlements: control, judiciary, investigative and intelligence.[42] Fiscal inspection does not limit itself to establishing a binding state (designations), establishing a factual state (executions), comparing the executions with designations and explaining the reasons of possible inconsistencies between the designations and executions. Fiscal inspection authorities and units undertake numerous measures which go beyond a traditional inspection model.[43]

A principle purpose of fiscal inspection, resulting from Fiscal Control Act, article 1, section 1,[44] is to protect the interests and property rights of the Treasury and to ensure efficiency of executing tax obligations and other payments due, which constitute the income of the Budget or of national earmarked funds.[45] Moreover, the purpose of fiscal inspection is to examine the concordance with property management law of other national legal persons and to prevent and reveal the crimes defined by articles 228 – 231 of the penal code; the crimes which are committed by employees or people having functions in organizational units that are subject to a Minister in charge of public finances. Fiscal inspection completes broader tasks than tax inspection as those tasks go beyond the issues regarding realization of tax obligation.[46] Nevertheless, it needs to be mentioned that the first and principal purpose of fiscal inspection is, as

[42] Piotr Pietrasz & Wojciech Stachurski, *Ustawa o kontroli skarbowej. Komentarz* 18 (2011).

[43] Wojciech Stachurski, *Kontrola skarbowa* in Cezary Kosikowski & Eugeniusz Ruśkowski, *Finanse publiczne i prawo finansowe* 784 (2008).

[44] Fiscal Control Act of September 28th, 1991 (unified act: Journal of Laws of 2011, No. 41 item 214).

[45] Fiscal inspection does not refer to subjects, whose benefits constitute solely the income of local government units.

[46] Dariusz Zalewski & Andrzej Malezini, *Ustawa o kontroli skarbowej. Komentarz praktyczny* 8ff. (2011).

emphasized by the legislative body, to protect property interests of the Treasury and to provide the efficient execution of tax obligations and other due payments, which constitute the income of the Budget.

The legislator has created a kind of inspection of tax obligations realization which is distinct from tax inspection. Taking the Fiscal Control Act regulations it may be stated that the legislative authority's intention was not only to separate this inspection from state inspection system and to emphasize this separation, but also to institutionalize the inspection. It is expressed in, among other things, setting up the fiscal inspection authorities and their organizational units. It is justified in the Fiscal Control Act, article 36, which assigns fiscal investigation as one of the forms of fiscal management realization. On the one hand, fiscal inspection constitutes the whole set of authorities and institutions which protect the interests and property rights of the Treasury within the scope defined by the Fiscal Control Act. On the other hand, it constitutes one of the kinds of fiscal management.[47]

Fiscal management realization involves certain measures which are undertaken by fiscal management inspectors and employees of organizational units of fiscal inspection, for instance fiscal investigation sections. Moreover, they conduct preparatory proceedings under the Code of Criminal Proceedings, the Petty Offences Procedure Code, the Penal and Fiscal Code and in the course of the cases within the scope of fiscal management. It seems vital to emphasize that inspection measures are conducted by a fiscal management inspector – independently or together with the entitled officials. Decisions in cases subject to the inspection and the outcome of the inspection are, however, issued by the head of the Treasury Control Office as the fiscal inspection authority.[48]

Inspection proceedings constitute an immanent part of fiscal management. Nevertheless, inspection proceedings shall not be considered as fiscal management, which constitutes a much broader concept. Within its scope there are both inspection proceedings and fiscal investigation.[49] Inspection proceedings are regulated in chapter 3 of the Fiscal Control Act.[50] They constitute a form of fiscal inspection authorities' powers.

---

[47] Jacek Kulicki, *Kontrola skarbowa. Komentarz do ustawy* 35 (1997).

[48] Andrzej Gorgol, *Kontrola skarbowa i odpowiedzialność za naruszenie norm prawa podatkowego* in Wanda Wójtowicz (ed.), *Prawo podatkowe – część ogólna i szczegółowa* 434 (2009).

[49] *Ibid.*, 35.

[50] In judicature, inspection proceedings are defined as every formalized proceedings conducted by fiscal control authorities in scope of their competence –

Inspection proceedings may be defined as a sequence of measures regulated by provisions, undertaken by its participants and initiated with a decision of fiscal inspection authority on instituting it, and concluded with the issuance of a resolution by fiscal inspection authority – generally – in a form of a decision or the findings of an inspection.[51] These proceedings are a particular kind of an administrative procedure, combining inspection and police powers as well as - typical of tax proceedings – judiciary powers.[52]

Inspection proceedings are tax procedures separate from tax proceedings, though according to article 31, section 1 of the Fiscal Control Act, within the scope that is not regulated by the act, the regulations of the Tax Ordinance Act are applied. In practice, due to appropriate referral to the Tax Ordinance Act regulations and partial regulations of the Fiscal Control Act, a unification of proceedings conducted by fiscal management authorities and by tax authorities has emerged. The same regulations, rules and the same course of action are applied, whereas the differences included in the act are irrelevant.[53] It should be mentioned that in the course of inspection proceedings, the tax inspection measures may be undertaken. They are undertaken within the scope of inspection proceedings and not as a distinct activity. In reference books it is accurately noticed that it is all about principal proceedings procedure and tax inspection measures overlapping each other, and not about distinct and independent procedures. Tax inspection measures are concluded with the moment of delivery a protocol of inspection to the inspected. However, this does not finish tax proceedings. At that moment tax proceedings may be still conducted but only based on the Fiscal Control Act and regulations of section IV of the Tax Ordinance Act.

Initiation of inspection proceedings occurs solely ex officio in the form of a resolution. The date of inspection proceedings initiation is the day of delivery of a resolution regarding initiating inspection proceedings to the inspected. As in the case of a tax inspection, initiation of inspection proceedings may occur in extraordinary proceedings, through showing the

---

a verdict of the Supreme Administrative Court of December 14th, 2007 (II FSK 1453/06), unpublished.

[51] Jacek Kulicki, *Kontrola skarbowa – wybrane zagadnienia. Kancelaria Sejmu Biuro Studiów i Ekspertyz – 208 Report 10* (2004).

[52] Wojciech Stachurski, *Prawny model kontroli skarbowej (copy of typescript)* 230-231 (2006); Similarly a verdict of WSA w Bialystok on May 5th, 2009 (I SA/Bk 93/09), LEX nr 558737.

[53] Aleksander Dąbrowski et al. in Dariusz Malinowski (ed.), *Postępowanie przed organami skarbowymi* 14 (2007).

identity card and identity signs to the inspected and subsequently through delivery of a resolution regarding initiation of inspection proceedings. Inspection proceedings differ from tax proceedings and tax inspection in that they are launched according to the inspection plan. It may be concluded with the outcome of the inspection – an act unknown to juridical proceedings and tax inspection.

As in the case of the tax inspection, the initiation of the inspection procedure can be fast-tracked. The person being investigated is shown official identification by the investigating officer and only later is a notification confirming the initiation of the inspection procedure sent. The inspection procedure differs from tax inspection in that it is initiated based on the plan of inspection. The final result is an act unknown to judiciary procedures or tax inspection.

In other cases, a final decision is made on basis of the Tax Ordinance Act. This happens, for instance, when tax is calculated by the head of the tax office, when it is calculated in accordance with excise duty, or when a case, while being investigated, falls under the statute of limitations. Giving a tax administrative unit the right to make a decision does not mean that it becomes a tax office.[54] Nevertheless, the ability to issue a decision as a result of the inspection procedure, makes this procedure quasi-jurisdictional.[55] The tax office, though, cannot make decisions which are outside their legal mandate, such as calculating and refunding taxes.

In view of the above, it has to be noted that the inspection procedure is a special administrative procedure. It is a tax measure. Although it combines elements of tax processes and fiscal processes, it is not a tax procedure, nor a tax inspection.

---

[54] Barbara Adamiak, *The model of double-instance tax procedure*, 12 State and Law 57 (1998).

[55] The tax law doctrine states that the ability to make tax decisions by tax offices should be abolished. However, the tax supervision itself is needed. Tax offices should exercise their supervision over public finances as well. Nevertheless, they should not have the right to make tax decisions, or to determine the outcome of tax inspection. The materials gathered during the inspection should be given to the right tax administration unit, which will make the decision. Refer to Cezary Kosikowski, *Repairing public finances in Poland* 342 (2011).

Tax procedures in France

General comments

The General Tax Code *(Code Général des Impôts- CGI)*, apart from the constitution, is the most important legal document regarding taxes. Given its complex structure, efforts have been made for years to simplify and systematise it, taking into consideration the protection of taxpayers' rights. As a result, the Book of Tax Procedures *(Livre des procédures fiscales – LPF)* has been created, which thoroughly regulates matters concerning the tax system in general.

It is worth mentioning the role which the doctrine and judicature play in the practical interpretation and application of law in France. Law protects taxpayers against the negative effects of a variety of ministerial instructions, acts and rulings, which taxpayers follow. The famous decree no. 83-1025 of November 28th, 1983, about relations between the administration and citizens states that the[56] citizens have the right to quote a wide range of guidelines,[57] circular letters[58] and instructions as long as they are not contrary to the law (article 1-3).[59] Moreover, article L-80A of the LPA says that if the taxpayer based their actions on the legal interpretation made by public administration, the administration cannot demand a higher tax payment, using a different interpretation of the same legal regulation.[60] Thus, the system effectively limits the negative effects of changes in the legal system and maintains a basic level of balance in relations between citizens and the tax administration.

---

[56] Décret n°83-1025 du 28 novembre 1983 concernant les relations entre l'administration et les usagers.

[57] Fr. directives.

[58] Fr. circulaires.

[59] This decree was substituted with decree no. 2006-672 of June 8th, 2006, however most of the regulations still hold to this day.

[60] Art. L-80A 'Il ne sera procédé à aucun rehaussement d'impositions antérieures si la cause du rehaussement poursuivi par l'administration est un différend sur l'interprétation par le redevable de bonne foi du texte fiscal et s'il est démontré que l'interprétation sur laquelle est fondée la première décision a été, à l'époque, formellement admise par l'administration. Lorsque le redevable a appliqué un texte fiscal selon l'interprétation que l'administration avait fait connaître par ses instructions ou circulaires publiées et qu'elle n'avait pas rapportée à la date des opérations en cause, elle ne peut poursuivre aucun rehaussement en soutenant une interprétation différente. Sont également opposables à l'administration, dans les mêmes conditions, les instructions ou circulaires publiées relatives au recouvrement de l'impôt et aux pénalités fiscales'.

The inspection procedure

The aim of this procedure is to check declarations of income and find, if any, mistakes and irregularities which will be corrected in the course of the readjustment procedure (*procédure de redressement*). In France, there are three main forms of tax inspection: formal inspection (*contrôle formel*),[61] control in accordance with documentation (*contrôle sur pièce*),[62] and detailed inspection at the tax office (*vérification approfondie/contrôle sur place*).[63] The last of the above mentioned inspections, when it concerns people, is defined as the comparative examination of a person's overall tax situation (*examen contradictoire de l'ensemble de la situation fis cale personele – ESFP*), whereas when it concerns entrepreneurs, traders, craftsmen, farmers or freelancers, it is defined as an accounting inspection (*controle de comptabilité – CDC*). The above mentioned division also influences the taxpayers' rights, which are much more developed and protected in the case of the ESFP inspection than in the CDC.

The above-mentioned procedures involve a wide range of resources which the tax administration may use to obtain essential information to establish regularities in declarations of income.

Those resources include, for example, a written **demand for clarifications**. When it only concerns supplementation of information, it is called *demande de renseignement*, and when it concerns clarifying already detected inconsistencies, it is called *demande d'éclaircissement.*

A further right of the tax administration is the demand for justifications (*demande de justification*), which usually involves giving statements about one's family situation or undeclared income.

What is also worth mentioning, is a separate procedure called droit d'enquête, which concerns the verification of invoices filed by the VAT[64] payers as well as the right to investigate people who, due to the fact they run fiscal warehouses, have special obligations.

All of the above-mentioned procedures need to be notified in a written form, which is sent by recorded delivery.[65] In the letter it must be

---

[61] Investigates declarations of income in relation to bills, finances and completion of declaration of income on time.

[62] Investigates declarations of tax in relation to filed documentation.

[63] Investigates declarations of tax in relation to ledgers, contracts, etc.

[64] Fr. TVA (Taxe sur la valeur ajoutée) amounts in France 19.6%.

[65] Envoyé en recommandé avec avis de réception.

specified exactly what information is required and how to reply.[66] The lack of reply is tantamount to enforcement of the ex officio taxation (*taxation d'office*). One of the important sections in the Book of Tax Procedures (LPF) concerns the statute of limitations on the right to execute the supplementary procedure (*droit de reprise*). According to the article L. 168 LPF, the statute of limitations (*prescription*) changes depending on the type of tax and how and when the tax obligation has been defined (*fait générateur*).[67] In general, however, the statute of limitations is a six-year period, commencing from the end of the year in which the tax obligation started (art. L. 186 LPF).[68] However, in cases when the tax administration abandons legal action as regards the implementation of the tax obligation (*action en vue de recouvrement*), the statute of limitations, according to article L.274 LPF, is a four-year period, commencing from the execution of the tax administration's decision (*mise en recouvrement du rôle*). It is also worth mentioning that the statute of limitations does not apply if it is discovered that the taxpayer was aware of their tax obligations (art. L.189 LPF).

The readjustment procedure

In France, the readjustment procedure comprises of four main modes: comparative mode (*redressement contradictoire*), ex officio taxation (*taxation d'office*), particular and regulating mode (*règlement particulière*), and mode of malpractice (*abus de droit*).

The comparative mode is viewed as the main one. It analyses the accuracy of accusations made against taxpayers. This mode applies to all taxpayers who complete self-assessment (*contribuables*). The first stage of this mode is to send a readjustment notice to the taxpayer (*notification de*

---

[66] According to article L.16 A LPF the taxpayer has at least two months to reply, with the possibility to extend that period by sending a written request. If the response is incomplete, the tax office can designate an additional 30-day period to provide missing information, otherwise, ex officio taxation will be initiated.

[67] In the case of local taxes, the statute of limitations is one year, starting from the beginig of the period, for which it is due (art. L.173), and in the case of income tax and corporation tax, the statute of limitations is three years, starting from the end of the year for which it is due.

[68] This period has been shortened from 10 years by regulation Loi n° 2008-1443 of December 30th, 2008 de finances rectificative pour 2008 article 52 VI :, the six-year statue of limitations concerns only tax obligations after December 31st, 2008; (le présent article s'applique aux délais venant à expiration postérieurement au 31 décembre 2008).

redressement),[69] which is a preliminary administrative decision. The final outcome can be changed by the actions of the taxpayer,[70] who may appeal to The Departmental Tax Commission (*Commission départementale des impôts*) for help, if the contentious issues can be supported with documentation.

Ex officio taxation takes place only in the few cases which are listed in the tax law (art. L.65 LPF). [71] These are cases of impeding legal proceedings, such as not filing or late-filing of the declaration of income, lack of reply to a demand for clarifications, obstructing an audit, or, for the self-employed, not assigning one's representative within the time stated in the tax law. If one of the above-mentioned situations occurs, the tax administration evaluates the basic taxation itself, based on the evidence and documentation at hand. Interest for late payment and the so-called additional fee (majoration de droits)[72] is added to this amount.

The particular and regulating mode refers to, above all, the mistakes and irregularities detected during the accounting inspection (art. L.62 LPF). This procedure is initiated by the taxpayer who has not deliberately made a mistake, by filing a revised declaration of income and paying the overdue tax, as well as the late payment penalty.

The last of the readjustment modes is the mode of malpractice, enforced by article L.64 and L.64B. It refers to all the actions undertaken by the taxpayer in order to lower their tax.[73] This mode is very similar to

---

[69] This period has been shortened from 10 years by regulation Loi n° 2008-1443 of December 30th, 2008 de finances rectificative pour 2008 article 52 VI :, the six-year statue of limitations concerns only tax obligations after December 31st, 2008; (le présent article s'applique aux délais venant à expiration postérieurement au 31 décembre 2008).

[70] The taxpayer has 30 days to reply; lack of reply means enforcement of the procedure.

[71] Art. L65 Dans les cas limitativement énumérés à la présente section, les revenus ou bénéfices imposables des contribuables et les éléments servant au calcul des taxes sur le chiffre d'affaires, des droits d'enregistrement et taxes assimilées ainsi que des taxes assises sur les salaires ou les rémunérations sont taxés ou évalués d'office.

[72] It is worth mentioning that within 30 days from receiving the readjusting notice, the taxpayer has the right to disagree, which can result in no action taken.

[73] Art L.64 LPF Afin d'en restituer le véritable caractère, l'administration est en droit d'écarter, comme ne lui étant pas opposables, les actes constitutifs d'un abus de droit, soit que ces actes ont un caractère fictif, soit que, recherchant le bénéfice d'une application littérale des textes ou de décisions à l'encontre des objectifs poursuivis par leurs auteurs,ils n'ont pu être inspirés par aucun autre motif que celui d'éluder ou d'atténuer les charges fiscales que l'intéressé, si ces actes n'avaient

the comparative mode, the only difference being the possibility to turn to The Consultation Committee for Malpractice (*Comité Consultatif pour la répression des abus de droit*) in cases of a conflict between the taxpayer and the tax administration. The Committee's ruling is significant regarding the burden of proof, as, if it decides in favour of the taxpayer, it is the tax administration which needs to prove the taxpayer's liability. However, if the Committee's decision favours the tax administration, the burden of proof falls upon the taxpayer. It is worth mentioning that the so-called tax rescript, a letter of positive judgement, protects the taxpayer against any negative repercussions.

The appeals procedure

The appeals procedure (*recours contentieux*) is initiated when the taxpayer does not approve of the amount of tax imposed by the tax administration on them. According to the general rule discussed in article R-196-1 LPF, the deadline for the appeal is December 31 of the second year after: receiving the demand for payment,[74] receipt of payment referral,[75] the payment of the tax, and the discovery of the basis of the appeal.

Filing an appeal does not halt the immediate enforcement of the tax administration decision; however the taxpayer can file a form called *sursis de paiement* and withhold the tax payment.

The tax administration, the chief executive of chief administration[76] to be exact, has six months to respond to the appeal.[77] In cases when the tax administration does not reply, it is assumed it gives its tacit approval (*accord tacite*) to the taxpayer's interpretation of the regulations. Additionally, according to article R.199-1 LPF, in cases where there is no reply, or within six months of the decision being issued, the taxpayer has

---

pas été passés ou réalisés, aurait normalement supportées eu égard à sa situation ou à ses activités réelles. En cas de désaccord sur les rectifications notifiées sur le fondement du présent article, le litige est soumis, à la demande du contribuable, à l'avis du comité de l'abus de droit fiscal. L'administration peut également soumettre le litige à l'avis du comité. Si l'administration ne s'est pas conformée à l'avis du comité, elle doit apporter la preuve du bien-fondé de la rectification. Les avis rendus font l'objet d'un rapport annuel qui est rendu public.

[74] Fr. mise en recouvrement du rôle.

[75] Fr. notification d'un avis de recouvrement.

[76] Directeur des services fiscaux.

[77] This period can be extended by a further 3 months, after written notification to the taxpayer.

the right to take the case to an administrative court, where The Code of Administrative Justice applies (*Code de ja justice administrative*).

Conclusions

The analysis of the tax regulations in Poland and in France shows that the tax procedures in both systems are similar, yet not identical. Both systems have inspection procedures. Their primary aim is to verify the amount of tax tax-payers declare. In case of any irregularities, the tax administration undertakes further procedures in order to calculate the correct amount of tax. In Poland, this procedure takes place during the tax process or the inspection process. In France, it takes place during the readjustment procedure. Both Polish and French legal regulations allow the taxpayers to file revised declarations of income. In this case, there is no need to initiate the judiciary proceedings.

THE RIGHT TO PUBLIC INFORMATION AS A CONSTITUTIONAL CATEGORY

PAWEŁ ROMANIUK

UNIVERSITY OF WARMIA AND MAZURY IN OLSZTYN, POLAND

Introduction

Openness in public administration is the opposite of secrecy and confidentiality in dealing with national authority, administration and in the relations between state bodies, local governments, and organizations of all kinds. Openness is a state of a relative lack of obstacles to be informed and be able to inform others, or to be able to seek information, request, receive and transmit (to communicate, disseminate) information. It is a state of relatively free access to information in a broad sense, the opportunity to review not only their individual case (if such information is in the possession of authorities and institutions), but also in common: social, political, national, regional cases. Openness in public administration is also relatively unfettered access to all kinds of information, documents, activities, subjects, authors. There is no prohibition on the provision, although, no arrest is not equivalent to the impossibility of disclosure (of the provision). This rule eliminates the barrier between the need for real insight and access.

Openness in public administration is also a measure that allows one to reduce or mitigate the distress caused by unavailability, unawareness, ignorance of things. Transparency is the realization of the right to information.[1]

Accountability is an issue equally important on a global, international, regional, national, local and individual scale. It is a condition of social communication that was already known in the distant past. Along with the complexity of interpersonal and international relations, information became a factor of particular value: long arms, good, a friend, but also the enemy. Transparency is a principle of conduct in the everyday sense, and

[1] Cf. Michał Bernaczyk, *Electronic gazettes, 4 Electronic Administration* (2006).

opens the way for institutional information; its free movement is thus also a means to achieving the objective.

In international relations, accountability is to encourage a noticeable transparency - in the shaping of the extent to which the methods of agreement, dialogue and mediation between states are possible. Authors and participants in the integration processes in Europe, while maintaining the necessary understanding of the particularities, must endeavour to find a common language, and that is not possible without exchange of information.

Accountability has become the conscious condition, and measure of progress, understanding, cooperation, necessary confidence, peace, alleviation of tensions, democratic relations and the use of human capabilities. It has become a means of control of public institutions and protection of the citizen, his fundamental rights and freedoms and individual development.[2]

Transparency in public life is therefore an important tool for creating social reality. It applies to a wide variety of functions:

1. cognitive,
2. communicative,
3. educational,
4. mediation,
5. protective,
6. control,
7. democratization.

Openness as a feature, is important in international, national, social and individual relations. The principle of transparency in public administration must (should) serve the general public, it must be useful. Legislation should therefore limit the maximum extent of possible violation of it or use in a manner inconsistent with the objectives which it is to serve.

One may speak of transparency within the system of state bodies and transparency as a principle in external relations with citizens and other entities outside the system and in many other situations. The principle of public administration has a direct link to the right to freedom of information and to related freedoms. Often, however, it is **wrongly identified** with the following freedoms: expression, speech, press, participation in public life, demonstration and association.

---

[2] See Michał Bernaczyk, *Right to public information only loses a political nature*, Rzeczpospolita - Everyday Law (June 1st, 2007).

Idea of transparency

The idea of transparency in public administration has undergone a process during the time of legislative development and has taken the form of the right to transparency in public administration, seen as a set of legal rights to penetrate the public administrative system. Accountability has become the rule, rather than the obligation of secrecy.

The consequence of the adoption of administrative transparency as one of the principles of administration is the passive obligation of the administration to respond, disclose information administered in accordance with public needs and interests, and an active duty to inform the government on its own initiative and to be consulted.

The boundaries between transparency in public administration, economic, political and other spheres are indefinable, because they are elements of a general right to information, the instrument of a principle of openness.

It is expressed in regulations governing the subject of access, entities in which information is available, entities entitled to access (the beneficiary), restrictions on access rights, the freedom to exercise the right to information (access procedure) and guarantees the exercise of the right to information (remedies).

Right to information in the files of international law

Information and the right of access to it, being a matter for the individual and collective existence, is the subject of a number of normative acts of an international character.

The most important acts being:

1. The Universal Declaration of Human Rights (Paris, December 10th, 1948, valid in 1953);
2. Convention for the Protection of Human Rights and Fundamental Freedoms, known as the European Convention on Human Rights, adopted by the Council of Europe (Rome, November 4th, 1950 valid in 1953);
3. International Covenants on Human Rights, which include the International Covenant on Economic, Social and Cultural Rights and the International Covenant on Civil and Political Rights (New York, 16 December 1966. Valid in 1976);

4. Final Document of the KBWE (Helsinki, August 1st, 1975) Together with supporting documents.[3]

The right to freedom of information is recognized and defined in acts and documents of an international character, which in time has undergone a process of **constitutionalization**. In many countries it has become a constitutional category, along with reaching consensus on the fact that it is not the state that should evaluate which values of fundamental rights are worthy of protection.

Freedom and constitutional rights are the symptomatic rights, which are called rules, a complex or complexes that sustain the various concepts of high axiological, ideological or practical significance.

In public law, it applies to identifying particularly important social rights of individuals, termed **civil rights** or **human rights**. Civil rights are understood as the constitutional provisions, and human rights as the standards contained in international declarations and agreements (UN Human Rights Declaration of 1948) and as certain universal moral principles, in particular the principles of social justice. These are the subjective public law entities, which differ from the rights of a private nature. The rights of citizens mentioned in the constitutions specify the position of the citizen in relation to the state.

The Constitution of April 2nd, 1997[4] the right to information considered in Articles 54 and 64

Article 54

1. The freedom to express their views and to acquire and disseminate information.

2. Preventive censorship of mass media and the licensing of the press shall be prohibited. Statutes may require the prior grant of concessions to operate a radio or television station.

Article 61

1. A citizen has the right to obtain information about the activities of public authorities and persons exercising public functions. This right also

[3] Cf. Irena Kaminska & Mirosława Rozbicka-Ostrowska, *Access to public information* (2007).

[4] Polish Constitution of the Republic of April 2nd, 1997 - Journal of Laws of 1997 No. 78, item 483 with subsequent amendments.

includes the acquisition of information on the activities of economic and professional public persons and other persons or organizational units in which they perform the tasks of public authorities and manage communal assets or property of the Treasury.

2. The right to obtain information shall ensure access to documents and entry to sittings of collective bodies of public authority appointed by universal elections, with the possibility of audio or video recording.

3. Restriction of the right referred to in paragraphs 1 and 2, may be solely due to those specified in the protection of freedoms and rights of other individuals and businesses and to protect public order, security or important economic interests of the state.

The party's right to information in the **Code of Administrative Procedure**[5] (CAP) is not formulated directly as their personal right. It follows from the provisions setting out the specific responsibilities of the state administration bodies, in particular:

Article 6 [**The principle of the rule of law**] Public Bodies operate under the provisions of the law.

Article 7 [**The principle of the rule of law**] In the course of their duty public authorities are the guardians of law and take whatever steps are necessary to ascertain the facts and to uphold the law, bearing in mind the public interest and the legitimate interests of citizens.

Article 8 [**Principle of enhancement of public confidence**] public administration bodies are obliged to conduct proceedings in such a manner to increase citizens trust in these bodies, and increase awareness and legal culture of citizens.

Article 9 [**The principle of informing the parties**] public administration bodies are obliged to properly and fully inform the parties of the facts and law, which may affect the determination of their rights and obligations subject to administrative proceedings. Authorities shall ensure that the parties and other persons participating in proceedings shall not suffer damage due to ignorance of the law, and to this end provide the necessary clarifications and guidance.

This principle is known as the principle obligation of authorities to provide factual information and the legal principle by the care of the authority for the interests of the parties and other persons participating in the proceedings, the principle of providing information to the parties, the principle of legal aid.

---

[5] See Act of June 14th, 1960 Code of Administrative Procedure - Journal of Laws of 2000 No. 98, item 1071 with subsequent amendments.

The current wording of Art. 9 was given in 1980 and significantly strengthened the position of the page. The provision of Article 9 formulates both the person, who is entitled to expect the performance of this obligation. The doctrine was addressed to the fact that '(...) this requirement excludes the pre-positioning as an enemy, who waits by a party to commit an error in assessing the impact of certain factors on the outcome of the case and use this error as an excuse to issue a decision unfavourable to the party. On the contrary - the authority conducting proceedings must do so with an open attitude, characterized by action in the interest of understanding'.

In the second sentence of Article 9, the state is obliged to inform, but in a different form than in the first sentence of Article 9. Administrative authority must not only ensure that the parties to the proceedings do not suffer injury, but for this purpose shall be obliged to provide the necessary guidance and explanations. It may not remain indifferent to the interests of the parties to the case.

The provision of Article 9 formulating an obligation on the side of public administration establishes the process to seek permission to meet that obligation, and that violation may lead to invalidity of the decision by an administrative court.

Article 10 [**Principle of participating parties in the proceedings**] § 1 Public administration bodies are obliged to ensure that the parties are involved in every stage of the proceedings, and before its decision to allow them to comment on the collected evidence and materials of submitted requests.

§ 2 Public authorities may derogate from the principle laid down in § 1 only in cases where the settlement of the case does not suffer delays because of the danger to human life or health or because of the threat of irreparable material damage. § 3 The public administration body is obliged to fix in the file, by way of endorsements, the reasons for not complying with the rule set out in § 1.

Article 11 [**Principle to explain the conditions for settlement of the matter**] of public administration authorities should explain the merits of the conditions to the parties which are taken into account in settling the case and so far as possible lead to the execution by the parties of the decision without the need for coercion.

Article 73 [**Sharing the parties to file**] § 1. In each stage of the proceedings the public authority is required to enable the review and preparation of documents in the case of these notes and write-offs. § 2. A party may request the authentication made by them of copies of the file or issue it with certified copies of the file, if it is justified by important interests of the parties.[6]

Article 74 [**Protection of confidential**] § 1. Provision of art. 73 does not apply to a file under protection of state secrets, or other records that the public authority does not disclose due to the importance of national interest. § 2. Refusal to allow parties to see a file, make notes and extracts, authentication of such copies or certified copies of the issue by way of a resolution, which is subject to appeal.

Freedom of speech in the press

Freedom of the press is part of freedom of expression, which consists of the freedoms of expression and freedom to receive and communicate information, which is also the source and foundation of the freedom of broadcasting, film and television. Freedom of expression is applicable in different forms: written, oral, printed, artistic or any other by the free press, by a narrow definition it may be the presentation of information in written form, and widely, agent of social (mass) media, which is a form of expression.

Freedom of the press is not therefore an isolated freedom and is not listed alone in either the European Convention or the International Covenant on Civil and Political Rights. The constitutional freedom of the press is also frequently associated with freedom of expression (Constitutions of Germany and Denmark), freedom of the press (The Constitution of Sweden). Sometimes it is regarded as specific and recognized as a separate constitutional freedom (such as in the Constitutions of Portugal and Greece).

Sometimes it is the subject matter of ordinary laws (in France). Poland, in the Constitution of 1997, provides the freedom of the press and other mass media (Article 14) and places it beyond the chapter on the freedoms and human and civil rights; so, it is not, according to the constitutional classification, either a personal, political, economic, social, or cultural freedom. It was placed in Chapter I, entitled 'The Republic', which indicates that they wanted to give it a special value and make it real.

It is worth noting that any information about public affairs is public information under the Act and subject to availability of social

---

[6] See Act of June 14th, 1960 Code of Administrative Procedure - Journal of Laws of 2000 No. 98, item 1071 with subsequent amendments.

development. **The most important piece of legislation is the Act of 6th September 2001 on Access to Public Information.**[7]

Entities required to comply with the Act, among others:

1. public authorities (including government and local government);
2. bodies representing the legal person;
3. local government bodies representing local government entities;
4. legal entities in which local governments have a dominant position within the meaning of Consumer Protection and Competition;
5. others (Article 4 of the Law on Access to Public Information).

The right to information includes the right to: immediately obtain public information, access to official documents, access to meetings of the collegial bodies of public authority formed by public elections. Ensuring access to public information in the shares at the highest level gives us to understand that those rights can not be simply a collection of technical and organizational terms. They must refer to certain ideals and values, raising the dignity of the law.[8]

The beneficiary of rights of access to public information in the light of the Constitution of 1997 is the citizen; also entitled to obtain information are public authorities and persons acting for the public from other entities performing public tasks, as required to provide it.[9]

What is surprising is the fact that there is some discrepancy in identifying the persons entitled to obtain information. The Constitution uses the phrase "citizen is entitled". There is no mention here, as in the rest of its provisions, of any specific features of an authorized entity.[10] Z. Witkowski classifies the criterion as being the norm of civil law that is strictly enjoyed only by persons holding Polish citizenship.[11]

A citizen may be entitled to seek the requested data, but the agency responsible for the provision cannot be held liable if the transfer of this information is impossible from a purely technical or an independent body impediment reason. I should also mention that the right to obtain public information is not unlimited.[12] It would be quite illogical and dangerous to disclose all information relating to the functioning of the state. It should be

---

[7] Act of September 6th, 2001 on Access to Public Information - Journal of Laws No. 112, item. 1198, as amended.

[8] Zbigniew Witkowski, *Constitutional Law* 46 (2006).

[9] *Ibid.,* 190.

[10] An example would be Article. 62 of the Constitution starting with repayment of 'Polish citizen has the right...'.

[11] Zbigniew Witkowski, *supra* 190.

[12] Judgement of the Constitutional Court of October 23rd, 2002 (Reference number K 41/02).

borne in mind here that there are those persons that could and would use such information for criminal purposes to the detriment of the general security in the country.

Notice of meeting local government bodies

Both the Organic Law and the Constitution expressly states that one of the public manifestations is the right of entry to the sessions of the council, or admission to sittings of collective public authority bodies formed by universal suffrage. Both acts leave no doubt that the deliberations of the municipal, county, or regional assembly are always open, and any attempt to prevent access to the meeting is possible only by clearly enabling legislation. The rule is that any council resolution shall be passed in an open vote, unless the law provides otherwise. The Act provides for this when votes are secret votes (in the case of roll-call votes appointing and dismissing the President, Vice Presidents or the legislative body, the choice of governor and other members of the board of county). Legislation contained in the statute of constitutional government, or the content of the Constitution expressly state public deliberations, and collective organs of public authority are formed by universal suffrage. No executive bodies in any of the grades of local government fail to comply with both of these criteria. The town mayor is selected by means of universal suffrage, but it is a monocratic body, while in the district and province self-governing committees of these units are collegial, but come from the choice made by the legislative body of (forming and control). Residents do not have a direct impact on their choice in the district and province.

In considering the issue of transparency of action of the executive (mayor, mayor of the city, district committee executive officer, the Speaker of the Provincial Council), two ways of understanding the disclosure should be distinguished in relation to these bodies:

a) **external openness** is to give everyone concerned the right to participate in the deliberations. The deliberations of the executive body are closed to outside observers. However, there is the possibility that the President has invited the press to such debates that take place, unless the issues being discussed are subject to statutory secrecy preventing unauthorized disclosure by the chairman. Product information is protected against unauthorized disclosure prescribed by law on the protection of classified information.

b) **internal openness** is widespread availability of the results of meetings of those bodies. To show the validity of the principle of transparency of the activities of the executive in local government one should raise the issue of disclosure of information and rules concerning making them available. These issues are regulated by the Law on Access to Public Information.

However, the deliberations of the meeting, in which the treasurer and secretary and other persons, who may be invited by the mayor, as well as district committee meetings and province committee meetings are closed to the public.[13]

Restrictions on disclosure of local government bodies

In discussing the issue, keep in mind that total transparency is not possible. There is no transparency as a principle of neutrality, because its existence is always clear concerning whose interest may limit the realization of whose subjective right. It is difficult to set a strict limit, when the principle of openness in local government is justified for being in the interests of the unit, or by reason of the common good. The right to information must not impair the efficiency of decision-making on public issues and possibilities of governance.

The Act requires the authority of government (and others) provide any information about public affairs. Exceptions are classified information. According to the Act the right to public information includes the right to promptly obtain such information, containing the current knowledge about public affairs. This right extends to any person. A person applying for public information shall not be required to justify the proposal (to demonstrate an interest in law or fact).

To provide access to public information:

Sharing public information by way of:

- a publication in the Bulletin of Public Information,
- making available on request,
- a display in offices, or in public places,
- an installation in public places to allow devices access to this information,
- admission to sittings of collective bodies of public authority formed by universal elections,
- a third party access to the administrative file.

[13] See Jerzy Hausner (ed.), *Public administration. General subjects* (2008).

It should also be mentioned that the **Public Information Bulletin**[14] is part of a policy of openness and accessibility to public information. The Public Information Bulletin is the official publication ICT - the primary source of providing information.

The main features of the Public Information Bulletin:

1. **Universality of access** - access to public information in the Bulletin is possible only through the main page of the Bulletin www.bip.gov.pl;
2. **Uniformity of pages** - The relevant pages of the Bulletin are created by the standards of a unified system of party;
3. **Ministry of Internal Affairs and Administration of the Public Information Bulletin**-specific regulation;
4. **Security** - Access restricted by user ID and password, server protection by the security module, at least once a day to copy the information into separate media.

If public information cannot be made available within 14 days, the person responsible is obliged to notify in this time the reasons for the delay and the date on which information shall be provided, not more than two months from the date of filing. If, as the result of providing public information request, the entity obliged to make it available sustains additional costs associated with that provision in the application process or for the transformation of information into the form specified in the request, this body may demand from the applicant a fee equal to the cost. Refusal to provide public information and the termination of the proceedings for information by a public authority shall be by decision.

Summary

The Law on Access to Public Information is an important element of a functioning state. Access to public information is a vital link between the rule of people occupying important positions in the administration and the partial social control implemented by the citizens.

Article 61 of the Constitution provides that the citizen has the right to obtain information about the activities of public authorities and persons exercising public functions. This right also includes the acquisition of information on the economic and professional activities of individuals, as well as other persons or entities, in which they perform the tasks of public

[14] Decree of the Minister of Internal Affairs and Administration of January 18th, 2007 on the Public Information Bulletin - Journal of Laws No. 10, item. 68, as amended.

authorities and manage communal assets or property of the State. The scope of the requested information is based on Article 61 of the Constitution, so it covers the right to obtain information on the activities of public authorities and persons exercising public functions, including access on the basis of Article. Paragraph 61. 2 to official documents. The nature of these documents are records of administrative matters, particularly giving administrative decisions (Judgment of the Supreme Administrative Court, 28.11.2003, ref. Act II SA 3412/03). If the authority refuses to provide the content of administrative decisions relying on the protection of personal data, it should be in the form of an administrative decision. If it is found that the documents are private documents and other materials subject to personal data protection, the public authority file sharing shall turn off (delete) such documents and materials or part thereof.[15]

It is worth knowing the law and to know that Polish legislation provides ample opportunities to obtain information about the activities of all public bodies. Of course, exceptions are situations where that information may be limited. Such restrictions are set out in specific acts, even on national security. Society is increasingly exercising its right of access to public information under the Act, and thus, indirectly and sometimes directly influences transparency, disclosure and regularity of the implementation of public tasks.

[15] Michał Zaremba, *Right of access to public information. Practical issues* (2009).

European Economic Interest Grouping as an Opportunity for Exercising Freedom of Establishment for Polish Entrepreneurs in the Internal Market

Katarzyna Pokryszka

University of Silesia in Katowice, Poland

Abstract

Freedom of establishment is considered to be one of the most important principles of the internal market of the European Union since it creates the right for the Union's entrepreneurs to commence and pursue economic activity in the territories of all Member States. The effectiveness of conducting cross-border business activity may be increased as a result of international cooperation between entrepreneurs. The author presents the most important provisions of Council Regulation 2137/85 on the European Economic Interest Grouping (EEIG) and of Polish law introducing the EEIG as a Union instrument created in order to support and develop the activity of European entrepreneurs in the internal market.

The article focuses on the analysis of the most essential features of the EEIG including the procedure of its formation and its nature as a legal entity, as well as the requirements referring to its members, its purpose and application in conducting business activity.

Owing to the fact that the idea of the EEIG is to create a legal framework for the international cooperation of entrepreneurs, the Council Regulation 2137/85 contains detailed stipulations concerning its membership. The basic rule is that members of the EEIG must be involved in conducting economic activity in the Union, but they may be natural persons who conduct any kind of business activity including professional services, as well as companies or firms in the meaning of article 54 of the Treaty on the Functioning of the European Union which are connected with the Union on the basis of the address of their registered or statutory office and central administration. The essence of the EEIG as an instrument for international cooperation is expressed by the provision according to which at least two members must originate from different Member States of the European Union.

The fundamental purpose of the EEIG and the aim of its creation are very interesting since it has an influence on the scope of the application of the EEIG and on the difficulties with the definition of its legal nature. The EEIG should be concentrated on facilitating the economic activity of its members and the improvement of the results of their activities. The ancillary nature of the EEIG for its members is emphasized as one of its essential features. As a legal entity the EEIG should not be focused on making profits for itself, but in the case of gaining profits resulting from its activity, they should be considered to be the profits of its members.

The legal basis of the internal structure and functioning of the EEIG in Poland are included in the provisions of the Act on the European Economic Interest Grouping and the European Company that became valid in May 2005.

Introduction

The establishment and proper functioning of the internal market is regarded as one of the most fundamental purposes of the European Union, which must be attained in order to promote sustainable economic growth in the Union.[1] The internal market is defined as an area without internal frontiers in which the free movement of goods, persons, services and capital is ensured in accordance with the provisions of the Treaty.[2] However, although not expressly indicated in the definition of the internal market, freedom of establishment is regarded as one of its most important freedoms. According to art 49 of the TFEU, this freedom enables citizens of the Member States to take up and pursue activities as self-employed persons and to set up and manage undertakings, in particular companies or firms within the meaning of art. 54 of the TFEU, under the conditions laid down for its own nationals under the law of the country, where such business activities are pursued. Entrepreneurs who conduct economic activities in the European Union also have the right to set up agencies, branches or subsidiaries on the territory of any Member State. Freedom of establishment is based on the prohibition of discrimination on grounds of

---

[1] Treaty on the Functioning of the European Union, art. 3. Consolidated version of the Treaty on the Functioning of the European Union (Official Journal C 115, 09/05/2008, 47-388), hereafter referred to as the Treaty or TFEU.

[2] TFEU, art. 26.

nationality. In light of the EU law, this fundamental rule of equal treatment with respect to economic activities, which is expressed in art. 49 of the Treaty, means that Member States are free to regulate the conditions of accession to the professions and business activities, as long as these conditions are not directly or indirectly discriminatory on the grounds of nationality.[3]

In practice individuals exercising freedom of establishment may encounter a number of obstacles that result from the differences in the legal systems of Member States, difficulties in recognizing professional qualifications, or transferring the official address of a company to another country. Efforts by the institutions of the EU to overcome these difficulties in order to establish a real internal market have resulted in the adoption of new legislation whose main purpose is to enable entrepreneurs to develop their business activities and to create legal instruments, which are applicable in providing cross-border services. The European Economic Interest Grouping is one of these legal instruments that may increase the opportunity to conduct business activities in the internal market by Polish entrepreneurs.

EEIG as a legal instrument for the international cooperation of entrepreneurs in the European Union

The idea behind the establishment of an EEIG

The European Economic Interest Grouping (EEIG) has been introduced into European Union law on the basis of the Council Regulation (EEC) No 2137/85 of July 25th, 1985, on the European Economic Interest Grouping.[4] The most important issues, which were taken into consideration by the European institutions as reasons for creating the European Economic Interest Grouping,[5] are explained in the preamble of the Regulation 2137/85. Firstly, the idea of establishing a new legal entity must be analysed in the context of the aims of the Union relating to ensuring the stable development of economic activities. This aim may be reached as a result of the proper functioning of the common

---

[3] Catherine Barnard, *The Substantive Law of the EU. The Four Freedoms* 299 (3rd ed. 2010).

[4] Council Regulation (EEC) No 2137/85 of July 25th, 1985 on the European Economic Interest Grouping, Official Journal L 199, 31/07/1985 P.0001 – 0009, hereafter referred to as the Regulation 2137/85.

[5] Hereafter referred to as the EEIG or the Grouping.

market, which should be based on conditions similar to those which are specific to a real, internal national market. The establishment of this single market is connected with the necessity of creating a legal framework, which shall assist natural persons, companies and other legal entities to adapt their activities to the conditions of the common European market and to effectively develop their international cooperation. However, this kind of cooperation may be constrained by legal, fiscal and psychological obstacles. An EEIG, as a legal instrument which will be used in order to remove them, strengthen international business relationships and support the efforts to achieve the principal aims of the Union, seems to be necessary.[6]

In the light of its aim and its application, an EEIG is considered to be quite a specific legal entity. It differs decidedly from traditional forms of concentrations, which are usually unable to meet the expectations of their members and often lead to the domination of stronger participants over the weaker ones. Under these circumstances the European Commission referred to the French model of economic interest grouping, which was adopted in France in 1967, as a more flexible but structured form of the cooperation of entrepreneurs. Following the French idea of the functioning of this entity, the activities of an EEIG should be focused on facilitating or developing the economic activities of its members and not on making profits for itself. Regulation 2137/85 came into force in August 1985, but it has only been applied since April 1st, 1989. Such a long period of time between the coming into force and application of the Regulation was justified in order to enable Member States to adopt the legal provisions necessary to complete the European law and familiarise themselves with the new opportunity for business cooperation.[7]

The essential features of an EEIG

An EEIG, as a legal instrument, which may be used by entrepreneurs in order to increase the results of their business activities, has very specific features that on the one hand are sufficient to realise this aim and are quite original in comparison with traditional forms of partnerships, companies or other forms of cooperation, but on the other hand, make the legal nature of an EEIG quite difficult to define. The most important features of an

---

[6] Preamble to the Regulation 2137/85 paragraph 1 and 2; see also Iwona Hykawy, *Europejskie Ugrupowanie Interesów Gospodarczych – nowa formuła współpracy gospodarczej w prawie wspólnotowym* in Marek Safjan et al., *Prawo wspólnot europejskich a prawo polskie. Prawo gospodarcze* 269 – 270 (2002).

[7] *Ibid.*, 270 – 272.

EEIG are emphasised in the provisions of the Communication from the Commission Participation of European Economic Interest Groupings (EEIGs) in public contracts and programmes financed by public funds.[8]

The regulations of the Communication provide that an EEIG is a legal entity, which has legal capacity, but its structure is flexible and not very formal so as to enable its members to cooperate in conducting economic activities and not be forced to resign from their legal and economic independence.[9] The Communication also sets forth that the main purpose of an EEIG is to support the economic activities of its members and to give them the opportunity to improve their results. Owing to the fact that the essence of an EEIG as a legal entity and the instrument of international economic cooperation requires a more precise explanation, the Communication identifies its most important characteristics. The Communication prescribes that the specific features of EEIG are the following:

- an EEIG has a Community nature,
- an EEIG has a legal capacity, but its members are autonomous,
- the activities of an EEIG must be ancillary to the economic activities of its members,
- stability and flexibility are the principal aspects of the structure of an EEIG,
- unlimited joint and several liability of members of an EEIG for its debts.[10]

Firstly, an EEIG must be considered to be an entity of a Community nature. In the light of the provisions of the Communication this means that it has a connection with the Union legal system, since an EEIG may be established and may commence and conduct its activities only according to the conditions laid down in the Union laws, which are now included in Regulation 2137/85. The fact that the Regulation refers to national laws and in practice the EEIG acts to a certain extent on the basis of the internal legal systems of the Member States, is not inconsistent with this principal rule. The Community nature of an EEIG should have a positive impact on its application in international business cooperation, since as an entity which is legally neutral, it will eliminate the entrepreneur's fear that one of

---

[8] Communication from the Commission Participation of European Economic Interest Groupings (EEIGs) in public contracts and programmes financed by public founds, Official Journal C 285, 20/09/1997 p. 0017 – 0024, hereafter referred to as the Communication.

[9] The Communication paragraph 1.

[10] Rafał Adamus, Europejskie Zgrupowanie Interesów Gospodarczych. Problemy wybrane, 3 Gazeta Sądowa 22-23 (2006).

them may have a more privileged position as a result of conducting economic activities in more familiar legal surroundings.[11]

The second notable characteristic of an EEIG is that it has legal capacity, but simultaneously it allows its members to retain their autonomy. The Communication emphasises that an EEIG has full and independent legal capacity, which makes it impossible to regard an EEIG as a purely contractual form of cooperation. It is worth mentioning that art. 1 par. 2 of the Regulation 2137/85 stipulates that an EEIG has the capacity, in its own name, to have rights and obligations of all kinds, to make contracts or accomplish other legal acts, and to sue and be sued. The European Union law does not confer a legal personality on an EEIG, but makes it possible for the Member States to take the decision of whether an EEIG registered on its territory should have a legal personality.[12] The provisions of the Communication also underline the fact that the specific legal structure of an EEIG may create a great opportunity for entrepreneurs to increase their profits since it has its own organs which represent its members, and in consequence they have a more powerful position in negotiations than they would have if they acted independently. The Communication emphasises that the managers, within the scope of representing members, act according to the rules, which are applicable to a limited company. This principle may have a significant meaning for the members since it enables them to present a common attitude towards proposals during negotiations concerning public contracts or when they seek loans or financial guarantees connected with public contracts, and it may also improve their opportunities to participate in public contracts and programmes financed by public funds.[13]

The third noteworthy characteristic of an EEIG is the ancillary nature of its activities. This feature is considered to be one of the most controversial and ambiguous characteristics of an EEIG, since it may cast doubt on the aim and scope of activities of an EEIG. This is the feature of an EEIG that differentiates it from companies, which traditionally operate in order to gain profits for themselves. By contrast, the main purpose of an EEIG is to develop and facilitate the economic activities of its members and to enable them to increase the results of their activities. However, it cannot operate in order to make profits for itself. Moreover, the activities of an EEIG must be connected with the economic activities of its members and it must not go beyond what is ancillary to their activities.[14] In order to

---

[11] The Communication paragraph II p.1.

[12] Art. 1 paragraph 2 and 3 of the Regulation 2137/85.

[13] The Communication paragraph II p.2.

[14] Art. 3 paragraph 1 of the Regulation 2137/85.

clarify these provisions, the Communication stipulates that the ancillary nature of an EEIG means that its activities must not replace the activities of its members. However, while being restricted to facilitate the activities of its members, an EEIG should not be considered to have only a subsidiary or minor role or to have a limited possibility to operate in the market.[15]

The fourth characteristic of an EEIG, which is emphasised in the Communication is its specific structure, which is stable and yet simultaneously very flexible. The Regulation 2137/85 gives the members of an EEIG a wide scope of freedom in the field of their contractual relations and decisions concerning internal organisations of an EEIG, in order to give this entity the best opportunities to adapt to the economic conditions of the market. The flexibility of an EEIG is reflected in almost all aspects of its functioning, including the establishment of an EEIG, its duration, as well as its financing and the principles according to which it operates.[16] Firstly, the provisions of the Regulation 2137/85 introduce only a minimum level of formalities that must be fulfilled in order to establish an EEIG. With a view to making the formation of an EEIG as simple as possible, the Regulation stipulates that it requires only the conclusion of a written contract and the registration in the Member State in the territory of which the EEIG has its official address. The flexibility of an EEIG manifests itself also in the period of time during which it may operate, since it may be established for an indefinite or a limited period, which may meet the expectations of its members in particular when they are interested in the realisation of projects that are for a limited time. Flexibility of an EEIG as a legal entity is essential in order to define the main differences between this entity and a company. In that respect, it must be emphasised that, in contrast to a company, an EEIG does not require capital when it is formed. Furthermore, there are no restrictions concerning contributions, all types of contributions are allowed, including cash and even industrial property. The other important reflection of the flexibility of an EEIG refers to its operation and its ability to transfer its official address from one Member State to another without losing its legal personality or capacity. The Communication emphasises that such a transfer cannot be regarded as a winding up of an EEIG and have such effects on its tax duties.[17]

The last important characteristic of an EEIG is related to its liability for debts. The Regulation 2137/85 prescribes that the members of the EEIG

[15] The Communication paragraph II p.3.

[16] The Communication paragraph II p.4.

[17] The Communication paragraph II p.4.

have unlimited joint and several liability for its debts of whatever nature. The consequences of such liability must be determined by the national law.[18] The justification for introducing this kind of liability is based on the necessity to provide the maximum level of effective protection for third parties entering into business relationships with an EEIG. The Communication indicates that the unlimited joint and several liability of the members of an EEIG should be regarded as a guarantee and an encouragement for the third parties to enter into economic relationships with the grouping, in particular to conclude an insurance agreement or to give it a loan, since they may rely on the financial position of one of its members. However, it must be pointed out that introducing the unlimited joint and several liability of the members of the grouping is also the consequence of the lack of a capital requirement.[19]

In conclusion it must be admitted that the EEIG is a new legal structure and it cannot be defined as a company; from the legal point of view its construction is rather that of a hybrid. On the one hand an EEIG is similar to partnership, in particular with respect to the principle of the unlimited joint and several liability of its members for its debts. On the other hand an EEIG includes some features of a limited company, which are reflected first of all in the rule that it has the capacity to act in its own name, but only the managers are authorised to represent the EEIG in respect to dealings with third parties, and their representative powers are directly based on the rules applicable to limited companies.[20] However an EEIG should be regarded as an entity that has more of the features of a partnership than a limited company. The basic features of an EEIG that confirm its similarity to a partnership are in particular:

- the purpose of the EEIG according to which its activities must be ancillary to the business activities of its members (in fact its members must have some common interests),
- specific criteria necessary to gain membership in the EEIG, restrictions concerning any changes in the members of the EEIG and the possibility of ceasing to participate in the EEIG,
- the prohibition to invite investment by the public (art. 23 of the Regulation 2137/85),

---

[18] Art. 23 paragraph 1 of the Regulation 2137/85.

[19] The Communication paragraph II p.5; see also Rafał Adamus, *Europejskie Zgrupowanie Interesów Gospodarczych-wolne zawody prawnicze*, 2 Europejski Przegląd Prawa 117-121 (2004).

[20] Art. 20 of the Regulation 2137/85, Communication paragraph I and II 2.

- the principle of unlimited joint and several liability of its members for the EEIG's debts.[21]

The scope of the activities of an EEIG

The economic purpose of the establishment of the EEIG is considered to be one of the most controversial issues related to its functioning, since it may make it quite difficult to determine the scope of the activities of the EEIG. The provisions of the Regulation 2137/85 stipulate that the purpose of a EEIG should be to facilitate or develop the economic activities of its members and to improve or increase the results of those activities. The Regulation emphasises that the aim of the grouping is not to make profits for itself. Additionally, the activities of the EEIG shall be related to the economic activities of its members and must not be more than ancillary to those activities.[22] In the light of these provisions, three questions connected with the functioning of the EEIG are deemed to have the most important meaning: the purpose of the EEIG, the profits resulting from its activities, and the ancillary nature of the entity.

First of all it is worth indicating that the purpose of the activities of the EEIG must be public, since it is an obligatory element of the contract for the formation of an EEIG, and such a contract must be filed at the appropriate registry in a Member State where the grouping has its official address. Member States are also required to ensure that anyone will have the right to inspect the documents in the registry and obtain full or partial copies. Moreover, this information, in particular the details that must be included in the contract are also to be published in the appropriate official gazette of the Member State.[23]

The purpose of an EEIG, which should be focused on facilitating or developing the economic activities of its members and improving or increasing its results, is regarded as a deciding factor in determining the object of the EEIG, which is conducting business activities. In this context the term 'business activity' should be interpreted as widely as possible and should encompass industrial, commercial, craft and agricultural activities as well as the provision of services. However the members of the grouping should identify the object of its activities precisely in the agreement on the

---

[21] Rafał Adamus, *Europejskie Zgrupowanie Interesów...* 23 (2006).

[22] Art. 3 paragraph 1 of the Regulation 2137/85.

[23] Art. 5 c), art. 7, art. 39 paragraph 1 of the Regulation 2137/85; see also Rafał Adamus, *Europejskie Zgrupowanie Interesów Gospodarczych. Komentarz* 53 (1st ed. 2006).

formation of the EEIG.[24] In principle, the purpose of the EEIG should be common for all of its members, however it is also acceptable that different members may be interested in the activities of the Grouping in different levels.[25]

In the light of the purpose of the activities of the EEIG, it may seem to be ambiguous if the Grouping is allowed to make profits, since it is basically established in order to support the development of the business activities of its members. According to art. 21 of the Regulation 2137/85, if the Grouping makes profits resulting from its activities, they should be deemed to be the profits of the members and they should be apportioned among members in the proportions laid down in the contract for the formation of the Grouping or, in the absence of any such provision, in equal shares. Taking into consideration this provision, it must be admitted that an EEIG is not prohibited from making profits, but they are always regarded as profits of its members.[26] In conclusion, making profits must not be the principal purpose of the activities of the Grouping.[27] In substance, the purpose of an EEIG is to indirectly enable its members to gain more profits.[28]

The essential feature of an EEIG, indicated in art. 3 of the Regulation 2137/85 and emphasised in the Communication,[29] is its ancillary character with respect to the activities of its members. The ancillary nature of the Grouping must obviously have a great impact on the scope of its activities, but on the other hand such a condition should not be regarded as an operational limitation that confines the Grouping to a subsidiary or minor role. In particular the Regulation does not prohibit an EEIG from

---

[24] Iwona Hykawy, *Europejskie Ugrupowanie Interesów Gospodarczych...* 285 (2002). This interpretation seems to be consistent with the provisions of the Regulation which refer to the scope of activity of its members. According to art. 4 paragraph 1 a,b of the Regulation 2137/85 the members of an EEIG may only be companies within the meaning of art. 54 of the Treaty on the Functioning of the European Union and natural persons, who carry out any industrial, commercial, craft or agricultural activity or who provide professional or other services in the Union.

[25] Rafał Adamus, *Europejskie Zgrupowanie Interesów...* 53 (2006).

[26] Peter Behrens, *Prawo spółek* in Manfred A. Dauses et al., *Prawo gospodarcze Unii Europejskiej* 526 (1999).

[27] Rafał Adamus, *supra* 53 – 54.

[28] Iwona Hykawy, Europejskie Ugrupowanie Interesów Gospodarczych... 288 (2002).

[29] Communication paragraph II p.3 – The ancillary nature of an EEIG's activity.

completely but temporarily taking over some of its members activities.[30] However it must be emphasised that an EEIG is intended to be a legal instrument for cooperation of the entrepreneurs and not integration. In effect, its activities must neither replace the activities of its members nor compete with them, since its aim is to improve the results of the activities of members and cannot eliminate them. This condition is directly expressed in the French provisions regulating the functioning of an EEIG - if the activity of an EEIG absorbs the activities of members, it will contribute to the nullity of the grouping, since in France the auxiliary nature of an EEIG is obligatory.[31]

The ancillary nature of an EEIG, reflected in the provisions, according to which its activities must not replace the activities of its members, also has an impact on the general prohibition of practising the profession by an EEIG with regard to the third parties.[32] This issue relating to the functioning of an EEIG is worth emphasising, since the Grouping may be established by the representatives of the free professions, who, in practice, are one of the biggest groups of entrepreneurs creating the groupings. However, in such a case, the aim of the EEIG may only be connected with facilitating the conducting of the free profession.[33]

Any abuse of the purpose of an EEIG or using it for different purposes than those indicated in the art. 3 of the Regulation 2137/85 may result in serious consequences. First of all, an EEIG whose aim, as indicated in the contract for its formation, is inconsistent with art. 3 of the Regulation, may be refused the right to register in an appropriate register in a Member State. Moreover, any inconsistency of the purpose of an EEIG with the law may, according to the internal law of the State where the EEIG has its official address, be regarded as a reason for the nullifying of the Grouping. In the light of the provisions of article 15 of the Regulation the consequence of the nullity of an EEIG is its liquidation.[34]

---

[30] Communication paragraph II p.3; see also Rafał Adamus, *supra* 54. The Communication refers to the statement of the Commission issued in 1991, where the Commission admitted that 'there is nothing to prevent an EEIG from carrying out some of the activities of its members for a limited period, for the purposes of performing site work, for example'.

[31] Rafał Adamus, *Europejskie Zgrupowanie Interesów...* 54 (2006); Iwona Hykawy, Europejskie Ugrupowanie Interesów Gospodarczych... 275 – 276, 286 (2002).

[32] Preambule of the Regulation 2137/85.

[33] Iwona Hykawy, *supra* 286.

[34] Rafał Adamus, *supra* 59.

However, it must be admitted that in practice many groupings conduct traditional business activities and from a practical point of view there is little opportunity to verify to what extent their activities are only ancillary to the activities of its members.[35]

The specific legal aspects of an EEIG in the light of the provisions of Polish law

A European Economic Interest Grouping that has its official address in the territory of Poland is subject to quite complicated legal regulation, which consists of a several levels of legal sources. The structure of this legal regulation is the consequence of a general reference to the internal law of the State in which the official address of an EEIG is situated, which is included in the provisions of the Regulation. The Regulation 2137/85 stipulates that the law is applicable, on the one hand for the formation of the EEIG, except as regards matters relating to the status or capacity of natural persons and to the capacity of legal persons and, on the other hand, to the internal organization of a EEIG is the internal law of the State in which the official address of the EEIG is situated according to the provisions of the contract for the formation of the grouping.[36]

The principal group of provisions concerning an EEIG are included in the of the Council Regulation (EEC) No 2137/85 of July 25th, 1985 on the European Economic Interest Grouping, which creates this supranational kind of legal entity.

In spite of the literal meaning of article 2 of the Regulation, the following group of provisions applicable to an EEIG are not provisions of the national law, but rather regulations of the contract for the formation of an EEIG. Such a conclusion must be drawn from the overriding character of the provisions of the Regulation. The Regulation indicates the scope of issues which may be regulated by members of the grouping in the contract. Their freedom concerning the regulation of these issues should be respected by the legislative authority of the State.[37]

---

[35] Aleksander Cieśliński & Eligiusz Jerzy Krześniak, *Podmioty ponadnarodowe* in 2 Aleksander Cieśliński et al., *Wspólnotowe prawo gospodarcze* 393 (2nd ed. 2007).

[36] Art. 2 paragraph 1 of the Regulation 2137/85.

[37] Adam Opalski, *Europejskie prawo spółek* 580 (2010); see also Rafał Adamus, *Europejskie Zgrupowanie Interesów Gospodarczych jako forum dla międzynarodowej współpracy pomiędzy osobami wykonującymi wolne zawody prawnicze*, 2 Radca Prawny, 102-103 (2007).

The functioning of an EEIG is subject to the provisions of the national law and its jurisdiction depends of the provisions of the Regulation. First of all, it should be emphasised that an EEIG with its official address in Poland is regulated by Polish law to the extent indicated in the Regulation and in the national law. The principal rules relating to an EEIG are included in the provisions of the Act of 4th March 2005 on the European Economic Interest Grouping and the European Company that came into force in May 19th 2005.[38] It is noteworthy that the Act on an EEIG and a European Company is applicable only to those issues that are not regulated in the European Regulation. There are also other provisions of Polish Law which are applicable to an EEIG that has its official address in Poland, in particular the commercial company code,[39] the civil code,[40] and the National Court Register Act.[41] The Polish Act on the EEIGs sets forth rules that determines the registration and certain principles of the organization of an EEIG in matters not regulated in the provisions of the Regulation 2137/85.[42]

The Polish Act on the EEIGs lays down the principal rule concerning the application of the appropriate provisions of Polish Law. According to this rule, in matters not regulated under Regulation 2137/85 and in the Polish Act on the EEIGs, an EEIG shall be governed accordingly by the provisions on registered partnerships.[43] However, taking into consideration the hybrid construction of an EEIG, the provisions referring to a registered partnership may not be exhaustive with respect to all aspects of the organisation of an EEIG. This is the reason why the Polish legislature, following the ideas introduced in German Law, decided accordingly to apply to an EEIG the provisions of a limited liability company in respect of the members of the management board.[44]

---

[38] Act of March 4th, 2005 on the European Economic Interest Grouping and the European Company - Journal of Laws of 2005, No.62, Item 551 with subsequent amendments, hereafter referred to as the Polish Act on the EEIG.

[39] Act of September 15th, 2000 Code of Commercial Companies - Journal of Laws of 2000, No. 94, Item 1037 with subsequent amendments.

[40] Act of April 23rd, 1964 The Civil Code - Journal of Laws of 1964 No. 16. Item 93, with subsequent amendments.

[41] Act of August 20th, 1997 on the National Court Register - Journal of Laws of 2001 No. 17. Item 209, with subsequent amendments.

[42] Art. 1 of the Polish Act on the EEIG.

[43] Art. 7 of the Polish Act on the EEIG.

[44] Art. 11 paragraph 1 of the Polish Act on the EEIG; see also Rafał Adamus, *Europejskie Zgrupowanie Interesów Gospodarczych z siedzibą w Polsce*, 9 Przegląd Ustawodawstwa Gospodarczego 5-7 (2005).

It is worth emphasising that according to the opinion of the representatives of the legal doctrine, the expression that the provisions are applicable 'accordingly' is usually interpreted in such a way that some provisions must be directly applicable, while other provisions are applicable with particular modifications and some of the provisions are not applicable at all.[45] As a result of the application of the provisions on a registered partnership to an EEIG with its official address in Poland, an EEIG has no legal personality. Furthermore, there are many important provisions concerning a registered partnership, which cannot be applicable to an EEIG in Poland. In particular, it is impossible to apply the legal definition of the registered partnership included in art. 22 of Polish Act of Commercial Companies to a Grouping, since, according to the European Union law, the essence of an EEIG is different, and both entities, although similar to each other to a certain extent, should be regarded as two separate legal institutions.[46] In conclusion, a European Economic Interest Grouping with its official address in Poland differs substantially, in terms of its legal construction and internal structure, from a typical registered partnership, which is considered to be its model.[47]

Conclusions

The European Economic Interest Grouping has been introduced into European Union law with the intention of creating an instrument for international cooperation between entrepreneurs that originates from different Member States and a legal framework, which will facilitate them adapting their activities to the economic conditions of the European internal market.[48] One of the fundamental principles of Regulation 2137/85 is to ensure that such an opportunity for the development of economic activities and increase in its results will be available for as wide a group of natural and legal persons as possible.[49] In principle, the Regulation provides only a few conditions that may restrict access to an EEIG. One of the most noteworthy conditions refers to the essence of an

---

[45] Józef Nowacki, *Odpowiednie stosowanie przepisów prawa,* 3 Państwo i Prawo 87 (1964); Antoni Witosz, *Konstrukcja Europejskiego Zgrupowania Interesów Gospodarczych w prawie polskim i niemieckim,* 1 Prawo Spółek 15 (2007).

[46] Rafał Adamus, *Europejskie Zgrupowanie Interesów Gospodarczych...* 5-7, 10 (2005).

[47] Antoni Witosz, *Konstrukcja Europejskiego Zgrupowania Interesów Gospodarczych w prawie polskim i niemieckim,* 1 Prawo Spółek 15,16 (2007).

[48] Preamble to the Regulation 2137/85 paragraph 1.

[49] Preamble to the Regulation 2137/85 paragraph 6.

EEIG and provides that only entities that conduct, at least additionally, business activities may be members of the groupings.[50] A second important provision that relates to the international character of an EEIG stipulates that the grouping must comprise of at least two members, who conduct business activities in different Member States.[51]

In light of these provisions it may seem that an EEIG should be considered to be a great opportunity for Polish entrepreneurs to commence cooperation with foreign entrepreneurs, develop their activities, and improve their results. But despite all of the opportunities that are connected with membership in a grouping, since the validity of the Act of the European Economic Interest Grouping and the European Company, EEIGs have not become very popular in Poland. In fact at the end of 2010 there were only two of them registered on the territory of Poland: the Polish-German Research Association ADHOC EEIG/ EZIG with its official address in Jelenia Góra, and the European Coordination Centre for Education, Energy, Health and Technology EUREKA EEIG with its official address in Warsaw.[52]

The relatively low level of interest in the establishment of an EEIG may be the result of some features connected with its structure and functioning. First of all, the restrictions concerning the purpose of the activities of an EEIG may be regarded as an obstacle to using this form of cooperation, particularly taking into consideration that entrepreneurs may choose the appropriate form of business relationship from a variety of options offered in the provisions of civil law or company law. A second important feature of an EEIG that may discourage potential members refers to its liability for debts. According to article 24 of the Regulation, members of the grouping have unlimited joint and several liability for its

---

[50] Rafał Adamus, *Europejskie Zgrupowanie Interesów...* 62 (2006); Iwona Hykawy, Europejskie Ugrupowanie Interesów Gospodarczych... 274, 289 (2002).

[51] Rafał Adamus, *supra* 64; Iwona Hykawy, *supra* 289. According to art. 4 paragraph 2 of Regulation 2137/85 a grouping must comprise at least: two companies, firms or other legal bodies, within the meaning of paragraph 1, which have their central administrations in different Member States, or two natural persons, within the meaning of paragraph 1, who carry on their principal activities in different Member States, or a company, firm or other legal body within the meaning of paragraph 1 and a natural person, of which the first has its central administration in one Member State and the second carries on its principal activity in another Member State.

[52] Adam Opalski, *Europejskie...* 579 (2010); 16 Aleksandra Gawrysiak-Zabłocka, *Prawo przedsiębiorczości i prawo spółek* 126-127 (2010). These information is also available on the website www.libertas-institut.com (list of all EEIG as to 9.12.2010) and www.krs-online.com.pl.

debts and other liabilities of whatever nature. These severe principles of liability along with high requirements concerning publications and restrictions with respect to the scope of its activities are not deemed to be justified.[53] Furthermore, in Poland additional problems may arise out of the quite complicated system of legal sources that regulates the functioning of an EEIG. This system may provide the formation of a legal entity whose structure is different in a majority of aspects from a registered partnership regulated under the Polish Code of Commercial Companies.[54]

On the other hand it must be emphasised that an EEIG as a European instrument for the international cooperation of entrepreneurs also has many advantages that may make it a really interesting alternative to traditional forms of companies. First of all, an EEIG must be considered as an instrument for international cooperation in business activities, but its originality is connected with the fact that it simultaneously enables the entrepreneurs to retain their independence. Moreover, an EEIG is a real opportunity to develop and improve the activities of its members and increase their results. In particular, an EEIG offers a great opportunity to conduct free professions, not only in the field of legal services. Within the framework of an EEIG, its members may, for example, look for new clients, broaden the territorial scope of their activities, exchange professional experiences or conduct joint business negotiations.[55] It is also worth emphasising that the formation of an EEIG is intended to be very simple and informal and, what is even more important is the establishment of an EEIG does not require any assets or contributions. This kind of flexibility of an EEIG seems to be particularly attractive for small- and medium-sized enterprises.[56] A very interesting feature of an EEIG, which should make it a really popular instrument of business cooperation on the internal market, is also the possibility to transfer its official address within the Union without losing its legal personality or capacity and without regarding such a transfer as a winding up of an EEIG.[57] All these notable features of an EEIG should result in an increase in the application of

---

[53] Adam Opalski, *Europejskie...* 579 (2010).

[54] Antoni Witosz, *Konstrukcja Europejskiego Zgrupowania...*15,16 (2007).

[55] Rafał Adamus, *Europejskie Zgrupowanie Interesów...* 55-56 (2006); Iwona Hykawy, Europejskie Ugrupowanie Interesów Gospodarczych... 286 (2002); see also the Communication paragraph II p. 2.

[56] Iwona Hykawy, *Europejskie Ugrupowanie Interesów Gospodarczych...* 307 (2002).

[57] Art. 13 of the Regulation 2137/85, the Communication paragraph II p.4.

EEIGs by Polish entrepreneurs as an instrument that may improve their competitiveness in the internal market.

Consumer Protection and Limits for National Legislatures in the Field of Electronic Communications: Some Reflections about the ECJ Judgments in Polish Cases

Alessandro Palmieri

University of Siena, Italy

Abstract

The recent developments in the European Court of Justice case law on the electronic communications package, contribute to more accurately define the boundaries of national rule-makers in this field. In particular, two references for a preliminary ruling from Polish courts have given the Court the opportunity to clarify the extent of consumer protection rules that aim to protect clients against the risks inherent in the bundling of different products and to facilitate number portability, so as to enhance competition in the telephone services market. In the first decision (case of Telekomunikacja Polska), the Third Chamber held that harmonised provisions concerning unfair B2C commercial practices preclude national legislation which, with certain exceptions, and without taking account of the specific circumstances, imposes a general prohibition of combined offers made by a vendor to a consumer; according to the judges, this principle applies to the rule that bans making the conclusion of a contract for the provision of certain services contingent on the conclusion, by the end-user, of a contract for the provision of other services. In the second judgment (case Polska Telefonia Cyfrowa), the Fourth Chamber ruled that the National Regulatory Authority could not ignore the costs incurred by mobile telephone network operators in carrying out the number portability service when it appraises whether the direct charge to subscribers for the use of that service has a negative motivational influence; the Authority retains the power to fix the maximum amount of that charge levied by operators at a level below the costs incurred by them, when a charge calculated only on the basis of those costs are likely to dissuade clients from making use of the portability facility. Both decisions reveal that legislators and agencies operating in Member States, while providing safeguard measures for consumers, ought to be fully aware of the interests of other market players and to pursue the objectives of the efficiency and openness of the market itself.

The Evolution of Electronic Communications Markets and the Need for Adequate Consumer Protection Rules

Over the past two decades the communications markets in Europe have known a radical evolution, having faced the problems stemming from extremely fast growth and from the urgent need to adapt old *cliches* to the 'spirit' of the Digital Age *we are living in.*[1] The European Union legislator attempted to conduct this process, and its main contribution was the preparation, in 2002, of a composite regulatory framework. Five Directives were enacted, with the aim of covering the entire spectrum of issues in a vast region, populated by all kinds of electronic communications services and networks, including those used for radio and television broadcasting. The full package was composed of five Directives: the Framework Directive,[2] the Authorisation Directive,[3] the Access and Interconnection Directive,[4] and the Universal Service Directive,[5] as well as the Directive on Privacy and Electronic Communications.[6] According to the views expressed by the European

---

[1] The advent of Digital Age has had repercussions even on the side of law; see Giovanni Pascuzzi, *The law of the digital age* in *Italian National Reports to the XVI International Congress of Comparative Law* 513 (2002).

[2] Directive 2002/21/EC of the European Parliament and of the Council of March 7th, 2002, on a common regulatory framework for electronic communications networks and services.

[3] Directive 2002/20/EC of the European Parliament and of the Council of March 7th, 2002, on the authorisation of electronic communications networks and services.

[4] Directive 2002/19/EC of the European Parliament and of the Council of March 7th, 2002, on access to, and interconnection of, electronic communications networks and associated facilities.

[5] Directive 2002/22/EC of the European Parliament and of the Council of March 7th, 2002, on universal service and users' rights relating to electronic communications networks and services.

[6] Directive 2002/58/EC of the European Parliament and of the Council of July 12th, 2002, concerning the processing of personal data and the protection of privacy in the electronic communications sector.

Commission,[7] all these Directives were connected with the purpose of developing and reinforcing the single market, and stimulating competition, while safeguarding public and user interests in this sector.[8] After seven years, this framework was modernised. Two new Directives were passed to amend the previous ones.[9] The revision was accompanied by the establishment of the Body of European Regulators for Electronic Communications (BEREC), an agency at European level, composed of one member per Member State, representing each National Regulation Authority (NRA).[10] The package in question contains consumer protection rules specific to the electronic communications sector, and reaffirms the intangibility of more general rules, such as those concerning unfair terms and distance selling.[11] The improvement of consumers' position, in terms of lower prices, better quality, and enhanced transparency of contractual conditions,[12] needs to be paired with robust policies in order to foster innovation and to encourage small and medium sized firms to compete against the giants still occupying large shares of the relevant markets.

---

[7] See the Information Society Policies at a Glance, http://tinyurl.com/4vekg4.

[8] For a comprehensive analysis of the regulatory framework, see Robert Bell & Neill Ray, *EU Electronic Communications Law* (2004); Mira Burri Nenova, *Communications and Competition Law* (2007).

[9] Directive 2009/136/EC of the European Parliament and of the Council of November 25th, 2009, amending Directive 2002/22/EC on universal service and users' rights relating to electronic communications networks and services, Directive 2002/58/EC concerning the processing of personal data and the protection of privacy in the electronic communications sector and Regulation (EC) No 2006/2004 on cooperation between national authorities responsible for the enforcement of consumer protection laws; and Directive 2009/140/EC of the European Parliament and of the Council of November 25th, 2009, amending Directives 2002/21/EC on a common regulatory framework for electronic communications networks and services, 2002/19/EC on access to, and interconnection of, electronic communications networks and associated facilities, and 2002/20/EC on the authorisation of electronic communications networks and services.

[10] Regulation (EC) No 1211/2009 of the European Parliament and of the Council of November 25th, 2009, establishing the Body of European Regulators for Electronic Communications (BEREC) and the Office.

[11] Universal Service Directive, art. 1(4).

[12] Hans W. Micklitz, *The Visible Hand of European Regulatory Private Law - The Transformation of European Private Law from Autonomy to Functionalism in Competition and Regulation*, 14 EUI LAW 22 (2008) argues that 'the privatization (liberalization) of former State monopolies in the sector of telecommunications, energy, and transport has raised the importance of contract law'.

Since 2009, the transposition in national legal systems of the amendments to the rules currently in force, has been greatly anticipated amongst legal scholars. In the meantime, the Court of Justice of the European Union (the institution that, before the validity of the Treaty of Lisbon, was named 'Court of Justice of the European Communities'; note that, even with its present appellation, the Court continues to be referred to as ECJ; accordingly, this abbreviation will be used in the following part of this paper) has sought to clarify many features of the present set of concepts, values and policies in the branch of communications.

Considering 2010 alone, and apart from privacy-related issues, the ECJ delivered seven judgments on this very subject. *Amongst this heterogeneous group,* the cases that came before the Court were almost equally divided between actions brought by the European Commission against Member States for failure to comply with their obligations (under Article 226 of the EC Treaty, now replaced by Article 258 of the FEU Treaty), on the one hand, and questions submitted by domestic judges, concerning the interpretation of specific provisions of the Directives comprising the communications package (under Article 234 of the EC Treaty, now replaced by Article 267 of the FEU Treaty), on the other.

It is easy to observe that the difficulties encountered at a national level arose especially with respect to the scope and the enforcement of users' rights pertaining to electronic communications networks and services. In addition, from a mere geographical point of view, it should be pointed out that the majority of rulings in the segment of time taken into account (five out of seven) originated from only two countries, namely Belgium (two decisions) and Poland (three decisions). Of course, the obvious close connection with a specific legal system does not mean that the statements made by the court are irrelevant in the context of other Member States. Indeed the ECJ's decisions, as experienced in many areas of law, have a strong influence on the reasoning of judges sitting in the higher courts in every European country, dealing with matters related to EU norms. This is particularly evident in the well-known judgment that compelled national courts, seised of disputes concerning a contract between a supplier and a consumer, to favour the interpretation of national law that would allow them to decline, of their own volition, the jurisdiction conferred on them by virtue of an unfair term.[13] Although the decision was rendered by the ECJ in reply to a question referred by a Spanish court, it had an enormous impact on the case law of various jurisdictions. In Italy for instance, the

[13] ECJ 27 June 2000, joined cases C-240/98 to C-244/98, *Océano Grupo Editorial and Salvat Editores* [2000] ECR I-4941.

Supreme Court, in the absence of clear statutory guidance in this regard, refused to apply the general principles set forth in the Code of Civil Procedure, and held that the proper forum for litigation involving consumer contracts was the district court sitting in the place where the consumer resides.[14]

Coincidentally, the recent 'Polish cases', especially those referred for a preliminary ruling, seem to be very significant, because the ECJ intends to set unambiguous guidelines upon which legislators and authorities could rely. Hence, these two cases - one concerning the linking of different communication 'products',[15] the other addressing the problem of telephone number portability[16] - will be further analysed in greater detail to illustrate some of the trends that characterise the evolution of regulatory tools in the field of electronic communications.

Combined Offers of Different Communications Services: Balancing Consumers' Interests with the Enhancement of Competition

Broadly speaking, one of the commercial practices that may distort competition, to the detriment of consumers and which is therefore often looked at with suspicion and mistrust, consists of the marketing of a combination of two (or, very rarely, three or more) services, artificially linked for the purposes of commercialization, in the form of a single, indivisible, offer.[17] The above mentioned practices are in contrast with European antitrust law (1) when they are planned or executed as the result of an agreement or another type of collusion between two or more undertakings, provided that the other requirements set out in Article 101 of the FEU Treaty are met, or (2) when they embody a strategy designed by a single firm acting alone, or by a group of several undertakings acting jointly, that holds a dominant position, in the meaning of Article 102 of the Treaty.

---

[14] See Italian Supreme Court ('Corte di Cassazione') August 28th, 2001, n. 11282, Foro italiano, I, 3587 (2001) (with a comment by Alessandro Palmieri, Foro esclusivo del consumatore e abusività della deroga convenzionale alla competenza per territorio: mai più in giudizio lontano da casa).

[15] ECJ March 11th, 2010, case C-522/08, *Telekomunikacja Polska.*

[16] ECJ July 1st, 2010, case C-99/09, *Polska Telefonia Cyfrowa.*

[17] The bundling of different services increases the sales of products with a lower demand (see Georg Wuebker & Hermann Simon, *Price Bundling. A Powerful Strategy to Increase Profit*, 14 The Journal of Professional Pricing (2005).

According to the European communications package, the regulatory powers conferred upon National Regulation Authorities interfere with the provision of combined services only in the presence of an extra-factor inherent in the market structure. In this legislation one finds two situations that call for appropriate intervention. Firstly, with regard to undertakings designated for the fulfillment of universal service obligations, the supply of additional services must be governed by regulators in order to assure that any client who asks for a specific service is not obliged to pay for facilities or services which are not necessary or not required for the service requested.[18] Secondly, the unreasonable bundling of services may be denounced by NRAs when they decide to impose special obligations on undertakings that appear to keep significant market power on a given retail market.[19]

What happens if a national legislator imposes obligations of that kind on all operators, even those which are neither designated for universal service nor identified as holders of a significant market power? This harsh approach was envisaged in the Polish Telecommunication Act, and coherently the local Authority ordered a company to desist from a practice consisting of making the conclusion of a contract for the provision of broadband Internet access services subject to the conclusion of a contract for telephone services. After the complaint filed by the addressee of the injunction, the judicial proceedings commenced; the plaintiff filed an appeal, where the matter was heard by the members of the Supreme Administrative Court, who doubted the compatibility of the aforesaid restriction (to the freedom of contract) with European communications law, and referred the case (labelled Telekomunikacja Polska) to the judges sitting in Luxembourg.

The Third Chamber of the ECJ decided to proceed to judgment without a prior opinion from the Advocate General. Despite that procedural choice, this was not an easy case, as evidenced by the complex analysis rendered, inspired by a global view of the European rules that protect consumers' concerns. The ECJ observed that, while the protection of consumers (and, more generally, of end-users, whether belonging to the wide group of consumers or not, as prescribed by EU legislation) is one of the pillars of the framework for the regulation of electronic communication services, the package does not provide for full harmonisation of consumer-protection issues. In this area of communication law, Member States only have the power to lay down more stringent standards than those set out in EU law;

---

[18] Universal Service Directive, art. 10(1) (not modified by the 2009 amendments).

[19] Universal Service Directive, art. 17(2) (not modified by the 2009 amendments).

in other words, deviations from the benchmark are strictly forbidden to the extent that they worsen the position of consumers. On the contrary, national legislatures are free to create and implement measures that are capable of strengthening the protection of those individuals, provided that they comply with the basic principles consecrated by the Treaties.[20]

For that reason, the way in which the Polish authority behaved, enforcing the national mandatory rule, was not objectionable in light of the Directives dealing specifically with the markets for the supply of communication services. However, the consistency of this attitude with electronic communications' harmonised law is not a safe harbour, because it does not guarantee immunity from the European legislation on the protection of consumers. To grant power to NRAs, when it is likely to rebound on consumers when so defined, could be disputed under this body of principles.

In particular, the combined offers made by an undertaking to consumers may breach the rules set out in the Directive concerning unfair business-to-consumer commercial practices (Unfair Commercial Practices Directive or, simply, UCPD).[21] The EU legislator banned all commercial practises that (1) are contrary to the requirements of professional diligence, and (2) may cause distortion of the economic behaviour of the average consumer whom it reaches, or to whom it is addressed, or of the average member of the group, when a commercial practice is directed to a particular group of consumers. Both requirements must be ascertained in order to demonstrate the illegality of the enterprise's conduct.

UCPD encompasses a black list of practices which are always deemed to be unfair, notwithstanding the context in which a trader engages. This classification aims to facilitate enquiries on suspected conducts, although some of the blacklisted practices are a 'mixed bag', and not all are drafted very precisely. Outside of this area, there is no presumption, not even a rebuttable one, of unfairness. The declaration of unfairness should be the

---

[20] According to the standard European notion, a consumer is a natural person acting for purposes which can be regarded as outside his of her trade or business. Note that Article 1:201 of the Principles of the Existing EC Contract Law (the so-called Acquis Principles) states that the word consumer means 'any natural person who is mainly acting for purposes which are outside this person's business activity'.

[21] Directive 2005/29/EC of the European Parliament and of the Council of May 11th, 2005, concerning unfair business-to-consumer commercial practices in the internal market and amending Council Directive 84/450/EEC, Directives 97/7/EC, 98/27/EC and 2002/65/EC of the European Parliament and of the Council and Regulation (EC) No 2006/2004 of the European Parliament and of Council.

outcome of a case-by-case determination conducted by the Authorities in charge of this duty (even acting on their own motion) and by the judges (investigating the claims stated by those who believe they have fallen victim to a certain practice). The problem is that national legislatures cannot add other presumptions to the ones included in Annex I to UCPD. Indeed, UCPD, belonging to the last generation of the laws intended to protect consumers, embraces the 'complete harmonization' philosophy, ceasing any attempt to escape from the chosen path.

This philosophy already led to the disapproval of national norms that aim to dissuade firms from selling packages of goods and/or services without including the possibility of choosing just one of the items.[22]

In VTB-VAB, the ECJ censured Belgian rules that inhibit vendors from making combined offers to a consumer, generally and as a preventative measure.[23] This decision was confirmed in Plus Warenhandelsgesellschaft, where a German provision was at issue, that vetoed in principle, without taking into account the specific circumstances of individual cases, the practices under which the participation of consumers in a prize competition or a lottery was made conditional on the purchase of goods or the use of services;[24] and once again in Mediaprint Zeitungs, in order to condemn a piece of Austrian legislation, laying down a prohibition in principle on commercial practices making the offer of bonuses to consumers subject to the purchase of goods or services.[25]

In Telekomunikacja Polska, the reporter recalls the first of these precedents (VTB-VAB), to state that, from the date on which the period for the transposition of UCPD expired, the Member States are prevented from prohibiting combined offers on a general basis; this foreclosure

---

[22] Under the current trend, it is arguable than several Member States will have to abrogate a certain number of still existing regulations of sales promotion; see Jules Stuyck, in Geraint Howells & Rainer Schulze (eds.), *Modernising and Harmonising Consumer Contract Law* 142 (2009); Damian Chalmers et al., *European Union Law: Texts and Materials* 99 (2010).

[23] ECJ April 23rd, 2009, joined cases C-261/07 and C-299/07 VTB-VAB and Galatea, La nuova giurisprudenza civile commentata, I, 1059 (2009) (with a comment by Giovanni De Cristofaro).

[24] ECJ January 14th, 2010, case C-304/08, Plus Warenhandelsgesellschaft, Foro italiano, IV, 173 (2010) .

[25] ECJ November 9th, 2010, case C-540/08, Mediaprint Zeitungs- und Zeitschriftenverlag (the Court added that the possibility of participating in a prize competition, linked to the purchase of a newspaper, did not constitute an unfair commercial practice simply on the ground that, for at least some of the consumers concerned, that possibility represented the factor, which determined them to buy that newspaper).

applies to every commercial sector, without any exception for the communication markets.

The Tricky Problem of Number Portability

Even the *Polska Telefonia Cyfrowa* judgment is heavily influenced by the need to balance the interest of the key players operating in the market. The basic idea is to avoid the sacrifice of the professional operators when there is an available solution that does not harm (or does not excessively harm) consumers.

When all over Europe the markets for the provision of telephone services were by and large characterised by the presence of national monopolists, owned or controlled by public entities, clearly the clients had no means by which to make choices other than to exit from the market (unimaginable, since the consequence would have been isolation). In the previous scenario, all the subscribers retained their assigned telephone number all life long, unless they moved to another address.

The situation changed radically after the implementation of the policy of opening the aforesaid markets, with the removal of barriers to competition. Various firms entered into the cores of the once impermeable sector, trying to erode the market shares of the incumbents. Antitrust rules undoubtedly play a major role in safeguarding the freedom of choice among the suppliers, but unfortunately, due to the technical peculiarities of communication services, one cannot rely entirely on the general prohibition of anti-competitive, cooperative and unilateral, conducts.

The opportunity to migrate to another provider was an essential constituent of the design to build a competitive and dynamic market; and, in order to ensure the effectiveness of this objective, the possibility to change should not be dampened by qualitative or quantitative obstacles, not justified by insurmountable technical barriers.[26]

A strong disincentive certainly resides in the necessity to modify one's previous number every time one finds it *economically rational and feasible* to withdraw from the old operator to enter into a new contractual

---

[26] According to Mira Burri Nenova, *Communications...* 86 (2007) 'Liberalisation allowed new players to enter markets, which accordingly gave consumers the opportunity to choose between operators, service packages and/or networks. This freedom of choice was created and is largely guaranteed by competitive processes in the markets (and thus indirectly by the antitrust rules). In communications, however, due to some technical predeterminations, this freedom might be harmed and needs to be secured by additional regulation. Number portability [...] could be seen as expression[...] of this need'.

relationship with another undertaking that offers the same service. Under this constraint, many subscribers may not profit from really valuable offers, because they are forced to evaluate the risk of not being able to be contacted by phone for a certain period of time, during which other users are not aware of their new number. This virtual 'black-out' could last for quite a long period, especially for those users who do not allow the disclosure of their personal data in paper and digital directories. In theory, the problem could be solved by communicating the change, but the burden associated with this task would usually be heavy and costly. How great would the loss be, not only for business entities, but also for private individuals! Difficulties are likely to multiply, as rapidly as the providers increase, striking a blow even to the so-called marginal consumers (or active choosers), that is to say the ones who possess, as compared with average consumers, a higher level of information on the value of different offers as well as on their variation through time and, relying on this information, would be willing to search constantly for the best combination. Undeniably, in this context, numbers could be of considerable economic or social value.

Even though the right to retain the old number is recognised, there are still challenges that threaten to undermine the exercise of this right. Enabling the number portability imposes expenses on the undertakings involved and it seems fair to pass these costs on to the clients. However the price charged for the implementation of the service endanger the genuineness of the client's decision. Relatively high figures have the effect of hindering potential movements.

Accordingly, it is crucial to formulate rules that do not discourage end users who desire to change provider without losing their number. The first step towards the full implementation of number portability dates back to 1997, when a sort of recommendation was issued to NRAs in order to 'encourage the earliest possible introduction of operator number portability whereby subscribers, who so request can retain their number(s)', and to ensure the availability of this facility by the beginning of 2000.[27]

Five years later, with the enactment of the telecommunications package, the original concise rule was replaced by a more detailed provision.[28] The objective to guarantee number portability is so important that one of the exceptional circumstances in which NRAs can impose

[27] Directive 98/61/EC, that amended Directive 97/33/EC of the European Parliament and of the Council of June 30th, 1997, on interconnection in telecommunications with regard to ensuring universal service and interoperability through application of the principles of open network provision (ONP).

[28] Universal Service Directive, art. 30.

obligations on undertakings that do not have market power relates specifically to the measures required to put into practical effect the facility of number portability.[29]

A controversy regarding this issue arose before the Polish courts, and concerned a mulct or financial penalty imposed by the President of the National Regulation Authority (UKE) on a company which charged high fees if the mobile phone operator were to be changed, thus violating the national rule at that time in force, which prohibited the setting of fees at such a level as to dissuade subscribers from making use of their right to transfer yet retain their number.[30]

The opposition proceedings against the fine finally came before the Polish Supreme Court that asked the ECJ to elucidate the powers of the Authority when it keeps under surveillance the conduct of the undertakings asked by their clients to use the facility of taking their numbers to other operators.

As the ECJ stated in 2006, in *Mobistar*, when it dealt with the interconnection charges between operators,[31] the NRAs enjoy a certain discretion in estimating the situation and defining the method which they deem most appropriate in making portability fully effective.[32] In *Polska Telefonia Cyfrowa*, the Fourth Chamber stresses the importance of taking account of the costs incurred by operators, in order to compare that amount with the fee they levy on the subscribers. In this regard, the Court follows the Advocate General's opinion, delivered at the sitting on April 15th, 2010. According to the Advocate General, the aforementioned costs are the most reliable source for extracting indicators that NRAs cannot ignore. Apparently, the Polish Authority was accused for having suggested

---

[29] Universal Service Directive, art. 8(3). On this issue, Mira Burri Nenova, *Communications...* 234 (2007), recommends great care in using these exceptional powers.

[30] The relevant provisions of the Telecommunications Act of 2004 was substituted in 2010; it currently states that a subscriber shall not be charged any fee for porting an assigned number.

[31] ECJ July 13th, 2006, case C-438/04, Mobistar, [2006] ECR I-6675. About this judgment, see Vincenzo De Falco, *Il complesso equilibrio tra attività di regolazione, esigenze del servizio universale e tutela della concorrenza nel mercato delle telecomunicazioni in Belgio*, Diritto pubblico comparato ed europeo 1861 (2006).

[32] According to Yves van Gerven & Anne Vallery, *Polska Telefonia Cyfrowa: Pricing of Number Portability: Cost- or Demand-Based?*, Journal of European Competition Law & Practice (2010), doi 10.1093/jeclap/lpq056, Polska Telefonia Cyfrowa ruling 'constitutes a welcome complement to the Court's existing case law on the topic'.

a methodology based mainly on demand, as emerged from a consumer survey. Indeed, the Advocate General observed that the best solution was probably to offer the portability service free of charge, but he acknowledged that, even though some countries adopt this strategy, the latter could not bind all Member States, in the light of the European rules; consequently, in the final paragraph of the opinion, where his proposal is synthesised, one cannot find any allusion to limits operating in favour of the end-users. On the contrary, in the Court's decision, the statement concerning the legitimacy of a charge in line with the costs incurred by the undertakings does not stand alone. The Authorities retain the power to declare illegal all the charges that, although in line with those costs, exceed the amount that a consumer can reasonably afford.

The ECJ bears in mind consumers' interests, but its reasoning could not be construed as a defence of consumers under any circumstance. The EU regulation effort does not argue strongly enough in support of the consumers! And the ECJ is not willing to take up the cudgels on behalf of the consumer! The *ex ante* determination of a ceiling for the charge is not allowed independently from a cost analysis, and once this analysis has been conducted, the regulatory measure ought to be upheld in light of its results.

The 2009 amendments, refurbishing the text of the 2002 provision on number portability, bring to the fore important adjustments, in order to enhance consumers' protection. The most important guarantee for a client who decides to port his/her number, is the determination of an upper limit of time for the activation of the number by the new operator. This period is very short indeed: the operation must be completed within one working day. This reform will constitute a great improvement for consumers, since, currently in the EU, it takes, on average, a much longer time.[33]

[33] Whereas in some EU countries, NRAs have already implemented the one working day requirement, on average, the end-user has to wait 8.5 days, for a mobile number, and 7.5 days, for a fixed number to be changed, with some customers facing a two to three week wait. Note that, according to the British government, the new obligation to conclude applies also to bulk porting (i.e., porting of of 25 numbers or more at once).

ARTICLE V(1)(B) OF THE NEW YORK CONVENTION: THE UNIFORM STANDARD OF PROCEDURAL FAIRNESS

KLÁRA SVOBODOVÁ

MASARYK UNIVERSITY IN BRNO, CZECH REPUBLIC

Abstract

Article V(1)(b) of the New York Convention enables refuse of recognition and enforcement of arbitral award in the case when the arbitration proceedings showed serious irregularities, which may be described as a breach of procedural fairness in arbitration. However, Article V(1)(b) does not contain the rule that would decide under which law it is necessary to evaluate what is included in the basic procedural principles. In other words, what law determines the standard of procedural fairness? The aim of this paper is to prove that Article V(1)(b) itself represents the uniform standard of procedural fairness. Therefore, it is not necessary to apply national law. The paper also analyses the scope of Article V(1)(b) and identifies which procedural irregularities lead to the refusal of recognition and enforcement of arbitral awards. The paper seeks to confirm that only the most serious irregularities cause the refusal of recognition and enforcement and that only this conclusion is in accordance with the pro-enforcement nature of the New York Convention.

Introduction

Article V(1)(b) of the Convention on Recognition and Enforcement of Foreign Arbitral Awards ('New York Convention' or 'Convention') enables refusal of the recognition and enforcement of arbitral award in the case when the arbitration proceedings showed serious irregularities, which can be described as the breach of procedural fairness in arbitration. In particular, Article V(1)(b) sanctioned the situation when *the party against whom the award is invoked was not given proper notice of the appointment of the arbitrator or of the arbitration proceedings or was otherwise unable to present his case.* However, Article V(1)(b) does not contain the rule that would decide under what law it is necessary to evaluate what is included in the basic procedural principles. In other words, what law determines the standard of procedural fairness? Is it the law of the enforcement state or the law of the state where the arbitration took place? Or does Article V(1)(b) represent the international substantive rule, the standard of procedural fairness? And if so, what is the scope of this standard?

The aim of this paper is to prove that Article V(1)(b) itself represents the uniform standard of procedural fairness. Therefore, it is not necessary to apply national law. The paper also analyses the scope of Article V(1)(b) and identifies which procedural irregularities lead to the refusal of recognition and enforcement of arbitral awards. The paper strives to confirm that only the most serious irregularities cause the refusal of recognition and enforcement and that only this conclusion is in accordance with the pro-enforcement nature of the New York Convention. The conclusions of this paper are mostly based on the case law of the Contracting Parties to the New York Convention.[1]

First of all, the recognition and enforcement under the Convention are briefly described. Secondly, the reasons for refusal of recognition and enforcement of arbitral awards are characterized. Then, Article V(1)(b) is analysed.

Recognition and Enforcement under the New York Convention

The New York Convention is the corner stone of the recognition and enforcement of foreign arbitral awards. At present it has 145 Contracting States.[2] In most of them the process of recognition and enforcement is realized under the conditions contained in the Convention. The application of national regulations of recognition and enforcement instead of the New York Convention is possible only due to Article VII of the Convention,

---

[1] The author of this paper obtained most of the case law and several other sources from the database Kluwer Arbitration, available at http://www.kluwerar bitration.com. The author had access to this database during her stay at the Hague Academy of International Law in September 2007 and July 2008. During the writing of this paper the author did not have full access to the database, so it was not possible to state unique electronic addresses at all places. These sources are therefore cited only as available from http://www.kluwerarbitration.com.

[2] See at http://tinyurl.com/2ohneu.

which contains the rule of maximal effectiveness. The New York Convention has strongly contributed to the simplification of the recognition and enforcement of arbitral awards in the international sphere and thus has increased the attractiveness of international arbitration as such.

The New York Convention concerns two main questions: the enforcement of arbitration agreements, and recognition and enforcement of foreign arbitral awards. This paper deals with the second question. The Convention does not regulate the process of recognition and enforcement itself.[3] Article III of the Convention binds the Contracting States to recognize arbitral awards as binding under the conditions laid down in the Convention. Article III also states that *there shall not be imposed substantially more onerous conditions or higher fees on the recognition and enforcement of arbitral awards to which the Convention applies than are imposed on recognition or enforcement of domestic arbitral awards.* Article III contains the obligation of Contracting States to recognize the awards if the conditions under the Convention are met.[4]

The procedural regulation of enforcement is in the hands of a state of enforcement. The Convention only states that the enforcement of foreign awards must not be substantially more onerous than recognition of domestic awards. The conditions of enforcement are laid down in Articles IV – VI of the Convention. National law contains the actual procedural rules.[5]

The conditions of recognition and enforcement are contained exclusively in the Convention. The Convention regulates the burden of proof, reasons for refusal of recognition and enforcement and documents that have to be supplied.[6] The party applying for recognition and enforcement has the obligation to supply documents under Article IV. The party against whom the recognition is invoked has to in principle prove a reason for refusal of recognition and enforcement.

---

[3] Naděžda Rozehnalová, *Rozhodčí řízení v mezinárodním a vnitrostátním obchodním styku* 325 (2nd ed. 2008); II Gary B. Born, *International Commercial Arbitration* 2708 (2009).

[4] Gary B. Born, *supra* 2717.

[5] Albert Jan Van Den Berg, *The New York Arbitration Convention of 1958* 236-239 (1981); Gary B. Born, *supra* 2708-2710 (2009).

[6] Phillipe Fouchard, *Fouchard, Gaillard, Goldman on International Commercial Arbitration* 968 (1999).

The reasons for refusal of recognition and enforcement

The reasons under the New York Convention can be characterized as follows. Firstly, the reasons can be divided into two groups. The first group contains reasons the court deals with only at the request of the party against whom the recognition is invoked.[7] The second group is formed by the reasons the court dealt with on its own volition.[8] Secondly, the list of the reasons is exhaustive. Thirdly, the Convention does not allow reviewing foreign awards as to their merits. And finally it is up to the court if it really refuses the recognition and enforcement even if the existence of one of the reasons is proved.[9]

If the court deals with the reasons for refusal of recognition and enforcement, the important question is under what law the court evaluates the reasons. Some of the reasons in the Convention are clearly based on the national law of a state. For example, both reasons contained in Article V(2) are governed by the law of the state where the recognition and enforcement are sought. On the other hand, Article V(1)(a) or Article V(1)(e) lead expressly to the law of the state where the arbitration took place *(lex arbitri)*. However, there are still reasons that do not mention any national law. What law is then applicable to them? There is also Article V(1)(b) among these reasons.

Article V(1)(b)

Article V(1)(b) of the New York Convention enables refusal of the recognition and enforcement of arbitral award in the case when the arbitration proceedings showed serious irregularities, which may be described as the breach of the procedural fairness in arbitration. In particular, Article V(1)(b) sanctioned the situation when *the party against whom the award is invoked was not given proper notice of the appointment of the arbitrator or of the arbitration proceedings, or was otherwise unable to present his case.* If the party is not given proper notice of the appointment of the arbitrator or of the arbitration, it cannot present its case in arbitration. However, Article V(1) is broader. Even if the party was informed, there can be a situation, when the party is not able to

---

[7] Article V(1).

[8] Article V(2).

[9] Albert Jan Van Den Berg, *The New York Arbitration...* 264-267 (1981); Alan Redfern, *Law and Practice of International Commercial Arbitration* §10-33 (2004); Phillipe Fouchard, *Fouchard, Gaillard, Goldman...* 967-971 (1999).

present its case for other reasons. Article V(1)(b) thus covers any serious procedural irregularity.[10]

Article V(1)(b) has to be construed in accordance with the so-called pro-enforcement bias of the New York Convention.[11] This provision leads to the refusal of recognition and enforcement of arbitral awards only in the case where the procedural irregularities were so serious that there was a violation of basic procedural principles of arbitration.

Basic procedural principles in the arbitration proceedings

Basic procedural principles are contained in all modern regulations of arbitrations. Even though the concepts used differ, it is possible to say that all modern regulations of arbitration guarantee the right to a fair trial.[12] The arbitrators are obliged to follow these principles, because their violation is penalised by the annulment of arbitral award. We can demonstrate this on several national regulations.

Under Article 18 of the UNCITRAL Model Law on International Commercial Arbitration[13] and under the Section 1042 of the German Code of Civil Procedure,[14] the parties shall be treated with equality and each party shall be given a full opportunity of presenting its case. The application of Article 18 is governed by Article 34(2)(a)(ii) which covers the right to be heard in a broad sense. Firstly, there is the situation where the party was not heard concerning the appointment of the arbitrators, which led to the improper composition of the arbitral tribunal. Secondly, Article 34(2)(a)(ii) covers the situation where the party was not able to take part in the arbitration proceedings. And finally, there is the situation where the party was not able to present its claims during the proceedings.

---

[10] Albert Jan Van Den Berg, *The New York Arbitration...* 306 (1981).

[11] II Gary B. Born, *International Commercial...* 2738 (2009).

[12] Gabrielle Kaufmann-Kohler, *Identifying and Applying the Law Governing the Arbitration Procedure–The Role of the Law of the Place of Arbitration* in Albert Jan Van Den Berg, *Improving the Efficiency of Arbitration Agreements and Awards: 40 Years of Application of the New York Convention*, 9 ICCA Cogress Series 356 (1998) available at http://www.kluwerarbitration.com.

[13] UNCITRAL Model Law on International Commercial Arbitration (1985 with amendments as adopted in 2006). Text available at http://tinyurl.com/7fl6mqj.

[14] The Code of Civil Procedure (*Zivilprozessordnung*) 10th Book (1998). English text available at http://tinyurl.com/7jocayb.

The same is true for Section 1059(2)(1)(b) of the German Code of Civil Procedure, which sanctions the non-application of the Section 1042.[15]

In the Swiss regulation, the principles contained in Article 182(3) of the Private International Law Act[16] are the reasons for the annulment of arbitral award.[17] Under Article 182(3) the parties are equal and their right to be heard in the adversarial proceedings has to be respected. The right to be heard in the adversarial proceedings includes two aspects. Firstly, there is the right to be heard as such, which enables the party to present the factual and legal side of the case including evidence. Secondly, it also includes the right to take part in the proceedings and to have representation. The principle of adversarial proceedings guarantees the party the right to express its position on claims and evidence of the other party.[18]

The French regulation has only the violation of the principle of the adversarial proceedings as the reason for the annulment of an arbitral award (Article 1502(4) of the New Code of Civil Procedure).[19] The principle is interpreted very broadly by French courts. It covers both the right to be heard, and the obligation of the parties to designate the decisive factual circumstances and the evidence to support the parties' claims. The arbitrators must not take into account the arguments or documents that were not dealt with in the adversarial proceedings. The Article 1502(4) thus covers a range of procedural irregularities, for example the violation of the equal treatment, violation of the right to be heard, or the use of the documents that were submitted to the arbitrators, but not to the other party.[20]

Section 68 of the English Arbitration Act[21] enables the annulment of arbitral award on the ground of serious irregularity concerning arbitrators, award or proceedings. Section 68 enumerates what serious irregularity means. These irregularities may lead to the annulment of arbitral award

---

[15] Jean Francois Poudret & Sébastian Besson, *Comparative Law of International Arbitration* 736 (2nd ed. 2007).

[16] Federal Code on Private International Law (*Bundesgesetz über das Internationale Privatrecht*) (1987). English text available at http://tinyurl.com/7vbmycw.

[17] See Article 190(2)(d).

[18] Jean Francois Poudret & Sébastian Besson, *supra* 736-737.

[19] New Code of Civil Procedure (*Le Nouveau Code de Procedure Civil),* Book IV (1981). English text available at http://tinyurl.com/3nx5arn.

[20] Jean Francois Poudret & Sébastian Besson, *Comparative Law...* 738-739 (2007).

[21] Arbitration Act (1996). Text available at http://tinyurl.com/3zf2bxa.

only if it would cause substantial injustice.[22] The first mentioned irregularity is the breach of basic principles under Section 33. Under this Section, the arbitrators are obliged to act fairly and impartially, to give each party reasonable opportunity to present its claims, and to express its arguments regarding the claims of the other party.

The Czech Act on Arbitration Proceedings[23] contains basic procedural guarantees in Section 18, which includes the principle of equal treatment of the parties and the principle of full opportunity to exercise the parties' rights.[24] The violation of these principles could invoke the sanction of the annulment of the award under Section 31(e). This ground applies if there is a fundamental violation of basic procedural principles.[25] The reasons for the annulment could be for example: the action notification or other important document was not delivered or sent, reasonable opportunity to express arguments was not given, the arbitrators refused to deal with the suggested evidence.[26]

Very interesting is also the application of Article 6(1) of the European Convention on Human Rights ('EHCR') in arbitration proceedings. As this is the topic for a separate paper, we will only mention basic points. The conclusion of the arbitration agreement is permissible under Article 6(1), if not concluded under constraint. Article 6(1) fully applies in the case of court proceedings relating to arbitration. The indirect application of Article 6(1) on arbitration is therefore not questionable. A court of a Contracting State deciding for example on the annulment of an arbitral award is bound by the ECHR. The direct application of Article 6(1) has both its proponents and opponents. At present, there is no clear opinion on this question. However, we can at present witness a significant shift from the initial strict rejection of the application of Article 6 in the arbitration proceedings.[27]

---

22 Jean Francois Poudret & Sébastian Besson, *supra* 746-752 (2007).

23 Act No. 216/1994 Coll. on Arbitration Proceeding and on Enforcement of Arbitral Awards (1994).

24 Alexander Bělohlávek, *Zákon o rozhodčím řízení a o výkonu rozhodčích nálezů* 143 – 145 (2004).

25 *Ibid.*, 238 (2004).

26 In detail see *Ibid.*, 238-242 (2004); Bohuslav Klein & Martin Doleček, *Rozhodčí řízení* 136-138 (2007).

27 See Sébastian Besson, *Arbitration and Human Rights*, 24 ASA Bulletin 395-416 (2006), available at http://tinyurl.com/85aplrk [March, 1st 2011]; Alexander Jaksic, *Procedural Guarantees of Human Rights in Arbitration Proceedings. A Still Unsettled Problem?*, 24 Journal of International Arbitration 159-172 (2007), available at http://tinyurl.com/78pmk2x [March 1st, 2011]; Neil McDonald, *More Harm than Good? Human Rights Considerations in International Commercial*

Article V(1)(b) as Uniform Procedural Standard

Article V(1)(b) does not contain a rule which would determine under what law we must evaluate what ranks among the basic procedural principles. In other words, under what law we have to assess 'the standard of fair trial.' The law of the state of enforcement or *lex arbitri* come primarily into account.[28] Both options have their support in the case law of national courts. However, a reference to the law of a particular state is unique in this respect. In the famous decision, *Parsons & Whitehorse Overseas v RAKTA the Court of Appeals for the Second Circuit,* concluded that Article V(1)(b) protects the application of the forum's standards of fair trial.[29]

German *Hammerstein Berlin* in the decision No. 20 Sch 02/08[30] applied *lex arbitri* to consider the question of whether the defendant was informed about arbitration. The court concluded that the statement of

---

Arbitration, 20 Journal of International Arbitration 523-538 (2003), available at http://tinyurl.com/73hr92j [March 1st, 2011]; Adam Samuel, *Arbitration, Alternative Dispute Resolution Generally and the European Convention on Human Rights. An Anglo-Centric View*, 21 Journal of International Arbitration 413-438 (2004), available at http://tinyurl.com/6udxhzx [March 1st, 2011].

[28] II Gary B. Born, *International Commercial*... 2740-2741 (2009).

[29] *Parsons & Whittemore Overseas Co. Inc. v Société Générale de l'Industrie du Papier (RAKTA)* (2nd Cir. 1974), cited according to Albert Jan Van Den Berg, *Why are some Awards not Enforceable* in Albert Jan Van Den Berg, *New Horizons in International Commercial Arbitration and Beyond* 297 (2005). In 1962 American company Overseas and Egyptian company RAKTA concluded the contract on construction of factory in Egypt. The construction was financed by the US Agency for International Development (AID). Before the construction was finished, so-called 'six days war' began between Egypt and Israel. Egypt expelled Americans from the country. AID informed Overseas, that it withdrew the financial support. Overseas terminated the contract on the basis of vis maior. RAKTA did not agree with this termination and commenced arbitration. The arbitrators decided in favour of RAKTA. RAKTA applied for enforcement of the award in the US.

[30] 20 Sch 02/08 (Kammergericht Berlin, Germany, April 17th, 2008), available at http://tinyurl.com/6mr7nxv [March 10th, 2011]. The claimant asked for enforcement of arbitral award rendered in Ukraine. The defendant alleged that due process was violated, since it did not participate in the proceedings. It had neither received the statement of claim nor the arbitral award. Also Bayern Oberlandesgericht applied lex arbitri the question whether the defendant was delivered the notice on arbitration proceedings. See *Seller v Buyer*, 4Z Sch 50/99 (Bayern Oberlandesgericht, Germany, March 16th, 2000), available at http://www.kluwerarbitration.com.

claim and arbitral award were sent to the defendant by registered letters that were returned to the Arbitration Court of Ukraine with the notice that they had not been collected by the defendant. Pursuant to Article 3(1) of the Ukrainian International Commercial Arbitration Law, the documents in that case were deemed to be properly delivered.

In cases where the courts apply a national standard of fair trial, they should take into account the international character of arbitration and so distinguish between national and international arbitration. This distinction leads to the fact that the refusal of recognition and enforcement of arbitral awards occurs only in the most serious cases.[31]

According to a number of views, Article V(1)(b) represents an international substantive rule. It is not therefore necessary to refer to any national law. Article V(1)(b) itself is the standard of the fair trial.[32] Foulard states that Article V(1)(b) is created in the substantive and not in the choice of law spirit. The New York Convention establishes international substantive rule and violation of this rule is sufficient to refuse recognition and enforcement of arbitral award.[33] Similarly, Poulterer and Benson conclude that in the absence of a conflict rule, Article V(1)(b) contains standard and uniform requirements.[34] According to Born, Article V(1)(b) has to be understood as a uniform international standard of procedural fairness. This is consistent with the aim of the New York Convention to create an international set of rules facilitating the recognition and enforcement of arbitral awards.[35]

This approach is also reflected in the case law of national courts where in many decisions there is no reference to national law. After all, violation of the principles of fair trial is primarily a question of facts, which has to be proved by a party.[36]

---

[31] II Gary B. Born, *International Commercial...* 2743 (2009); Albert Jan Van Den Berg, *The New York Arbitration...* 298 (1981).

[32] Albert Jan Van Den Berg, *supra*; Julian D.M. Lew et al., *Comparative International Commercial Arbitration* 711 (1999); Phillipe Fouchard, *Fouchard, Gaillard, Goldman...* 967-971 (1999); Jean Francois Poudret & Sébastian Besson, *Comparative Law...* 986 (2007); II Gary B. Born, *supra* 2745; Loukas A. Mistelis, *Arbitrability-International and Comparative Perspectives* in Id. & Stavros L. Brekoulakis, *Arbitrability International & Comparative Perspective* 1 (2009).

[33] Phillipe Fouchard, *Fouchard, Gaillard, Goldman...* 986 (1999).

[34] Jean Francois Poudret & Sébastian Besson, *Comparative Law...* 835 (2007).

[35] II Gary B. Born, *International Commercial...* 2744-2745 (2009).

[36] Loukas A. Mistelis, *Arbitrability-International and Comparative...* 711 (2009); See also the following decisions 9 Sch 01/08 (Oberlandesgericht Karlsruhe, Germany, July 4th, 2008), available at http://tinyurl.com/6mr7nxv [March 10th, 2011]; 9 Sch 02/05 (Oberlandesgericht Karlsruhe, Germany, March 27th, 2006)

Violation of the principles of fair trial is also covered by Article V(2)(b) as a part of public policy of the state of enforcement. In this case, the courts base standards on their national law.[37] The standards of *lex arbitri* could be covered by Article V(1)(d). Therefore, it is not necessary

---

available at http://tinyurl.com/6mr7nxv [March 10th, 2011]; 9 Sch 12/04 (Oberlandesgericht Köln, Germany, October 26th, 2004), available at http:// www.kluwerarbitration.com; *Film distributor v Film producer*, 4 Z Sch 13/02 (Bayerisches Oberstes Landesgericht, Germany, November 22nd, 2002), available at http://www.kluwerarbitration.com; *Shipowner v Cattle and meat dealer*, 5 U 89/98 (Oberlandesgericht Stuttgart, Germany, October 18th, 1999), available at http://www.kluwerarbitration.com; *Manufacturer v Exclusive distributor*, 16 SchH 01/99 (Oberlandesgericht Schleswig, Germany, June 24th, 1999), available at http://www.kluwerarbitration.com; 11 Sch 04/98 (Oberlandesgericht Dresden, Germany, October 20th, 1998), available at http:// www.kluwerarbitration.com; *Shipowner v Time charterer* (Oberlandesgericht Hamburg, Germany, July 30th, 1998), available at http://www. kluwerarbitration.com; 6 U 110/97 (Hanseatisches Oberlandesgericht Hamburg March 12th, 1998), available at http://www. kluwerarbitration.com; *Seller v Buyer* (Bundesgerichtshof, Germany, April 26th, 1990), available at http://www.kluwerarbitration.com; *G SA v T. Ltd.* (Tribunal Fédéral, Switzerland, January 12th, 1989), available at http://www.kluwerar bitration.com; *Italian party v Swiss company* (Bezirksgericht Zürich, Switzerland, February 14th, 2003), available at http://www.kluwerarbitration.com; *Netherlands seller v Swiss buyer* (Obergericht Basel, Switzerland, June 3rd, 1971), available at http://www.kluwerarbitration.com; *De Maio Giuseppe e Fratelli snc v Interskins Ltd.* (Corte di Cassazione, Italy, January 21st, 2000), available at http://www.kluwerarbitration.com; *Dalmine SpA v M. & M. Sheet Metal Forming Machinery AG* (Corte di Cassazione, Italy, April 23rd, 1997), available at http://www.kluwerarbitration.com; *Conceria G De Maio & F. snc. v EMAG AG* (Corte di Cassazione, Italy, January 20th, 1995), available at http://www. kluwerarbitration.com.

[37] Jean Francois Poudret & Sébastian Besson, *Comparative Law...* 835 (2007); Julian D.M. Lew et al., *Comparative International...* 711 (1999); Albert Jan Van Den Berg, *The New York Arbitration...* 299-300 (1981); *Construction company v Painting contractors,* 34 Sch 019/05 (Oberlandesgericht München, Germany, November 28th, 2005), available at http://www.kluwerarbitration.com; *Trading company v Buyer,* 9 Sch 01/03 (Oberlandesgericht Köln, Germany, April 23rd, 2004), available at http://www.kluwerarbitration.com; *Seller v Buyer,* 1 Sch 12/01 (Oberlandesgericht Stuttgart, Germany, December 6th, 2001), available at http://www.kluwerarbitration.com; 2 Sch 04/99 (Hanseatisches Oberlandesgericht Bremen, Germany, September 30th, 1999), available at http://www. kluwerarbitration.com; *Seller v Buyer,* 8 Sch 01/99 (Oberlandesgericht Brandenburg, Germany, September 2nd, 1999), available at http://www. kluwerarbitration.com; 6 U 110/97 (Hanseatisches Oberlandesgericht Hamburg, Germany, March 12th, 1998), available at http://www. kluwerarbitration.com.

for Article V(1)(b) to refer to any national law. It can represent the substantive rule itself.

3.3 The Scope of the Article V(1)(b): The Content of the Substantive Rule

The range of procedural irregularities potentially falling within the scope of Article V(1)(b) is broad. However, not all of them may lead to refusal of recognition and enforcement of arbitral awards.

3.3.1 The Party was not Given Proper Notice

The first irregularity is stated explicitly by the text of Article V(1)(b) – the party against whom the award is invoked was not given proper notice of the appointment of the arbitrator or of the arbitration proceedings. The situation where the party was not notified at all will be a serious irregularity. Notification has to be proper. The notion 'proper' has to be interpreted as meaning adequate or appropriate.[38] The question of whether the notice is adequate depends on the circumstances of a particular case.[39] Adequacy refers to time (whether the party was notified early enough), the way of notification, and its content. A short period for appointing an arbitrator, preparing a defense or notifying the oral hearing does not generally lead to the refusal of recognition of arbitral award.[40] The courts examine whether the party was able or not to appoint an arbitrator or to attend the oral hearing.[41] According to the prevailing opinion, the notification does not have to meet any formal requirement laid down by national laws applicable to judicial proceedings.[42] *Bezirksgericht Zürich*[43]

---

[38] Albert Jan Van Den Berg, *The New York Arbitration...* 303 (1981); Julian D.M. Lew et al., *Comparative International...* 711 (1999).

[39] Albert Jan Van Den Berg, *The New York Convention: Summary of Court Decisions, In The New York Convention of 1958: A Collection of Reports and Materials Delivered at the ASA Conference held in Zürich on 2nd February 1996* 39 (1996).

[40] See *De Maio Giuseppe e Fratelli snc v Interskins Ltd.* (Corte di Cassazione, Italy, January 21st, 2000), available at http://www.kluwerarbitration.com; *ILET – Industria Legnami Trentina S.r.l. v Ditta Holzindustrie Schweighofer* (Corte di Cassazione, Italy, November 16th, 1992), available at http://www. kluwerarbitration.com.

[41] Albert Jan Van Den Berg, *The New York Convention...* 40 (1996).

[42] *Ibid.*, 39; II Gary B. Born, *International Commercial...* 2750 (2009); Julian D.M. Lew et al., *supra.*

[43] *Italian party v Swiss company* (Bezirksgericht Zürich, Switzerland, February 14th, 2003), available at http://www.kluwerarbitration.com. The parties concluded a licence agreement that contained an arbitration clause. A dispute arose between the parties and the Italian party commenced arbitration at the Swiss Chamber of Commerce in Italy. The arbitral tribunal found in favour of the Italian party.

points out that there are no formal requirements in international arbitration for the delivery of documents abroad. It is also not necessary for the party to obtain all the communication from the arbitrators. It is enough if the party obtains vital information such as request for an answer to the action. This conclusion was reached by the *Oberlandesgericht Karlsruhe* in decision No. 9 Sch 01/08.[44] The notion proper in Article V(1)(b) also includes the 'proper' representation of the party in the arbitration proceedings.[45]

The notification of the appointment of the arbitrator includes also the notification of the name of the arbitrator. This fact led to the refusal of the recognition of arbitral award in the frequently cited decision of the *Oberlandesgericht Köln*.[46] The arbitration proceedings were conducted under the Arbitration Rules of the Copenhagen Arbitration Commission for Trade in Grain and Feeds. Under these rules, the parties did not know the names of the arbitrators, except for the chairman of the arbitral tribunal. The parties received the copy of the award, which was signed only by the chairman. The German court deciding on the enforceability of the award came to the conclusion that this was contrary to Article V(1)(b) of the New York Convention, which requires that the party was notified of the appointment of the arbitrator.[47]

The Party was Otherwise Unable to Present the Case

The notion 'the party was otherwise unable to present the case' can include any serious procedural irregularity, in particular the breach of the equal opportunity of the right to be heard. The equal opportunity means that both parties shall be given the opportunity to raise their claims and to

---

[44] 9 Sch 01/08 (Oberlandesgericht Karlsruhe, Germany, July 4th, 2008), available at http://www.kluwerarbitration.com. Arbitral award was rendered in Lithuania under the Arbitration Rules of the Arbitration Court of the Commercial Arbitration Court in Vilnius. The plaintiff requested a declaration of enforceability of the award in Germany. The defendant contended that the arbitral tribunal violated its right to be heard, since it had not received notice of all communications from the arbitral tribunal and because the tribunal had refused to change the date of the oral hearing even though it was aware that the defendant was not available on that date.

[45] Albert Jan Van Den Berg, *The New York Arbitration...* 311 (1981); *K Trading company v BMW AG*, 4Z Sch 005/04 (Bayerisches Oberstes Landesgericht, Germany, September 23rd, 2004), available at http://www.kluwerarbitration.com.

[46] *Danish Seller v German Buyer* (Oberlandesgericht Köln, Germany, June 10th, 1976), cited according to Albert Jan Van Den Berg, *Why are some Awards...* 297 (2005).

[47] Albert Jan Van Den Berg, *The New York Arbitration...* 305 (1981).

present evidence to support their claims. However, if the party refuses to participate in the arbitration proceedings, it waives this opportunity.[48] Arbitral awards rendered in the defendant's absence do not as such constitute the reason for refusal of the recognition and enforcement. *Oberlandesgericht Hamburg*[49] states that there is no reason for refusal of recognition under Article V(1)(b). The defendant was duly informed of the arbitration and could present its case. The arbitrators also complied with due process, which dictates that a party may not be affected by a legal measure unless it has had the opportunity to express itself thereon. Whether the party does indeed express itself, is its own affair. The defendant knew that the arbitrators had been constituted and that the plaintiff's claim would be settled in arbitration. Hence, it should have taken care that its interest be considered in the proceedings.

The Court of Appeals for the Second Circuit in the Avco case[50] held that the right of the defendant to be heard was breached. Avco was not

---

[48] Albert Jan Van Den Berg, *The New York Arbitration...* 307 (1981); Phillipe Fouchard, *Fouchard, Gaillard, Goldman...* 986 (1999).

[49] *Shipowner v Time charterer* (Oberlandesgericht Hamburg, Germany, July 30th, 1998), available at http://www.kluwerarbitration.com. In 1996 the shipowner chartered the vessel M/S A to the defendant. The parties signed a summary agreement drawn up by the defendant which referred to a charter party that the defendant previously concluded with a third party on a NYPE standard form. This latter charter party contained an arbitration clause. A dispute arose between the parties. The shipowner informed the defendant that it intended to commence arbitration in London and requested it to appoint an arbitrator. The defendant appointed Captain S as its arbitrator for all disputes under the charter party concerning M/S A. In the arbitration proceedings, the defendant required and obtained a postponement of the time limit to file a statement in reply, due to the absence of its general manager. The defendant ultimately did not file any statement. No oral hearing was held. The shipowner claimed hire and interest. The award granted its claim.

[50] *Iran Aircraft Industries and Iran Helicopter Support and Renewal Company v Avco Corporation* (2nd Cir. 1994), cited according to Albert Jan Van Den Berg, *Why are some Awards...* 298 (2005). The arbitral award was rendered by the Iran – US Claims Tribunal. After the preliminary hearing, the chairman of the arbitral tribunal expressly asked Avco not to burden the arbitrators by lots of invoices. Instead, the chairman approved the way, which Avco had suggested – submitting the book of account of the debtors that was audited. Neither the Iranian party, nor the Iranian arbitrator took part in this hearing. Avco submitted the affidavit that the book of account corresponded to the original invoices. Before the oral hearing on merits took place, the chairman resigned. During the hearing the Iranian arbitrator requested submitting the invoices. The arbitrators finally refused the claims of Avco that were based on the book of account.

aware that the arbitrators required the invoices to prove the claims. After the arbitrators had convinced Avco that it had used the right way to prove its claim, they rejected its claim for the lack of evidence. The arbitrators denied Avco the opportunity to assert claims in a meaningful way.

Equal opportunity of the right to be heard does not mean that in the arbitration proceedings an oral hearing necessarily has to be held. The possibility or necessity of the oral hearing depends mainly on the agreement of the parties, arbitration rules and *lex arbitri*. If a party asks for oral hearing and its request is automatically rejected, this may be the reason for refusal of recognition.[51] The fact that the arbitrators refused to change the date of the oral hearing because the defendant was not able to take part, is not in principle a ground for refusal of recognition. *Oberlandesgericht Karlsruhe* in the mentioned decision No. 9 Sch 01/08 states: The fact that the defendant was prevented from attending the hearing was not relevant, because the defendant (as a legal person) in any event required a legal representative for the proceedings and could have made sure that a suitable representative would be able to attend the hearing.[52]

The arbitrators have a duty to inform the obligated party about the allegations and evidence submitted by the other party and to allow the party to react to them. Violation of this principle may lead to the refusal of recognition of arbitral award under Article V(1)(b). The same applies in the case where the arbitrators rely on the facts which were not alleged by the parties, and arbitrators did not give the parties the opportunity to comment on these facts (the surprising decision).[53] Not so certain is the case where the arbitrators based their decision on the legal determination that was not proposed by either party. According to some courts, it is also the surprising decision. Other courts are inclined to the opinion that the legal determination is the matter of the arbitrators.

The reason for refusal of the recognition under Article V(1)(b) is the situation where one party is given a certain advantage and the principle of

---

[51] Albert Jan Van Den Berg, *The New York Arbitration...* 307 (1981); II Gary B. Born, *International Commercial...* 2746 (2009).

[52] Similarly see 9 Sch 02/05 (Oberlandesgericht Karlsruhe, Germany, March 27th, 2006), available at http://tinyurl.com/6mr7nxv [March 10th, 2011].

[53] See *Manufacturer v Exclusive distributor*, 16 SchH 01/99 (Oberlandesgericht Schleswig, Germany, June 24th, 1999), available at http://www.kluwerarbitration.com. The court concluded here that it was not a surprising decision, because the arbitrators explained what had led them to the new assessment of the factual and legal situation and the defendant had the opportunity to express itself.

equal treatment is breached. The arbitrators have the discretion as regards the question of what evidence will be produced in the arbitration proceedings. Only the situation in which the arbitrator does not allow the party to submit substantial evidence, will lead to the refusal of the recognition.[54]

The scope of Article V(1)(b) also includes the question of impartiality and independence of the arbitrators. Where the arbitrator is not impartial and independent, the party has no real opportunity to present its claims.[55]

The question of the reasoning of arbitral award was also considered under Article V(1)(b). Most of the courts concluded that the absence of reasoning does not constitute a ground for refusal of recognition. However, according to some courts, the right to put forward the claims also includes the right to reasoning of arbitral award.[56]

Conclusion

According to the theory, Article V(1)(b) represents the international substantive rule, the standard of fair trial. It is not necessary to refer to the national law of the particular state when applying this provision. National courts very exceptionally applied the law of the state of enforcement or *lex arbitri*. The author of this paper disagrees with the reference to the law of the state of enforcement. The standard of fair trial of the state of enforcement is used where the violation of fair trial is examined as part of public policy under Article V(2)(b).

When assessing the breach of fair trial, most courts do not refer to national law, but evaluate this question autonomously, only under the New York Convention. During the existence of the Convention, the case law

---

[54] II Gary B. Born, *International Commercial...* 2751-2753 (2009); *Film distributor v Film producer*, 4 Z Sc 13/02 (Bayerisches Oberstes Landesgericht, Germany, November 22nd, 2002), available at http://www.kluwerarbitration.com; *Seller v Buyer*, 1 Sch 12/01 (Oberlandesgericht Stuttgart, Germany, December 6th, 2001), available at http://www.kluwerarbitration.com; *Manufacturer v Exclusive distributor*, 16 SchH 01/99 (Oberlandesgericht Schleswig, Germany, June 24th, 1999), available at http://www.kluwerarbitration.com; *Bank A v Bank B* (Landesgericht Hamburg, Germany, September 18th, 1997), available at http:// www.kluwerarbitration.com; *Dalmine SpA v M. & M. Sheet Metal Forming Machinery AG* (Corte di Cassazione, Italy, April 23rd, 1997), available at http://www.kluwerarbitration.com.

[55] II Gary B. Born, *International Commercial...* 2755 - 2756 (2009).

[56] II Gary B. Born, *International Commercial...* 2758 - 2759 (2009).

has clarified the rules or principles, the violation of which in the arbitration proceedings may lead to non-recognition under Article V(1)(b).

At this point, we have to recall that the courts of the Contracting Parties to the ECHR are bound by Article 6(1). If the courts determine the recognition and enforcement of arbitral award, which was made in arbitration proceedings that were contrary to Article 6(1), the recognition will most likely be refused. The question of direct application of Article 6(1) in the arbitration proceedings was mentioned above. The conclusion of the arbitration agreement is not contrary to Article 6(1). By concluding the arbitration agreement, the parties do not waive all rights under Article 6(1). The extent of their application in arbitration is not clear. If the court of the Contracting State to ECHR recognizes an arbitral award, which is contrary to Article 6(1), it may be responsible under the ECHR. A limited review of arbitral awards is not in conflict with the ECHR and is in conformity with the principle of party autonomy.[57] The situation whereby the courts refuse to recognize and enforce arbitral awards only if there is a clear and serious violation of rights under Article 6(1), is not contrary to the ECHR.

[57] Alexander Bělohlávek, *Rozhodčí řízení, ordre public a trestní právo* 210-213 (2008).

THE RULES OF BIOSAFETY IN THE CARTAGENA PROTOCOL AND IN THE REGULATIONS OF THE WORLD TRADE ORGANIZATION

PIOTR KRAJEWSKI

UNIVERSITY OF WARMIA AND MAZURY IN OLSZTYN, POLAND

There are no relevant provisions in the law of the World Trade Organization in biotechnology, which sometimes leads to a state of uncertainty connected with biosecurity and trade in genetically modified organisms. It is worth analyzing the overlaps or differences of these regulations with other important documents on this issue. It would be proper for instance to check whether the principles and rules contained in the Cartagena Protocol might somehow be helpful in solving the problems of biosafety.

Issues of compliance with the provisions of the Cartagena Protocol and the WTO

In the Cartagena Protocol one sees several aspects which are in conflict with the provisions of the World Trade Organization. This mainly applies to: a) the importance of harmonization with international standards of environmental and health risks, b) acceptable criteria for risk assessment and management (particularly the precautionary and the socio-economic aspects principle), c) the procedures for consent after prior information about the import of genetically modified organisms (including the different decomposition of the burden to provide proof) d) rules of the identification of GMOs; e) lack of a clause of the total absence of trade restrictions, f) any restrictions on exchange of GMOs (mainly imports - exports) established by the states that are not the parties.

(a) The above mentioned doubts in the light of WTO rules cause numerous problems. The international standards of harmonization of environmental and health risks relate to the concept that the provisions of the Cartagena Protocol cannot be interpreted as restricting the right of Parties to take actions ensuring a higher level of protection, preservation and sustainable use of biological diversity than that called for by the Protocol. The condition is that such actions are corresponding with its objective, provisions, and the Party's other obligations resulted from international law.[1] The States may include other bilateral, regional and multilateral agreements on trans-boundary movements of genetically modified organisms, on condition that such agreements and arrangements are compatible with the objective of the Protocol and that they would not become a reason for a lower level of protection than provided by the Protocol.[2] Basically, the Protocol - by setting a minimum standard of protection - enables the states to establish more rigorous internal provisions through arrangements and regional or bilateral agreements. In the light of WTO rules it is easy to notice that this model of organization is contrary to the unconditional promotion of the harmonization of provisions provided (in particular) in the Agreement on the Application of Sanitary and Phytosanitary Measures (SPS) and the Agreement on Technical Barriers to Trade (TBT).[3] The difference is very significant. Despite the existence in the protocol of the clause about commitment to comply with international obligations,[4] it should be noted that in the same article more rigorous measures are allowed to provide a higher level of protection than the assumed minimum requirements. What is more, the countries are appointed to perform the task of integrating and complementing the existing regime in this regard. In the SPS and TBT Agreements one observes some 'reluctance' to such regulations; these agreements inhibit them, favouring 'flattening' them to the level of international standards.[5] The World Trade Organization is a promoter of the general harmonization (including all countries) of sanitary and environmental protection regulations, resulting in the continual erosion of the respective state powers. In other words, more restrictive national or regional regulations - in relation to international standards - concerning the exchange of genetically modified organisms, from the perspective of the WTO, are not well appreciated.

---

[1] Cf. Article 2, paragraph 4 of the Cartagena Protocol.

[2] Cf. Article 14, paragraph 1 of the Cartagena Protocol.

[3] Cf. paragraph 6 of the Preamble, Article 3 of the SPS Agreement and paragraph 3 and 4 of the Preamble, Article 2, paragraph 4-6 and 9 of the TBT Agreement. The term of harmonization in agreements concerns submission to other standards, for instance these included in Codex Alimentarius.

[4] Cf. for instance Article 2, paragraph 4 of the Cartagena Protocol.

[5] Cf. Article 3, paragraph 2 of the SPS Agreement and Article 2 Paragraph 5 TBT Agreement.

(b) There are also some objections of comparative analysis of the precautionary principle as a criterion for risk assessment and management in the Cartagena Protocol and the provisions of the WTO (mainly the SPS Agreement). In the SPS Agreement the requirement of valid scientific evidence and the adoption of appropriate sanitary and phytosanitary measures as equivalent to the precautionary principle in the absence of scientific certainty, appears rather exceptionally. Moreover, 'implementing appropriate risk management strategies and/or monitoring the living modified organisms,' clearly provided in the Protocol,[6] is entirely unfamiliar to the SPS Agreement, to which each risk and scientific uncertainty assessment must have been subject to scientific rigour.[7] The same thing happens with the socio-economic aspect of the impact of GMOs on the conservation and sustainable use of biodiversity. According to the Protocol,[8] any of the States-Parties may take into account this aspect when considering a decision on import that is in the stage of the analysis of risk management. The same or similar aspects of the WTO regulations are not considered at all in the process of adoption of restrictive measures.

(c) In a quite different manner, we approach the mechanism of the prior informed consent in cases of imports of GMOs, which in the light of the provisions of the GATT, SPS and TBT Agreements, appears as a difficult to justify barrier of the trade between countries. Depending on the document, such a consent is considered as an unnecessary or exaggerated measure, not provided for international standards, lacking scientific rationality, or inconsistent with the conditions on which these agreements make such mechanisms.[9] Moreover, it is worth recalling that the procedure for making decisions on import of GMOs implies that the burden of proof to the potential harm should lie on the state - the party of exports. However, the reversal of the normal method of proving appears contrary to the principles adopted in the WTO system, especially in the GATT. The General Agreement on Tariffs and Trade lays a duty of presenting evidence contained in Article XX upon the state imposing restrictions.

(d) Noticeable differences also appear in the issue of identification of GMOs. This obligation, provided by the Cartagena Protocol, in the light of WTO regulations can be treated as unnecessary, exaggerated or without scientific bases limitation. This commitment combines with the need to

[6] Cf. paragraph 4 and 8, point f) of the Annex III to the Cartagena Protocol.
[7] Cf. Article 5, paragraph 4 of the Annex A of the SPS Agreement.
[8] Cf. Article 26, paragraph 1 of the Cartagena Protocol.
[9] Cf. Annex C of the SPS Agreement.

ensure the documentation accompanying[10] living modified organisms intended for consumption, processing or as animal feed, not intended for deliberate release into the environment[11] and destined for contained use and deliberate release into the environment clearly designating them as living, as well as any requirements for safe handling, storage, transport and use.[12] Non-compliance of these provisions with WTO regulations cannot be excluded, because there is a lack of international standards in this area[13] that could be used to assess the preventive measures suggested by the Protocol. Therefore, we may consider that the approach to this issue by the decisive bodies of the World Trade Organization can be very stringent, since it appears that only the provisions of sectoral agreements (SPS and TBT) may be applied here.

(e) What is also controversial in the Cartagena Protocol is the absence of a general clause about not implementing the trade restrictions, which may be interpreted as a permission to take protective measures contrary to the principle of privilege and the principle of equal treatment of domestic and imported products adopted by the WTO, especially if we take into account that the draft protocol of 1999 contained such a clause.

(f) We may also mention the lack of conformity in the case of eventual restrictions on exchange (Transboundary Movements) of GMOs adopted by the States Parties to the Cartagena Protocol towards the countries that are not parties to it, but which are WTO members. The Protocol (in contrast to the Convention on Biological Diversity) contains a regulation, which states it may take place in accordance with the objective of this Protocol.[14] This implies the need to ensure an adequate level of biosafety in accordance with the precautionary principle. This provision differs from the others found in different agreements related to environmental issues. Agreements on issues of trade towards non-parties are much more restrictive.[15] However, the Cartagena Protocol is far from imposing

---

[10] In the Protocol, there is not specified whether it is specifically identifying (for instance in the form of labelling), or any other less obliging, the general form of identification of GMOs.

[11] Cf. Article 18, paragraph 2, point (a) of the Cartagena Protocol.

[12] Cf. Article 18, paragraph 2, points (b) and (c) to the Cartagena Protocol.

[13] In the present situation, the Cartagena Protocol can be treated as a set of international standards.

[14] Cf. Article 24, paragraph 1 of the Cartagena Protocol.

[15] For example, prohibition on import and export imposed by The Montreal Protocol on Substances That Deplete the Ozone Layer (1987) and The Basel Convention on the Control of Transboundary Movements of Hazardous Wastes and Their Disposal (1998).

restrictions, suggesting the conclusion of bilateral, regional and multilateral agreements on transboundary movements of GMOs with non-parties. However, there is the possibility of placing restrictions on trade of GMOs with non-parties.[16] Referring to the need of keeping an adequate level of biosafety, we may for instance prohibit GMO imports from the countries that do not accept the precautionary principle (in a manner and under rules adopted by the Cartagena Protocol), as a basic parameter of trade in these goods.

The need to seek an objective assessment of existing legislation on biosafety, in the era of rapid development of technologies based on the use of genetically modified organisms, requires a closer consideration of the issue of hypothetical conformity of at least some trade restrictions imposed by the Cartagena Protocol, with the limits set by the World Trade Organization.

Principles of biosafety in the light of Article III, paragraph 4 of the GATT

For a proper indication of the Protocol restrictions on GMOs that are reflected in the provisions of the WTO, it is worth mentioning the role of GATT in biosafety issues. The assumptions of non-compliance of biosafety rules with GATT mainly concern the prohibition of quantitative restrictions on imports of certain products.[17] In trade in genetically modified organisms the principle of equal treatment of domestic and imported products contained in Article III is especially important. It is particularly important to clarify whether the restrictions provided by the Cartagena Protocol (relating for example to procedures for obtaining prior authorization, the marking and identification obligation, and possible import prohibitions) may be in conflict with Article III, paragraph 4 of the General Agreement on Tariffs and Trade, that is, the obligation to provide the imported products an analogous (not less favourable) treatment in matters affecting their commercialization, comapared with similar goods of domestic origin.[18]

---

[16] In compliance with the requirement of equal or higher level of protection than that dictated by the Cartagena Protocol. Cf. Article 24, paragraph 1 and Article 15, paragraph 1 of the Cartagena Protocol.

[17] Cf. Article XI and III (that is the principle of equal treatment of domestic products and imported products) of the GATT.

[18] A similar clause is contained in Article 2, paragraphs 1 of the TBT Agreement. There is lack of such regulation in the SPS Agreement. The reference was made to sanitary and phytosanitary measures, such as control procedures, inspection and

The prohibition of the introduction of such internal restrictions is connected with two problems:

a) the possibility of applying restrictions (applicable to GMOs) resulting from the use of certain processes or methods for producing genetically modified organisms;

b) the use of the similarity criterion of imported genetically modified organisms with homologous genetically unmodified products of domestic manufacture, without which one cannot speak of infringement of this prohibition.

Limitations resulting from the manufacturing process (a) gave the opportunity for numerous discussions about certain judgments[19] preceding the validity of the WTO agreements. It was pointed out that the restrictions (for which the circumstance was a definite production process) should not be considered in the light of Article III, paragraph 4, but Article XI and alternatively justified by the exceptions set out in Article XX.[20] Currently that position is slightly different; it concerns the applicability of Article III of the GATT to the restrictions imposed due to the use of certain processes or methods of manufacturing of GMOs, noting that some of them did not comply, with 'the test of national clause' referred to in that provision.[21]

---

acceptance. In paragraph 1, point (a) of Annex C, one reads that 'such procedures are undertaken and completed without undue delay and in a no less favourable manner for imported products than for like domestic products.'

[19] Cf. U.S. - Restrictions on Imports of Tuna (U.S. - Tuna I) the panel report (not adopted), doc. DS21/R of September 3rd, 1991; US – Restrictions on Imports of Tuna (US – Tuna II) the panel report (not adopted), doc. DS29/R of June 16th, 1994.

[20] Evaluation of biosecurity in the light of the WTO law requires, to some extent, also knowledge whether the specificity of production of genetically modified organisms and products affect the nature of the restrictions placed on the provisions of the Cartagena Protocol. It is seen that the dissimilarity of restrictions is due to: a) the application of the methods by which GMOs are obtained, and thus how to change the properties and characteristics, b) the use of biotechnology processes that do not influence the physical properties of products. The latter is rather unwillingly welcomed in WTO law. By the way, it should be noted that the area of application of the Cartagena Protocol only covers the living modified organisms, that is the organisms with new combinations of genetic material, retaining the ability to replicate and transmit the revised combination of DNA.

[21] A suggested division of restrictions for (a) arising from the characteristics of the product and (b) the used process (methods) has not resulted from the content of documents. However, the texts of the SPS and TBT Agreements allow in a way, the limitations resulted from the methods of production (cf. the definition of the technical provisions in point 1 of Annex A of the TBT Agreement and the

After finding some compatibility of restrictions concerning GMOs in the Cartagena Protocol and Article III, paragraph 4 of the GATT, it should be checked whether these restrictions are in accordance with these provisions. Of course, much depends on the circumstances of a particular case. Generally, however, one may say that provided limits, in principle, appear to be consistent with Article III, paragraph 4, because they relate to products which do not resemble domestic products. We have here again the issue of similarity of imported GMOs and their national not genetically modified equivalents. If this kind of similarity has been demonstrated, it would have been a breach of regulations contained in Article III, paragraph 4[22] by all States Parties to the Cartagena Protocol, as their right to take into account the different treatment of GMOs and related domestic products. However, we should exclude the possibility of legal acceptance of the concept of substantial equivalence as a normative standard corresponding to the requirement of similarity provided by the WTO. In some respects, these two conditions did not differ so much.

It is possible that GMOs, due to the principle of substantial equivalence, will be considered as homologous to products of national production. Small differences arising from the presence of transgenic DNA or protein may be considered negligible for the physical properties of these products. On the other hand, the criterion of health risk and possibly also organic risk is problematic. Scientific data in the system of the WTO rules are important. Due to the incomplete knowledge of the nature of GMOs, uncertainty can influence the reduction of significance of the equivalence criterion.

We cannot exclude that national restrictions on the trade of genetically modified organisms may be negatively judged in the light of Article III, paragraph 4 of the GATT. Doubts arise primarily from the similarity criterion, which has its source in the preferences and habits of consumers. This lack of trust may ultimately decide the legal status of genetically modified products in relation to the unmodified products.

---

definition of sanitary and phytosanitary measures in point 1 of Annex A of the SPS Agreement).

[22] Cf. Article 1, paragraph 1 of the GATT and Article 2, paragraph 1 of the TBT Agreement.

Principles of biosafety in combination with the principles of protection of natural resources contained in Article XX Point (g) of the GATT

Measures taken by states to ensure bio-security on their own territory, seen as inconsistent with Article III, paragraph 4 or Article XI of the GATT, in the light of exceptions included in Article XX,[23] may seem justified. Such an approach, however, interferes with the requirement of presentation of evidence: there is a responsibility on the plaintiff (affected by constraints) to show violation of Article III and XI, due to the exceptions provided by Article XX, a duty to demonstrate the relationship between constraints imposed by specific dispositions is borne by the defendant.

There are only two exceptions included in Article XX of the GATT, which are important in bio-safety issues. The first exception (point (g)) is a justification for the measures introduced due to conservation of non-renewable natural resources, if such measures are effective in combination with restrictions on domestic production or consumption.[24] The second (point (b)) permits restrictive actions if they are necessary to protect human, animal, plant or public health.[25] In both cases, the measures taken (according to Article XX) may not make unjustified discriminatory or arbitrary operations, or restrictions that are contrary to international trade rules. The uniqueness of Article XX, paragraph (g), results mainly from the subject of regulation (that is biological resources) and the objective of protecting biodiversity, which is the basis of this provision, is a more precise indication of the main tasks, namely conservation of non-renewable natural resources. The protection of biodiversity, involving the conservation and sustainable use of the existing diversity not only within

---

[23] Article XX contains a list of exceptions allowing for restrictions on trade contrary to the principles of privilege clause, national treatment and prohibited quantitative restrictions.

[24] Application of this exception was evident in the two disputes brought by countries that are members of the WTO against the USA (U.S. - Standards for Reformulated and Conventional Gasoline and U.S. - Import Prohibition of Certain Shrimp and Shrimp Products). The measure can be considered compliant with Article XX, paragraph (g) only if three conditions listed in it are satisfied.

[25] Article XX Point (b) clearly shows that the parties have the right to introduce restrictions on trade, provided that the restriction is 'necessary' to achieve the objective of protecting public health. In other words, the restriction, which is not connected with health or which has no effect on health, cannot be imposed. Moreover, the tool chosen to achieve must be 'necessary'.

species and between species, but also between ecosystems, takes the nature of the primary value, and without doubt it is the area covered by the application of Article XX, paragraph (g). It means that the protection of biological diversity is more important than conservation measures aimed at saving individual species. Species protection is treated as a component of a much broader initiative - conservation of biodiversity.

An absolute prerequisite for the possible use of biosafety measures suggested by the analyzed regulation is only the protection of natural resources. However, it appears that the crucial bodies of the World Trade Organisation rather freely interpret the content of Article XX, paragraph (g). On the basis of the law it should be noted that there is a required dependence of measures, which are the subject of controversy and conservation of natural resources[26] - it means that they must be somehow related to the aim.[27]

Moreover, the measures to ensure biosafety under Article XX, paragraph (g), may not be 'applied in a manner, which would constitute a means of arbitrary or unjustifiable discrimination between countries where the same conditions prevail, or a disguised restriction on international trade.' The required prerequisites are carefully analyzed so one may have the impression that a certain freedom granted in Article XX, paragraph (g) was compensated in some way with a rigorous interpretation of the initial part of this legal standard. This situation requires a certain balance, finding some balance between these - to some extent conflicting - requirements in a manner which prevents their mutual exclusion. The best solution is probably to consider each case separately, with consideration of all relevant circumstances.[28] Individual treatment, in addition to reducing the possibility of placing equally treating procedures, certainly carries the risk of arbitrary decisions. However, it gives a guarantee of special treatment of cases, which - because of the special qualities and importance to the economy and population of the region - require it in the general opinion.

---

[26] Cf. The Appellate Body Report of the United States - Standards for Reformulated and Conventional Gasoline(U.S. - Standards for Reformulated and Conventional Gasoline of May 20th, 1996, WT/DS2/R, p. 19, 22-29). The USA in support of its position contended that the measure was justified under Article XX.

[27] Cf. US – Shrimp I, paragraph 141.

[28] In this way, in 'the shrimp case' (as well as in 'fuel case'), the questionable measures, even if initially regarded as equitable in the light of Article XX, paragraph (g), were considered to be contrary to the 'content' rule (with an indication on the initial part), and therefore discriminatory. Cf. US – Shrimp I, paragraph 159.

It is not entirely clear what such an analysis should take into account and how this balance should be defined. Should it be similar to a specification, on one hand of the costs and benefits manifested in negative effects of trade exchange arising from the use of controversial measures, and on the other hand, benefits of environmental protection? May we omit in such an analysis many other difficult to determine factors such as socio-economic reactions and preferences of consumers towards biotechnology? Of course, such an approach gives the Dispute Settlement Body of the World Trade Organization broad discretionary power in determining the circumstances or factors indicating the 'equilibrium' of the case, and thus - the solution. However, it may seem difficult to accept in the initial part of Article XX the role of the legal 'standard'.

The international community towards the protection of environmental resources

Some of the principles and basic standards adopt the nature of the evolving common law. Decisive significance in the light of Article XX GATT depends upon: the principle of protection and sustainable use of biodiversity, the principle of equitable sharing of the benefits of biogenetic resources, the prevention principle and the precautionary principle that stand at the base of the Cartagena Protocol. They are the legal expression of the contemporary concerns of the international community to maintain sustainable development. It does not affect the functioning of the WTO, which is required to check whether certain trade restrictions fall within the 'influence' of either of these principles and whether they become the rules consistent with the principle of protection of common interests, contained in Article XX, or relevant provisions of other treaties.[29]

Assigning the appropriate rank to the environmental standards does not significantly affect the significance of their interpretation. Granting the provisions of the Convention on Biological Diversity a more contractual nature than customary nature enables them to function as the main parameter of interpretation of WTO law. In the case of the Cartagena Protocol, recognition of restrictions on GMO may be understood as a supposition (and even as a prerequisite) of compliance with Article XX of the GATT, even in relation to third countries under the Protocol. The approach is changing, going from an interpretative level to analysis of the potential conflict between the WTO rules and standards of 'ecological

[29] Cf. Riccardo Pavoni, *Biodiversità e biotecnologie nel diritto internazionale e comunitario* 342 (2004).

treaties' which reflect a concern for the common interest of all mankind. It seems that the only dispositions that are able to prevail over conflicting provisions of the WTO are those belonging to *ius cogens*.[30]

A more controversial issue is the solution for standards based on the changing of customary law. Taking into account the specificities of the lex specialis, it is noted that these standards would be considered to be applicable (or even as a prevailing), provided that the WTO agreements do not explicitly or implicitly provide for the exclusion of their application.[31] It is therefore difficult to determine when an explicit criterion or default of a customary rule of exclusion is applicable.[32]

The most controversial situations encountered are at the interface between the WTO law contained in the conventions and environmental regulations. The first obstacle in finding a solution is the need to distinguish the position of third countries in the treaties for the protection of the environment and members of the WTO. One should reflect whether the question about the existence of the criteria and principles capable of mitigating the negative consequences of compliance with the rules invalidates treaties with third countries in 'environmental agreements' which are an expression of general interest. When it comes to the states parties of both, the WTO and the 'ecological agreements' (successive or preceding the first ones), it is suggested that 'environmental agreement' should prevail because of the principle of good faith. In this case, it may prevent another party from claiming the benefits of compliance with the obligations of the GATT or the WTO. In this case, this advantage should lead not only to breach of WTO rules, but above all, to prevent the initiation of proceedings by the State affected by the restrictions provided for environmental agreements.[33]

This hypothesis can be acceptable, mainly because of the fact that the WTO Dispute Settlement Body has shown particular interest in the principle of good faith. This principle seems to be extremely important in the interpretation of the introduction of Article XX of the GATT,

---

[30] Under such an assumption, this advantage should be reflected at least suspending the effectiveness or use of a controversial provision in the WTO (cf. Paolo Piccone & Aldo Ligustro, *Diritto dell'Organizzazione mondiale del commercio* 630, 647 (2002)).

[31] The only case of exclusion of customary rules clearly provided by the WTO system, applies the principles of international responsibility of states for the consequences of tort. *Ibid.*, 631.

[32] Riccardo Pavoni, *Biodiversità e biotecnologie...* 344 (2004).

[33] Cf. Paolo Piccone & Aldo Ligustro, *Diritto dell'Organizzazione mondiale...* 648 (2002).

according to which the measures authorized by exceptions mentioned in this article may not be used for discrimination or to mask the restrictions on international trade. Thus, in the case of shrimps, the Appellate Body directly stated that the ratio of this introduction lies precisely in respecting the principle of good faith and what results from it, which is what resists the abuse of law (in particular the right to invoke the exceptions of Article XX).[34]

The logic of the reasons of the Appellate Body may therefore suggest that the imposition of trade restrictions under the existing multilateral agreements, namely the Cartagena Protocol, is a sign of good faith and willingness to comply with the provisions contained in it, and extra restrictions are somehow justified by Article XX of the GATT. This approach, however, is entirely dependent on the adoption of the 'external' to the WTO rules and standards.[35] Moreover, in situations of conflict between WTO rules and regulations contained in 'the ecological agreements' the WTO Dispute Settlement Body - as it seems - does not have the ability to create any standardization recommendations, if another treaty is to replace the provisions of the WTO. Regarding the deficiency of relevant WTO rules, such an approach could complement the ambiguities of law and the position of the WTO Dispute Settlement Body would then have only a declarative character. However, we should remember that every situation of legal uncertainty would be an opportunity to make unfair (or even dishonest) trade restrictions, which in the absence of other mechanisms would significantly lengthen the time of the resolution of the controversy between the parties. Therefore, the competent bodies of the WTO should take the responsibility of decision making even if it is connected with the 'sacrifice' of one of the rules from this untouchable system.[36]

It seems that difficult in resolve issues arising from the predominance of environmental standards have a raison d'etre only in the theoretical field, and the WTO Dispute Settlement Bodies always manage to use the

---

[34] This kind of abuse was found for example in avoiding talks by the USA, which were aimed at concluding an agreement on the protection of sea turtles with the countries affected by shrimp import prohibitions. Cf. US – Import Prohibition of Certain Shrimp and Shrimp Products, of 6.11.1998, WT/DS58/AB/R, paragraph 158.

[35] It should be noted, that this is possible only in terms of purely interpretative level through a broad interpretation of Article XX of the GATT. Cf. Pavoni, p. 346-347.

[36] Riccardo Pavoni, *Biodiversità e biotecnologie...* 347 (2004).

general principles of law, already used to interpret tensions emerging at the intersection of trade law and the environmental protection law.

Principles of biosafety under Article XX, Point (b) of the GATT

Although biosafety regulations are generally associated with Article XX Point (g) of the GATT, one should not forget about the exception contained in paragraph (b) of that article, which concerns the protection of human health and life, animals and plants. The specific provisions on the safety of food and feed (containing GMO) are contained in the SPS Agreement, but we may point out some concerns about the rapid spread of genetically modified plants and animals. The dual purpose (the protection of human rights and biodiversity) of the Cartagena Protocol therefore creates a system of protection against risks arising from uncontrolled trade of such organisms.[37] This requires demonstrating the advisability of entering the rules and their compliance with the protocol. To justify these bio-security measures, one must therefore demonstrate their connection with Article XX Point (b) of the GATT, namely the protection of human health or life. In other words, they must be geared for protection and control of the actual and reasonable risk to human health.[38] The product covered by the restrictions must therefore represent real (scientifically proven) threat to human health. This may be treated as a 'test' of the assessment of admissibility of implementing GMO trade restrictions. It is hardly likely that the bio-safety measures taken based on the precautionary principle would be able to pass this test, even if the solutions are dependent on the individual case and the manner of understanding and application of this principle. These issues have not been thoroughly tested, so it may be expected that the trade restrictions towards GMO trade referring to Article XX Point (g) shall require scientific evidence that would demonstrate that the measures are actually designed to protect natural resources and that they will be used only in exceptional situations.

Is there any justification for the requirement of providing scientific proof provided by the exceptions in Article XX of the GATT? Assuming

---

[37] '[...] the objective of this Protocol is to contribute to ensuring an adequate level of protection in the field of the safe transfer, handling and use of living modified organisms [...] that may have adverse effects on the conservation and sustainable use of biological diversity, taking also into account risks to human health'. Cf. Article 1 of the Cartagena Protocol.

[38] Cf. EC - Asbestos, Panel Report, paragraph 8.182.

that this condition is the reason for the exceptions included in Article XX,[39] it may be assumed that the adoption of the SPS Agreement increases the importance of this requirement as a parameter for assessing the fairness of the trade restrictions dictated by sanitary and ecological reasons.

On the other hand the case of asbestos is an example of a 'migration' of the normative concept of the SPS Agreement and in connection with the jurisprudence of the GATT Agreement.[40] The effect of this could be a change of the rigour of the decisions on matters relating to Article XX. Referring to the case of meat with hormones,[41] the Appellate Body emphasized that the risk underlying the measures taken to protect health, not only can be quantified, it may also be expressed using qualitative methods.[42] Moreover, the Appellate Body confirmed the possibility of adopting trade restrictions, even based on less significant or divergent positions of research in relation to the position prevailing at the time.[43]

The most important issue awaiting clarification is whether the scientific approach to the problem is a sufficient motive to interfere with state law in order to clarify the level of environmental and health protection for a given territory. Even if it clearly results from the SPS Agreement, the same may not be said about remedial measures to be taken under Article XX of the GATT.[44] In the case of asbestos (which was after all proved to be harmful), the Appellate Body did not knowingly and intentionally interfere in government decisions. It seems that this should not have taken place, particularly in the absence of scientific certainty as to the harmlessness of introduction to the environment and the market of a growing number of genetically modified organisms.

Restrictive provisions in the protection of biodiversity

As shown above, taking security measures based on Article XX Point (b) of the GATT is justified only if they are necessary to protect the life or health of humans, animals and plants. This condition is combined with the

---

[39] The results of the research is the default condition for both the exceptions set out in Article XX of the GATT, as well as many other aspects of the WTO system.
[40] Cf. EC - Asbestos, Panel Report, paragraph 8.180.
[41] The Case EC - Hormones have been decided on the base of the SPS Agreement.
[42] Cf. EC - Asbestos, the Appellate Body report, paragraph 167, EC - Hormones, the Appellate Body report, paragraph 186-187.
[43] Cf. EC - Asbestos, the Appellate Body report, paragraph 178; EC - Hormones, the Appellate Body report, paragraph 194.
[44] Cf. EC - Asbestos, Panel Report, paragraph 8.210.

need to prove (by the initiating state) the lack of alternative means of complying (or at least being consistent) with the GATT, so that relating to Article XX Point (b) sometimes proves to be fruitless, because the trade always treats the disposal of state preventive measures as unjustly restrictive. This condition, however, was not treated as a criterion corresponding to the principle of proportionality, containing the requirement of balancing the interests of market and environmental protection.

The WTO jurisprudence seems to be more focused on the completion of the condition of finding and balancing the expectations of trade and biosafety,[45] taking into account: a) the effectiveness of measures taken, b) the common interests or values protected by these measures, c) the impact of the effects resulting from the application of international trade. In this context, the Appellate Body, without indicating any preference among the proposed three criteria, has changed - at least apparently - the approach to the requirement of placing the least restrictive limitations on trade (in line with criterion (c)). On the one hand, this explains why certain measures may be considered necessary (according to Article XX), even if they are more restrictive than others. Furthermore, they can also be advantageous if their impact on the trade balance would be insignificant or negligible. Besides, the adoption by the state of less restrictive measures should not always be perceived as the best solution, since their evaluation depends on the expected effect of the interaction of three of these factors and the granting of preferences to one of them, due to the nature of the case.[46]

That is why the most important criterion of those assessed by the WTO bodies is the necessary condition of joint business or values protected by the controversial measures. It should be noted that the concept of joint business appears in the jurisprudence of the World Trade Organization concerning the impact on the environment. Referring to the principles of the common interest of mankind - the need to protect the most important components of the ecological environment for its preservation - particular attention is given to the fact that certain restrictive measures are adopted in accordance with the Agreement (Protocol on Biosafety) based on that principle. It is logical, therefore, that the restrictive measures taken under this Agreement, are intended to protect the vital interests of the whole community. They should thus easily (or even automatically) pass 'the

[45] Cf. Korea – Measures Affecting Imports of Fresh, Chilled and Frozen Beef (Korea – Beef), Apellate Body report, doc. WT/DS 161/AB/R I WT/ds169/AB/R z 11/12.2000.

[46] Riccardo Pavoni, *Biodiversità e biotecnologie...* 352 (2004).

necessity test'. There are agreements for such aims not only by state parties, but the entire international community.

The proposed solution requires, however, verifying whether it has a chance of implementation in practice and whether the WTO Dispute Settlement Body will treat remedial measures as necessary. But there is no absolute certainty that the acceptance of such measures will be influenced by demonstration of the absence of scientific certainty of dangers of genetically modified organisms, or that they will not be dominated for instance by economic-commercial arguments. These concerns arise from the similarities of 'the necessity test' and analysis of the costs and benefits - that is, costs which are a consequence of reduction of trade and profits due to the need to increase the level of environmental protection.[47]

The conclusions from the method of settling the controversy which uses a 'necessity test' do not explain everything. It seems quite possible that the high level of uncertainty associated with the likelihood of adverse effects of GMOs, can greatly affect the shape of a 'necessity test' the proposed Article XX, paragraph (b) in the version suggested by the WTO law. In other words, the lack of solid scientific basis may prompt the bodies of the WTO to grant remedies a secondary role protecting the joint business or preferential treatment of modifying international trade. Particularly drastic biosafety regulations - like the total ban on imports - may be considered as not necessary because of the possibility of using less restrictive measures (for example appropriate labelling, traceability and monitoring). It is possible, because the evaluation of 'the test of necessity' is to use the wide discretionary powers of the WTO, also in the situation where according to agreements on environmental protection, the measures were adopted to protect the joint business of mankind.[48]

---

[47] Considerable freedom enjoyed by the WTO bodies in recognition of certain restrictive measures as extremely important for the protection of joint business, makes the restrictions on trade (moratoria or prohibition of imports) prevail over economic interests and dictate a solution, which less restrictive features are at the discretion of the state. In this case, the necessity test can significantly affect the regulatory autonomy of states in the environmental and health safety.

[48] It should also be noted that the criterion of science not only affects the real evidence of protection by limiting actions, but also in the analysis of compliance with the element of necessity.

The assessment of biosafety rules in the SPS and TBT Agreements and Article XX of the GATT

The need to extend the analysis of biosafety in the context of international law requires an examination of the effects of possible conflict between the SPS and TBT Agreements and the General Agreement on Tariffs and Trade. Article 11, paragraph 3 of the SPS Agreement says that 'nothing in this Agreement shall impair the rights of Members under other international agreements.' This regulation, usually ignored in doctrine, in some way resembles the safeguard clause of other international conventions. It should provide the advantage of these conventions in the event of a conflict with the SPS Agreement.[49] These types of clause[50] - especially if they are expressions of conformity - are unable to resolve hypothetical differences between successive agreements. However, they may indicate the need to adapt to each of their controversial applications. On the other hand, Article 11, paragraph 3 gives the impression of exceptional standards in the WTO system. We could suppose that it introduces a kind of internal restriction of the use of the WTO law, that can scarcely be combined with the general principles, such as the prohibition of expanding or restricting the rights and obligations of members. At the same time, the same standard is an important signal of the affect of the WTO on international law, particularly on existing treaty obligations. It should be the subject of increasing attention of bodies deciding about controversies, which would enable comprehension of its meaning.

In the case of the possibility of uniting the WTO law with the Protocol, one must consider how the rule of interpreting in the light of the general interest of the international community connected with environmental protection applies in relation to the SPS Agreement and TBT Agreement. The adoption of specific measures suggested by environmental regulations for the common interest of mankind, should lead to the adoption of a

---

[49] Cf. Article 30, paragraph 2 of the Vienna Convention on the Law of Treaties, 'When a treaty specifies that it is subject to, or that it is not to be considered as incompatible with, an earlier or later treaty, the provisions of that other treaty prevail'.

[50] According to Article 11, paragraph 3, the SPS Agreement in no way limits the rights of the WTO Members under other international agreements. One may see some similarity with the Article 22, paragraph 1 of the Convention on Biological Diversity, which notes that 'the provisions of this Convention shall not affect the rights and obligations of any Contracting Party deriving from any existing international agreement'.

special precautionary approach in the process of researching the violation of the WTO regulations.

The issues arising from a statement of the SPS and TBT Agreement from Article XX of the GATT require attempts to clarify, namely the difference in the obligation to provide evidence for the two proposed cases. While the defendant (the State which has introduced measures with a view to raising the level of biosecurity) must demonstrate compliance with the requirements of Article XX, a complainant (who wants to show losses on this account) must prove the violation of these conditions; the conditions on which the SPS and TBT Agreement make the admissibility of the protective action of sanitary / phytosanitary and technical measures.

An interesting effect of this combination is associated with the element of 'necessity' occurring in the controversial regulations, which is very important in the SPS and TBT Agreements. In the SPS Agreement, this concerns Article 2, paragraph 1 and 2 (similar to Article XX, Point (b) of the GATT). It concerns the possibility of ensuring the necessary measures to protect the life or health of humans, animals or plants, and the requirement that 'measure is applied only to the extent necessary to protect human, animal or plant life or health'.[51]

More important - as it seems - is Article 5, paragraph 6, which indicates that with the introduction of protective measures, it is required to ensure 'that such measures are not more trade-restrictive than required to achieve their appropriate level of sanitary or phytosanitary protection, taking into account technical and economic feasibility'.[52] In order to demonstrate the violation of this provision, the claimant must demonstrate three elements to prove that the measures are more restrictive than necessary. This occurs only if there is an alternative to them (a) objectively available, technically and economically possible, (b) able to provide the level of protection deemed sufficient, (c) significantly less restrictive of trade.[53]

We are dealing with a different case than the 'necessity test' (developed in conjunction with Article XX of the GATT and the issue of restrictions on imports of beef); a form of assessment. First of all, it does not seem to have a particularly large impact on trade, given that the alternative

[51] Article2, paragraph 2 of the SPS Agreement.

[52] Article5, paragraph 6 of the SPS Agreement.

[53] The footnote 3 of the SPS Agreement 'for purposes of paragraph 6 of Article 5, a measure is not more trade-restrictive than required unless there is another measure, reasonably available taking into account technical and economic feasibility, that achieves the appropriate level of sanitary or phytosanitary protection and is significantly less restrictive to trade'.

measure must be clearly less restrictive than the provision at issue. It seems that in the analysis, there would be some space to take into account the common interests or values provided in the regulation.

Similarly to Article XX of the GATT, it should be noted that the outcome of a 'necessity test' laid down by the SPS Agreement is largely dependent on scientific data. In the case of restrictions on agricultural products[54] the WTO bodies excluded validity of alternative measures (plant health testing of each product, instead of each type of product, as required by a controversial measure to reduce), as adopted in the light of scientific assessments lacked sufficient evidence that would demonstrate that the adopted restrictions are able to maintain the level of protection required by Japan. In this situation, the scientific criterion worked for necessity of the introduction of controversial measures, but there may also be a different situation, against the restrictions on the marketing of GMOs, which generally do not have such well-documented impact on the environment as conventional products. It should be noted that the WTO system, and particularly in the SPS Agreement, to determining the level of protection is the prerogative of the State,[55] which should be taken into account by the decisive authorities. This approach is changing when bodies based on scientific data look for an alternative measure which would enable the achievement of the same level of protection. The division between postulating the adoption of the alternative measure and demand of reduction in the level of protection, seems to be extremely subtle.

Similar issues are also raised in Article 2, paragraphs 2 of the TBT Agreement, which stresses that technical regulations should not restrict trade more than necessary to achieve a legitimate objective, taking into account the threats that may develop. Just as in the SPS Agreement, the technical provisions seem to be necessary to achieve the aim - in this case, an appropriate level of environmental protection. Indication of less restrictive means at the disposal of the state requires consideration of many factors. These factors, however, differ from those required by Article 5, paragraph 6 of the SPS Agreement. In place of the technical and economic feasibility of implementing the adopted restrictive measure (according to Article 5, paragraph 6 SPS), Article 2, paragraph 2 of the TBT Agreement, requires taking into consideration the risk of damage caused by the departure from implementing the permitted purpose, such as manifested by a lower level of environmental protection.

---

[54] Cf. Japan – Measures Affecting Agricultural Products (Japan – Agricultural Products), Appellate Body Report, doc.

[55] Cf. Australia - Salmon, paragraph 199.

It is somewhat like comparing the costs and profits. This is a problem because this method is strictly scientific, and in the choice of restrictive measure that the environmental risk analysis depends on, it is difficult to determine the degree of probability of such risks. The consequences related to it (especially in relation to trade in GMOs) are evident. This 'inconvenience' is offset by the need (expressed clearly in Article 2, paragraph 2 of the TBT Agreement) to take account of common interests and values, make arrangements and agreements provided for setting goals. This means that it is this last criterion, which is joint business and common values, that should determine the choice of acceptable adopted mitigation measures in accordance with the Protocol on Biosafety.

LEGAL MODELS OF ARTIFICIAL PROCREATION IN EUROPE AND POLISH LAW

ANETTA BRECZKO
AND JOANNA RADWANOWICZ-WANCZEWSKA

UNIVERSITY OF BIAŁYSTOK, POLAND

Some remarks on the moral and legal status of the human embryo

The phenomenon of the creation of human life is losing its traditional natural character. With medical advancement comes the possibility of observing the development of the human being from the very beginning. This provides a basis for precise planning of the moment of conception and selection of appropriate reproductive cells, as well as for the creation of life in entirely artificial conditions. The conception of a child need not involve even casual relations of an intimate nature between two people. It may take the form of a medical service – a procedure performed using gametes provided by either the future parents or anonymous donors – or may also be the subject of a surrogate motherhood agreement.

With medical advances in the area of reproduction, the problem of the legal subjectivity of the human embryo becomes more and more significant. The practical situations, which arise along with new medical capabilities are often of the nature of *casus perplexus*.

In the field of bio-jurisprudence we observe a whole spectrum of views concerning the legal status of the human embryo: from its being regarded as a thing (an object at the disposal of the reproductive cell donors and the doctors), to its being treated as the equal of a human person, entitled to full legal protection. Although the need is perceived today to protect the human dignity of a conceived being, it is also increasingly often regarded as permissible to destroy an embryo. Some even deny the embryo (particularly when *in vitro*) a status in family law, regarding the cell donors not as parents, but as persons connected to the embryo only by a genetic link and some imperfectly defined legal relationship.

If we accept that the embryo is a person and has the status of a subject equal to that of a person who is already living, then it ought to be subject to the same legal protection, which would exclude any interference in the domain of reproduction, since any such action would compromise the dignity of the *nasciturus*. It is therefore appropriate to seek a new legal definition of a person, which would distinguish the concept of 'human being' from 'human person' and would serve to define the extent of legal protection to which each is entitled.

It would seem that the 'dignity of a human person' is not the same as the 'dignity of a human being'. This conclusion is implied by the very fact that we differentiate the concepts of human person and human being. Since a 'human being' (an embryo) does not have the status of a subject equal to that of a 'human person' (a person already living), it should also not be ascribed the same dignity, just as the dignity of an animal cannot be made equal to the dignity of a person.

The 'potential life' of a person should not therefore be equated with life already existing. Indeed, even after a person is born it is becoming increasingly justified to differentiate (graduate) the 'quality of life' – for example, the quality of life of a 'human person' in a permanent vegetative state is not comparable to the quality of life of a healthy person.

In matters of human subjectivity it is undoubtedly easier to achieve a consensus on a legal than on a moral plane. From the perspective of jurisprudence it is becoming more and more widely accepted that the legal status of a human foetus changes according to its stage of development, capacity for life, etc. No great disputes are aroused by the 'gradation' of legal subjectivity.

European standards set only minimum requirements in relation to the protection of human rights in the process of medically assisted reproduction, including protection of the conceived child itself. Regulatory formulations set the direction for the interpretation of particular laws. The overriding interpretative directive should be taken to be the duty to protect human dignity and the precedence of the good of a human being over the interests of the community or of science.

Of fundamental importance is the Convention for the Protection of Human Rights and Dignity of the Human Being with regard to the Application of Biology and Medicine (known as the Bioethics Convention).[1] It is implied by Article 1 of that Convention that the definition of the concept of "person" is left up to national law. The degree of legal protection is differentiated. Every 'human being', regardless of its personal status, is subject to protection at least as regards its dignity and

---

[1] Text of the Convention available at http://tinyurl.com/72gw3uq; [August 10th, 2010].

identity, while integrity and other basic rights and freedoms are guaranteed only to a 'person'. The minimum level of protection is therefore defined by the obligation to respect the dignity and identity of every human being.

Among the fundamental regulations relating to human embryos, worthy of particular attention are the recommendations of the Parliamentary Assembly of the European Council from 1986 and 1989. These protect the dignity of the human embryo and foetus.[2] The first of them defines ways of using human embryos for diagnostic, therapeutic, scientific, industrial and commercial purposes. The second recommendation addresses the issue of their use in scientific research.

Attention should be drawn to the provisions of the European Union Charter of Fundamental Rights, which forbid eugenic practices intended for the selection of persons, as well as reproductive cloning.

Detailed regulatory guidelines concerning artificial reproduction are laid down by the European Parliament and Council Directive of 31st March 2004 on setting standards of quality and safety for the donation, procurement, testing, processing, preservation, storage and distribution of human tissues and cells.[3]

One may not disregard the importance of certain executive directives: 1) on certain technical requirements for the donation, procurement and testing of human tissues and cells;[4] 2) on traceability requirements, notification of serious adverse reactions and events and certain technical requirements for the coding, processing, preservation, storage and distribution of human tissues and cells.[5] These directives oblige Member States to guarantee health safety by introducing legal regulations and controls over the circulation of reproductive cells.[6]

European standards are intended to provide only a minimum of protection for the human embryo. Due to the freedom left for the legal regulation of issues relating to human reproduction, it is possible to take account of the main directions of bioethical debate and dominant values in a particular country. Individual European countries adopt their own regulatory measures in this field, often diametrically different. There is a visible division between countries that give precedence to technical

---

[2] No. 1046 of September 24th, 1986 and no. 1100 of February 2nd, 1989.

[3] No. 2004/23/EC; OJ L 102/48.

[4] No. 2006/17/EC; OJ L 348/38.

[5] No. 2006/86/EC; OJ L 294/32.

[6] *Modele regulacyjne wspomaganej prokreacji w świetle standardów konstytucyjnych* in Leszek Bosek & Michał Królikowski (eds.), *Współczesne wyzwania bioetyczne* 157 (2010).

progress (including the UK and France) and those that accept the priority of the person (such as Germany and Switzerland).

Techniques of artificial fertilization and surrogate motherhood – moral and legal uncertainties

Artificial fertilization is a term used to refer to medical techniques which are intended to bring about the conception of a child other than through the natural act of sexual intercourse between a woman and a man. As M. Safjan notes: 'In a period of a few decades, legal and deontological views and evaluations relating to the phenomenon of artificial reproduction have undergone fundamental change – from resolute prohibition towards increasing tolerance and permissiveness'.[7] Today artificial fertilization is most often regarded as a method of treating infertility. It makes it possible to realize the desire, characteristic of the majority of people, to have a child.

Methods of artificial fertilization are divided into two groups: 1) homological methods and 2) heterological methods. In the homological case, the sperm and ovum come from the couple who are trying to have a child. In the case of heterological methods, at least one of the gametes originates from a third person.

In considerations of the subject of artificial reproduction, the following issues in particular are addressed: 1) artificial insemination; 2) *in vitro* fertilization; and 3) surrogate motherhood.

Artificial insemination refers to *in vivo* artificial fertilization. Sperm (collected earlier from the man) is introduced into the female reproductive organs in order to fertilize the ovum. Fertilization thus takes place within the mother's body, as it does in the process of natural reproduction. In the case of artificial insemination surplus embryos are not created, and therefore no issue arises with the freezing and destruction of zygotes or their inappropriate treatment as objects. There is also no pre-implantation diagnosis. Also absent is the potential risk of harm to the mother's health, as hormonal stimulation is not used.

It should be emphasized that artificial insemination procedures have been known since the end of the 18th century, which means that it has been possible to verify their medical and social value. Although at first they were accused of going against good customs and fundamental legal principles, over time they became generally accepted. Nonetheless the Catholic Church continues to oppose even this apparently morally neutral

---

[7] Marek Safjan, *Prawo wobec ingerencji w naturę ludzkiej prokreacji* 13 (1990).

method, seeing in it the substitution of masturbation (as a means of obtaining sperm) for the marital act. It should be added, however, that in international and European Union law, basic standards have been developed with regard to the legal problems which might arise in relation to artificial insemination.

Still controversial is the moral and legal evaluation of the permissibility of artificial insemination outside marriage. In an era when there is a noticeable tendency to treat informal partnerships on a level with formal marriage relations, this issue is gradually becoming blurred. The view is increasingly widespread that limiting the availability of artificial insemination only to married women would be both a limitation on the principle of equality and a form of discrimination.

The question arises of the moral and legal evaluation of artificial insemination of a single woman with sperm from an unrelated donor. Fundamental controversies relate to the need to determine whether there exists in general a right to control one's own genetic material, and what the nature of that right is. The permissibility of such control results from the general right of a person to control his or her body. It is legitimate to conclude that reproductive cells are not things, and that, being the source of life, they are not comparable with any other products of the body. Without going into the debates on this subject, it should be mentioned that the fundamental function of cells of this type ought to have an effect on the rights of the person from whom they originate. Such rights cannot be of an absolute nature, as they are related to the specific nature of human genetic material. The donor, though not having the right of ownership, should nonetheless have defined rights to that material, and in particular the right to oversee the way in which the donated reproductive cells are used.

A further important question relates to the permissibility of *post mortem* insemination, using the previously donated sperm of a man after his death. The dominant view of this possibility can be seen to be negative. However it is increasingly common to hear voices of approval for the practice as the right of a woman, implied directly by her freedom in the sphere of reproduction. Insemination is regarded in this case as a kind of continuation of the marriage. Since the treatment is performed in accordance with the wishes of the deceased husband, it is hard to view it as going against good customs and morals. *Post mortem* artificial insemination is finding supporters in an ever increasing number of European countries. It can be expected that in time it will become accepted and legally regulated in Poland as well.

More moral and legal doubts undoubtedly arise in connection with *in vitro* fertilization. M. Safjan notes that 'In vitro fertilization (…) opens up possibilities never previously existing for human interference in the biological processes of the creation of life, and consequently gives rise to completely new ethical and legal problems. The danger of instrumentalization of the processes of creation of human life appears here on a much greater scale than in the case of artificial insemination, a real possibility arises of breakage of the natural time continuity of biological processes relating to conception, pregnancy and childbirth, and the dilemmas become more marked in relation to the division of social and legal parenthood from biological parenthood'.[8] The author points out that the *in vitro* method makes it necessary to resolve the fundamental legal and ethical problem concerning the legal status of the embryo prior to implantation. He indicates the fundamental doubts concerning the bounds of permissibility of medical experiments, whose subject is conceived human life. He predicts that 'there will be an ever more forceful striving for the creation of a perfect human being, and consequently for the 'technicalization' and 'medicalization' of procedures of artificial reproduction'.[9]

It is indisputable that the fundamental controversies surrounding *in vitro* methods are particularly concerned with the moral and legal status of the embryo. The human embryo *in vitro* constitutes a specific form of human life, genetically determined. Matters of dispute include differences in defining the value of this 'potential human life'.

Representatives of Christian perspectives on this issue state that the artificial creation of embryos is morally unacceptable: 'Procedures of assisted fertilization may not interfere in the natural process of passing on life, namely the marital sexual act. The Church explains that every child has the right to be the fruit of the love of its parents and cannot be a result of technical manipulations'.[10]

Representatives of liberal (non-religious) positions point out that the technique of artificial fertilization of a method of treating the disease of infertility. In their view there are no moral contra-indications to 'test-tube' fertilization. They also state that the life created by artificial fertilization has the same value as that conceived by natural means. It is a potential life, from which in time a person will develop.

---

[8] Marek Safjan, *Prawo wobec ingerencji...* 77 (1990).

[9] Marek Safjan, *Prawo wobec ingerencji...* 78 (1990).

[10] *Bioetyczne problemy nowej cywilizacji w świetle katolickiej nauki społecznej* in Leszek Bosek & Michał Królikowski (eds.), *Współczesne wyzwania...* 63 (2010).

Every *in vitro* fertilization procedure gives rise to the issue of surplus embryos, which are not used for implantation. Serious dilemmas thus arise regarding the selection, storage, destruction, etc. of these embryos.

From a Christian perspective, particularly a Catholic one, since the embryo is a person from conception, any selection of embryos in order to choose the 'best' ones for implantation, freezing of embryos, and so on '(...) opens the doors to the tragic results of a culture of death'.[11]

From secular standpoints these issues are viewed quite differently. The moral controversies concerning the selection, storage and destruction of embryos are reduced by the view that the human embryo is not yet a person. It is merely a developmental phase of a potential person, and thus as a 'human being' is not entitled to the same subjective status as a 'human person' ('natural person') who has already been born. In these considerations there is a visible concern that the legal sanctioning of the principle of the 'sanctity of every human life' by making a person a full legal subject from the moment of conception would call into question the entire legitimacy of *in vitro* methods.

With the practice of *in vitro* techniques, it becomes ever clearer that legal definitions not only of 'humanity' but also of other terms – 'family', 'motherhood', 'fatherhood', etc. – are inadequate. Not long ago these terms did not require precise legal definition – they were understood intuitively. With the spread of *in vitro* fertilization, terminological doubts began to arise as to how to explain the meanings of these categories. A good example is the concept of 'parenthood'. Alongside the classical formula of legal parenthood there appeared over time competing concepts such as 'biological parenthood', 'sociological parenthood', 'genetic parenthood', and so on. It is noticed that the practice of medically assisted reproduction 'upsets' the concepts of family relationships, which have developed over the centuries in particular countries' legal systems. The question now needs to be asked whether the reference point for these relationships is to be biological origin. In opposition to the opinion, which held sway until recently, that *mater sempter certa est*, doubts now arise more and more frequently in relation to disputes over motherhood.

Surrogate motherhood is not, in medical categories, a separate technique for the artificial conception of a child. It is nonetheless a form of reproduction associated with artificial insemination and *in vitro* methods. It involves the practice of bearing a child for another woman (or for married or unmarried partners) with the intention of handing the child over to her (or them) after it is born.

---

[11] *Ibid.*

Surrogate motherhood agreements raise a number of moral questions, and the very idea of surrogate motherhood is a very controversial expression of freedom in the sphere of reproduction, since it upsets traditional legal values. Questions are frequently asked about the subjectivity and dignity of a person, bodily integrity and the boundaries of freedom in making use of one's reproductive capabilities.

Another reason why issues of surrogate motherhood are the subject of moral discussion is that the natural desire for parenthood and freedom in the sphere of reproduction are somehow in a collision with the laws of economics and the 'process of production' of a person in a borrowed womb. There is a clash between the concept of having a child and the dehumanization of the human reproductive process.

Surrogate motherhood agreements are intended, as a rule, to enable couples to satisfy their desire for a child in cases of infertility. Occasionally, however, there are cases where the motivation is the convenience of a woman who does not want to carry a child out of fear that the pregnancy might harm her appearance, career, etc.

Let us look at the nature of surrogate motherhood. Most generally, its essential feature is that a surrogate mother, who is at the same time the biological mother, conceives and gives birth to a child without the intent of raising it or accepting any parental responsibility in the future.[12] This is most often done for appropriate remuneration, and more rarely on a voluntary basis. Two basic types of surrogate motherhood are distinguished: partial and full.

Partial surrogacy occurs when the woman who is to give birth is artificially inseminated with the sperm of an unrelated man (usually an anonymous donor). The biological mother is then also the genetic mother, but is not the sociological mother, as the child is handed over after birth to the parents who ordered the surrogacy service.

In the case of full surrogacy, an embryo is implanted into the womb of the woman who is to give birth. Here the biological mother is neither the genetic nor the sociological mother. If the donor of the ovum is the woman who wishes to raise the child, then she, as genetic mother, also becomes the sociological mother. If the donor is a woman unrelated to either party, then the genetic mother is neither the sociological nor biological mother.

Depending on who donated the sperm, surrogate parenthood gives rise to further complication of family relationships. There is a clear ethical problem particularly when surrogate motherhood is used by same-sex couples.

---

[12] Marek Safjan, *Prawo wobec ingerencji...* 135 (1990).

Surrogate motherhood agreements began to be used many years ago in various countries, thus requiring legislators to adopt appropriate legal rules.[13] The legal aspects of such an agreement are related to its content, which includes the following elements: 1) definition of the child as the subject of the agreement together with giving up of the rights to the child; 2) definition of actions connected with conception and giving birth to the child, as the surrogate motherhood service involves making available one's own body; 3) determination of additional contractual stipulations (e.g. concerning a specific diet to be followed during pregnancy or an undertaking to abort a defective foetus). Where the matter is regulated, the law provides for specific claims, such as legal suits for determination and denial of motherhood, for handing over of the child after birth, for taking away of the child after birth, for compensation for breach of contract by either of the parties, and for denial of fatherhood.[14]

A permissive view of surrogate motherhood is becoming more and more common among philosophers and ethicists of non-religious provenance. Such a view is generally taken by supporters of utilitarianism, consequentialism and deontological theories of rights, who find arguments in favour of permitting the use of surrogacy agreements in practice.

The spectrum of legal positions with regard to surrogacy agreements ranges from 1) prohibition and punishability of surrogate motherhood and forms of intermediation (e.g. in some US states, France, the Netherlands, Sweden and Switzerland); 2) through the absence of regulation and claims of impermissibility due to inconsistency with social norms (e.g. in Poland); 3) to the permissibility of the practice (e.g. Belgium, the UK, Israel, Hungary, Australia and some US states). International organizations such as the WHO permit surrogate motherhood, although they disallow forms of intermediation. A close link is seen between the legalization of surrogate motherhood agreements and the ethical and legal acceptance of artificial insemination and *in vitro* fertilization. Comparative analysis shows, however, that most legal systems lack any kind of regulation of the issue of surrogate motherhood. As M. Działyńska notes, in recent years there has even been a strengthening in the trend towards restricting or completely prohibiting surrogate motherhood. The main reason for this is

---

[13] It is sometimes remarked that an analogous form to surrogate motherhood was known in antiquity, as is implied by biblical texts concerning the giving of birth by a slave for her mistress in the case of Sarah (Gen. 16, 1–6) and Rachel (Gen. 30, 1–6).

[14] *Prokreacja medycznie wspomagana* in Jerzy Stelmach et al. (eds.) *Paradoksy bioetyki prawniczej* 82 (2010).

the uncertainty as to the fate of the child conceived by this method, as well as the commercial motivation for the undertaking in most cases.[15]

In spite of the moral and legal uncertainties, surrogate motherhood agreements are also concluded in Poland, as seen at least from the large number of advertisements in the media. They function within the domain of legal indifference, not having been prohibited by Polish law. This social practice is also reflected in court judgements.

It should be noted that, until the 2009 amendment to the Family and Care Code,[16] the Polish legal system provided no clear and unambiguous regulation concerning a child's origin on the mother's side. The mother of a child was assumed to be the woman shown as the mother on the birth certificate. The changes to the law explicitly defined the mother to be the woman who gave birth to the child, and hence the surrogate mother where applicable.

Considering the social extent of the phenomenon, it would seem necessary, in Poland as well, to formulate legal rules that comprehensively and unambiguously regulate the conditions and procedure for concluding surrogate motherhood agreements and a system of supervision for such agreements. Another reason for doing this is that such agreements are usually the result of an attempt to realize a desire for motherhood, which cannot be attained by other means. Very often the surrogate mother's motivation is not the remuneration, but the desire to help someone close to her – for example when the child is carried by a sister or the mother of the woman, who is not able to carry a full-term pregnancy. In any case, such agreements cannot be disregarded, as there will always be those who wish to realize their desire for parenthood at any price, and those who for various reasons, most often self-interested, want to help them. The suggestion made by many, that surrogate motherhood agreements should be considered legally void on the ground of their being contrary to social norms, is not entirely convincing. This attitude will not remove the problems which arise together with the surrogate motherhood agreement.

Legal models for regulation of the status of human embryos and artificial reproduction

There is no single 'rational' standard for the regulation of artificial reproduction, and in particular *in vitro* methods. The laws of European

---

[15] *Problematyka prawna macierzyństwa zastępczego* in Tadeusz Smyczyński (ed.) *Wspomagana prokreacja ludzka. Zagadnienia legislacyjne* 116 (1996).

[16] Journal of Laws No. 220, item 1431.

countries in this field differ significantly. A common feature is the lack of explicit prohibition of *in vitro* fertilization.[17] Regulatory differences result from differences in constitutional traditions and socio-axiological conditions. This is linked to differences in approach to the legal status of the human embryo.

L. Bosek distinguishes four basic regulatory models of the status of a human embryo: 1) the naturalistic model; 2) the original model; 3) the autonomous (individualistic) model; and 4) the dignity model.[18]

The naturalistic model is characterized by legal prohibitions on interference in reproductive processes. It is encountered mainly in the countries of South and Central America. It entails an absolute prohibition on experiments on embryos, and also excludes *in vitro* fertilization methods.[19]

In most countries the 'original model' still applies, with an absence of legal regulation as to the status of the human embryo. It is noted that just 30 years ago this was the case in every country's legal system. The legal gaps in this area, which still exist today are the result of either biotechnological backwardness, or else a conscious decision by legislators to leave the sphere of reproduction subject to free market forces.[20] This state of affairs must be assessed negatively, if only because of the possible dangers to human life and health. It is unacceptable to have a situation where anyone (not having the necessary medical knowledge or satisfying suitable conditions) can offer reproductive medical services, even if this is in accordance with the normal democratic principle that everything that has not been prohibited is permitted. Social relations of this type are sufficiently important, both for individuals and for society as a whole, that they ought to be reflected in legal norms. The original model cannot be reconciled with European tradition and European Union law.

The autonomous model is characterized by the fundamental legalization of intervention in the nature of human reproduction, subject to state control and the consent of the interested party. This model has been introduced in practice in the United Kingdom by way of the Human Fertilisation and Embryology Act. British legislation demonstrates a

---

[17] Leszek Bosek, *Refleksje wokół prawnych uwarunkowań wspomaganej prokreacji,* 45 Diametros 20 (2009).

[18] *Modele regulacyjne wspomaganej prokreacji w świetle standardów konstytucyjnych* in Leszek Bosek & Michał Królikowski (eds.), *Współczesne wyzwania...* 156 (2010).

[19] Kazimierz Complak, *Godność człowieka w orzecznictwie konstytucyjnym Ameryki Łacińskiej*, 279 Przegląd Sejmowy 3 (2007).

[20] Leszek Bosek & Michał Królikowski (eds.), *supra* 156.

marked biotechnological optimism, associated with freedom of reproduction and the freedom to experiment. Such a model is also reflected – at least partially – in the laws of Belgium, France, the Netherlands and Spain, although in no other European country has it been implemented directly, at least partly because of incompatibility with the Bioethics Convention, which the UK has not signed. However, similar measures have been adopted in certain US states (such as California).[21]

An autonomous approach is also taken in the laws adopted in France. The French bioethical law of 1994 was based on principles proposed by N. Lenoir, a member of world bioethical bodies. She indicated the following principles: 1) respect for the human body and its non-commercial nature; 2) the principle of informed consent; 3) the principle of protection for the genetic heritage of the human race.

The formula 'respect for the human body' does not answer the question of whether the human embryo possesses a 'human body'. It would be going too far to conclude from it that a foetus is subject to the same protection as a living person. The same applies to the claim that the prohibition on commercialization applies equally to the foetus as to a person who is already living. Certainly, however, legal protection is associated with the concept of a 'human being', although it cannot be compared to the protection given to a 'human person'.

The principle of informed consent refers to a fundamental dimension of human freedom, expressed in the right to be properly informed, and then to submit to biomedical actions having consciously given one's consent.

The principle of protection of the genetic heritage of the human race applies directly to the embryo, and is linked to the perception of a need for progress, human self-creation, scientific autonomy and therapeutic benefits. It finds justification in utilitarianism, the deontological theories of rights, and consequentialism. Protection of this heritage does not mean that the foetus is to be treated as an object – it is, after all, entitled to the dignity appropriate to a 'human being'.

The foregoing principles form the basis for legal regulations in the sphere of bioethics in France. They have been adapted to civil law, as is reflected in numerous legislative acts. The terms 'human person' and 'human being', indicating the gradability of the embryo's legal protection, have become a part of legal language. The measures adopted imply an

---

21 *Modele regulacyjne wspomaganej prokreacji w świetle standardów konstytucyjnych* in Leszek Bosek & Michał Królikowski (eds.), *Współczesne wyzwania...* 158 (2010).

open attitude to experiments on the human body, and a marked biotechnological optimism.

The French regulations can be classified as closest to the British autonomous model, although the measures adopted in France are not as radical as those found in British law. For this reason, a better description of this standard would be as a model of limited autonomy.

The last of the models listed – the dignity model – protects human embryos and the genetic integrity of humanity. This is reflected in practice in the laws adopted in Germany: *On protection of embryos* and *On prohibition of trading in children and surrogate motherhood*. The measures adopted in German law give priority to the dignity of a person from conception. This translates into the legal status of an embryo as a legal subject, comparable with a 'human person'. The concerns about scientific risk, which are noticeable in German law are associated with a marked biotechnological pessimism. The German model has been transferred to Switzerland and to Italy.[22]

As regards the legal regulation of artificial reproduction, in Europe two standards are noted, developed in the late 1980s and early 1990s in the countries with the highest levels of biotechnological progress: the United Kingdom and the Federal Republic of Germany.

The British model for artificial reproduction prefers reproductive and experimental freedom, which is reflected in:

1. legalization of the creation of human admixed embryos;
2. permissibility of destruction of human embryos with the consent of the genetic parents;
3. possibility of creating surplus embryos, their preservation and destruction even against the will of the genetic parents (after five years);
4. absence of restrictions on who can have access to *in vitro* fertilization procedures;
5. possibility of creating embryos *post mortem*;
6. public funding for techniques of artificial reproduction.

British law prevents a disabled person from pursuing claims resulting from the actual fact of being born with an undesired genetic composition. The UK also has highly developed institutional regulations. The market is supervised by the Human Fertilisation and Embryology Authority.

The British model is not applied in its full extent in any other European country. It is however partly reflected in the laws of Belgium, the

---

[22] *Modele regulacyjne wspomaganej prokreacji w świetle standardów konstytucyjnych* in Leszek Bosek & Michał Królikowski (eds.), *Współczesne wyzwania...* 159 (2010).

Netherlands and Spain, where there is again an absence of restriction on who has access to procedures, and the creation of surplus embryos is legal. However in most countries there are numerous restrictions on what actions may be performed and who has access to treatment.

An example of the latter type of restriction is the fact that *in vitro* procedures are usually restricted to married couples or heterosexual partnerships (as in Denmark, Norway and Austria). Sometimes the use of methods of artificial reproduction is also available to homosexual couples (as in Sweden). Sometimes *in vitro* fertilization (and even artificial insemination) are denied to single women and same-sex partners, and in the case of non-married heterosexual partners require that they have been together for at least two years (as in France). A frequent type of restriction is a limit on the woman's age (e.g. a maximum age of 45 in Denmark).

Moreover some countries' legal regulations lay down restrictions on the circulation of reproductive cells. The use of other women's ova may be prohibited (as in Austria). An *in vitro* procedure is only permitted if at least one of the gametes comes from the married or unmarried partners themselves (e.g. France, Sweden). The number of embryos created in a cycle may be restricted to the number which is necessary to achieve pregnancy (as in Austria).

The German regulatory model for artificial reproduction legalizes *in vitro* fertilization while at the same time protecting the dignity of the human embryo. It prevents a human being from being treated as an object, and protects the integrity and identity of the human embryo. The features of this model are as follows

1. it is not permissible to create embryos for purposes other than reproduction;
2. the number of embryos created per cycle is limited to three, and they must be immediately transferred to the woman's body;
3. the routine preservation of human embryos is not permitted except as a result of a higher need (such as the woman's illness);
4. cloning is prohibited;
5. surrogate motherhood agreements are not permitted;
6. manipulation of the human genome is completely prohibited;
7. genetic selection of embryos is not permitted, including pre-implantation testing;
8. public funding of *in vitro* fertilization is limited to married couples.

Although German law does not explicitly lay down who has access to *in vitro* methods, there are restrictions resulting from extra-legal professional ethical norms, which permit the technique only for married and unmarried couples.

The legal situation closest to the German model is that of Italy. There are also aspects of this model in the law of Switzerland.[23]

Comparative legal analysis shows that techniques of assisted reproduction are not the subject of explicit legal prohibitions in European countries, except for cloning and, partially, surrogate motherhood. A tendency towards the regulation of *in vitro* methods is noted, reflected in restrictions (more or less narrow) on the actions permitted and on who has access to treatment.

Polish debate concerning methods of artificial reproduction in the context of the constitutional provisions on right to life

It must be agreed that the reference point for considerations concerning the regulatory model for artificial reproduction in Poland should be the constitutional guarantees. The Polish Constitution refers to the 'dignity of a person', which is the source of freedom and rights, is inviolable, and must be respected and protected by the public authorities (Article 30). The text of the constitution lays down an obligation to provide every person with 'legal protection of life' (Article 38). Everyone has the right to protection of their private life, family life, honour and good name, and to decide about their personal life (Article 47). Everyone also has the right to protection of health (Article 68). The aforementioned provisions might form a good basis for statutory regulations providing a distinction between the concepts of 'human being' and 'human person'.

The adoption of a naturalistic regulatory model for the status of the human embryo, prohibiting all intervention in the natural reproductive processes, would require changes to the constitution to include reference to the protection of life from the moment of conception.

The constitution of Poland does not lead directly to prohibitions on artificial reproduction. Also it may not be concluded from its text that medical interventions on the human body might violate or threaten the guarantee of respect for human dignity, unless it is connected with eugenic selection, which is prohibited in accordance with Article 3(2) of the Charter of Fundamental Rights.[24] Detailed bases for the legal protection of

---

[23] *Bioetyczne problemy nowej cywilizacji w świetle katolickiej nauki społecznej* in Leszek Bosek & Michał Królikowski (eds.), *Współczesne wyzwania...* 40 (2010).

[24] *Modele regulacyjne wspomaganej prokreacji w świetle standardów konstytucyjnych* in Leszek Bosek & Michał Królikowski (eds.), *Współczesne wyzwania...* 159 (2010).

embryos are found in judgements of the Polish Constitutional Court. That body has stated explicitly that a conceived child is subject to such protection and is entitled to personal dignity; however the degree of protection depends partly on its stage of development.

Irrespective of the differences of opinion as to which of the regulatory models for the status of the human embryo and artificial reproduction is best suited to Polish conditions, there is a clear need for Polish legislators to take a position on these issues.

In Poland, procedures involving artificial fertilization and implantation of embryos in the mother's body are carried out despite the lack of legal regulation. It can be concluded that since the law does not prohibit them, they lie within the zone of legal indifference. These socially significant issues are regulated solely by the norms of customary law, which have already come to take shape as a consequence of medical practice. A particular role is undoubtedly played by the Code of Medical Ethics.

Polish law is in need of a comprehensive set of changes and additions. In seeking optimum measures, it seems appropriate to consider the legislative solutions which have been adopted in other countries.

Five draft laws have been put forward in relation to *in vitro* procedures: 1) for an amendment to the Act on transplantation – an expert proposal submitted by the Federation for Women and the Nasz Bocian association (known as M. Balicki's proposal); 2) for an Act on protection of the human genome and the human embryo and a Polish Bioethics Council (proposal of J. Gowin); 3) for an amendment to the Act on transplantation (*in vitro*) and the Family Code, and an Act on basic human rights and freedoms in applications of biology and medicine and on the creation of a Polish Bioethics Council (proposal of the team of M. Kidawa-Błońska); 4) for an Act on protection of the human genome and human embryo (proposal of B. Piecha); 5) for an Act on prohibition of *in vitro* fertilization and manipulation of human genetic information (proposal of T. Wargocka).

All of the proposals would prohibit human cloning, trading in embryos and gametes, experiments on embryos, and the creation of hybrids. They provide for the creation of a Bioethics Council and contain regulations, supplementing those of EU directives, on the actions of laboratories and clinics holding human tissues, gametes and embryos.[25]

The proposal authored by M. Balicki is based on the British model. It provides that:

---

[25] *Bioetyczne problemy nowej cywilizacji w świetle katolickiej nauki społecznej* in Leszek Bosek & Michał Królikowski (eds.), *Współczesne wyzwania...* 37 (2010).

1. *in vitro* techniques are to be generally available to couples and to single women;
2. these techniques may be used not only to treat infertility, but also to avoid genetic diseases;
3. the number of embryos created and implanted depends solely on medical indications;
4. surplus embryos are to be frozen or destroyed, or possibly passed on for adoption;
5. the decision on the fate of surplus embryos is to be made by the biological parents;
6. embryos may be tested, with the selection of those which have the best potential for "normal development" and are free of genetic defects;
7. a child adopted as an embryo is entitled to know its origin.

In turn the proposal of the team of M. Kidawa-Błońska, which is intended to allow all persons with such a need to make use of modern infertility treatment methods, lays down that:

6. *in vitro* techniques are to be generally available to heterosexual couples;
7. they may be used solely for treatment of infertility;
8. the destruction of embryos, which are capable of development is prohibited;
9. the number of embryos created and implanted is to be regulated solely by medical considerations;
10. embryos with the best development potential are to be selected for implantation;
11. pre-implantation diagnosis can be carried out for diseases which are currently routinely considered an indication for abortion.

The proposal of T. Wargocka appears to be extremely radical, being based on assumptions which are entirely out of step with international standards. Under the proposal:

- the creation of embryos *in vitro* would be a criminal offence subject to two years' imprisonment;
- usage of human embryos would be prohibited, including their implantation.

Somewhat less extreme is the proposal of B. Piecha, under which:

- the creation of embryos *in vitro* would be prohibited;
- already existing frozen embryos would be subject to either implantation to their biological mothers, or adoption;

- if the biological parents do not consent to adoption, the fate of the embryo would be decided by a court (with proceedings as in the case of adoption of a born child).

Realistically, in Polish conditions, the proposal with the best chances is that of J. Gowin. This alludes to the German model, and is based on the following assumptions:

1. *in vitro* methods can be used only to treat infertility;
2. the creation of surplus embryos is prohibited;
3. all embryos, regardless of their chances of normal development, should be implanted immediately, unless there are medical contra-indications;
4. *in vitro* treatment would be available only to married couples;
5. the method would not be available to women over 40 years of age or persons with diseases or 'genetic impairments';
6. compensation cannot be claimed for giving birth to a child with genetic defects;
7. the freezing of ova is proposed instead of the freezing of embryos;
8. it is forbidden to place gametes from another woman in a woman's body for reproductive purposes, hence the use of surrogacy agreements is directly forbidden;
9. in exceptional circumstances a court may allow the implantation of a human embryo in another woman (for example in case of the death of the genetic mother, withdrawal of consent for implantation, or the elapse of two years from the embryo's date of creation).

L. Bosek points out that from a formal standpoint Gowin's proposal is precise and well synchronized with basic constitutional principles, and the restrictions contained in it have legal and social justification.[26] However the restrictions it would make on methods of artificial reproduction and who has access to them are very far-reaching. They block autonomy in the sphere of reproduction for single persons, partners in unformalized relationships, women of reproductive age who are not able to get pregnant naturally. The proposal's assumptions practically exclude the possibility of experimenting on embryos, which is important for the development of medicine. This proposal does not entirely correspond to medical standards and public expectations, especially when the scale of the treatment carried out in Poland at present is taken into account. A realistic assessment is that

---

[26] *Bioetyczne problemy nowej cywilizacji w świetle katolickiej nauki społecznej* in Leszek Bosek & Michał Królikowski (eds.), *Współczesne wyzwania...* 58 (2010).

it is a symptom of political consensus and an attempt to reconcile religious values with liberal standards.

It would seem that the aforementioned legislative proposal does not take account of social changes and the common use of *in vitro* methods and surrogate motherhood. In a way it confirms the state of hypocrisy existing in Poland, including in the legislative sphere. Social problems whose dimension is significant from a legal standpoint are marginalized, creating the impression that they do not really exist.

CONTINUING OR BREAKING WITH THE CONSTITUTIONAL SYSTEM OF POLISH PEOPLE'S REPUBLIC? LEGAL CONSIDERATIONS IN THE CONTEXT OF THE 1989 TRANSFORMATION

HANNA DUSZKA JAKIMKO
AND EWA KOZERSKA

OPOLE UNIVERSITY

Two hundred years after the 1789 French Revolution, the ideological aspirations (in the spirit of "Liberty, Equality and Fraternity") of which led to the reorientation of the absolutist state into a republic, there also occurred the desired and significant changes in the countries of Middle-Eastern Europe, closely dependant (after World War II) on the Soviet totalitarian regime, in the direction of democratization of the socio-economic and political relations. Without a doubt, the impulse for the significant political changes in this region of the Old Continent, described by historians as "Autumn of Nations", was provided by the events taking place in Poland, culminating in the talks around the "round table", between the ruling group and the political opposition. As it turned out, the leading and sublime thesis, popularized by the dissident groups, specifically characteristic of those countries, postulated the need of a qualitative revolution of the politico-legal system in almost every area of public life. In practical use, the "improved" system was to realize the desired guarantees of freedom and legal equality, additionally stimulating the growth of the so far suppressed intellectual and economic potential of the emerging civil societies. The driving force of this transformation had to be both a substantive discussion and formal actions, which would allow the realisation of the expectations of the "oppressed" societies. It should be noted that in Poland, on the field of systemic changes, creative aspirations were provided not only by the conclusions of the agreements in Magdalenka, but also the talks at the broad public forum, revealing different (often immature, inefficient and even utopian) idealistic projects on the subject of the perspective of forming the country.

One of the many groups belonging to the elite, and participating with interest in the politico-legal "dispute" over the shape of the Republic of Poland, was the representatives of legal science and legal practice. Their activity was expressed on the pages of specialist journals, thematic publications and during the proceedings of the nationwide scientific conferences or general assembly meetings of legal corporations. A special, and often substantial activity in the controversy regarding the above-mentioned issues, could be noted in the leading legal periodicals, representative of the mentioned intelligentsia group (showing a great variety of worldviews)[1]. The analysis of the articles published in those journals has revealed the rudimentary dilemmas of the time, concerning the issue of the systemic continuity of the Polish state, and, thus, reflections on the recognition (and its range) of the legal tradition of the PRL or breaking with it and a possible reference to the constitutional achievements of the interwar period. Their attention was rightly centered around the merit of the constitution, because, under the "new" socio-political and economic conditions, it was to assume the role of the fundamental normative act, ordering the internal structure of the state and its law. Especially, it was to redefine the systemic status of the state, its authorities and individual citizens, and, at the same time, solve the issue of eliminating the inconveniences of the transformation period. A breakthrough, and also controversial postulate, was the adopted constructive position on the issue: to maintain the temporary systemic solutions, or repeal the constitution of 22.07.1952, with its subsequent amendments and generally cut off from any connotations associated with it.

Expanding the issues outlined above, it should be noted that great lawyers (often regarded as influential authorities), publishing in the scientific legal periodicals in the years 1989 – 1991, usually expressed the

---

[1] The conducted research has shown that an activity on the issue of the systemic profile of Poland in the period we are interested in, that is 1989 – 1992 (before the entry into force of the so-called Little Constitution of 24.04.1992) that was especially rich in its contents, we can find on the pages of the popular journal "Państwo i Prawo". To a lesser extent, the mentioned issues were the subject of interest on the pages of other specialist legal periodicals, such as "Ruch Prawniczy, Ekonomiczny i Socjologiczny", "Studia Prawnicze" or "Przegląd Sądowy". Of course, it is important to remember that an important voice in the public discourse belonged also to magazines and journals, that is "Tygodnik Powszechny", "Polityka", "Rzeczpospolita", "Gazeta Wyborcza", etc.

unequivocal conviction about the need to derogate from the "socialist" model for the new and "eloquent" sounding "democratic legal state". The term "legal state" present since 1989 both in the Polish legal and juridical language, became the synonym of the reform of the state that was to free the individual from the arbitrary actions of the state power.[2]

From this moment on, the rule of legal state became the value in chief, determining the future legal system, its axiology and the legislator's preferences regarding legal regulations of the country.[3]

The revised constitutional document of 1952, which, in the opinion of many legal authorities, "radically" transformed the monocentric ruling system into a pluralist political order, they treated as temporary and transitional. [4] For example, in the opinion of professor Wojciech Sokolewicz, the resolution passed on 7.04.1989, regarding the changes in the constitution, caused the "deepest" changes of this act in its history, revealing the "new philosophy of governance", guaranteeing its practical realization. He was also confident that the constitutional amendment of 29.07 created the "legal conditions for the qualitative change of this system", as the arrangement of parliamentary political forces after the June

---

[2] Cf. Marek Zirk-Sadowski, *Instytucjonalny i kulturowy wymiar integracji prawnej*, in *Zmiany społeczne a zmiany w prawie. Aksjologia, konstytucja, integracja europejska*, 35 (ed. Leszek Leszczyński, Lublin 1999).

[3] See more Marzena Kordela, *Rola zasady państwa prawnego w budowie aksjologii państwa*, 175 in *Zmiany społeczne a zmiany w prawie.....*

[4] Such an opinion can be found in the article by Janina Zakrzewska (Judge of the Constitutional Tribunal from 1989 to 1995), *Nowa Konstytucja Rzeczpospolitej*, 4 Państwo i Prawo 3 (1990); Wojciech Sokolewicz (member of the Legislative Council to the Prime Minister from 1984 to 1992, expert of the Parliamentary Constitutional Commission from 1990 to 1991, Judge of the Constitutional Tribunal from 1993 until his resignation in 1999), *Rzeczpospolita Polska - demokratyczne państwo prawne (Uwagi na tle ustawy z 29 XII 1989 o zmianie Konstytucji),* 4 *Państwo i Prawo* 12 (1990); Zdzisław Czeszejko-Sochacki (constitutional law professor, Judge of the Constitutional Tribunal from 2001 to 2010), *Projekt nowej konstytucji (Przegląd zagadnień węzłowych)*, 7 Państwo i Prawo 3 (1991); Mirosław Wyrzykowski (professor of legal science, Judge of the Constitutional Tribunal from 2001 to 2010), *Legislacja – demokratyczne państwo prawa, radykalne reformy polityczne i gospodarcze,* 5 Państwo i Prawo 17, 20 (1991); Karol M. Pospieszalski & Zygmunt Ziembiński (prominent professors of law, working during this period at the Adam Mickiewicz University in Poznan), *Konstytucja rocznicowa czy konstytucja wiekopomna?*, 1 Ruch Prawniczy, Ekonomiczny i Socjologiczny, 19, 20 (1991); Kazimierz Działocha, *Państwo prawne w warunkach zmian zasadniczych systemu prawa RP*, 1 Państwo i Prawo 13 (1992).

elections led to "radical" systemic reforms[5]. This way of looking at the short-term systemic solutions – illustrated even in the titles of some articles – introduced in the April and December modifications of the constitution, was, surprisingly, reviewed as thorough. However, in its content there were elements of phraseology and institutional relicts, which might have been the evidence for keeping the systemic continuity.[6] As evidence, there is not only the fact of having kept in its title (also after the December amendment) the not too sublime date of the enactment (22.07) of the constitution of 1952, which deliberately referred to the "shameful" anniversary of the July Manifesto imposed by the Soviet authorities, but also keeping, until the changes in December, the name of the country, whose top authorities (the President, Senate and Parliament) terminologically represented the PRL, still referred to as a socialist country.[7]

What is more, as K.M. Pospieszalski, Z. Ziembiński and W. Sokolewicz unanimously noted in their articles, the legislators of the time, and also the specialists in the field of constitutional law, did not have any clearly specified idea on the concept of the state, apart from the declared need for negating its socialist character. [8] The professors of Adam Mickiewicz University mentioned above, might have properly depicted the constitution of Poland of the transformation period, stating that "new content was poured into and old vessel, but the old vessel arouses resentments." [9] In their opinion, the temporary and fully insufficient

---

[5] Wojciech Sokolewicz, *Kwietniowa Zmiana Konstytucji*, 6 Państwo i Prawo, 3 (1989); Wojciech Sokolewicz, *Rzeczpospolita Polska...*, (n. 4), 12.

[6] A similar opinion was expressed by Marek Smolak, *Wykładnia prawa a zmiana społeczno-polityczna,* in *Studia z filozofii prawa*, 163 (ed. Jerzy Stelmach, Kraków 2001).

[7] Maintaining those systemically important parts of the constitution remained connected with the contents of the "Round Table" agreements of 05.04.1989, in which there are no establishments on this matter. See *Porozumienia okrągłego stołu* in *Konstytucje Polskie 1918-1998* 285-91 (ed Tadeusz Mołdawa, Dom Wydawniczy Elipsa 1999).

[8] It is worth noting that professor Janina Zakrzewska, demonstrating the need to change the constitution of 1952, unsuitable for the social realities, proposed also a concept of state marked by social elements; in *Nowa konstytucja* ..., p. 11 Similar standpoint was taken by Sylwester Zawadzki (a member of the State Council in the years 1985-1989, a member of the "Round Table " proceedings), *Nowa konstytucyjna definicja polskiej państwowości,* 5 Państwo i Prawo, 13, 22-3 (1990).

[9] K. M. Pospieszalski, Z. Ziembiński, "Konstytucja rocznicowa...", p. 20. Against the background of reflections on systemic continuity in the transformation period of the Polish state, it is worth referring to the observations made on this matter by

modernization of the act showed also the striking inconsistency of regulations and led to many difficulties in the process of enforcing the law, thereby lowering its prestige.[10]

The indicated problems of systemic continuity corresponded closely with the need of adopting an adequate naming terminology of the state and its organs, adequate to the new Polish reality. It was therefore necessary to settle the issue of whether to systemically refer to the pre-war tradition of the Second Polish Republic, referring to the constitutional rules of 17.03.1921, or to create, on the basis of the temporary solutions that were in force at that time, a significantly modified and optimal construction for forming the country or to completely abandon the previous order and create a constitution not burdened by the socialist past. It can be said that a constructive discussion in that direction was not undertaken during the meetings in Magdalenka.[11] Also the theoreticians and practitioners of law and other opinion-creating groups, as there was no consensus in the case of the aware recognition of the continuation of one of the two pre-war legal systems,[12] were unable to adopt a radical attitude that would break with the constitutional achievements after the year 1940.

---

the eminent writer and statesman, Alexis de Toqueville of France, who, on the pages of the treatise *Dawny ustrój i rewolucja* (Znak 1994), aptly argued that revolution is always a continuation of the old regime.

[10] Ibid, at 22; W. Sokolewicz, "Kwietniowa zmiana…", pp. 8 – 9; Andrzej Kubiak, *Państwo prawne – idea, postulaty, dylematy* 7 Państwo i Prawo 15. Undoubtedly, these discrepancies in the law and the accompanying pragmatic problems, - as referred to by the then Ombudswoman professor. Ewa Łętowska - a disturbing phenomenon of "agnosticism" or "constitutional nihilism" in the behavior of state organs, Ewa Łętowska, *Wystąpienie Rzecznika Praw Obywatelskich w Sejmie,* 5 Państwo i Prawo 9-10 (1990).

[11] It may be puzzling that there was no unequivocal position on this matter, especially from the political opposition. Could it be that, having so many issues concerning the political system to deal with, they didn't notice, or knowingly agreed to maintain the existing status quo regarding the name of the state, whose authorities, eventually giving it the name of the Republic of Poland, didn't clearly break with the PRL tradition.

[12] J. Zakrzewska writes about public sentiment for the March constitutional regulations, which, in turn, professor Ludwik Dembinski of international law considered to be immature and weak. See Janina Zakrzewska, Supra, at 4 and Ludwik Dembiński, *Uwagi o ustroju III Rzeczpospolitej*, 28 Tygodnik Powszechny 1 (1990). The opinions concerning the April constitution and the you express the critical attitude, both towards the legality of its enactment, as well as its antidemocratic character. See the authors cited above and K. M. Pospieszalski, Z. Ziembiński, Supra, 20.

Indeed, they expressed the opinion of the need of breaking with the PRL tradition, crucial evidence of which was to be the symbolic transfer of the state insignia by the emigrant president to his counterpart chosen in the free elections in Poland in December 1990.[13] What is more, there were even voices that postulated treating the new post-communist reality as the Third Republic of Poland; a country which was not to rely on standards and experiences of the Second Republic or the post-war period, but, on the basis of verified European projects, and has the chance to become a real democratic state.[14] However, it should be noted here that, on the basis of the newly enacted constitutional principles, most of the columnists on the pages of Państwo i Prawo proposed developing values and interpretation of the regulations, which would allow, in the name of legal certainty and trust for the majesty of law, to maintain, under certain circumstances and legal relations, the previous state of affairs, discussed in detail below.[15] Theoretically reconciling – using proper arguments – the many inconsistencies and contradictions in the law, they expressed the agreement to use the current legal system in the new, allegedly "radically" different, socio-political and economic reality. In the absence of derogation of the existing legislation, it was assumed that in the first stage of the transformation, the existing legislation was to be adapted to the requirements of the legal state and the international standards of protections of human rights through its interpretation.[16] Interpretation of law played a very special role in the transformation process: its political involvement aimed to maintain the continuity of law, adapt the existing legislation of law to the requirements of the legal state and defined the direction and dynamics of the socio-political changes. Interpretation of law was thus regarded as an "effective instrument to solve social and political problems related to the systemic transformation of the state."[17]

---

[13] Id, at 20.

[14] Ludwik Dembiński, supra, 1.

[15] See the reflections of professor Andrzej Wasilewski of Adam Mickiewicz University on the importance of "the guarantee of the relative continuity" of the normative order, which he closely connects with the postulate to protect trust, the sense of legal certainty and clarity, computability and predictability of the actions of the state. In his opinion, these principles require respect in the process of enacting and enforcing the law, and may be departed from only in "exceptional" cases, which - quite vaguely – he justifies with the extraordinary needs, which do not cause negative consequences for the constitutional principles, Andrzej Wasilewski, *Aktualizacja porządku prawnego – potrzeby i rygory*, 5 Państwo i Prawo 3,4 (1992).

[16] Cf. Marek Zirk-Sadowski, supra, 40; Marek Smolak, Supra, 162-163.

[17] Marek Smolak, Supra, 162-163.

This important role was also reflected in the growing activity of courts. It was a process of “transferring the politico – social role of creating the law to the level of its enforcement” in so that the court could adjust the meaning of legal terms to the social needs of the existing legislator.[18] It is visible, for example, in the adjudication of the Constitutional Tribunal, concerning the exegesis of the legal state ideology, where the “lack of the new constitution didn’t prevent the Constitutional Tribunal and judicature from identifying a number of democratic principles of the legal state, not explicitly formulated anywhere.”[19] And so the catalogue of values which, according to the Constitutional Tribunal, directly or indirectly results from the legal state ideology, is “enormous but not exhaustive, because of the very nature of the legal state as an open concept.”[20] However, as noted by M. Kordela,[21] the analysis of the adjudication of the Constitutional Tribunal allows us to identify the following within the content of legal state values: a) the systemic political values, such as the constitutional and legal order, representative democracy, separation of powers, the autonomy of parliament, legislative freedom of parliament, independence of the judiciary, freedom of political parties, powers of local government, secularism and neutrality of the state; b) systemic legal values, which include the principles of legalism, formal rule of law, non-retroactivity of the law, the principle of citizens’ trust in law, equality in law or protection of acquired rights; c) systemic economic values associated with freedom of management, property protection, autonomy of the economic subjects. From this basic specification it is easy to ascertain that it was the interpretation of law that largely constituted the process of political and social transformation in Poland after the year 1989. However, as pointed out by M. Smolak, this process of incorporating the interpretation of law into the constitutional and systemic transformation was a real political trend; instrumentalization of the interpretation of law.

The change of the political system, occurring in the years 1989-1990, as W. Lang noticed, did not annul the previous axiological foundations of the Polish legal system.[22] The criticism, as the author claimed, “was directed not at the axiology of the July constitution and the whole of the

---

[18] Id., at 164.

[19] Marek Zirk-Sadowski, supra, 40.

[20] See more . Marzena Kordela, supra, at 175 .

[21] For the discussion and indication of the specific values of the rule of legal state and the extensive adjudication of the Constitutional Tribunal on this subject see Marzeana Kordela, supra, at 175.

[22] Wiesław Lang, *Aksjologia polskiego systemu prawa okresie transformacji ustrojowej*, in *Zmiany społeczne a zmiany prawie…*, p. 52.

legal system of the PRL, but on the functioning of the legal and political system, contradictory with the declared principles and violating them in practice (for instance, by the existence of censorship violating the freedom of speech). They also pointed to the absence of legal instruments that would allow their realization (the absence of the freedom of strike, judicial control of the legality of normative acts, the control of the compliance of acts with international contracts)." [23] Therefore, the systemic transformation only caused changes in the hierarchy and preference of values at the foundation of the axiology of the legal order: stressing the superior position of the individuals and their freedom in relation to the social values, the state and the political system as constitutional values; eliminating the contradictions between the rudimentary rules of the political system and the axiology of the legal order; priority of individual property and acquired rights in relation to other forms of property; stressing the idea of freedom of economic activity.[24]

It should also be noted that in the face of the sudden and fully unexpected (though declared) systemic modernization, which occurred in the spring of 1989, the Polish society, with the political opposition at the forefront, could not very well, under the new circumstances, find the politico-legal consensus that would satisfy at least the majority of its citizens. Undoubtedly, as Z. Ziembiński rightly noticed, the political and economical system continuously ruling since 1945 had led to the destruction of the attitudes typical of a democratic society and disturbed the process of selecting elites that would be able to elaborate a detailed and real systemic program. The changes of that time, he ascertained, unfortunately justified the thesis that the process of totalitarization of the system proved to be easier than the process of its democratization.[25] A similar analysis was also conducted by the sociologist Jerzy Szacki, who, on the pages of Res Publica, argued that the influence of the previous system, lasting for more than half a century, on all areas of life, including the monopoly to control them, has left its mark on the process of degradation and disorganization of the society. He warned against changing the "lyrical model of socialism" (described by the sociologist and essayist J.Strzelecki) into the lyrical model of democracy.[26]

---

[23] Id, at. 52.

[24] Id, at 52-53.

[25] Zygmunt Ziembiński, *"Lex" a "ius" w okresie przemian,* 6 Państwo i Prawo, 3,4 (1991); see also Andrzej Wasilewski, Supra, at 3.

[26] Jerzy Szacki, *Marzenia i rzeczywistość polskiej demokracji*, 5 Res Publica 10, 16-17 (1991).

The problem of creating a truly democratic political system forced, as the renowned theoretician of law, Z. Ziembiński, claimed, undertaking actions in the direction of outlining general axiological assumptions, which would designate the character of the currently valid legal system. Its proper functioning in the post-communist socio-political structure required an inner integrity of content and clearly defined legitimization of rules, guaranteed by rules (of validation and exegesis) designating, in turn, the conception of the sources of law. As the result of this deep reflection on values, which should be realized by the systemic order, it became necessary to find a balance between lex and ius, that is the "letter" and the "spirit" of the law[27]. The authors publishing in "Państwo i Prawo" all noticed that this system of legitimate values was to be significantly filled with the catalogued constitutional principle, with the idea of the "democratic legal state", already formulated in the first article of the amended version of the 29.12 constitution,[28] at the forefront.

As it was stressed, using determinants of operative and political power adequate to the temporary conditions, this constitution was to be prioritized and meaning was to be given to the other valuable and binding principles of the constitution and thus the whole legal order. The ideal of the rule of law, especially the formal rule of law and the legality of the state at the stage of creating and enforcing the law, and subjecting normative acts, obligatory for the citizens,[29] to constitutional review were

---

[27] In the context of deliberations on adopting a new Polish constitutional axiology, adequate to the new conditions, and the ability to execute it in practice, there was a debate on the advisability of appealing to natural law, which, in the opinion of J. Zakrzewska, supra, at 11, and Z. Ziembiński, supra,.at 4-5, is difficult to catalog and does not provide detailed decisions, such as procedural.

[28] According to A.Wasilewski, the general constitutional principle expressed in Art. 1 of the constitution imposed on the state to recognize, in a formal sense, the separation of powers, judicial independence, and to respect the rule of law and, on the material level, it manifested itself in the guarantees used to implement the compliance with the law of all state organs, protections of fundamental civil rights and liberties, the pivotal role of law in the legal system, judicial protection against acts of power and review of constitutionality of all legal norms, A.Wasilewski, supra, 3.

[29] Jerzy Wróblewski, *Z zagadnień pojęcia i ideologii demokratycznego państwa prawnego (analiza teoretyczna)*, Państwo i Prawo, 6, 3 (1990). Andrzej Kubiak being a bit critical about this principle (as an unnecessary constitutional phrase – even tautology – requiring state authorities to fulfill the obligation of the rule of law, inscribed in their competence) and evaluating it in programmatic terms, argued that it causes problems at the level of definition which will always have to be primarily the subject of decisions of the **adjudication practice** of state

identified with the leading principle (deriving from the 19th century German doctrine of Rechtsstaat).[30] It was assumed that, for the safety of law and legal certainty, much more attention should be paid to the letter of law, even inherited from the previous political regime (apart from extremely unfair decisions) than to relate to the rules of justice or a particular morality that professor Tadeusz Zieliński, first-term senator in the Republic of Poland, thought of as a higher legal order, calling it at the same time "the law written on the stars."[31]

Against the background of many controversial voices concerning the role and meaning of the guiding principle in the first article of the constitution, consideration was given to a catalogue of constitutional principles that would be compatible with it and sanctioned. Principles such as legal certainty, predictability of law, non-retroactivity, and stability related to the principle of the citizens' trust in law, was not and could not have been, as professor S. Wronkowska pointed out, "interpreted as demanding an unchanging law." [32] Although these are particularly important values in the situation of systemic transformation, the changing politico-social and economic circumstances required, more than once, a significant change in legal regulations or modification of existing norm. Such changes, concerning the fundamental principles of law, the system of the state, the political culture, the axiological and praxeological values, should, according to the doctrine, take into account the following: 1) legal state directives of unchanging character; their abuse would mean the abuse of the values behind this concept; 2) preserving the integrity of the legal system as a whole regardless of arguments of political nature; 3) respect for fundamental rights and liberties of the individual; 4) maintaining the stability of the rules of legislation and the resulting constitutional and statutory guarantees; 5) maintaining an adequatly long vacatio legis, for

---

authorities using the constitution, especially the Constitutional Tribunal, in "Państwo prawne..." p.19 A negative attitude towards this principle was adopted by the politician Jan Olszewski who brought it down to the level of a rule protecting the communist nomenclature; see more Jan Olszewski, *Państwo przede wszystkim*, 153 Rzeczpospolita 3 (1991) and maintained in a similar spirit, the article of the Judge of the Supreme Court in the years 1990-1998, professor of law Adam Strzembosz, *Rzeczpospolita Polska państwem prawnym – czy naprawdę?*, 234 Rzeczpospolita 2 (1991).

[30] See more Karol Jonca, *Ewolucja pojęcia "państwa prawnego" w niemieckiej doktrynie prawnej*, 7 Przegląd Prawa i Administracji 210, 213-228 (1976).

[31] Interview with prof. Tadeusz. Zieliński, W poszukiwaniu nowego sensu prawa, 157 Rzeczpospolita 3 (1991).

[32] Sławomira Wronkowska, *Zmiany w systemie prawnym (Z zagadnień techniki i polityki legislacyjnej),* 8 Państwo i Prawo, 3 (1991).

making transitional regulations and entitle the subjects whom it may concern, to decide, under the circumstances indicated by the legislator, whether their cases are to be adjudicated on the basis of the old or the new rules.[33]

Similarly important issues in the time of systemic transformation were the issues of the acceptability of retroactive legal acts. Such a situation, usually causing disapproval and violating the principle of trust in the legislator, could be justified by the existence of important reasons and expectations of subjects whom it may concern; on the other hand it should respect the postulate of protecting (respecting, maintaining) the acquired rights as fundamental for the idea of the legal state. In accordance with the decisions of the Constitutional Tribunal, the principle of protection of acquired rights is a norm valid under the constitution, limiting the acceptability of depriving the citizens of previously established personal rights and expectations, has "important and omni directional axiological justification. It supports the credibility of the state and its organs in relations with its citizens, whose trust is the condition for the effectiveness of exercising the state power. Taking away from the citizens the powers conferred to them is also highly unfavorable for the state of the legal awareness of the citizens. In such cases they lose the respect for the idea of law itself, as they do not find in the acts a reliable measure for protecting their rights."[34] However, one must ask whether this postulate should apply equally to every right. It is rightly considered that the discussed principle should be realized thoroughly and in a holistic manner in reference to rights acquired by agreement "because of the respect for the will of the parties making the agreement and their responsibility for forming their legal positions by an act of will."[35] Surely the issue of acquired rights in the time of systemic changes showed the complexity of the processes of legal-systemic changes in Poland of the 90s and the conflict between the "extreme conservatism and radical revolutionism", on the one hand acknowledging their indisputability and inviolability in accordance with the clause of rebus sic stantibus, on the other, allowing – in the process of rationalization of law – the possibility of their verification.[36]

---

[33] Cf. M. Wyrzykowski, Supra, at 25-28, also S. Wronkowska, supra, 12.

[34] See the Constitutional Tribunal ruling no. K 8/88. The importance of the principle of acquired rights in the time of the systemic transformation was discussed by Tadeusz Zieliński, *Ochrona praw nabytych – zasada państwa prawnego*, 3 Państwo i Prawo 3 (1992).

[35] S. Wronkowska, supra, 11.

[36] See more T. Zieliński, supra, at 10-11.

In sum, in the time of the transformation of the Republic of Poland, consideration was given to the name of the state and its political system, and also to determining the normative and political interpretation of the amended constitution of 1989, adequate to the temporary circumstances (especially in the context of the values and constitutional principles respected at the time), with the rule of the democratic legal state and associated with it and, already mentioned ideas, such as legality and legitimacy the executive, judiciary and legislative authorities, protection of acquired rights, non-retroactivity of the state, the right to trial at the forefront. The finally accepted exegesis of the constitutional legal regulations was to affect the compatibility of the hierarchically subordinate acts, essential for avoiding the often occurring contradictions with the amended constitution (for instance, the act on citizenship, organization and financing of social security, and other acts on retirement pensions, housing regulations, etc.). The disputed matter required legal solutions in the area of redefining justice, especially redefining the position and competence of the Constitutional Tribunal, the Supreme Court, the Supreme Administrative Court and marking the profile of the adjudication doctrine in the process of enforcing the law. This question of politicization of law enforcement became at that time one of the most serious issues of the philosophical reflection on law.

The conducted research has shown that the historical situation of Poland in the late 80s and early 90s mobilized the specialists in science and legal practice to a theoretical reflection on accepting axiology of the legal order compromise for the time of the transformation and on the systematization of honored values. An effort was also made to find a legal doctrine on the field of desuetude and exegesis of legislation enacted under the PRL rule and still in force in the period of socio-political and economic changes. The analysis of selected articles allowed the conclusion that the mostly heterogeneous postulates expressed by their authors, showed the tendency to a moderate attitude towards complex legal changes. Despite their agreement on the need of repealing the 1952 constitution, there were no radical proposals of breaking up with the existing doctrine and normative system, which was often substantiated with the thesis of stability and safety of the state.